THE
ENCYCLOPEDIA
OF BEER

THE
ENCYCLOPEDIA
OF BEER

Christine P. Rhodes, General Editor

Pamela B. Lappies, Project Editor

Contributing Editors:
Thomas Bedell, Alan Eames, Fred Eckhardt, Robert Haiber,
Karl F. Lutzen, Alan John Pugsley, Peter V. K. Reid,
Christine P. Rhodes, and Mark Stevens

A Henry Holt Reference Book
Henry Holt and Company
New York

A Henry Holt Reference Book
Henry Holt and Company, Inc.
Publishers since 1866
115 West 18th Street
New York, New York 10011

Henry Holt® is a registered trademark
of Henry Holt and Company, Inc.

Published in Canada by Fitzhenry & Whiteside Ltd.,
    195 Allstate Parkway, Markham, Ontario L3R 4T8.

Library of Congress Cataloging-in-Publication Data
The encyclopedia of beer / Christine P. Rhodes, general editor; contributing
editors, Tom Bedell . . . [et al.].—1st ed.
p.   cm.—(A Henry Holt reference book)
Includes bibliographical references.
1. Brewing—Encyclopedias. I. Rhodes, Christine P.
II. Series: Henry Holt reference book.
TP568.E53   1995   95-24963
641.2'3—dc20   CIP

ISBN 0-8050-3799-3

Henry Holt books are available for special promotions and premiums.
For details contact: Director, Special Markets.

First Edition—1995

Created and produced by Storey Communications, Inc., Pownal, Vermont
    M. John Storey, President; Martha M. Storey, Vice President; Pamela B. Art, Publisher;
    Catherine Gee Graney, Managing Editor.

Editorial assistants: Barbara Bacchi, Judith Cooper, Polly Estes, Elizabeth McHale, Barbara Jatkola, Chris Meyer,
    Louise Lloyd Prescott, Jessica S. Reardon, Donna M. Sprague, Gwen Steege, and Gayle Thompson
Text design: Cynthia N. McFarland
Text production: Susan Bernier, Greg Imhoff, Wanda Harper Joyce, Meredith Maker, Cynthia N. McFarland,
    Robin O'Herin, and Jessica S. Reardon

Printed in the United States of America
All first editions are printed on acid-free paper.∞

10 9 8 7 6 5 4 3 2 1

The Great American Beer Festival, American Homebrewers Association, and *Zymurgy* are all registered trademarks of the Association of Brewers. All
style guidelines from the Great American Beer Festival were reproduced with the written permission from the Association of Brewers.

CONTENTS

CONTRIBUTING EDITOR PROFILES

THOMAS BEDELL is an author, freelance writer, and editor. His work has appeared in dozens of general interest and specialty publications, including *Beer: the magazine* and *All About Beer*. An award-winning homebrewer, Bedell is also a certified beer judge. He lives in Williamsville, Vermont.

ALAN D. EAMES is a beer consultant, historian, and writer. He is a regular contributor to such beer periodicals as *All About Beer* and *Beer: the magazine* and the author of *Secret Life of Beer*, *A Beer Drinker's Companion* and the *Oldenberg Beer Drinker's Bible*. Eames is a founding director of the American Museum of Brewing History & Fine Arts in Fort Mitchell, Kentucky, and established the $3 Dewey's Ale House in Portland, Maine. He lives in Brattleboro, Vermont.

FRED ECKHARDT is a writer and publisher who has specialized in sake, beer, and brewing-related subjects for more than a quarter century. A contributor to and regular columnist for *All About Beer, Celebrator Beer News,* and *Southern Draft Beer News,* Eckhardt also contributes to *American Brewer, Zymurgy, The New Brewer,* and other periodicals. He is the author of *A Treatise on Lager Beer, Essentials of Beer Style*, and *Sake (U.S.A.)*. Eckhardt lives in Portland, Oregon.

ROBERT HAIBER, a freelance writer specializing in beer history, is an internationally recognized beer expert and certified beer judge. He is the founder of the North American Guild of Beer Writers and coauthor of the book *A Short but Foamy History of Beer*. Haiber lives in La Grangeville, New York.

KARL F. LUTZEN is the coauthor of *Homebrew Favorites: A Coast-to-Coast Collection of More Than 240 Beer and Ale Recipes*. He is also co-editor of the computer-accessible public domain beer recipe books *Cat's Meow* and *Cat's Meow 2*. Lutzen lives in Rolla, Missouri.

ALAN JOHN PUGSLEY has a degree in biochemistry from Manchester University. A brewmaster, he is President and majority owner of Peter Austin & Partners (Contracts), Ltd., a company headquartered in Portland, Maine, that designs and installs microbreweries and pub breweries worldwide. Pugsley is also a part owner of Kennebunkport Brewing Co./Shipyard Brewer in Portland, where he lives.

PETER V. K. REID is the editor of *Modern Brewery Age.* He frequently writes about beer, and his work includes extensive reporting on the evolution of the brewing industry. A graduate of Hobart College, Reid lives in Weston, Connecticut.

CHRISTINE P. RHODES, who has served as editor as well as advertising and marketing director of *Modern Brewery Age,* is a freelance writer and editor whose specialty is beer and brewing. She lives in Providence, Rhode Island.

MARK STEVENS is the coauthor of *Homebrew Favorites: A Coast-to-Coast Collection of More Than 240 Beer and Ale Recipes.* Stevens has written for *All About Beer* magazine and he co-edited the computer-accessible public-domain beer recipe books *Cat's Meow* and *Cat's Meow 2* Stevens lives in Beltsville, Maryland.

INTRODUCTION

BEER: A JOURNEY

The art of brewing is thousands of years old. Through hieroglyphics, cuneiform characters, and artifacts, beer historians have traced the roots of brewing back to the women of ancient African, Egyptian, and Sumerian tribes some 8,000 years ago. Things in the beer world have changed quite a bit since 6000 B.C., and today we find ourselves in the midst of an exciting and ever-changing industry that supports over 600 breweries in the United States alone. Despite the growth of the industry — particularly that of the microbrewing, brewpub, homebrewing, specialty beer, and import segments — there has not until now been a compendium of information available. It is our hope that *The Encyclopedia of Beer* will clarify every question you ever had about beer but were afraid to ask. From Abbaye to Alken Maes, hops to hefe-weizen, original gravity to Oktoberfest, and zwickel cock to Zythos — and everything in between — we hope to help you on your journey to discover all you ever wanted to know about beer and brewing.

To help you use this book, you need to know how beer is classified — and it is classified in a variety of ways. The color, alcohol content, amount of fermentables, style, type of ferment, and season may all be used to differentiate various beers. Most beer merchants identify each beer by the country in which it was produced. This classification is less than satisfactory, as most countries produce beers that are similar to those in other countries. For instance, many Norwegian, Swiss, and even Thai beers are very similar in style, content, color, and method of ferment to German, Czech Republic, and Dutch beers. Australians, Japanese, Canadians, and Mexicans make beers that are virtually indistinguishable from those made in the United States. Fiji, Nigeria, Hong Kong, and Singapore produce beers quite similar to those made in Great Britain. Belgium produces very distinctive beers, but even its beers are beginning to be copied in the United States, mostly by microbrewers and specialty brewers. Many Americans try to distinguish beer based on whether it is pale or dark in color. Others look for ales or lagers, which are also known as warm- or cold-fermented beers.

The classification system used in this book is based broadly on the system devised by beer critic and writer Michael

Jackson. He has identified approximately 41 different beer styles, and his work has been expanded upon, first by Fred Eckhardt in *Essentials of Beer Styles* and then by Charlie Papazian in the style guidelines for the Great American Beer Festival.

As is true with any classification system, there are arbitrary distinctions in this book, especially where the styles blend into one another. There is always the classic argument about when an ale is truly an ale. The purist would say that an ale is a top-fermented beer, but that is an oversimplification. The United States brewing industry says that an ale is a beer that is warm-fermented (above 60°F, or 15.5°C) during part of the ferment, no matter what type of yeast is used. This book's classification system allows for both possibilities. Some Belgian Trappist beers are produced from three ferments, using three yeasts, and perhaps three different temperatures. There is more to beer than yeast — a lot more to the world of beer than most people ever imagined.

When we talk about beer in this book, there are several points of reference. Original gravity, alcohol content, bitterness units, color, type of fermentation, and aging are among these points.

Original Gravity

The extract content is a measurement of the fermentable ingredients available at the start of the ferment that can be converted to alcohol. This is a direct result of the quantity of grains is used in the mash. If a large amount of grain used, the wort will have a high extract content and the beer will be strong in alcohol content. If a small amount of grain is used, the wort will have a low extract content and the beer will be weak. This density can be called original extract (a percentage of the total volume). If it is a measurement of the specific gravity at the start of the ferment, it may be called original gravity or original specific gravity. In this book, extract content is called original gravity (OG).

At the end of the ferment, some of the original extract will remain. This usually consists of unfermentable sugars called dextrins. Dextrins, combined with alcohol, are what give beer its flavor. An extract measurement of the finished beer, which is a measure of the nonfermentables as they appear and as they have been modified by the presence of alcohol, is called the apparent extract. This measurement also is called the final or terminal extract or gravity, or the beer extract or gravity. In this book, this figure is designated final gravity and is given in degrees Plato (i.e., percent).

Alcohol Content

The ferment with yeast generates about equal amounts of alcohol and carbon dioxide, plus a tiny percentage of other by-products. The alcohol content is presented by volume in this book.

Bitterness

Hops give beer aroma, flavor, and a slightly bitter taste. Hops were originally used as bactericide — that is, they helped prevent souring of the beer. Hops come in many forms: whole hops, or flowers (natural form), pellets, concentrated syrup, and even hop oils. These forms each have a different effect on beer. There are some 20 to 30 hops varieties. The measurable effect of hops is usually expressed as International Bitterness Units (IBU), which are parts per million (mg/L) of alpha acid, the major flavor element in hops.

Color

The color of beer may range from very pale (as in Budweiser) to very dark (as in Guinness Stout). Most of the color is the result of the malts used in the mash. Most malts are pale malts; they produce lighter-colored beers. Dark beer is the result of using malts that have been roasted to some degree. Darker malts add much more flavor to beer than pale malts. Budweiser has no dark malts, while Guinness Stout has a variety of them. Not until the beginning of the 19th century did it become possible to brew pale beer. At that time, brewers learned how to control the temperature during the malting process. Pale malts were later used to produce pale beers.

Color is expressed in degrees SRM (Standard Reference Method), or just SRM, which is similar to, but not quite the same as, the old Lovibond measure, which is still used to measure the color contributions of malts. The higher the SRM number, the darker the beer is. The European Brewery Convention (EBC) also has color descriptors that are somewhat related to SRM. The relationship is variable as follows:

1 degree EBC = 2.65 degrees SRM less 1.2

1 degree SRM = 0.375 EBC degree plus 0.46

Method of Ferment

Another variable in beer production comes from the type of yeast used and the fermenting temperature. The higher the temperature, the faster the ferment (and its effects), because the speed of all chemical changes doubles (or halves) for each 18°F (10°C) temperature change.

A beer fermented at very high temperatures will have some harsh character notes, while a beer fermented at very low temperatures will have very mellow and moderate taste factors. Moreover, yeasts are sensitive to temperature and will function only within certain temperature ranges. For the most part, this range is about 58°F to 100°F (14° to 38°C). This type of yeast is called *top-fermenting yeast* because it works through the body of the beer and then collects on the surface (where it can be skimmed to garner a new yeast crop for use in the next brew). The beer produced by such yeasts is called ale.

If the temperature drops too low, top-fermenting yeasts will go into a defensive posture by constructing a protective wall around themselves (sporulating) and will actually die if they are then subjected to high temperatures. However, not all yeasts operate in this fashion.

Lager is brewed with yeasts that do not sporulate when they get cold. These yeasts will keep working slowly right up until they are almost frozen. The benefit here is that cold-fermented beer is protected against souring bacteria and hence can be made with fewer hops (less bitterness) and a weaker alcohol content (longer drinking pleasure). When this cold-fermented beer is cold-aged, the result is a very mild and mellow beverage. These yeasts ferment throughout the body of the beer and then settle to the bottom of the vessel — hence the terms *bottom-fermenting yeast* and *bottom ferment*.

There is also a fermentation style known as a *spontaneous ferment*.

Aging System

The final variable in beer production is aging. For most of brewing history, beers were not aged; when the ferment was finished, the beer was deemed ready to drink. At some point it was discovered that beer, particularly stronger beer, would improve if it was allowed to stand for a period of several weeks or even months. This type of beer became popular in Bavaria, for example, where it was brewed in the fall, stored through the winter, and then consumed in the late spring. It was a great improvement over beer that had not been aged in this way. Some monks then discovered that if they stored this beer in deep caves and covered it with ice harvested from nearby lakes, the end product was even more delicious. As a result, pale, cold-fermented, cold-aged beers called lager (from the German *lagern,* "to store") were invented.

Conditioning Method

In the mid-19th century, beers came to be conditioned. Brewers found that if the fermenting vessel was closed tightly (bunged), carbon dioxide would build up. When the beer was drawn, it foamed up and had a different, most interesting taste. Brewers carried this idea further and added fermentable extract after the aging cycle to produce this wonderful taste. This conditioning process was carried out by both British and continental brewers.

The British added sugar syrup to their casks, which were then partially closed. When the ferment revived (after aging), the beer had a lovely, almost velvety taste. This came to be known as cask-conditioning.

Continental and American brewers closed their casks, allowing the gas pressure to build up. Early in the century brewers added sodium bicarbonate (baking soda) to their casks, which "carbonated" the beer artificially. Later they began adding newly fermenting wort to the casks, then closing them, which produced carbon dioxide saturation. This method became known as kraeusening (the addition of newly fermenting beer at the kraeusen, or heavy foam, stage).

Toward the end of the 19th century, beer came to be bottled, and a ferment in the bottle was encouraged by the addition of yeast and a small amount of sugar (in the manner of champagne). This resulted in well-carbonated, bottle-conditioned beers. Brewers later discovered that they could capture the carbon dioxide released early in the ferment and add that back to the beer at the time of bottling or kegging, for the purpose of conditioning. This is how most beers are carbonated today.

The Beer Summary

Any description of beer styles entails a wide range of possibilities. This is natural for a beverage that comes in such a huge variety of styles. These styles vary in strength from 2 to 13 percent alcohol by volume; in color from very pale to very dark brown; in taste from modest to mind-boggling; and in hoppiness from very low to exceedingly high. Styles can be in the form of lager beer or ale beer, and a wide range of varietal and seasonal possibilities is available.

This book explains the factors involved in the manufacture of various beer styles (ingredients, malts, methods, and specifications). In some cases, the Great American Beer Festival style guidelines are quoted. These guidelines have been summarized with the permission of that organization.

Budweiser: The Beer Summary

Let's look at a particular beer and summarize some of its specifications, including fermentables and nonfermentables, alcohol strength, bitterness, and color. The most popular American beer is Budweiser lager, for which the following information is available.

Original Gravity. This is the amount of fermentables at the beginning of the ferment. The original gravity is 11 degrees Plato or 1.044. British brewers use specific gravity in lieu of original gravity, but they drop the decimal (1044). That value is often shown on the label, since the beer's tax rate is tied to gravity. On the European continent, some countries (such as the Czech Republic) require that the original gravity in degrees Plato be on the label as a percent, hence the confusion about the alcohol content of some European beers. The degree (or percent) Plato is not the same as alcohol content; it is the original gravity of that beer.

Final Gravity. This is the measure of the nonfermentables, or apparent extract (beer extract). For Budweiser, this is 2.1 degrees Plato. The final gravity represents the apparent configuration of the beer as it is altered by the presence of alcohol. It consists mostly of unfermentable dextrins.

Alcohol Percent Strength. The alcohol strength of Budweiser is 4.7 percent alcohol by volume.

Hop Bitterness. Bitterness is 10.5 IBU.

Color. Budweiser's color is 2.7 SRM.

Budweiser and some other beers are described below using these parameters.

Original Gravity	Final Gravity	Alcohol by Volume	IBU	SRM
Budweiser 1988				
11/1.044	2.1	4.7%	10.5	2.7
Bass Pale Ale (England) 1982				
11.8/1.047	2.9	4.7%	19	9.8
Guinness Extra Stout (Ireland) 1982				
13.2/1.052	2.8	5.5%	50	60
Spaten Club Weisse (Germany) 1982				
12.5/1.050	2.5	5.1%	14	6

Now that you have an understanding of the type of information that we use in this book to describe beer, let's talk about how to use the *Encyclopedia* itself.

All the major terms used in our previous discussion, along with 900 or so more, are listed as main entries. These main entries vary in length, and will often direct you to cross-references that will provide you with related, pertinent information to the entry that you initially chose. Some of you might be familiar with a particular beer brand, but not with the brewery that made it well-known. By looking to the brand name itself, you will be directed to a cross-reference on the brewery. All cross-references are noted at the end of the main entries to which they correspond. A list of sources used by our contributors is also included in the bibliography in case you are interested in reading some in-depth discussion of a particular topic.

Selecting the beers and breweries to include was a difficult task, since there were thousands of breweries from all over the world to choose from. We have chosen to profile those that are most interesting in terms of their history, their influence, and their products.

Finally, we have used several abbreviations throughout the text. They are:

ABV   alcohol by volume
IBU   International Bitterness Unit
OG   original gravity
SRM   Standard Reference Method

This should get you started. Grab your favorite brew, dig in, and enjoy the journey.

— Fred Eckhardt and
Christine Rhodes

THE
ENCYCLOPEDIA
OF BEER

ABBAYE

A general name for a top-fermented, bottle-conditioned ale of the Trappist order currently available from only six breweries in the world. Abbaye beer or Trappist beer is not a single style of beer, but is a protected appellation in Belgium and the Netherlands that refers only to beer brewed by and under the control of the Cistercian Trappist monks. The standards are guaranteed by the governing body. Each Trappist beer is distinctive, in the manner of Belgian ales.

At one time, there were more than 500 monasteries in Europe. Trappist monasteries can be traced back to the 1600s, when a monk named Rancé founded a monastery at La Trappe in Normandy.

During the 17th and 18th centuries, the nobility wrested power and brewing from the church throughout Europe. In France, the Revolution of 1789 crushed the power of the church. Monasteries were looted, and their lands were seized and sold off. Monastic life therefore ceased for 40 years, and it took the monasteries many more to reestablish themselves.

During the 1930s, all Trappist monasteries brewed beer, but their beers were found only at the monasteries. Not until after World War II did their products become available outside the monasteries. By the late 1950s, commercial breweries had produced copies of Trappist beers, and in the early 1960s the Orval Monastery petitioned the Belgian Trade and Commerce Tribunal in Ghent for a legal appellation of origin for Trappist beers, which was granted in 1962. Commercial beers in this style, therefore, must be called abbey beers, not Trappist. Only the six Abbaye or Trappist breweries are entitled to use the word *Trappiste* on their beer labels.

Today, the six Benedictine monasteries of the Trappist order that brew their own beer in Belgium and the Netherlands are:

• Chimay (Abbaye de Notre-Dame de Scourmont), in the French border province of Hainaut. It was founded in 1850.

- Orval (Abbaye de Notre-Dame d'Orval), in the province of Luxembourg, near the rivers that form the border with France. It was founded in 1070.
- Rochefort (Abbaye de Notre-Dame de St. Rémy), near Dinant in the province of Namur. It was founded in 1230, began to brew in 1595, then started brewing again in 1899.
- Schaapskooi (Abdij Koningshoeven), the abbey in the Netherlands, is near Tilburg in North Brabant. It was founded in 1884.
- Westmalle (Abdij der Trappisten), in the province of Antwerp. It was founded in 1794 and began to brew in 1836.
- Westvleteven (Abdij Sint Sixtus) in West Flanders. It was founded in 1899.

Together the six breweries have as many as 20 different beers (mostly strong ales). All are made on monastery grounds. Some are exported to the United States.

In general, Trappist beers have the following characteristics: 12.5–23.2/ 1.050–1.095 OG/ 5–9.5 Belge, 2.6–5.6 final gravity, 5–11 percent alcohol by volume, 20–45 IBU, 3.5–20 SRM, and low pH (3.9–4.3). They usually include candy sugar and sometimes even spices. They are all top-fermented, usually at very warm temperatures as high as 85°F (29°C), and either with a yeast strain that has a multiple bacterial complement or with different yeasts for the primary and secondary ferments and even for the tertiary ferment. All are bottle-conditioned, usually with yet another yeast. None of

these conditions is a requirement, since Trappist beers can be anything the monasteries want them to be. All, however, are fruity and estery in taste, often with a quite distinctive character.

Orval

The oldest of the Trappist beers is Orval (Abbaye de Notre-Dame d'Orval) at Villers devant Orval. Founded in 1070, this monastery was rebuilt a number of times over the centuries. Its beer is certified by the Brussels School of Brewing to be a totally natural beer with no artificial ingredients or flavorings. Three separate yeast strains are used in the triple ferment, along with Belgian-grown and malted barley (three kinds), white candy sugar, and German and English hops. The usual initial (primary) ferment is followed by a second ferment. The second ferment takes place during the 2-month aging process at a temperature of 59°F (15°C). During this ferment, the beer is dry hopped. A third ferment takes place in the distinctive bottle, after the addition of a champagne-style dosage of yeast. When bottled, the beer is allowed to age for at least 3 months. Orval Trappist Ale has an original gravity of 13.7/1.056/5.6 Belge and 6 percent alcohol by volume.

Chimay

The first monastery to sell its beer to the public and label it Trappist was Chimay. The three Chimay beers — Chimay Red (the original), Chimay Grand Reserve (blue cap in Belgium), and Chimay Cinq (white in Belgium) — are the best known of all Trappist beers and are available in the United States.

Westvleteven

The Westvleteven Abdij Sint Sixtus is the smallest of the monasteries. Its beer is St. Sixtus. The St. Sixtus beer found in the United States is an abbey beer that is not brewed by the monastery itself but is brewed under license by the St. Bernardus Brewery in nearby Watau.

Rochefort and Westmalle

The beers of the monasteries of Rochefort and Westmalle are found in the United States from time to time, but they do not seem to be regularly available.

La Trappe

The Koningshoeven Monastery at Schaapskooi in the Dutch province of Brabant, just across the border from Belgium, started its brewery in 1884 to finance the monastery.

Original Gravity	Final Gravity	Alcohol by Volume	IBU	SRM
Chimay Red 1987				
15.4/1.063/6.2 Belge	2.3	7%	Unknown	≈20
Chimay White 1986				
18.3/1.071/7.1 Belge	2.6	8%	Unknown	≈6
Chimay Grand Reserve 1985 (blue)				
19.8/1.081/8.1 Belge	2.6	8.9%	Unknown	≈16
La Trappe Tripel 1988				
17/1.070/7 Belge	4	7%	Unknown	≈10
Orval 1985				
13.7/1.056/5.6 Belge	2.5	6%	24	≈8

See ABBAYE DE NOTRE-DAME DE ST. RÉMY.

ABBAYE DE NOTRE-DAME DE ST. RÉMY, ROCHEFORT, BELGIUM

A small, secluded Trappist brewery in the Ardennes, St. Rémy has been a holy site since the 13th century, and monks have brewed there since the late 16th century. Today the monks produce three beers under the Rochefort label, designated by their original gravity (in degrees Belge) as "six," "eight," and "ten."

The beers are brewed with German malt and hops, and like many Trappist brewers, the monks of St. Rémy add candy sugar to the brew. White sugar is used for priming. The beers are bottle-conditioned.

See ABBAYE, BOTTLE-CONDITIONED BEER, HOPS, and MALT.

ABBEY BEER

Any top- or bottom-fermented beer produced by a commercial brewery under license of a monastic order. Belgian custom lends the term *Trappiste* only to beers brewed in Trappist monasteries, or under license from a Trappist monastery. Secular breweries label similar beers *Bière d'Abbaye* or *abbey beer*. German and Austrian brewers use the terms *Klosterbräu* and *Stiftsbräu* to describe their commercial products. In 1962, the Orval monastery obtained an appellation injunction forbidding the use of the name *Trappist* by any but the brewing monasteries themselves. The commercial brewers, therefore, had to call their beers something else, and the generic term for these many beers and beer styles became *abbey.* General guidelines for them are similar to those for Trappist beers. In theory, an abbey beer can be any style the brewer wishes, but the Trappist guidelines are usually followed.

Dubbel and Tripel Beers

The terms *Dubbel* and *Tripel* refer to gravity or density. The old brewers often drew off the earliest wort (the heaviest) to make a double- or triple-strength brew. The later draw (near the end of the wort run) might be used to produce a "single," or simple (small) beer. These are similar to English and American brewers' use of *XX* and *XXX.*

The Trappist abbey of Westmalle was the first to brew Dubbel and Tripel Trappist beers. This occurred after World War II.

Dubbel. A not very hoppy brown ale, with an original gravity of 15.3–17.1/ 1.063–1.070/6.3–7 Belge, Dubbels are made from mostly pale Pilsner malt, dark candy sugar, and a small amount of amber and caramel malts for color. They are 6–7.5 percent alcohol by volume, 18–25 IBU, and 10–14 SRM. Up to three different yeast strains might be incorporated, and the brewing temperature might be allowed to rise to 86°F (30°C). The beer is bottle-conditioned.

The Great American Beer Festival guidelines for Belgian-style Dubbel are 12.5–17.5/1.050–1.070 OG, 6–7.5 percent alcohol by volume, 18–25 IBU, and 10–14 SRM.

Tripel. A strong (some at barley-wine

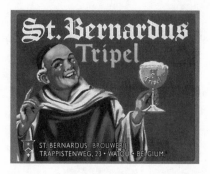

strength), very pale (3.5–5.5 SRM) beer brewed mostly from Pilsner malt and white candy sugar, with an original gravity of 17.1–23.2/1.070–1.095/7–9.5 Belge, 7–10 percent alcohol by volume, and 20–25 IBU. Up to three different yeast strains and fairly high brewing temperatures might be used, and the beer is bottle-conditioned. The Great American Beer Festival guidelines for Belgian-style Tripel are 17.5–24/1.060–1.096 OG, 7–10 percent alcohol by volume, 20–25 IBU, and 3.5–5.5 SRM.

As the summaries below indicate, not all abbey ales fit the Dubbel/Tripel description fully.

Original Gravity	Final Gravity	Alcohol by Volume	IBU	SRM
Affligem Tripel Abbey 1985				
17.4/1.071/7.1 Belge	3.1	8%	≈20	≈14
Augustijn 1985				
16.3/1.067/6.7 Belge	2.6	7.5%	≈20	≈16
Grimbergen Tripel 1985				
19.6/1.080/8 Belge	2.4	9%	≈20	≈6
St. Sixtus Belgium Abbey Ale 1982				
18.7/1.075/7.5 Belge	2.4	9.8%	11.2	≈38

See BARLEY WINE and DOUBLE, TRIPLE, AND QUADRUPLE BEERS AND ALES.

ACA CHICHA

A sacred corn beer made by Native American women and by the Inca Sun Virgins for their leaders at Cuzco, now in Peru. Also called Chicha.

See CHICHA and LATIN AMERICAN BREWERIES.

An Inca drinking Aca Chicha, a type of maize beer brewed in Peru since about 200 B.C.

ACCUMULATION TABLE

Generally, a mechanized table in which a motor causes the round top to rotate. The table is placed at the end of a bottling line in small microbreweries. Bottles accumulate on the table without knocking into each other and hence scuffing the labels. The table also might be located in overspill areas in case of stoppage, such as before the labeling machine.

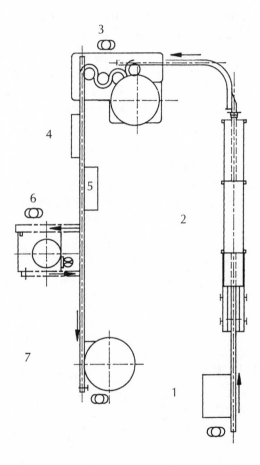

Sections of a bottling line include 1 — the dump table, 2 — the rinser, 3 — the filler/crowner, 4 — the inspection eye, 5 — the accumulation table, 6 — the labeler, and 7 — the accumulating table.

ACERBIC

A description of an acidic or sour taste.

ACETALDEHYDE

A substance that is normally produced during the fermentation process but decreases as the process progresses and the beer ages. Excessive levels of residual acetaldehyde give beer a cidery or green apple–like taste. It also can produce a breadlike or solventlike character at higher concentrations. One common cause of acetaldehyde is the excessive use of cane or corn sugar in the beer. Other causes can be pitching too little yeast or under-aerating the wort. A bacterial infection also may convert the ethanol to acetaldehyde and water. In most cases (except for bacterial infection), a long, cold aging should reduce the amount of acetaldehyde in the beer.

ACID

See pH and WATER.

ACID REST

A step at the beginning of the mash during which the temperature is held at about 90°F (32°C). This is done to correct the pH (increase the acidity) of the mash by causing a naturally occurring salt known as phytin

to form phytic acid. More often a brewer will simply correct the pH by using gypsum and dispense with the acid rest. The acid rest is usually used in a traditional decoction mashing schedule, such as would be used for producing a lager or German wheat beer, and it is also the first step of a step mash.

ACROSPIRE

Part of a kernel of barley that grows during the germination phase of the malting process. Malt that contains acrospires at least three-quarters the seed length in size is considered to be highly modified.

The modification and growth of the acrospire and rootlets during malting is broken down into stages in the illustra-

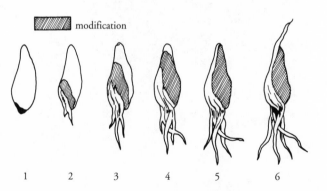

modification

1   2   3   4   5   6

tion. At first (1) there is no modification. Then (2) the rootlets first appear and the acrospire begins to grow, with the modification beginning at the bottom of the grain. Modification continues upward and outward (3) until the acrospire is about half the length of the kernel. When the acrospire is about three-quarters the length of the kernel (4), modification is almost complete. Only the tip remains hard and steely. The acrospire is fully grown (5) when it has achieved full modification but has not sprouted. It has overgrown (6) when germination has gone too far.

See BARLEY.

ADA

An abbreviation for apparent degree of attenuation, a measurement of the effectiveness of the yeast in consuming sugars in beer.

ADAMBIER

See DORTMUNDER BEER.

SAMUEL ADAMS

See BOSTON BEER CO.

ADAM'S ALE

An old English/Scottish term for water.

ADDITIVE

Anything added to beer other than malted barley, adjunct grains, hops, water, and yeast, as well as some flavorings added to specialty beers, such as fruits or spices. Typically, additives are chemicals or enzymes added at any point in the brewing process to alter the physical properties of the beer so that it is more stable in commercial distribution and therefore appeals to a mass-market economy. Some homebrewers and craft brewers also use additives, particularly clarifiers such as isinglass, Irish moss, and some gelatins.

Some types of additives are alkalines, acids, and minerals to adjust water chemistry; enzymes that affect the mashing process to change the sugars or dextrins — for example, to produce a diet (light) beer or malt liquor; clarifiers to enhance protein removal and thereby eliminate haze; heading agents to improve head retention (carbonation); and yeast nutrients to encourage vigorous fermentation.

See CLARIFIER; FRUIT, VEGETABLE, HERBAL, AND SPECIALTY BEERS; GELATIN; ISINGLASS; and IRISH MOSS.

ADJUNCT

A grain other than malted barley added to beer as a source of fermentable sugars. Some typical adjuncts are corn, rice, oats, and wheat.

Adjuncts are used — primarily by megabrewers — to create a special flavor, to enhance or reduce some property of the beer, or to cut costs by substituting cheaper grains for the more expensive malted barley. For example, oats are added to oatmeal stout to create a unique flavor.

Unmalted barley or wheat is added to improve head retention.

Breweries are not required by the United States government to list adjuncts or any ingredients used in their products.

ADRIANNE BROWER BIERFESTEN

An annual beer festival held in late June in Oudenaarde, Belgium, to celebrate the birth of the famous painter by this name, born in Oudenaarde in 1605.

AERATION

The process of supplying oxygen to the wort. To provide the best possible fermentation, the wort must be thoroughly aerated. This can be done in any number of ways, but in all cases the wort should be near yeast-pitching temperatures — anywhere below 80°F (27°C). The cooler the wort, the more soluble the oxygen will be. When the wort is aerated at higher temperatures, it can become oxidized, leading to a paperlike off-flavor.

A simple method of aerating wort is to allow the cooled wort to splash into the fermenter while filling it. Other methods include stirring vigorously with a spoon or wire whisk or using an aquarium air pump, a 2-micron or smaller air filter, and a sanitized air stone. Without an adequate supply of dissolved oxygen, the yeast cannot reproduce properly, leading to a stuck fermentation, an off-flavor, and a greater risk of ruined beer.

See FERMENTATION, HOT SIDE AERATION (HSA), and YEAST.

AFRICAN BEER

Beer has been brewed in Africa for approximately 8,000 years, from the great commercial brewing dynasties of ancient Egypt to the tiny huts of remote villages. The first Europeans to explore Africa found a staggering number and variety of beers brewed by tribes everywhere. Beer was a critical component in the daily diet of African peoples, and beers brewed from indigenous grains and grasses varied

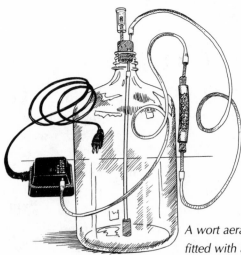

A wort aeration assembly. The wort aerator consists of a cork fitted with an airlock and a length of ¼-inch copper tubing. The copper tube is attached to a length of polyethelene tubing, which in turn connects to an aquarium aeration stone.

according to the availability of fermentable materials. Palm sap, cassava flour, barley, sorghum, millet, and, after its introduction by Arab traders, maize all figured into the brewing of more than 100 native beer styles. Some of these ancient ingredients are still used in modern, commercially brewed beers.

Most African beers taste like thin, sour porridge, with a hint of raisins in the finish. Varying in strength from mild, milky brews to unusual ceremonial concoctions close to barley wine in strength, native beers continue to be an important part of many Africans' diet.

Throughout Africa today, many tribes drink beer through hollow reed straws stuck in a communal beer pot. The villagers sit around the pot gossiping and telling stories. The beer straw is at least 5,000 years old and can be seen in ancient Egyptian hieroglyphs and Middle Eastern tablets dating to 4000 B.C.

Many of Africa's ancient tribal customs are threatened by modernization and industrial development. In Kenya, for example, teetotaling President Daniel arap Moi banned all homebrewed beer in 1989. "I am not prepared to lead a drunken nation," he said, banning even ceremonial brews.

AGING

The process of allowing fermented beer to sit, undisturbed, until it is potable. Aging allows the yeast and other particles to settle and helps remove fermentation by-products, reducing off-flavors. Aging also allows

the aromatics to mellow and meld, creating a more pleasant aroma.

If the beer is to be bottle-conditioned, aging is even more important. A small amount of sugar is added to the beer, which still contains active yeast. The beer is then bottled, and the yeast consumes the sugar, producing carbon dioxide and thus carbonating the beer.

Some beers require very long aging periods, others quite short periods. Barley wines and strong ales often must be aged for months or years.

AIR COMPRESSOR/DRYER

A piece of equipment that generates air at a delivery pressure suited to a particular bottling line, generally 60 psi (414 kPa) and up. Typical applications are the drive mechanisms of bottle rinsers, the pistons of bottle fillers, air diaphragm pumps, and automatic label glue dispensers.

An air dryer should be installed at the discharge point of air from the compressor to remove moisture from the air. If the air circulated to the application points is wet, it will ultimately cause problems.

AIR DIAPHRAGM VALVE

A valve activated by air generated from an air compressor. These valves are often found in totally automated systems at larger breweries where computer signals and instructions activate the partial or full opening of the valves. They are not generally found in microbreweries where valve control is usually manual.

AIWF BEER & FOOD FEST

The American Institute of Wine & Food (AIWF) held its first Beer and Food Fest in lower Manhattan in 1990. The event was so popular that it has become an annual event.

The first event was put together with the help of Matthew Reich, whom some people see as a pioneer in contract brewing with the work he did to promote New Amsterdam Beer. Keynote speakers included Fritz Maytag of Anchor Brewing Co., who revived the art of small craft brewing on the West Coast, and Bert Grant of Grant's Brewing in Yakima, Washington.

The highlight of the first festival, held at the South Street Seaport, was the appearance of Julia Child. The famous cookery expert made the nearly revolutionary statement that beer was no longer confined to accompanying hot dogs. Subsequent speakers have included Michael Jackson, Charlie Papazian, and Bruce Aidells, coauthor (with Dennis Kelly) of *Real Beer and Good Eats: The Rebirth of America's Food and Beer Tradition.*

The emphasis is not just on the beer, but on food as well. Steve Hindy, AIWF member and partner of the Brooklyn Brewery, says, "In many ways the renaissance of the beer industry that has given birth to hundreds of small breweries parallels the rebirth of the wine industry several years ago. Today, varietal wines account for roughly half the volume of wine sold in America. Microbrewed beers account for about two percent of the beer consumed in America [in 1995], but their share is growing rapidly.

"Beer is a wonderful accompaniment to food. There are traditions of matching beer and food in the great brewing nations of the world: Britain, Belgium, and Germany. Among American chefs, the craft-brewing revival in the United States has spawned a fresh interest in the combination of beer and food."

The AIWF events pair some of New York's most talented chefs with some of the country's most talented microbreweries. "These matches have resulted in some inspired pairings of beer and food — not just beef carbonade and hot dogs and sauerkraut," Hindy says.

In 1995, some of the 24 pairings included the Water Club's Mustard Cured Smoked Salmon with Dock Street Amber, Les Halles' Classic Cassoulet Toulousaine with Sierra Nevada Pale Ale and Porter, the Tribeca Grill's Ceviche of Red Snapper with NY Harbor Ale Dark, First's Steamed Mussels in a Wasabi Broth with New England Oatmeal Stout, and the Hudson River Club's Venison Apple Chili with Anchor Steam.

"Beer may never be a substitute for wine at the table," Hindy says, "but an informed palate may find it has its place. I would argue that amber lagers and ales make a much better beverage with a salad than wine, and a rich stout enhances the pleasure of a chocolate dessert in a way no wine or liquor could. But the idea of the event is to let people make their own choices. We think they may find themselves calling for the beer list the next time they eat out."

The event is usually held in mid-March. The AIWF also holds an annual International Beer Festival in January. The first, in 1994, matched more than 60 imported beers with food prepared by 25 New York restaurateurs.

ALBANY/SARATOGA INTERNATIONAL MICROBREWERIES FESTIVAL

A 2-day beer festival that hops from one New York city to the other in late February or early March each year. In 1995, the festival moved from Saratoga Springs to Albany. The venue may change, but the goal is the same — to benefit local charities such as the Albany Institute of Art and History and youth sport programs.

Northeast brewers, beer distributors, and homebrew suppliers take part. There are guest speakers and raffles of beer paraphernalia, T-shirts, and beer dinners, as well as homebrewing demonstrations to help the fund-raising.

ALCOHOL

A class of oxygen-containing organic chemical compounds containing a hydroxyl group attached to a saturated carbon atom. Many compounds fall into this category, but in the case of beverages, ethyl alcohol, C_2H_6O, is the pertinent compound. It is a by-product of fermentation, in that yeast converts sugars to carbon dioxide and ethyl alcohol. Trace amounts of higher alcohols, also called fusel alcohols, are produced during fermentation. These are unwanted additions to beer. Alcohol also acts as a preservative in beer.

See FERMENTATION.

ALCOHOL STRENGTH

The alcohol content of beer. Alcohol strength is a major descriptor of its character. Fermenting with yeast generates about equal amounts alcohol and carbon dioxide, plus a tiny percentage of other by-products. The alcohol content is expressed in two ways: by volume and by weight. An alcohol content of 4 percent by weight means 4 weight units of alcohol (i.e., grams) are dissolved in a total of 100 units (grams) of water (or beer). This is a comparison of the weight of the alcohol with the weight of the total beverage, and it is the way the United States brewing industry measures alcohol content.

The United States wine industry and most foreign brewers express the alcohol content of their beer by volume. An alcohol content of 4 percent by volume means that 4 teaspoons of alcohol are mixed with 96 teaspoons of liquor water, for a total of 100 teaspoons. Since alcohol weighs only 79.6 percent as much as water, a beer that is 4 percent alcohol by volume is only 3.2 percent alcohol by weight (79.6 percent of 4). Hence, the volume measurement is always larger than the weight measurement by a factor of about 126 percent. Most people are more familiar with alcohol by volume. That is the measurement used in this publication.

In most of the world, alcohol strength must be shown on the label. In the United States, however, listing alcohol strength was not even allowed until recently, and it is still not required by law in most states. The Bureau of Alcohol, Tobacco and Firearms, which governs the labeling of beer, has opposed alcohol strength labeling on the theory that people will search out strong beers and that brewers will use that in their marketing strategies, vying with each other for the "strongest" beer.

ALE

A top-fermented beer that is the oldest of all brews. From the Old English *alu*. Ales

In 1542, writer Andrew Boorde distinguished ale and beer in his Dyetary. Ale, he said, was made of water and malt, while beer was made of malt, hops, and water. Hops were a late addition to brewing ingredients, as some did not care for the strong, bitter taste hops impart.

tend to be stronger than bottom-fermented beers, and come in a variety of colors. Throughout much of history, ale was an unhopped brew. Primitive, spontaneously fermented ales, still found in remote places, are made from diverse materials such as corn, manioc, rice, and grasses.

ALE AS RENT

In Saxon times in England, rents and taxes were paid all or in part with homebrewed ale. In an age when the sale of surplus beer was often the only source of hard currency, common folk considered good beer the equal of gold. Feudal landlords often stipulated payments of beer rather than coins.

In pharaonic Egypt, and even earlier in Mesopotamia, measures of beer defined the minimum wage of the day. Thus, rents, tithes, and tributes were commonly in the form of assets. Throughout the ages, landlords eased the pain of annual rent days by providing beer to the rent-paying rabble.

ALE ASSIZES

A legal term literally meaning "session," but also used to refer to a jury, the sittings of a court, and sometimes the ordinances of a court or assembly. Also called *assises*.

Ale assizes were periodic legal proceedings that began in medieval England and were usually held at the county level. During the proceedings the court heard all matters of dispute relating to the sale and manufacture of ale and bread. Fines and penalties were typically handed down to errant or dishonest brewsters and innkeepers for such offenses as watering or otherwise debasing ale.

Adulteration of products such as ale, bread, butter, coffee, tea, and other foods was such a common practice that regulations drawn up by the crown, in its office as protector of the poor, were needed to protect citizens from unscrupulous traders. Adulteration took many forms but was often concerned with the sale of inferior goods to ignorant consumers. All Assizes also protected the offender from enraged citizens seeking vengeance. It is recorded that in Nürnburg, Germany, in 1444, a man was burned alive on a pile of adulterated saffron he was trying to palm off. Two years later, a woman and two men met with identical fates.

Assizes, in the sense of ordinances or enactments of courts or legislative bodies, such as the assize of bread and ale, played an important role in the economic system of that period. As early as the reign of John, and for a period of 500 years thereafter, the observance of assisae venalium was enforced. It was considered an important regulatory duty of legislatures to fix the price of goods such as ale, bread, and fuel, as well as to guard against adulteration, deceit, and scandal against the trade guilds.

During the Renaissance, the regulatory rights and, indeed, the strength of trade guilds were lessened by the enormous growth of trade and personal wealth of the merchants. The need for the crown to regulate was greater than ever, though the main objective was the protection of trade and commerce, not consumers.

More recently, assizes have been held during one month in each season of the year, replacing the practice, which dated back to before the Magna Carta (1215), of annual sessions at Westminster. Today judges of the High Court of Justice hold sessions in the various counties, similar to the way that United States circuit courts meet.

ALE BENCH

A long, low plank bench traditionally located outside an alehouse. The village idiot, ale knights, and alewives were customarily found upon this rude seat passing the time of day.

ALEBERRY

A traditional ancient drink made from hot ale, toast, honey, sugar, and assorted spices. This concoction was usually served hot. From the term *ale bree* or *brin* (broth).

ALE-BUSH

A term applied to heather tops, ivy, and evergreens that were hung from poles to mark the location of an alehouse. Festival wine booths also were draped with ivy in honor of Bacchus, the Greek god of wine. Both customs survived the Roman occupation of Britain.

The custom of hanging an ale-bush from a sign post is repeated in numerous cultures throughout the world today, including remote areas of Peru, Africa, Eastern Europe, and Mongolia. Wherever in the world floral displays and ale-bushes announce "beer for sale," that beer will have been made by women.

ALE-CONNER

An official whose duty it was to inspect commercial beers for purity. Custom required the ale-conner, or ale-founder, to enter the premises and seize a quantity of any brew served. The sample beer was then poured on the seat of a wooden bench. Sitting down in the puddle of beer, the ale-conner would allow his leather overalls sufficient time to dry. Upon arising, he would observe whether his britches stuck to the bench. If they did, he concluded that sugar had been added to the brew.

British custom dictated that if the ale-conner's pants stuck to the seat, a more potent beer had to be produced. In Germany, however, sticky beer was prized.

In Britain, ale-conners were appointed by nearly every manor house to assay taxable unfermented sugar content. These bureaucrats dragged shifty brewsters in to borough-court, or court-leet. At such sessions, fines and less pleasant penalties were handed down. Condemned beer was seized and given to the poor. John Shakespeare, father of the poet and playwright, was employed as an ale-conner.

In London, the office of ale-conner dates to the first charter of William the Conqueror. In deference to this ancient custom, the lord mayor of London is still required to don the ale-conner's uniform every 10 years to ritually inspect a selected local pub.

ALECOST

See ALE-GILL.

ALE DRAPER

The owner of a pub or an alehouse keeper. The name dates back to early Anglo-Saxon Britain.

An ale draper is an alehouse keeper, such as the woman shown here in the entryway to her establishment.

ALE FLIP

A drink of venerable but acquired taste. Directions for making an ale flip are as follows: To a pint of ale, add crushed ice and one egg. Shake, do not stir.

ALE-GAFOL

In early Anglo-Saxon Britain, a tribute or rent of ale paid by a tenant to the lord of the manor. In 852 A.D., the abbot of Medeshampstede, present-day Peterborough, rented some land at Sempringham to Wulfred. One of the conditions of the lease was that Wulfred should each year deliver to the cleric 2 tuns of pure ale and 10 mittans (measures) of Welsh ale.

Ale was frequently the form of payment for tolls (called tollester) charged by lords. In one Gloucestershire manor, it was customary for a tenant to pay 14 gallons of ale as a toll whenever he brewed ale to sell.

See ALE AS RENT.

ALE GARLAND

See ALE-BUSH.

ALE-GILL

A ground weed (Nepeta glecoma) that has been used for centuries to bitter beer. Also called gill-over-the-ground, cat'sfoot, alehoof, alecost, alehove, and ground ivy.

ALE HALL

An English term for a beer shop. The ale hall was among the most ancient of institutions. Perhaps the oldest written lease concerns a beer hall dating to pharaonic Egypt. The terms *ale hall* and *beer hall* fell

Ale halls are among the most ancient of institutions.

into disuse in the early 19th century, when it fell out of fashion for large numbers of people to drink beer socially. During the Industrial Revolution, in both the United States and England, beer came to be associated with unemployment and idleness.

ALE, HEATHER

An ancient brew said to be hallucinogenic. This legendary beer was the daily drink of the Picts, early inhabitants of the British Isles. The secret of making this mind-altering brew lay in the knowledge of which variety of heather had hallucinogenic properties. Small commercial English brewers have recently tried to replicate this brew.

ALEHOOF

See ALE-GILL.

ALE HORN

A large animal horn used as a cup, often with a metal or wooden stand to allow the horn to rest upright. Usually from oxen or cows, these vessels held about a half-pint of beer.

The ale horn assumed political significance following the Norman invasion of Britain in 1066. During that time, the occupying Normans required their Saxon subjects to drink beer only in the company of a Norman, presumably in an attempt to prevent beer-induced rebellions. This practice gave rise to a ritual called "peg-drinking." A large common horn was passed among a group, with each person's measure clearly marked by a wooden peg. The idea was to prevent drunkenness among the Saxons and to

prevent anyone from drinking more than his share. The expression "take him down a peg" survives to this day.

See PEG TANKARD.

ALEHOUSE

A drinking establishment. As the social center of any settlement or village, the alehouse played an important role in the social development of human society. Young and old, rich and poor shared news and gossip while they drank.

It is difficult today, in times when many things associated with drinking carry a negative connotation, to understand the respect the alehouse once enjoyed. In the

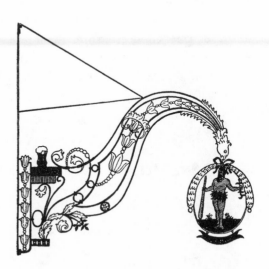

Elaborate signs marked the location of alehouses and became an art form in their own right.

Middle Ages, the alehouse was regarded in much the same way as some people today regard a house of worship. In spite of drunkenness, the alehouse was a serious setting for discussing and resolving legal and domestic matters. "Alehouse testimony" — any statement made on

Interior view of a typical 18th century alehouse. Alehouses were gathering places for family and friends.

one's oath in a licensed public house — carried the same weight as something said in a court of law. Goods and chattel, including children and wives, could be sold, pledged, or otherwise encumbered. In contrast, today any pledge made under the influence of alcohol is not recognized under the law, and barroom chat is taken as idle conversation.

The universal appeal of conversation over beer has made the alehouse central to many of the world's uprisings, from the American Revolution to Adolf Hitler's Munich (Beer Hall) Putsch. Alehouses remain among the first institutions closed down during times of social upheaval.

In Western tradition, and as far back as ancient Sumer, alehouses were usually controlled by women. These establishments were similar in function to modern-day brewpubs. Of particular interest is the Siduri (a woman brewer or tavern keeper), who dispensed beer, advice, and sexual favors to King Gilgamesh in the world's oldest written narrative, penned some 5,000 years ago.

As perhaps the world's first commercial enterprises, alehouses attracted the usual slew of draconian rules, regulations, and especially taxes. In the first written book of law, the Code of Hammurabi, alehouse keepers were the target of a wide array of restrictive laws. Infractions by brewsters for crimes such as accepting money instead of brewing ingredients as payment for beer resulted in the death penalty.

ALE KNIGHT

An old English expression, now obsolete, for one who spends life primarily among the ale pots. Also refers to an ale-drinking companion.

The term most likely had several nuances depending on the users' social class. To a person of the upper class, from which knights were drawn, the phrase "ale knight" might have been a derisive one directed at those of lower classes, who did all their fighting and brawling in public houses rather than in battle or at tournaments. To public house drinkers, to whom knights were anything but friendly, the phrase was a jibe at knightly pretenses. It would be an insult to all knights to have riffraff refer to themselves as knights of anything.

This class distinction lingers to this day in England, where, in many public houses, there is often a bar for blue-collar workers and one for the genteel classes.

> "Come all you brave wrights,
> That are dubbed ale-knights . . .
> Know malt is of mickle might."
> —*Wits' Recreations*

ALE-POST

See ALE-STAKE.

ALE-STAKE

A broom or stick originally placed upright in front of an alehouse to advertise "ale for

The ale-pole, a synonym for ale-stake, was often decorated with vines from the hop plant, a key ingredient in the brewing of beer. Here the ale-poles are being used to train hop vines.

sale." In some places, the broom or stick was found over the door. Eventually, the ale-stake, instead of being placed flat against the building, was set perpendicular to the building. Before long, someone thought of hanging a sign from the ale-stake. The symbolic connection between the broom and the brewster survives today in Latin America and Africa.

The ale-stake indicated to the public that ale had been freshly brewed at that location. The practice of putting out an ale-stake dates back to Saxon times, when alehouses were identified by the use of a long pole hanging from the establishment.

An ale-post, or ale-stake, was placed outside a location to indicate that ale had been freshly brewed and was available.

In the late 1400s, English law required the ale-stake to be removed from sight when no ale was available for sale. Permanent display of this sign indicated a commercial enterprise. Officials regulated overzealous brewsters by limiting the size of their signs to 7 feet.

ALEWIFE

An Old English term for the landlady of an alehouse. Throughout Western history, women presided over the making of beer. Not until the medieval church entered the brewing and saloon business did men gain a foothold in this traditionally female occupation. Brewsters, not brewers, continue their exclusive craft among many peoples today.

Legends abound of dishonest alewives who fleeced their drunken customers with adulterated beer and short measures. Severe punishment, far worse than those dealt to larcenous male brewers, befell those who were caught.

In Old England, alewives were recognized by their bright red caps. "Mother Red Cap" was a phrase commonly used when addressing alewives.

At one time, London's Fleet Street was home exclusively to alewives and hatmakers. A few brewsters achieved great fame through their skill in making "fine ale," which meant potent beer. The cost of a drink was always in proportion to its alcohol content.

Mother Louise was a celebrated alewife in her time (ca. 1678), known for her beer and her outdated clothing.

Because beer was thought to be critical to good health and longevity, any brewster caught selling inferior beer was believed to have committed a spiritual as well as a legal offense. An errant brewster often suffered excommunication from the church. In a rural English church dating from this period, a stone altarpiece features an unscrupulous alewife being carried into hell by a demon.

During the Middle Ages, the art of brewing was thought to border on witchcraft. Alewives were regarded with some suspicion, particularly if they were physically attractive. Although the alehouse catered to both sexes and all ages, people believed that brewsters were not to be trusted around men. Ironically, brewsters of the ancient world were the first to feature sexually alluring women in clay tablet advertisements. English alewives also realized the benefits of having comely young women about the premises.

In the 19th century, as men gained control of taverns, they realized that allowing attractive young women into the bar was good for business only so long as the men's wives did not find out. No woman of good conscience would allow her husband to drink with such temptation at hand. Thus, the all-male bar was created to placate troubled wives.

ALE YEAST

The yeast whose genus and species are *Saccharomyces cerevisiae*. This type of yeast forms colonies that can be supported by the surface tension of beer. These colonies create a thick layer of foam on top of the fermenting beer, which is why ale yeasts are commonly called top-fermenting yeasts. They readily ferment the sugars fructose, galactose, glucose, mannose, maltose, maltotriose, sucrose, and xylulose.

Ale yeasts work best at 55° to 70°F (13° to 21°C), and ferment beer very rapidly. As a result, they tend to produce more esters and other fermentation by-products than do lager yeasts. This is not necessarily a bad situation, and in fact some ale yeasts are prized for the particular esters they impart to beer.

See YEAST.

ALGARROBA BEER

A Latin American beer made from a variety of beans. It was a dietary staple of the Chaco Indians.

BROUWERIJEN ALKEN MAES WAARLOOS, BELGIUM

Alken Maes is a moderately large Belgian brewery with an annual capacity of 2,000,000 hl (52, 835, 692 gal.). It is partly owned by Kronenbourg and is perhaps best known for its Maes Pils (imported into the United States by Thames America of San Rafael, California). Maes is a very pale Pilsner of light body, with a touch of spicy hop character.

Alken Maes also produces the Grimbergen Abbey beers: Grimbergen Dubbel,

Grimbergen Optimo Bruno, and Grimbergen Tripel. These beers are brewed under contract for the Grimbergen Abbey, a common practice for abbeys that no longer operate their own on-site breweries.

Alken Maes produces a wide range of labels, including Cristal Alken, Cuvee de L'Ermitage, Golding Campina, Goliath, Judas, and Kronenbourg. Before the Kronenbourg alliance, the brewery was owned partly by England's Watney, and it still produces Watney's ales for the Belgian market.

Alken Maes also brews Miller beers under license for the European market. For a time, it produced a hoppy, full-bodied

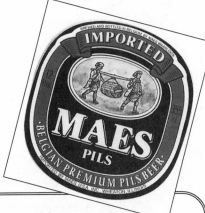

Maes Pils

A crisp, light-bodied Pilsner that is smoothly malty and delicately hopped. A distinctively Belgian take on the classic Bohemian style.

Miller Pilsner, very much in the European style. Miller is said to have specified a return to the more prosaic Genuine Draft formulation.

ALLIED BREWERY TRADERS' ASSOCIATION

G. W. C. Lemmens, Chairman
85 Tettenhall Road
Wolverhampton, West Midlands
WV3 9NE United Kingdom
0902 22303; Fax 0902 712066

An association of brewers dedicated to the issues confronting the industry in the United Kingdom.

ALLIED LYONS PLC, LONDON, ENGLAND

Allied Lyons, a division of Allied-Tetley, is one of Britain's larger brewing corporations, although brewing is only one part of this company's operations. The group also makes cider, wine, port, and sherry and has a food division.

Among the beer brands produced by Allied Lyons are Double Diamond, Alloa's, Ansell's, Holt's, and the Ind Coope brands. Most of the Allied brands are regional U.K. labels, but Double Diamond is imported into the United States, where it is handled by Barton Beers of Chicago, Illinois. Double Diamond is imported into Canada by Imported Beer Co., Mississauga, Ontario.

ALPHA ACID

Any of three major hop acids (humulone, cohumulone, and adhumulone). Alpha acids are bitter, but they do not dissolve well in wort in their original form. By boiling the hops with the wort, some percentage of the acids can be isomerized into iso-alpha acids, which are more soluble in wort.

See HOPS.

ALPHA ACID UNIT (AAU)

A unit for measuring alpha acids, also known as the homebrew bittering unit (HBU). It is used to calculate the amount of bittering hops being added to wort. The AAU value equals the weight of the hops times the percentage of alpha acid in the hops. For example, 1 ounce (30 g) of 6.8 percent alpha acid hops is 6.8 AAU; 2.5 ounces (74 g) of 5.3 percent alpha acid hops is 13.25 AAU. This calculation does not take into consideration any of the many hop utilization factors.

See HOMEBREW BITTERING UNIT (HBU), HOPS, and INTERNATIONAL BITTERNESS UNITS (IBU).

ALPHA AMYLASE

The enzyme that is primarily responsible for breaking down the starch in malted barley into fermentable sugars. Alpha amylase and beta amylase together form what is commonly known as diastase.

See ENZYMES.

ALT

From the German word for "old," broadly used to describe any top-fermented German beer.

ALTBIER

Literally, "old beer," or, more accurately, beer made in the old style. From the German *alt,* meaning "old." Today altbier refers to any prelager beer style, since bottom/cold-fermented lager beer is the major beer type of modern Germany and central Europe. The altbier in one's glass or mug in Germany depends on where one is. In Munich, the altbier is *alt-Bayrisches dunkeles,* "old Bavarian dark," which is a dark (cold-fermented) lager. In Dortmund, the altbier is a top/warm-fermented beer that is usually dark in color. Cologne (Köln) is famous for its Kolsch, which is a pale top/warm-fermented altbier that is also cold-aged in the lager style. The most famous altbier is that of Düsseldorf, which is produced in a similar way but is darker and has a stronger hop taste. The altbier of Münster is paler and a bit tart, with a healthy 40 percent wheat malt in its grist.

German authorities loosely define altbier as beer that is produced from pale or medium-colored malts (10 to 12 degrees Lovibond) of the Munich and Vienna types, with 11 to 12 percent extract (11 to 12 degrees Plato) in the original gravity. This can then be supplemented with 10 to 15 percent wheat malt and up to

10 percent crystal malt, plus additional dark malts (1 percent) to produce a final color at about 10 to 16 SRM. The mashing method usually involves a two-and-one-half- to three-hour step infusion mash (122–125°F [50–52°C] to 144°F [62°C] to 158°F [70°C], then mash-off at 172°F [78°C]), followed by a one-and-one-half to two-hour wort boil. Hopping is usually with flavoring hops only (Hallertauer, Spalt, Northern Brewer). Bitterness is around 28 to 40 IBU, or even higher.

The ferment is with top-fermenting yeast pitched at warm temperatures not lower than 54°F to 68°F (12°C to 20°C). This is followed by a lagering period at cold temperatures of 39°F to 41°F (4°C to 5°C) for 14 days, instead of the 3 weeks or longer for lager beer. Sometimes altbier brewers add hops during this aging cycle in what could be called "dry hopping."

This combination of an "old" top-fermenting production with the "new" bottom-fermenting aging is sometimes called a hybrid brewing method. Many ale brewers follow the warm ferment with a cold aging cycle but do not call their beer altbier.

The Great American Beer Festival (GABF) guidelines for Düsseldorf-style Altbier are 11–12/1044–1048 OG, 4.3–5 percent alcohol by volume, 25–35 IBU, and 11–19 SRM. Neither the GABF nor the National Beer Judge Certification Program recognizes German ale types other than Kolsch and wheat ales in competition guidelines.

Original Gravity	Final Gravity	Alcohol by Volume	IBU	SRM
Pinkus Alt (Münster) 1980				
11.4/1045	2.7	4.8%	≈28	≈12
Von Appels Alt (Münster) 1983				
12.3/1049	1.3	5.6%	Unknown	Unknown
Rheinisch Alt (Reinland) 1980				
11.8/1047	2.9	4.6%	26.5	Unknown
Widmer Alt (Portland, Oregon) 1985 (in Düsseldorf style)				
11.5/1047	2.5	4.7%	45	≈28

See DRY HOPPING, KOLSCH, and WHEAT BEER.

AMAZON BLACK BEER

A type of black beer brewed in Brazil that reached its height of popularity in the 19th century. Although seldom acknowledged by today's beer experts, the art of black beer brewing thrived as late as the 1920s in Brazil's cities. One beer historian identified and cataloged more than 50 commercially made beers popular in Rio de Janeiro as recently as 1950. This beer originally derived its opaque color from cereal grains roasted over acrid smoke fires of native hardwoods.

When European colonists arrived in South America in the 1500s, they observed the wide variety of American Indian brews and were impressed with the smoky-tasting black beers of the jungle interior. Applying traditional European beer technology and using locally available grains and tubers, brewers produced hybrid black ales that represented the best of both worlds.

Black beer is a black lager brewed in Brazil using barley, hops, water, and yeast. Black beers, such as Xingu from the Brazilian brewer Cascador, replicate, as much as possible, traditional beers brewed by early peoples of the Amazon River basin. Barley is a substitute for manioc, and hops for lupine. All milling, malting, and other aspects of the brewing process are performed by hand.

The earliest Western accounts of black beer by the natives of the Amazon region date to 1557. Many Amazonian Indians placed great significance in black beer as a beverage used in religious and social ceremonies. This primitive brewing was done with dark roasted corn or manioc root; fermentation was initiated by wild yeasts. The ancient malting process was accomplished by tribal women who chewed the starchy root to convert the starches to fermentable sugars.

Among locally available Brazilian black beers are Black Princess and Perola Negra. Xingu Black Beer is available in the export market throughout the United States and Europe.

See BLACK BEER.

AMBER AND RED BEERS

Beers that are defined by their amber or red color. For the most part, the brewer or in the case of larger operations, the marketing arm of a brewery, makes this determination. If the brewer calls it an amber beer, that is what it is, although it may be only 4 SRM or a fairly dark 26 SRM. Most amber beers are in the 5.5- to 17-SRM range. Red beers are generally a bit darker (to about 20 SRM) and a shade redder than those called amber. Some red beers are called copper beers, and vice versa.

There are two major lines of red and amber beers: ales and lagers (that is, top- and bottom-fermented beers, respectively). Most amber and red ales are made in the United States. They are closely related to pale ales and so-called Irish or Scottish ales. Amber and red lagers are often brewed according to the central European Vienna beer tradition. Amber and red beers are usually not aggressively hopped nor assertively flavored, although that is not always the case. Some American "reds" are aimed at the market niche carved out by George Killian's Irish Red, a popular beer produced by the Coors Brewing Co. that is neither Irish nor especially red. Instead, it is a lager more in the style of the Vienna beer tradition, with mellow shades of red.

The color of these beers is usually obtained by the use of colored malts, especially darker crystal malts, Vienna malts, and Munich malts. These are occasionally augmented by even darker malts such as British amber, chocolate, and black malts.

Original Gravity	Final Gravity	Alcohol by Volume	IBU	SRM
Dos Equis Amber Lager (Mexico) 1986				
10.9/1.044	2	4.6%	22	≈18
Newman's Albany Amber Ale (New York) 1986				
10.5/1.042	2.3	4.5%	18	≈10

Original Gravity	Final Gravity	Alcohol by Volume	IBU	SRM
Leinenkeugal Red Lager (Wisconsin) 1994				
12.5/1.050	3.5	4.8%	20	24
George Killian's Irish Red (Colorado) 1987 (lager ale)				
15.5/1.062	2.8	6.8%	17	≈18

See ALE, IRISH ALE, PALE ALE, and VIENNA BEER.

AMERICAN ALE

See LAGER ALE.

AMERICAN AMBER ALE

See PALE ALE.

AMERICAN BEER

American beer appreciation is heavily biased by the many styles and variations of beer and brewing that have been invented and popularized in the United States. Among these are American lager, sometimes called industrial beer; American malt liquor; sparkling lager ale or cream ale; light beer; low-alcohol beer; and 3.2 beer (beer with an alcohol content of 3.2 percent alcohol by weight, or 4 percent by volume); common beer, which is often credited with being the only indigenous American beer style; American wheat beer; and American fruit beer. In addition, the United States brewing industry is credited with the development of the heavy brewing system of production, which has been adopted by most major brewers around the world.

American brewers have been very inventive, but mostly at the instigation of brewery marketing departments. Most such innovations have been at the expense of taste.

See AMERICAN LAGER; COMMON BEER; FRUIT, VEGETABLE, HERBAL, AND SPECIALTY BEER; HEAVY BREWING; LAGER ALE; LIGHT BEER; MALT LIQUOR; and WHEAT BEER.

AMERICAN BREWERIANA ASSOCIATION, INC.

Christine Galloway, Executive Director
P.O. Box 11157
Pueblo, CO 81001
719-544-9267

This organization comprises collectors and historians interested in beer, beer advertising, and collectibles. It has more than 300 books on beer, breweriana, and brewing in its lending library. The organization also offers individuals a chance to exchange labels, coasters, napkins, and crown caps from different breweries and publishes a bimonthly magazine on breweriana.

AMERICAN BROWN ALE

See BROWN ALE.

AMERICAN CREAM ALE

See LAGER ALE.

AMERICAN HOMEBREWERS ASSOCIATION

Karen Barela, President
P.O. Box 1679
Boulder, CO 80306
303-447-0816

The American Homebrewers Association is a subsidiary of the Association of Brewers that caters to the needs of homebrewers, hobby brewers, and all those interested in homebrewing. Membership is $33 per year and includes a 1-year subscription to *Zymurgy* magazine, which is published five times per year.

See ASSOCIATION OF BREWERS.

AMERICAN LAGER

A very pale, cold-fermented lager of medium alcohol content (around 4 to 5 percent alcohol by volume). Sometimes called North American Standard. This style has been adopted in most parts of the world except Europe, particularly in the United States, Canada, Mexico, Australia, and Japan.

American lager has a minimal taste profile from 6-row barley malt and grain adjuncts (especially processed corn) and minimal (threshold level) hop content, at around 8 to 17 IBU. Original gravity is 10–11.5/1.040–1.046. Color is typically less than 3.5 SRM. There are four levels of production in this beer type: economy, standard, premium, and super premium.

Economy beer is made to be sold at a lower price, although the ingredients are not necessarily of lower quality. In fact, this beer may simply be a weaker version of a company's standard brand. In some cases, it is aimed at the 3.2 beer market. This beer must have no more than 4 percent alcohol by volume (3.2 percent alcohol by weight, hence 3.2 beer). In states with 3.2 requirements (Utah is one), beer with more than 4 percent alcohol by volume can be sold only in specially licensed liquor stores. Three-point-two beer was first legalized in the United States in 1933, just before the repeal of Prohibition. When Prohibition was actually repealed, the states were given the option of staying "dry" (no alcohol sales at all) or regulating sales of alcoholic beverages in any way they chose. Many states opted to limit alcohol beverage sales to 3.2 beer. Later, some states allowed 18- to 21-year-olds to drink this weaker beer. Today 3.2 beer is usually a watered-down version of a brewery's regular product. In some cases, an economy beer is the company's regular product sold for less under another name.

Standard beer is usually beer with a slightly lower original gravity and alcohol content, a higher percentage of adjuncts (compared with a company's premium or super premium brands), and perhaps a slightly lower hop content. In many cases, however, it is simply the company's regular product sold under a different name for a lower price.

In 1977, the Master Brewers Association of the Americas (MBAA) defined the average and acceptable range for United States lagers as follows: 11.4/1.045 OG (range 10.7–12.1/1.043–1.048), 4.65 percent alcohol by volume (range 4.3–4.9 percent), 2.5 final gravity (range 2–3.1), 16 IBU (range 10–23 IBU), and 3 SRM (range 2.4–3.8 SRM).

Premium and super premium beers are usually almost the same. Most brewers call their top-of-the-line brand "super premium," but the differences between this and their premium are often only cosmetic. Super premium beers sometimes have a lower adjunct ratio or higher-quality adjunct (such as rice instead of corn) than premium beers, and occasionally they contain some more expensive 2-row barley malt and more, or at least higher-quality, hops.

The American standard has been to produce beers with a higher alcohol content, as well as beers with fewer calories and/or a low alcohol content. In Europe, the American style has been modified (higher bitterness and fewer adjuncts) to produce what we call international lager. This style has been copied around the world.

Many countries have adopted the American lager style and created their own variations. The Japanese created dry beer, while the Canadians created ice beer as variations.

The Great American Beer Festival guidelines for American Lager call for very light body, slight bitterness, and mild flavor: 10–11.5/1.040–1.046 OG, 3.8–4.5 percent alcohol by volume, 5–17 IBU, and 3–4 SRM. The guidelines for American Premium Lager are as follows: 11.5–12.5/ 1.046–1.050 OG, 4.3–5 percent alcohol by volume, 13–23 IBU, and 2–4 SRM.

American dark lager is a closely related substyle. During the 1960s, some dark lagers were actually the brewery's regular beer with caramel color added. Recent American darks, such as Miller's Lowenbräu and Henry Weinhard's do contain dark and caramel malts, although grain adjuncts account for a healthy part of their makeup.

The Great American Beer Festival guidelines for American Dark Lager are as follows: 10–12.5/1.040–1.050 OG, 4–5.5 percent alcohol by volume, 14–20 IBU, and 10–20 SRM. Adjuncts are allowed.

Original Gravity	Final Gravity	Alcohol by Volume	IBU	SRM
Bohemian Club 1980 (economy 3.2)				
9.8/1.039	2.3	4%	13.5	2.5
Budweiser 1981				
11/1.044	2.1	4.7%	15	2.7
Budweiser 1987				
11/1.044	2.1	4.7%	10.5	2.7
Miller High Life 1986				
11.4/1.046	2.4	4.8%	15.5	≈2.7
Coors Banquet 1982				
11/1.044	2.1	4.7%	14.5	2.3

Original Gravity	Final Gravity	Alcohol by Volume	IBU	SRM
Molson Canadian 1986				
11.7/1.047	2.1	4.9%	13	≈2.7
Superior (Mexico) 1986				
10.9/1.044	2.5	4.3%	17	≈2.7
Swan Export Lager (Australia) 1989				
11/1.044	1.15	5.2%	17	3.16
Henry Weinhard Private Reserve 1980 (super premium)				
12/1.048	3	4.6%	16	2.7
Henry Weinhard Special Reserve Dark 1980 (compare with regular Henry Weinhard above)				
11.4/1.046	2.6	4.7%	15	≈15

See DRY BEER, ICE BEER, INTERNATIONAL LAGER, LIGHT BEER, and MALT LIQUOR.

AMERICAN MALTING BARLEY ASSOCIATION, INC.

Michael P. Davis, Executive VP
735 North Water Street, Suite 908
Milwaukee, WI 53202
414-272-4640

The primary purpose of this nonprofit trade association is the research and development of new malting barley varieties for use in brewing.

The association also publishes a newsletter, Gleanings.

AMERICAN PALE ALE

See PALE ALE.

AMERICAN SMOKED BEER

See RAUCHBIER.

THE AMERICAN SOCIETY OF BREWING CHEMISTS

Steven C. Nelson, Executive Officer
3340 Pilot Knob Road
St. Paul, MN 55121
612-454-7250

The American Society of Brewing Chemists (ASBC) is dedicated to the analysis of raw materials, supplies, and products for the brewing and malting industries. The organization holds an annual conference at which chemists associated with the ASBC present technical papers dealing with timely issues and experiments within the brewing industry. The ASBC also publishes a quarterly journal in which these technical papers are presented in written form.

AMERICAN STOCK ALE

See ENGLISH STRONG ALE.

AMINO ACID

Any of a class of organic acids that are the building blocks of proteins. A required nutrient for the fermentation of yeast.

See FERMENTATION and YEAST.

AMYLASE

An enzyme that breaks down the starch in malted barley into fermentable sugars. There are two amylase enzymes: alpha amylase and beta amylase. Alpha amylase breaks starch into glucose and maltose. Beta amylase breaks starch into maltose. Amylase enzymes function best at a mash pH of 5.2 to 5.4 and a temperature of 149° to 155°F (65° to 68°C).

See ENZYMES.

ANCHOR BREWING CO. SAN FRANCISCO, CALIFORNIA

Anchor Brewing Co. was a failing regional brewery when Fritz Maytag, heir to the Maytag washing machine fortune, bought a stake in it in 1965 "for the price of a good used car." Some years later, Maytag became sole owner, and in a highly disciplined fashion he rebuilt the business and learned how to brew traditional beer styles. He resuscitated Anchor's Steam Beer brand, trademarked the term *steam beer,* and paved the way for a new generation of brewing entrepreneurs in the process. Philosophically and practically, Maytag's Anchor was the inspiration for the microbreweries that would follow many years later. Anchor Brewing Co. now produces a full range of specialty beers, and Maytag continues to serve as an eloquent spokesman for the craft beer revolution.

The hallmark beer in the Anchor portfolio is its Steam Beer. In the late 19th century, a number of steam beer breweries operated on the West Coast. The term seems to have referred to the "steam" that burst from beer kegs when they were tapped. (Without refrigeration, carbonation in the warm barrels built up pressure.) The "steam" also may have referred to the use of steam power in the breweries. After Prohibition, only one brewery seems to have clung to the steam appellation, and that was Anchor. Today it remains the one and only steam beer.

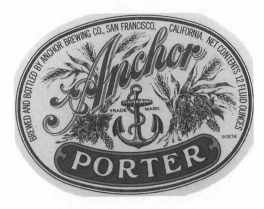

Anchor Liberty Ale

Anchor Brewing Co. conceived this beer as a Bicentennial tribute to America. This fine, all-malt, dry-hopped ale was first brewed in 1976, many years before any of today's microbreweries were more than a gleam in the eye of their founders. Liberty Ale is a delicious example of the brewer's art, with a richly floral hop bouquet and a nicely balanced hop-malt body.

Anchor has lovingly preserved the steam beer production process. First, carefully selected malted barley is crushed in a 6-row grain mill, mashed, and lautered. During the boil, fresh hops are added at different stages. After straining, the wort goes to a hot tank and then into a settling area. Once the wort is cooled, a bottom-fermenting yeast is pitched. Fermentation takes place in wide, shallow, stainless-steel fermenting vessels as cool, filtered air circulates through the fermenting room. The use of open fermenters is very unusual today, though still practiced by some Old World plants.

Once fermentation is complete, the beer is transferred to the aging room and kraeusened. This is an old German technique for natural carbonation. After the beer has been in the aging tanks for a few days, a quantity of newly fermenting beer is added. The tanks are then sealed, and a slow secondary fermentation takes place. During this period, carbonation develops. The brewers report that kraeusening produces a finer bubble and gives the beer a creamier head.

The beer is then finished — that is, filtered and pasteurized. Many small breweries do not have the equipment or inclination to finish the beer as carefully, but the brewers at Anchor know that carelessness in the final stages can dramatically increase the perishability of beer.

Anchor draught beer has been traditionally packaged in old-style kegs that are sealed with a wooden bung. The timeless sight of an Anchor worker bunging the kegs with his great mallet is a fitting symbol of the company's commitment to traditional brewing.

See COMMON BEER and NINKASI.

ANHEUSER-BUSCH
ST. LOUIS, MO

The largest brewing company in the United States is also the largest in the world. The company is especially known for its flagship product, Budweiser, which has become something of an American consumer icon. One out of every four beers sold in America is a Budweiser, and although the brand is no longer growing in the United States market, Anheuser-Busch is marketing it aggressively overseas and now sells the brand in over 60 countries.

Despite its monolithic stature, Anheuser-Busch is a family company, controlled by the descendants of its founding families. The brewery that would become Anheuser-Busch started up in 1850, but it was bankrupt by 1857, when it was purchased by a wealthy local soap magnate named Eberhard Anheuser.

Eberhard's ownership of the brewery may have led to a meeting between Eberhard's daughter and Adolphus Busch, a young brewing supply salesman. However the meeting occurred, the two were soon married, and Busch pitched in at the brewery, which was then called the E. Anheuser & Co. Brewing Association. When Anheuser died, the company changed its name to the Anheuser-Busch Brewing Association.

The beers of Bohemia were then all the rage, and there were numbers of American Pilsners, and even a few Budweisers. The latter took their inspiration from the city of Budweis, known for sweet, golden lagers. Adolphus Busch adopted this beer style as his own and quickly built it into a strong local brand. He was also canny enough to protect the name Budweiser, albeit only in North America. Busch soon began shipping the brand all over the United States, and Anheuser-Busch was one of the country's largest brewers when Prohibition hit in 1919.

Eberhard Anheuser purchased the original company that was to become the largest brewing company in the world when it went bankrupt in 1857.

Adolphus Busch, the son-in-law of Eberhard Anheuser, worked at the brewery then called the E. Anheuser & Co. Brewing Association. After Eberhard Anheuser died, Busch changed the company name to Anheuser-Busch Brewing Association.

During Prohibition, the company subsisted by selling brewer's yeast malt extract and Bevo, a rather popular malt-based nonalcoholic beverage. Once Prohibition ended, Anheuser-Busch began its gradual and hard-fought accession to the top tier of the United States brewing industry. The company now holds a 45 percent share of the United States market, with a stated goal of 50 percent in the not too distant future.

The company is now expanding aggressively around the world, with sales and distribution agreements in Asia, South America, and Europe. The latter continent has been somewhat troublesome for Anheuser-Busch, since a small Bohemian brewery also brews a Budweiser brand. The trademark conflict has kept American Budweiser out of Europe, and in most of Europe, the American version must be labeled simply "Bud." The mighty Anheuser-Busch has been courting the Czech government–owned Budvar brewery for many years, with an eye to buying it. Lately, emissaries from St. Louis have set up offices in Budweis, built a local community center, and stepped up their efforts. Many Europeans have decried this potential union, and the British beer enthusiasts association, Campaign for Real Ale (CAMRA) sends out periodic protest missives. Anheuser-Busch has promised to maintain the distinctiveness of the Czech Budvar, when and if it gains control, and an examination of the company's track record would tend to support its trustworthiness.

Although Anheuser-Busch is often pilloried for personifying everything wrong with American mass-market brewing, the company has a remarkable hold on tradition, which a visitor to the company's flagship brewery in St. Louis can easily see.

The Anheuser-Busch Brewery complex in St. Louis, Missouri, as it appeared in 1866

The Anheuser-Busch brewery is one of the few late-19th-century American breweries still used for the production of beer.

While brewery tours at most big American breweries can be tedious affairs, visiting Anheuser-Busch in St. Louis is like walking back in time.

It is one of the few late-19th-century American breweries to have survived intact, and one of only a handful still used for the production of beer. Of those, this has been the only one so lovingly maintained. The brickwork is clean and repointed, and old buildings are simply turned to new tasks instead of being razed. Like most American breweries, Anheuser-Busch no longer malts barley on-site, but the old malthouse still stands, now used for office space.

New buildings have been added, but wherever possible, the company has built them in the grand 19th-century style typical of that era's breweries. Small European-style fountains burble here and there, and in the center of it all sits a gem of a stable, home of the lead team of Budweiser Clydesdales.

The Clydesdales may be trite commercial symbols to many, but at heart they are another tie to the past. Many European breweries still maintain ceremonial draught teams, but Anhesuer-Busch is alone among United States brewers in doing so.

When it comes to brewing, Anheuser-Busch is a strange mix of utilitarianism and tradition. The Anheuser-Busch brewing staff has historically been made up of former German nationals, and German-accented English is still common in Anheuser-Busch brewhouses.

To use one example, Anheuser-Busch's brewers take great care in brewing the flagship Budweiser: They use a proportion of two-row barley, eight varieties of imported and domestic hops and the Budweiser yeast. Fresh yeast is propagated weekly from the St. Louis Budweiser culture and flown in sealed vessels to the other 11 Anheuser-Busch breweries.

After Budweiser has finished fermentation, it is aged in tanks that contain a bed of beechwood strips. This is an old tradition still used by a few small Bavarian and Bohemian breweries, ostensibly to help clarify the beer. It is an odd practice, being fairly labor intensive and likely providing only incremental benefit. Anheuser-Busch keeps on with it, however, and it is a common sight in Anheuser-Busch breweries to see brewers trundling great stacks of beechwood chips through the brewery in silver, bullet-shaped hand carts made expressly for that purpose.

In other areas, the company has diverged from tradition over time. Budweiser differs from the Bohemian beers that inspired it by employing a percentage of rice as an

Budweiser

Served cold, Budweiser can be superbly refreshing. (Although Bud employs eight varieties of excellent hops, the brewer has reduced the hopping almost to the threshold level, so serving it cold will not submerge its slender, though subtly appealing, hop character.) Light-bodied, smooth and creamy. A malty sweetness is evident, and the beer has an attenuated hop bite.

An aerial view of the Anheuser-Busch Brewing Co. complex, St. Louis, Missouri

Michelob

In the 1940s and 1950s, Michelob was a malty, draught-only specialty beer, much sought by the beer enthusiasts of the time. In later years, Anheuser-Busch adulterated the recipe with rice and put it in a can. Michelob today is a typical American lager, perhaps slightly meatier than some, but with little else to distinguish it from its lightly flavored brethren. Although the brand is classified as a "super premium," this designation has not prevented it from entering a prolonged slide, losing over three million barrels of volume over the past decade. One analyst has noted that the volume that Michelob has lost could easily account for the rise of the entire specialty beer segment (microbrews, contract brews, etc.), which in 1994 was approaching three million barrels. Anheuser-Busch has experimented with numerous specialty beers recently, and the next logical step might be to rejuvenate Michelob (which, like Budweiser, is named after a Bohemian town) as a contemporary specialty beer.

adjunct. Budweiser has also become measurably less bitter over time, according to some analysts, and its bitterness is now substantially below that of the Bohemian beers that inspired it. The final result is the light-bodied, lightly flavored lager that we know as Budweiser.

Whatever changes the company has made to the recipe over time, no one can argue with the results — a beer that sold over 40 million barrels a year almost a hundred years after its inception. In a world of fleeting brand loyalty, Budweiser endures.

Today the company is led by August Busch III, a fourth generation descendant of Adolphus. His son August IV, a graduate of the German brewing school VLB, is gradually ascending through the company hierarchy.

Of late the company has had great success with the beer of the moment — ice — and is also working on some more traditional styles, including the odd ale, and even a wheat beer.

See BEER IN THE WOOD and KRAEUSENING.

ANHEUSER-BUSCH CORPORATE LIBRARY

One Busch Place
St. Louis, MO 63118
314-577-2669

The largest brewing company in the world owns and operates one of the most impressive brewing libraries as well.

ANTIVACUUM VALVE

A valve that is located on tanks that are enclosed and often under pressure, such as enclosed fermentation tanks and bright beer tanks. The valve opens automatically at a set negative pressure to prevent a vacuum from occurring and thus alleviate the threat of a tank's caving in. These tanks can be under 1 to 30 psi (7 to 207 kPa) of pressure. When they are emptied without top pressure or atmospheric pressure, a vacuum will occur, ultimately causing a tank, no matter how large, to collapse. Normally, there is a constant top pressure of carbon dioxide or another gas over the beer in the tank being emptied. This gas replaces the liquid as it is removed and thus prevents a vacuum. If someone forgets to give the tank top pressure or if the gas runs out, the antivacuum valve will automatically open as the vacuum occurs, allowing air into the tank to prevent a collapse.

An antivacuum valve should be located at the top on every appropriate tank and regularly tested for its ability to function. This is one of many safety features found in breweries.

APACHE CORN

A corn-based beer seasoned with mind-altering herbs such as jimson and tiswin (poisonous hallucinogenic weeds) and brewed by the Apache Indians of what is now Arizona. The United States government banned tiswin brewing in the 1880s. Versions of this beer are still made in several rural areas of South America.

APPLES

See FRUIT.

AROMA

All the essences and sensations perceived by smelling a beer. A beer's aroma is made up of myriad chemical compounds, some present in hops and malt, others produced as by-products of fermentation by yeast. More than 16 million different odors are detectable by the human nose, but only a few dozen are likely to be pronounced in beer. Beers often are described as having a "malty" or a "hoppy" aroma. However, beer judges look for subtle aromas that indicate potential problems in the brewing process. These aromas can be described as "plastic," "cardboard," or "buttery," or by other adjectives associated with certain chemical compounds.

AROMATIC HOPS

Hops with high concentrations of essential oils, which are very volatile. They are driven off during the wort boiling and can be lost in storage. For this reason, aromatic hops are added toward the end of the boil or in a hop back, where the hot wort filters through the hops just before being cooled or in the secondary fermenter during dry hopping. Aromatic hops also can be added to the cask when producing real ales.

The essential oils of hops are made up of more than 200 compounds, with 3 oils —

Aromatic hops have high concentrations of essential oil.

humulene, myrcene, and caryophyllene — making up 80 to 90 percent of all hop oils. No combination of these 3 oils alone provides all the aromatic or flavor characteristics of hops. Some combination of the many other minor compounds must be present to provide all the desirable qualities in an aromatic hop.

See HOPS.

ASAHI BREWERIES LTD. TOKYO, JAPAN

Asahi is the second largest of Japan's big brewing combines, and it holds a market

Asahi Super Dry

The hallmark of dry beer is its very attenuated flavor. The idea is that it hits the palate and then just stops, eliminating the "finish" that beer enthusiasts rhapsodize over but not every consumer seems to embrace. (Many contemporary consumers consider the "finish" an "aftertaste.") When Super Dry hit the market in 1987, Japanese consumers went wild over it, and dry beer was soon the rage. The other major brewers quickly launched their own dry beers, and by 1989 dry beers accounted for 40 percent of the Japanese market. The craze quickly spread to the United States and Canada, where every major and regional brewer soon had a dry product. By 1991, however, the dry beer market share in Japan was down to 23 percent and shrinking monthly. The North American dry beer market also went south.

Asahi Super Dry is still produced for the Japanese market and in the United States. It is a pale, light-bodied beer with few noticeable beer characteristics.

share of about 25 percent. Asahi maintains 7 breweries with an annual capacity of 18,175,000 hl (480,144,350 gallons). Within its breweries, Asahi operates a total of 28 bottling lines, 16 canning lines, and 8 kegging lines. The company also has 4 laboratories. (Japanese brewing chemists are known the world over for their meticulous research into every aspect of brewing science.)

The brewery's best-known product is Asahi Super Dry, which was introduced in 1987. This is the beer that kicked off the dry beer wave in Japan and North America.

Asahi produces several other brands for the Japanese market, including Asahi Pure Gold, Asahi Draught Beer "Z," Asahi Super Premium, Asahi Draft Beer Horoniga, and Asahi Original Ale 6. The company also produces Coors under license in Japan.

See DRY BEER.

ASOCIACION LATINOAMERICANA DE FABRICANTES DE CERVEZA

Jose-Maria de Ro-mana, Coordinator
  General
Prolongacion Arenales 161 San Isidro
Lima 27 Peru
Apartado Postal 1642
Lima 100 Peru
22-32-25 or 41-55-83
Telex 21002 (025202) PB HCSAR

ASOCIACION NACIONAL DE FABRICANTES DE CERVEZA

Fernandez de la Hoz
7, 28010 Madrid, Spain
34-1-593 27 70 or 34-1-593 28 13
Fax, 34-1-448 97 12
Telex, 44629 ANFAC E

The Spanish association formed to promote the beer industry in Spain serves as an advisory group to the brewers.

ASSOCIATION DES BRASSEURS DE FRANCE

25 Boulevard Malesherbes
75008 Paris
France

The Association des Brasseurs de France (Association of Brewers in France) is quite similar to those in other parts of the world. It handles the legal and industry concerns of the breweries in France.

ASSOCIATION OF BREWERS

Charlie Papazian, President
Cathy Ewing, Vice President
P.O. Box 1679
Boulder, CO 80306-1679
303-447-0816

The Association of Brewers was founded in 1978 as the American Homebrewers

Association. Since then it has seen several organizational changes. It is now an incorporated, nonprofit association attempting to educate the public about the quality and beneficial aspects of beer. The association publishes two magazines, *The New Brewer* ($55 per year) for commercial brewers and *Zymurgy* ($33 per year) for homebrewers. It also operates Brewers Publications, publishing books related to brewing.

The Association of Brewers produces two national beer conferences, the National Microbrewers Conference and the National Homebrewers Conference, each year. In addition, the association sponsors the Great American Beer Festival, one of the United States's best-known and most respected events relating to American beer products.

The association's Institute for Brewing Studies is dedicated to small-scale brewers and focuses on continuing education for them. Membership in the institute is open to anyone interested in or involved with the commercial brewing industry. The organization has a sliding membership fee scale, and all members receive a subscription to *The New Brewer.*

The American Homebrewers Association is the arm of the Association of Brewers dedicated to homebrewers and hobby brewers.

See AMERICAN HOMEBREWERS ASSOCIATION.

ATTEMPERATION COILS

A coil in an open-top fermentation vessel that (1) cools down a fermentation after it has reached its final gravity or (2) controls the temperature during active fermentation. Generally, attemperation coils have three full turns that are located evenly throughout the part of the vessel holding the beer (not the yeast headspace).

Chilled water or a food-grade propylene glycol solution is passed through the coil, removing heat from the body of the beer until the required temperature is reached. The size of the vessel determines the diameter of this attemperation coil and how far off the sidewall it is located.

In this type of open-top fermentation vessel, where the ratio of surface area to depth is nearly 1:1 (a very important factor with different yeast metabolisms), cooling is more effectively achieved with an internal cooling coil as opposed to an external jacket.

ATTENUATION

The characteristic of yeast to stop fermenting at a certain alcohol level, regardless of the supply of available food and nutrients. This level varies with each strain of yeast. Most beer yeasts are capable of fermenting up to 8 percent alcohol by volume; wine and champagne yeasts can reach 18 percent alcohol by volume. The apparent degree of attenuation (ADA) is a measure of a yeast's attenuativeness. A yeast that has an ADA of 70 percent will be expected to convert 70 percent of the dissolved sugars into alcohol.

See ADA.

AUDIT ALE

A brew that English lords traditionally gave to tenant farmers when the farmers' land rents were due. Also, a special brew which was offered to students at universities in earlier times to soften the blow of the posting of grades.

AUGER

A screw conveyor that moves crushed or uncrushed grain to its destination. Care must be taken that kernels are not over-cracked as they pass through the auger. This is especially important when setting mill crush for milling and mashing simultaneously. The mill should not be set too fine, as further breakage will occur if the auger is to convey crushed malt to the mash tun.

AUGSBURGER ROT

See STROH BREWING CO.

AUGUSTINER-BRÄU WAGNER, MUNICH, GERMANY

Founded in 1328 as Augustiner-Kloster-Bräuerei, an Augustine monastic brewery, this brewery was secularized in 1803 and purchased by the Wagner family some years later. The company operates out of a 19th-century facility that malts its own barley and uses very traditional brewing methods. The company still ships some of its local draught beer in wooden casks.

Augustiner beers are local favorites in Munich — no small distinction in a city that boasts several world-famous lager brewers (Spaten, Hacker-Pschorr, Löwenbräu, and Paulaner). The brewery moved to its current location in the late 19th century but still maintains a *gasthaus* at its former site on the Karlsplatz, the city's pedestrian mall. The gasthaus offers half-liters of all the Augustiner specialties.

Augustiner also maintains a *biergarten* (beer garden), the Augustiner Keller, a few blocks from the city's main train station. The beer garden can accommodate up to 5,000 people and is a favorite of Munich natives.

Augustiner produces several brands that are poured at its gasthaus and beer garden, as well as in other establishments in Munich. Among these brands are Augustiner Helles, Edelstoff, Pils, Maximator, Heller Bock, Octoberfestbier, Dunkel, and Weiss.

See BOCK BEER, BOHEMIAN BEER, and WHEAT BEER.

AUTOCLAVE

A piece of equipment used in laboratories to sterilize growth media, glassware, and utensils when preparing for yeast propagation and plating procedures for general quality-control swabbing techniques for plant sterility checks.

BRÄUEREI AYINGER
AYING, GERMANY

The Ayinger brewery is located in a small town not far from Munich. It is owned by Bräu Franz Inselkammer, a graduate of Germany's Weihenstephan brewing college

The fine family of Ayinger beers

Celebrator Dopplebock

A strong, dark brew with a powerful malty character. The beer's sweetness is all-embracing, but not overpowering, and its heartiness recalls its origins as a monastic recipe, from a time when strong beers were used as "liquid bread" to sustain monks through their fasts. The ornate label is the work of Charles Finkel, a talented illuminator/illustrator and founder of the beer importing firm Merchant du Vin Corporation of Seattle, Washington. Celebrator is one of several Ayinger beers brought to the United States by Merchant Du Vin Corporation.

and a celebrated German brewer. (The honorary Bräu title is traditionally bestowed on independent brewery owners/brewers.)

The Inselkammer family has farmed in the area for decades and grows a substantial portion of its own barley. Ayinger also does its own barley malting, an increasingly rare practice among brewers.

Ayinger beers are lagered for 3 to 6 months, a long period by American standards, and are Millipore filtered under sterile conditions before bottling. The company exports its more robust beers but refuses to export its helles beers and Pilsners because they are too fragile to transport great distances.

Bräuerei Ayinger produces a full range of beers, including Ayinger Altbairisch Dunkel, Ayinger Jahrhundert, Maibock, Octoberfest-Märzen, Bräu-Weiss, Amber-Weiss, and Crystal Weizen. Perhaps the company's best-known beer in the American market is Celebrator Dopplebock, recognizable by its billy goat hang tag and colorful label with heraldic goats

59

A cooper at work at the Ayinger Brewery

rampant. Celebrator is also available in Canada on a specialty basis. Ayinger beers are imported into the United States by Merchant du Vin, Seattle, WA.

See BOCK BEER, DOPPELBOCK, OKTOBER-FEST BEER, and WHEAT BEER.

AZTEC BEER GODS

The beer of the Aztec people is called Aca Chicha, or Chicha. A drunken Aztec was considered under the influence of a spirit or god. The gods of beer took the form of a rabbit — a creature that the Aztecs thought had no common sense.

Chief among these deities was Ometochtli. Other gods of the brewing vat included Petecatl and Tequechmecauiani. The latter protected the Sendecho (beer drunkard) from accidental death by hanging.

Of sterner stuff was the god Teatlahuiani, whose divine duty it was to pursue drunks to death by drowning. The god of "the morning after" was Quatlapanqui. His associate was Papaztac. Tepoxtecatl, the beer god of the two-rabbit day of the Aztec calendar, was the patron of those fortunate (or unfortunate) enough to have been born on that day. These people were deemed destined for a life of drunkenness, and thus were exempt from any restrictions on their beery behavior, public or private.

See ACA CHICHA and CHICHA.

BACHELOR ALE

A brew sold at a stag party to provide a nest egg for the groom-to-be.

BACTERIA

Species of microscopic organisms whose single-celled or noncellular bodies are round, rodlike, spiral, or filamentous. They can and do exist on any surface — in water, soil, and air — but no pathogenic bacteria can survive in beer. They are entirely unwelcome anywhere in the beer-making process. Certainly, some strains of bacteria can improve a beer, but bacteria mutate far too quickly to provide a consistent effect, and experimentation with them should be avoided. The brewmaster must be sure to sanitize all surfaces that the unfermented wort (and ultimately the beer) will come in contact with.

Normally, steam or chemical sanitation can keep bacteria in check. Some bacteria will end up in the final product, as full sterilization of all equipment, beer lines, fermenters, bottles, and so on, is not possible. But when an adequate quantity of yeast is pitched, the bacteria's growth will be inhibited. A solution of 1 tablespoon (about 15 ml) of chlorine bleach in 1 gallon (about 4 L) of water is enough to sanitize any beer surface, provided that the solution is left on the surface for 20 minutes or more, then rinsed off with hot tap water. Chlorinated sanitizing solutions cannot be left on stainless steel and other metals for extended periods, as the solutions are corrosive.

See ACID REST.

BALANCE

See WATER.

BALCHÉ

A type of mead made by the Yucatá Maya. Quinine and an alkaloid extract from the bark of the Balché tree (*Lonchocarpus longistylus*) was added to the mead. This gave it a purgative nature. Balché was a sacred drink that the Maya believed purified body and soul.

BALLANTINE ALE

At one time one of the best-selling ales in America. Originally based in Albany, New York, the Ballantine Brewing Co. began producing its ale and India Pale Ale in the 1830s, when Peter Ballantine came to the United States from Scotland. In the decades that followed, the brewery relocated to Newark, New Jersey, and later the Ballantine beers were produced in Rhode Island by Narragansett and in Indiana by Falstaff. The Pabst Brewing Company in Milwaukee, Wisconsin, now brews ale with the Ballantine label.

The Ballantine ale can — immortalized by artist Jasper Johns — proclaimed it to be "America's largest selling ale," and in the 1960s and 1970s that was undoubtedly true.

See BEER IN THE WOOD, INDIA PALE ALE, and PABST BREWING CO.

The Ballantine Brewery in Newark, New Jersey, was a massive complex of buildings housing the various elements of the company.

BALLING

A measurement of the density of wort based on the amount of dissolved sugar in the liquid. Traditionally used in Europe, it has largely been replaced by the Plato scale.

See DENSITY.

BALL VALVE

A manual or automated valve that has a ball seated within its body and a hole through in one direction but not the other. A ball valve allows for very fine liquid flow control.

BAPTISM BEER

A beer brewed to celebrate a child's birth or baptism, then stored until the child reached his or her majority, at which time it was consumed. At a time in Christian history when infants who died before baptism were thought to go directly to hell, this dedication was often performed the same day a child was born.

BARLEY

A grassy grain that is the raw material from which beer is made. The ears of the plant produce the kernels of grain used to make malt. The grain grows in either 2 or 6 lateral rows of kernels. This is what a brewer or maltster is referring to when he or she talks about 2-row malt or 6-row malt. (There is actually a permutation of 6-row barley in which two of the rows grow together; this is called 4-row barley but is not commonly used in brewing.) Wispy strands of a hairlike substance called awn grow along the ear. Awn is much like the silk of corn.

Each kernel of barley is essentially a seed. It consists of a hard external husk, a large mass of starch called the endosperm, and an embryo area near where it is broken off the stem. The embryo area includes the acrospire, which grows out from the grain during the germination phase of the malting process.

The husk is important in malting because it distributes moisture evenly to the endosperm. It is also important to the brewer in that the husk serves as a filter for the mashed liquor during the sparging stage. The endosperm contains the starch that will be converted to sugar and ultimately form the basis of the beer. The acrospire breaks down the starch as it germinates; the length of the acrospire signals the extent to which the starch has been

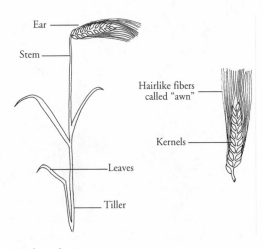

Barley plant

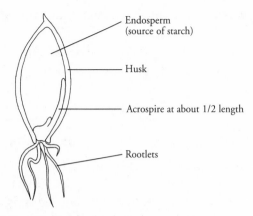

- Endosperm (source of starch)
- Husk
- Acrospire at about 1/2 length
- Rootlets

Germinating barley kernel

modified.

When selecting barley, the maltster looks for plump, round kernels. Historically, physical appearance was the most important selection factor, but today maltsters also consider a number of other factors. Low nitrogen content is now the primary criterion in selecting good barley. The nitrogen content should be no more than 1.6 percent. If the grain is being used for purposes other than making pale ale malt, it can contain somewhat more nitrogen — up to 1.9 percent for lager malt and 2.5 percent for distillery malts.

Most barley is sown in the spring, although winter varieties, such as Maris Otter, also are used for malting. One way that a farmer can reduce the nitrogen content of the barley is to plant early, but this goal must be balanced by the need to avoid cold weather, which can damage young plants.

When examining barley for suitability for brewing purposes, the grain can be cracked open and the starchy endosperm examined. Barley contains about 60 to 65 percent starch by weight. If the endosperm is white and looks like flour or meal, it is good for brewing. If it is gray or translucent, it would be better left for other purposes. Typically, the maltster also looks at other factors, such as grain size, which is determined by using a set of sieves.

When barley is harvested, it typically contains about 15 to 25 percent water. Drying is typically done by pumping hot air through the harvested barley. Historically, cut barley was left in the field in tall sheaves to be air dried, but this resulted in uneven drying and encouraged infection or infestation. Barley is usually dried to a moisture level of about 9 to 14 percent before being stored. Grain with

The general stages of barley cultivation are depicted in this illustration of an ancient Egyptian barley field.

more than 16 percent water is unsuitable for storage. Although barley sold on the open market varies in moisture content from 9 to 25 percent, higher prices are paid for grain with a low moisture content.

Another factor that the malt buyer looks at is the condition of the grain. He or she does not want grain that is crushed or otherwise damaged. The maltster also does not want grain contaminated with other feed grains, grasses, weeds, or dirt.

After the raw barley is sent to the maltster, he or she usually precleans the grain to remove any debris. At this time, the maltster also grades the kernels by size so that similar-size grains will be malted together, ensuring uniform germination.

Thousands of strains of barley are available, but some are preferred for malting because they have shown a tendency to produce plump grains, resist disease, or withstand harsh weather. Some types used today or in recent decades include Chevalier, Archer, Spratt, Klages, Imber, Maris Otter, Harrington, and Goldthorpe.

BARLEY WINE

A synonym for strong ale. The word came into use in Britain at the turn of the century. It refers to beer (usually ale beer) with an alcohol strength approaching that of wine (7 to 15 percent alcohol by volume). Beer of such strength is not continually produced by any brewery, although it is becoming more common, particularly in the United States. Barley wines require a long aging period, ranging from 6 months to several years. Some barley wines are fermented with a combination of yeasts, including champagne yeast, which is better able than ale yeasts to cope with the high-alcohol environment.

The United States Bureau of Alcohol, Tobacco and Firearms has outlawed the mixture of beer and wine and the use of any label that hints at such a mixture. Therefore, this type of beer is likely to be labeled "barleywine-style ale."

A number of early British brewers were noted for their barley wines, even though they were not called by that name. In his *Science of Brewing* (1805), Richardson, whose first name is unknown, described a "Strong Burton ale" at an original gravity of 1.110 (26.2 degrees Plato). Richardson is credited by some with the invention of the hydrometer, and his measurements allow us to determine the alcohol content of the beer. The beer's final gravity of 1.013 (3.2 degrees Plato) would, if correct, yield a stunning alcohol content of 13.1 percent alcohol by volume. Richardson's description of beer production methods and hop usage allow us to speculate further as to bitterness, and we can guess that to be about 83 IBU. But this beer's color will probably remain a mystery, although surely it was relatively dark, at around 30 to 40 SRM.

Another famous British barley wine of more recent vintage is Thomas Hardy's Ale from Eldridge, Pope & Co. in Dorchester, England. The beer is named after the writer, who mentioned the brewery in his writings. This beer ages well and is supposed to improve in the bottle (it is bottle-conditioned) for at least 5 years and perhaps as long as 20.

The first modern American barleywine-style ale was brewed at the Anchor Brewing Co. in San Francisco in 1975 and was called Old Foghorn. It was originally bottled in 6.4-ounce champagne splits, but since 1980 it has not been bottled and is available only on tap.

Barley wines and barleywine-style beers should have an original extract of at least, and probably above, 18/1.072, with an alcohol content of more than 7.5 percent by volume. Top-fermenting yeast is normally used, although some American brewers are experimenting with wine or champagne yeasts (also top-fermenting yeasts). British pale malt is the common grist agent. Some American brewers use United States 2-row barley plus some colored malts, including crystal or caramel malt. Additional ingredients might include sugar, molasses, and, in the case of at least one American beer, maple syrup. Hops are usually British types such as Kent Goldings or American variants such as Fuggle or Willamette.

The Great American Beer Festival guidelines for Other Strong Ales state that "any style of beer can be made stronger than [regular] . . . [the goal] . . . should be a balance between . . . character and alcohol." The guidelines for Barley Wine, which should have an estery and fruity character, are 22.5–30/1.090–1.120 OG, 8.4–12 percent alcohol by volume, 50–100 IBU, and 14–22 SRM.

Original Gravity	Final Gravity	Alcohol by Volume	IBU	SRM
Richardson's Strong Burton Ale 1805				
26.2/1.110	3.21	3.1%	≈83	≈40
Thomas Hardy's Ale 1985				
29.9/1.127	8.11	2.5%	≈100	≈30
Worthington Burton 1889				
21.5/1.088	7.5	9.8%	≈80	≈30
Anchor Old Foghorn (California) 1975				
25/1.105	8.1	9.1%	32	≈16
BridgePort Old Knucklehead (Oregon) 1987				
22.5/1.092	9	9.1%	55	≈34

See ABBEY BEER, BURTON ALE, DOPPELBOCK, ENGLISH STRONG ALE, and STOUT — IMPERIAL.

BARM

The froth of yeast on top of fermenting wort (also called barm beer), the foam on a glass of beer, or another word for brewer's yeast. As a verb, *barm* means to pitch (add) yeast to wort.

BARMY

A term used to describe someone whose brains are as the barm (foam) on beer. A modern equivalent would be "airhead."

BARREL

See BEER IN THE WOOD.

BARREL, 31-GALLON

The standard industry volume measure. Although there are no actual 31-gallon (177 L) barrels, volume is taxed based on this measure. While such barrels may have existed at one time, it is certain that a full 31-gallon barrel would be a daunting transportation challenge. As a result, half-barrels (15.5 gallons or 50 L) and quarter-barrels (7.75 gallons or 29L) are the largest packages available to consumers.

A barrel can refer to a casklike container for beer, such as the one shown here, or to a measurement for beer equivalent to 31 gallons or about 117 liters.

BASS PLC
BURTON-ON-TRENT, ENGLAND

Bass PLC is Britain's largest brewing conglomerate, owning Bass, Charrington, Wales and West Ltd., and Tennent. The

M. T. Bass, Esq., of the famous Bass PLC Brewery in England

company brews a score of brands under these names and others.

The Bass Brewery, founded in 1777, is located in Burton-on-Trent, the historical home of pale ale. There the company brews its famous Draught Bass (not to be confused with the Bass Ale sold in the United States, a somewhat different product) and Worthington White Shield, a noted bottle-conditioned ale.

The Bass Brewery was once known for its Burton Union System, an archaic fermenting system that involved interlinked wooden casks. The fermenting beer bubbled up through hoses into common troughs, then settled back into the casks. This system is said to have provided a unique flavor profile. Unfortunately, the brewery decided that it was no longer cost-efficient to use this system and removed it from the brewery.

The company's flagship Draught Bass is cask-conditioned, a practice followed by

Bass Ale

The Bass Ale familiar to American consumers is somewhat different from its draught counterpart in the United Kingdom. It is produced at the Bass brewery in Burton-on-Trent, but it has a higher alcohol content (5 percent by volume), is hopped differently, and is filtered and pasteurized. The result is a beer that bears little resemblance to the Draught Bass of England but has been very successful in the United States. In 1993, Bass Ale was the 11th most popular import brand in the United States, with sales of 246,000 barrels. It is a copper-colored, full-bodied brew, with a smooth, malty body and assertive hopping.

many of Britain's ale brewers and the odd American microbrewery. Under this system, a cask is delivered to a pub, where it is cellared while it matures at a carefully controlled temperature. While in the casks, natural carbonation develops.

The British "tied house" system, in which pubs are owned by particular breweries, has allowed the maintenance of this system, for the brewery can dictate to publicans the proper conditions for storage and maintenance of the beer. Tied houses are prohibited in the United States, a largely beneficial regulation, but one that makes cask-conditioned ales a dicey proposition. The rise of brewpubs in the United States has opened the door for more cask-conditioned ales, since the pub brewer has full control over the product from start to finish.

Bass Ale is imported to the United States by the Guinness Import Co. of Stamford, Connecticut and to Canada by Guinness International. The company is beginning to export some of its other beers (Tennent's Lager, for example) under the aegis of a new importing operation, Bass Brewers Worldwide.

The Bass Brewery's instructions for bottling beer ca. 1880 were:

1. Ale should not be bottled during summer, or in warm weather. Home bottling should be completed by the end of June at the latest. Summer-brewed ale should, however, be bottled as soon as it gets into condition.

2. When ale is received, it should be at once placed, bung upwards, on a scantling in the cellar, so as to allow the porous spiles to work; when thus placed it must be left undisturbed.

3. Each cask is usually provided with one or more porous pegs in the bung, which will carry off the gas generated by fermentation. It will only be necessary to make any alteration with regard to these pegs in the case of their having become so much clogged that the cask would burst if the requisite vent were not given; or in the opposite case of a tendency in the beer to become flat, when hard spiles must be substituted.

4. The cellar ought to be well-ventilated, kept perfectly clean, and as cool as possible. Underground cellars are usually the best.

5. Immediately after the beer is bright and sparkling, and in a quiet state, not fermenting, it is in the proper condition to be bottled.

6. If, from any cause, the ale should not become fit for bottling in the usual time, it will generally be sufficient to pass it through the grounds again, i.e., roll it over and put it up again on the scantling.

7. Ordinary bottling taps, with long tubes reaching almost to the bottom of the bottle, are recommended. All taps, pipes, and vessels used for ale should be kept scrupulously clean.

8. The bottles, when filled, should be corked without delay.

9. The bottles should be piled standing upright. Should the ale be sluggish in ripening, the bottles may be laid down; but this is seldom necessary.

10. Bottled ale is never fit to be sent out under a month. It takes at least that time to acquire the bottled flavour.

11. As the ale ripens in the bottle, a sediment is thrown down. In uncorking a bottle, therefore, be very careful to avoid disturbing this.

12. In decanting, pour out the ale in a jug, carefully keeping back the sediment within the bottle.

See ALE, BURTON UNION SYSTEM, LAGER ALE, and MARKET SHARE.

BASS, WILLIAM

The founder, in 1776, of the Bass Brewery at Burton-on-Trent, England. Bass is now one of the largest brewers in the world. As an early producer of India Pale Ale, Bass has nearly always been involved in the export market. The brewery's symbol, the red triangle, became the first registered beer trademark in 1890.

See BASS PLC.

BAVARIAN BEER

Bavarian-style beer is one of the four great 19th-century beer styles to come out of central Europe. The others are Bohemian, Dortmunder, and Vienna. The Bavarians were the first to brew lager beer. During the Middle Ages, they found that storing their beer in deep caves during the winter months greatly improved beer. Bavarian styles are considered "dark" in the United

States, but they are actually dark amber to brown in color (14–30 SRM) with a medium alcohol content (4.8–6.3 percent by volume) and an original gravity of 12–14.5/1.048–1.058. A malty character is predominant, and the taste is smooth, almost like caramel, with little or no burnt-grain harshness. Ingredients used are Munich malt, including colored malt, plus black malt (sparingly) and caramel malt. These beers are brewed with water at about 250 ppm hardness. The bitterness level, which is around 20 to 30 IBU, should be well balanced so as not to dominate the malt flavors. The modern Munich style, called Munich dunkel (a Bavarian variation), was originally developed by Gabriel Sedlmayr of the Spaten-Franziskaner-Brau in Munich early in the 19th century. Closely related are American dark lagers, which are a little lighter in body than the Munich dunkel.

The archetype of the Bavarian brewing style may well be the Kulmbacher type, which originated in the city of Kulmbach and inspired the brewers of Munich. Kulmbacher beer is heavier and richer than Munich dunkel or American dark lagers, and has an original gravity of up to 14–15/1.057–1.062. Kulmbacher is normally darker in color.

The city of Erlangen, in the Nuremberg-Franconia area of Bavaria, also is noted for its dark Bavarian style. Erlanger is a little heavier and darker than the original Bavarian style, an original gravity of 13–13.5/1.053–1.055.

The Great American Beer Festival guidelines for European Dark/Münchener Dunkels are 13–14/1.052–1.056 OG, 4.5–5 percent alcohol by volume, 16–25 IBU, and 17–20 SRM.

In the rest of Germany, dark beers are called dunkels or occasionally *schwarzbier,* which means black beer. Schwarzbiers contain dark malts, have an original gravity of 12/1.048, and employ Pilzen-type hopping (25 to 45 IBU).

Original Gravity	Final Gravity	Alcohol by Volume	IBU	SRM
Ayinger Alt-Bayrisches Dunkel 1985				
13/1.052	3.8	4.9%	23.5	≈30
Spatenbräu 1867				
13.1/1.053	4.5	4.1%	≈30	≈40
Erlanger 1875				
13.1/1.053	3.4	5.1%	≈38	≈40+
Kulmbacher 1887				
15.3/1.063	4.5	5.6%	≈35	≈40+

See AMERICAN LAGER, BLACK BEER, MÜNCHENER DUNKEL, and MUNICH HELLES.

BAVARIAN WHEAT BEER

See WHEAT BEER.

BEATING THE BOUNDS

An old English church custom practiced during the Christmas holidays in which the local vicar would lead a parade of the devout around the bounds, or borders, of the parish at night. This torch-lit procession would stop at every house along the way for ale, which church law required to be available.

BRAUEREI BECK & CO. BREMEN, GERMANY

Founded in 1873 as Kaiserbräuerei Beck & Co., the company operates the Haake-Beck Brauerei of Bremen. The brewery produces Haake-Beck labels for its home market and exports Beck's to foreign markets, including the United States and Canada. It owns an American importing subsidiary, Dribeck Importers of Greenwich, Connecticut.

BEDE-ALE

A festival in old England whereby "an honest man decayed in his fortune is set up again by the liberal benevolence and contribution of friends at a feast; but this is laid aside at almost every place" (William Prynne, "Canterburie's Doome," 1646).

The practice of the bede-ale was no doubt abused. The more giving and kind the guest might be, the more tipsy he would have to become to help his unfortunate friend or neighbor. There are, accordingly, records of the prohibition of this custom.

BEECHWOOD AGING

See ANHEUSER-BUSCH, BEER IN THE WOOD, and KRAEUSENING.

BEER

Any alcoholic beverage made by fermenting grains and usually incorporating hops. In general (in the United States), the term refers to a beverage that has been fermented to an alcohol level of less than 5 percent alcohol by volume (4 percent alcohol by weight). Most Americans think of lager beer when they use the word *beer,* but other types of ferment also are correctly called beer. In England, the word *beer* is usually used to indicate an ale with a lower alcohol content. The English word *beer* is from the Latin verb *bibere,* "to drink." Originally, the English word *beer* referred to a beverage that had been brewed with hops, as opposed to ale, which had been brewed without hops.

See ALE and LAGER BEER.

BEER AND THE TEMPERANCE MOVEMENT

See PROHIBITION.

BEER CAMP

Whether Beer Camp can rightly be called a beer festival or a 3-day party is not immediately clear. As some of the promotional literature for this event puts it, "There are no tents, no canoes, no campfires, but beer camp in Kentucky really pours out the good times."

Held at irregular intervals (though usually twice a year, in March and September) at the Oldenberg Brewery in Fort Mitchell, Kentucky (across the river from and 5 miles south of Cincinnati), the event itself is a little irregular. There are beer tastings, brewery demonstrations, and a chance to tour the Oldenberg Brewery.

The first Beer Camp was held in March 1992, with about 40 people on hand. Attendance has risen regularly, and the event usually sells out. (The 175 slots for the March 1995 camp were filled almost 5 months in advance.)

The Oldenberg Brewery Complex is situated on the Drawbridge Estate, which includes the Drawbridge Inn, Coyote's Country Music and Dance Hall, the American Museum of Brewing History and Arts, J. D. Brew's Brewpub, and a gift shop.

Campers arrive on Friday afternoon and leave on Sunday afternoon. One of the first things they do is meet their "counselors" under the hospitality tent on the hotel grounds. Then they confront the close to 300 international beers ready for sampling.

Saturday's events include putting on Beer Camp T-shirts and taking the Beer Campers Oath never to join a temperance society. The ceremonial tapping of a keg and the morning's first beer follow.

A beer scavenger hunt in the museum is a typical way to introduce campers to one of the glories of the complex, the Haydock collection of beer memorabilia. Herb and Helen Haydock of Wisconsin spent more than 30 years acquiring the more than 1 million items that make up the collection, a mind-boggling array of beer bottles, cans, coasters, posters, glasses, openers, trays,

The Oldenberg Brewery in Fort Mitchell, Kentucky, is the home of Beer Camp.

T-shirts, hats, and glasses are among the Beer Camp paraphernalia available to attendees.

signs, labels, matchbooks, tap knobs, and more. There are so many items that all of them cannot be displayed at once.

In addition to beer tastings, Beer Camp includes lectures, homebrewing demonstrations, talks about responsible drinking, discussions of the microbrewery revolution, and goods prepared with beer. Local homebrew clubs take part in the demonstrations, which may get as esoteric as how to do hot rock brewing. The lectures, by various beer professionals and writers, run the gamut from the history and cultural significance of beer to its nutritional aspects and how to taste and compare different beers.

In the evening, dining and drinking take place in the Great Hall, a mammoth assembly area bedecked with flags and breweriana. A stage and dance floor are set up for the night's merrymaking. Also known as Coyote's Country Music and

Dance Hall, it is the setting for a Saturday night barbecue and line dancing. Campers can also expect to see a local troupe of actors perform some medieval temperance plays.

There are even graduation ceremonies on Sunday, complete with diplomas.

BEER CANS

The first can used for packaging beer was introduced in 1934 by the American Can Company for the Gottfried Krueger Brewing Company located in Richmond, Virginia. Pabst Brewing Company and the Joseph Schlitz Brewing Company both introduced canned beer the following year after observing the success of Krueger Brewing's endeavor.

Canning appeals to the brewers' sense of frugality. Major brewery canning lines are able to process more than 1,500 cans per minute. Also, aluminum is superior as a package due to its lightness and strength. Aluminum accounts for money saved each year in transport costs as compared to glass, since aluminum is so much lighter than glass and therefore less costly to ship. As an added bonus, it is completely impervious to light, thus eliminating problems associated with glass bottles.

See BOTTLES and BOTTLING.

BEER ETYMOLOGY

The English word *beer* is from the Latin verb *bibere*, to drink. In other languages beer is spelled: *bier* (German, Flemish, and

Dutch), *bière* or *cervoise* (French), *olut* (Finnish), *cerveza* (Spanish), *cerveja* (Portugese), *cerevisia* (Latin) and *birra* (Italian).

SPELLING	ORIGIN/LANGUAGE
bier	German, Flemish, Dutch
bière	French
birra	Italian
cerevisia	Latin
cerveja	Portugese
cerveza	Spanish
cervoise	French
olut	Finnish

BEER FESTIVALS

Considering the antiquity of beer, it seems safe to say that the first beer festival was also antediluvian. Surely, whoever stumbled upon the intriguing property of barley to produce a beverage of great interest was in a festive mood in short order. Once the rest of the tribe was clued in, the festivities undoubtedly began.

Some beer festivals have gained the sheen of tradition, none more so than Munich's Oktoberfest, which highlights beers from major breweries. There are some such festivals in the United States, but a beer festival in America today is likely to mean a showcase for craft-brewed beers — those produced by microbreweries, brewpubs, and the like.

As a rule, these festivals gather dozens of smaller breweries together in a banquet

Once European phenomena, beer festivals are now held around the world, in large cities and in small towns, reflecting the growing popularity of beer in society today.

room, convention hall, or city park and charge admission for a few hours' sampling of the kegged beer provided. Festival glasses are usually given out, and 2-ounce pours are standard. There are usually food booths, music of some sort, large crowds, and not enough bathroom facilities.

Daniel Bradford, director of the Great American Beer Festival for 10 years, says, "When I started I'm not sure there was another beer festival showcasing micro-brewed beers. Now there are well over one hundred in a given year. Before I became publisher of *All About Beer* magazine, I was doing six a year myself."

The burgeoning market for craft beers has fed right into the burgeoning market for festivals. Brewers could easily spend all their weekends on the road. Consumers could become beer groupies. Festivals offer producers and festivalgoers an opportunity to showcase their beers and a chance to sample new beers.

Festivals come in many shapes and sizes, from profit-making ventures for the hosts to nonprofit fund-raisers. Some are limited to a few local breweries; others pack in as many beers as possible, which are not always easy to keep in top condition.

Not everyone in the beer world is enamored of festivals or their proliferation. Brewers and importers sometimes feel that festivals promote a frenzy of sampling that is less than felicitous. In addition, they usually have to pay a fee to have their beers represented. This, combined with the expense and work involved in traveling to and participating in a festival, outweighs any benefits.

Other brewers and distributors enjoy festivals and believe that they are worthwhile ventures. But they are careful to pick their spots and often send representatives to do their pouring for them.

Some state brewing organizations and other hosts hold invitational festivals — those limited to the state's breweries or others invited by the brewers themselves.

Some festivals have a wide-open admission policy; others require tickets and advance reservations.

The greatest challenge facing the festivalgoer may be the eternal complaint, "So many beers, so little time." The facts of beer festival life require a plan of attack. To sample as many beers as possible and still maintain vehicular safety, a designated driver is a must.

A tasting strategy also is essential. Should selections be limited to beers never tasted? All stouts? Old favorites? Small samples of as many beers as possible? Frequent samples from a select list?

As the beer calendar continues to expand, some festivals will undoubtedly fall by the wayside, although there is little evidence of that happening yet. For now, festival sponsors continue to come up with different ways of presenting beers to the public. In 1994, for example, Arcata, California, held a Bebop & Brew Festival, a confluence of 25 microbreweries and brewpubs with a jazz festival. The event coordinator turned away big brewers; let festivalgoers attend just the jazz festival, just the beer tasting, or both; and gave the proceeds to the Arcata Foundation to help local nonprofit organizations. On the other coast, the Brooklyn Brewery ran a continuing series of Great Beer and Music Festivals, where concertgoers could choose from a dozen or so microbrews while listening to local music groups.

Of course, it is always possible to mimic the original beer festival merely by opening a bottle of brew at home and marveling at the intriguing properties of barley malt.

See ADRIANNE BROWER BIERFESTEN; AIWF BEER AND FOOD FEST; ALBANY/ SARATOGA INTERNATIONAL MICROBREWERIES FESTIVAL; BEER CAMP; BELGIAN BEER FESTIVALS; BOOK AND THE COOK, BOSTON BREWERS FESTIVAL; BUFFALO BEER FESTIVAL; CALIFORNIA BEER FESTIVAL; CANNSTATTER WASEN; COLORADO BREWERS' FESTIVAL; FRÜHJAHRS STARKBIER-FEST; GREAT AMERICAN BEER FESTIVAL; GREAT BRITISH BEER FESTIVAL; GREAT CANADIAN BEER FESTIVAL; GREAT EASTERN INVITATIONAL; GREAT NORTHWEST MICRO-BREWERY INVITATIONAL; GREAT SOUTHERN BREWER'S FESTIVAL; GREATER NEW YORK BEER EXPO; KQED INTERNATIONAL BEER & FOOD FESTIVAL; NEW YORK BIERFEST; NORTHWEST MICROBREW EXPO; OKTOBER-FEST — MUNICH; OKTOBERFESTS; OREGON'S BREWERS FESTIVAL; POPERINGE HOPPESTOET; RHODE ISLAND INTERNATIONAL BEER EXPOSITION; ROCK, RHYTHM & BREWS; SCHÜTZENFEST; SCOTTISH BEER FESTIVALS; SOUTH BAY BEER FESTIVAL WINTERFEST; SOUTHEASTERN MICROBREWERS' INVITA-TIONAL; and WICHITA FESTIVAL OF BEERS.

BEER GARDENS

Technically, a beer garden is a roofed, out-door offshoot of a beer hall, a large room where beer is served. But the terms have come to be almost interchangeable. *Bier-gartens* and *bierkellers* are still abundant in Germany, as they once were in the United States, largely because of German immigra-tion and the German contribution to the lager beer industry in the mid-1800s. According to Stanley Baron's classic book *Brewed in America*, beer gardens were established throughout the United States wherever German immigrants settled — from Ohio and Wisconsin to New York and even Texas.

It may be hard to imagine San Antonio, Texas, as a hotbed of beer gardens, but apparently it was once just that. German settlers arriving in town in 1844 (before Texas was even a state) discovered an earnest pioneering spirit but no earnest spirits of libation. That changed in 1855, when a German brewer named William Menger began the first local brewery. It became so popular and such a draw that Menger built a hotel, right on Alamo Square. By then the population of San Antonio was about one-third German, and the beer gardens bloomed.

Baron characterized the American beer gardens as immense — capable of accom-modating up to 1,200 guests — with cheap beer and food, as well as music: "[They] were visited mainly on Sundays. . . . These beer-gardens are generally spoken of approvingly, because they provided enter-tainment for simple hard-working families, and offered a wholesome antidote to the corrupt and licentious gin-dives or 'danc-ing parlours' that were also current. . . . At the beer-gardens, entrance was free."

British beer writer Michael Jackson has said, "In Germany, people go to church in the morning and the beer gardens in the afternoon; in England, where no one goes to church at all, the nexus of sociability is

The most widely known beer festival is Octoberfest, often celebrated in beer gardens such as this one in Munich.

the pub. That nexus has been steadily destroyed in the United States since Prohibition. Places to enjoy beer are difficult to find, and too frequently are dark and gloomy 'Set 'em up, Joe' bars, where guys sit around telling how badly life has treated them and why their women left them."

Beer historian Alan Eames has made a similar point, stressing that the great value of beer and beer halls was how they leveled the classes: "I think if I had to say one thing about beer, above all others, it is that beer is a democracy. From the very beginning of human settlements and civilization, when you walked through those swinging doors in Sumeria or Babylon, you were on democratic common ground. You were able to speak to your boss on an equal basis. This was the value of the tavern or the public house, and the beer gardens.

"What a wonderful notion in and of itself — a beer garden: Let's drink outdoors, have the whole family, listen to some music, dance in the sunshine and fresh air!"

But, as Jackson has pointed out, those days all but vanished during Prohibition, and American bars barely recovered. When repeal of Prohibition came in 1933, Eames said, "someone forgot to tell the saloon owner, 'Hey, you can open the windows now.'"

Perhaps the lack of great taverns is not worth getting in a snit about, although the premise of sociologist Ray Oldenburg's book *The Great Good Place* is that the fewer such congenial hangouts we have the less of a civilization we become. The strokes we get from family and work are not enough, he maintains, and we forgo the warmth, wit, and diverse sociability of "third places" at our own risk. The particular synergy that takes place between conversation and alcohol consumption (in moderation, of course) contributes to the individual and common good, Oldenburg argues: "Some folks can't concede there's such a thing as a good bar, but if you don't have them, I don't believe you have a community."

As with other things in the world, what goes around comes around. The beer garden is, in many ways, being revived at festivals around the country and in some places more literally than others.

See BEER FESTIVALS and GREAT EASTERN INVITATIONAL.

THE BEER INSTITUTE

Patrick T. Stokes, Chairman
1225 I Street NW, Suite 825
Washington, DC 20005
202-737-2337

The Beer Institute is perhaps best known as a clearinghouse for statistics related to the beer industry. It represents more than 90 percent of domestic brewers and suppliers to the industry. The institute is a valuable source of brewing statistics, tax information, and growth numbers for the beer industry. It publishes the *Brewer's*

Almanac, which is available to nonmembers for a fee.

THE BEER INSTITUTE LIBRARY

1225 I Street NW, Suite 825
Washington, DC 20005
202-737-2337

This Washington, DC–based organization serves as a unified voice for the larger brewers in the United States The Beer Institute Library is open to the public.

BEER IN THE WOOD

A few brewers in Great Britain and Belgium actually do "age" some of their beers in oak barrels for various lengths of time, in much the same way that wine makers do. The practice undoubtedly

Beer was aged "in the wood" in closed wooden fermenters lined with resin in the 19th century.

adds tannins to the beer and has some effect on the flavor, no matter how short the contact period or how benign the wood. The barrels are made of English, German, or Polish oak, which contains fewer tannins and is harder than and imparts less taste than French or American oak. In general, however, beer is not a wood-aged product.

Wood Fermenters

Nineteenth-century continental brewers usually fermented their beer in open wooden fermenting vessels. This was followed by aging the beer in closed wooden fermenters. Such vessels, though made of wood, were lined with resin (pitch), which protected the beer from contact with the wood. In Great Britain, wooden fermenters were generally painted with whitewash (slaked lime or calcium oxide), which served the same purpose as resin. British brewers could use whitewash because their beer would be in the fermenter only a week or two at most, while continental brewers left their beer in the fermenter for months.

In the 20th century, metal fermenting vessels generally replaced wooden ones. The most famous wooden fermenting system was at the old Pilsner Urquell brewery in Czechoslovakia, rebuilt after World War II. Wooden vessels at this brewery are currently being phased out in favor of glass-lined and stainless-steel vessels.

Beer Service from Wood

In the United States, a number of small brewers are experimenting with cask-conditioned beers. It is possible that cask-conditioning may regain a foothold here, but actually serving cask-conditioned beer from a wooden vessel may be just a dream, as wooden casks and barrels are nearly impossible to obtain in the United States, and maintenance of them is even more difficult.

Although the British still serve from wooden vessels, "cask-conditioned" more and more means that the beer was conditioned in a stainless-steel or aluminum cask rather than a wooden one. In Germany, the relatively few old countertop 20 L (5.2 gallon) wooden casks are sometimes replaced with stainless-steel replicas that are covered with insulation made to look like wood.

British casks are barrel-shaped, not cylindrical like American beer kegs. They come in several sizes: the rare wooden barrel is 36 imperial gallons (43.2 U.S. gallons, or 164 L); the "pin" is 4.5 imperial gallons (5.4 U.S. gallons, or 20.4 L); and the "firkin" is twice the size of the pin. The conditioning process takes place while the cask is in a horizontal position, cradled in a wooden stand. The beer also is served from this position.

In the United States and central Europe during the 19th century, the beer was prepared with the cask, or keg, on its side. When it was ready to serve, the keg would be placed upright on a counter for tapping. Serving casks, like the fermenters discussed previously, were lined with pitch or resin.

Beechwood Aging

Budweiser is touted as being a "beechwood-aged" beer. This promotes the image of huge beechwood barrels filled with beer stacked in the brewery, where the beer slowly ages over the years. Of course, that is not what beechwood aging is all about. The beechwood aging process is not "aging" at all. Anheuser-Busch, the manufacturer, follows the age-old tradition of clarifying its beer in a process known as kraeusening. In kraeusening, a clarifying agent — in this case, beechwood chips — is added to the beer for a few days at most.

See CASK-CONDITIONED BEER and KRAEUSENING.

BEER JUDGE CERTIFICATION PROGRAM

BJCP
c/o *Celebrator Beer News*
P.O. Box 375
Hayward, CA 94543

The Beer Judge Certification Program, formerly run by the American Homebrewers Association and the Home Wine and Beer Trade Association, but now independent, is a program by which homebrewers, master brewers, and those simply interested in judging beer can become certified and, in the process, learn about how beers are judged in competitions.

BEER KING

"That, Osirus, there founded the dynasty of beer Kings" appears to be the first reference to the concept of royalty based on beer and brewing, dating to about 2800 B.C. in pharaonic Egypt. The institution "lords of beer" refers to Pelusium, the all-time beer capital of the world. Now a wasteland called Tell-el-Farama, this barren, windswept site was once Egypt's northernmost Nile port, exclusively devoted to the large-scale import and export of an enormous variety of styles of beer. At no other place or time did beer attain such enormous stature and significance as in pharaonic Egypt.

BEERMIRA

See PATRON SAINTS OF BEER.

BELGIAN BEER

Belgian beer is most remarkable and varied. Not even the Germans produce anywhere near the stunning variety of beers made in Belgium. With the exception of giant Stella Artois, whose beers have an international flavor, very few taste-alike beers are made in Belgium. To paraphrase Newton, the size of Belgium is in inverse proportion to the greatness of its beers. British beer critic Michael Jackson says, "No other country can match Belgium in the individuality and stylistic diversity of its beers, nor in their gastronomic interest."

Unfortunately, Belgium's beers are disappearing. Specialty beer production, which once dominated the market, is down to less than 15 percent. Fewer than 150 of the more than 3,000 breweries in operation around 1900 remain. The future of Belgium's beer heritage may well rest elsewhere.

Belgians still have about 400 brands of domestic beer from which to choose — and some 60,000 taverns in which to drink them. Belgium has been called the "land of pubs" because there is one café for every 170 people. Note that this is down from 1900, when there were more than 200,000 pubs, or one for every 32 people.

The current popularity of Belgian beers in the United States and Europe is due almost entirely to the efforts of Michael Jackson. His first book, *World Guide to Beer* (1976), contained eloquent descriptions of the beers of Belgium. Jackson almost single-handedly popularized lambic and other fine Belgian beers. His descriptions and enthusiasm led American importer Charles Finkel, of the Seattle-based Merchant du Vin, to bring the first samplings of lambics and fruit-flavored lambics into the United States. The Belgian government recently presented Jackson with the prestigious Mercurius Award for his promotion of the Belgian brewing industry and its beer styles.

The Belgians classify their beers in four categories — III, II, I, and S *(Superiour)* — in order of strength, designated by original gravity. In the United States and Germany, strength is expressed in degrees Plato, a measurement of the percentage of fermentable sugars in the original wort. In England, strength is expressed as specific gravity. The Belgians use a similar system, adopted from the French. For example, the specific gravity of a wort might be 1.044,

which is 1044 British (multiply specific gravity by 1,000) and which the Belgians would translate as 4.4 degrees Belge — that is, drop the 1 and move the decimal point two places to the right. One degree Belge is about 2.5 degrees Plato. The Belgian gravity is normally printed on the label in that country. Following is a list of the four classes of Belgian beer and their original gravities.

Class S 6.2 degrees Belge and up (1062+ British, 15.1 degrees Plato)
Class I 4.4–5.4 degrees Belge (1044–1054 British, 11–13.3 degrees Plato)
Class II 1.6–3.8 degrees Belge (1016–1038 British, 4–9.5 degrees Plato)
Class III less than Class II

The Belgian tax on beer is based on these classes.

Belgian brewing methods are described in detail in *Belgian Ale* by Pierre Rajotte and *Lambic* by Jean-Xavier Guinard. Belgian brewers use some very interesting ingredients, which are discussed in the following sections.

Sugar

Sugar is almost never used in American and German beers, and only occasionally by the British. The Belgians, however, often use processed sugar. They commonly use invert sugar, particularly for re-ferment in the bottle, but they prefer candy sugar (crystallized sugar) for most purposes. This is particularly true in the production of strong beers. Candy sugar allows an increase in original gravity without having to use additional barley malt or other grains, yielding a lighter-bodied, or softer, product with modified aromatics. The three varieties of candy sugar are pale, light, and dark.

Malt

The one essential ingredient in any beer is enzyme-active barley malt. Belgians prefer Pilsner malt for very pale beers such as Tripels and wits. Some brewers use the darker British pale malt in their ales and Munich malt in darker beers. In addition, caramel (crystal) malts add color and character to beer. They are available in a wide range of colors and are used in most dark Belgian brews. Dark roasted malts are seldom used in Belgian beers.

Hops

Belgian hop production is very low, so most brewers use foreign aromatic hop, especially Saaz, British Kent Goldings, and Yugoslavian Styrian, which are much preferred to American varieties. Belgian beers are not highly hopped, with the exception of lambics, which are made with old hops, not fresh ones.

The different regions of Belgium produce many varieties of beer, but the most popular style is Belgian Pils, a standard international lager that has a 75 percent market share in Belgium. There are a number of distinct Belgian styles, perhaps as many as 60, including abbey beer, Belgian golden ale, Belgian strong ale, Belgian white beer, Belgian brown and red ales, lambics, saisons, and Trappists. As Pierre Rajotte notes in *Belgian Ale,* "Trying to classify

Belgian styles is like attempting to impose guidelines on the Belgian brewmaster's creativity." As the Belgians say, *Brouwen is een kunst* (Brewing is an art).

See ABBAYE, ABBEY BEER, BELGIAN BROWN AND RED ALES, BELGIAN GOLDEN ALE, BELGIAN STRONG ALE, BELGIAN WHITE BEER, LAMBIC, and SAISON BEER.

BELGIAN BEER FESTIVALS

According to Tim Webb, who wrote *The CAMRA Guide to Belgium and Holland,* now in its second edition, there are no

Although the number of formal beer festivals in Belgium has dwindled, the interest in specialty beers remains high, and informal ongoing beer festivals such as the one depicted here are the norm in many places.

large town beer festivals in Belgium comparable to the Oktoberfest in Munich, Germany, and even events sponsored by individual breweries (such as the Wieze Oktoberfesten) have been discontinued. But Belgium brewing has not fallen off, and interest in specialty beers remains high. At some point, usually in early September, the Objectieve Bierprovers (Objective Beer Tasters) hold a 2-day festival in Antwerp to assess beers grouped around some general theme. The same sort of thing goes on in Louvain. If there is one thing a Belgian university student learns to do, it is drink beer, so there is a sort of ongoing beer festival in the town, put on at intervals by different student clubs.

See POPERINGE HOPPESTOET.

BELGIAN BROWN AND RED ALES

Sharp, acidic beers called Flanders brown and red (or copper) ales. Sometimes called *zuur* (sour) beers. These tart beers are usually from a top ferment by yeast, plus various *Lactobacilli* (similar to those active in yogurt) and occasionally even *Brettanomyces,* a wild yeast. They have their roots in medieval and Renaissance brewing.

Rodenbach Grand Cru and Bios are two such beers. Bios is from the family brewery Brauereij Bios van Steenberge, founded in 1789 in Dutch-speaking Flanders. The beer was first made in 1890 by Paul van Steenberge, ironically while he was studying under Louis Pasteur in Paris. Bios is made from barley malt, wheat, water, hops,

and yeast and is bottle-conditioned. Its original gravity is 13.5/1.054/5.4 Belge with 6.3 percent alcohol by volume.

Rodenbach Gran Cru is a classic example of West Flanders red beer. It is a dark, cherry-colored, bottle-conditioned ale from Roeselare in Flanders. A sharp beer that is aged in oak barrels for 2 years, it is occasionally found in the United States. Although it is common to condition beer in wooden fermenters, it is rare that an American or German brewery would let its beer touch the wood itself.

Rodenbach Grand Cru is strong (6 percent alcohol by volume), with an original gravity 15/1.060/6 Belge. The beer is brewed from 80 percent malt (2-row summer and winter barley, 6-row summer barley, and caramel malt) and 20 percent corn grits, using whole hops (Brewer's Gold from Belgium and Kent Goldings from England). Five different yeast and *Lactobacillus* strains are used in the ferment, which involves adding a new yeast at nearly every stage of the operation. This beer is heavily primed with sugar at the finish, which contributes to its intense dryness.

Another brown beer long available in the United States is Goudenband (Golden Band), an Old Brown *(Oud Bruin)* from the Liefmans Brewery (now owned by Riva) in Oudenaarde, west of Brussels. Dark and tart, Goudenband is a special beer (15/1.060 OG, 6 Belge) sometimes found in paper-wrapped, champagne-finish liters and jeroboams. The production is noteworthy in that the wort boil lasts 6 hours (Budweiser is boiled for about 80 minutes). Belgian brewers regularly use long wort boils to add color and concentrate the wort. This beer has six malts, four hop varieties, and an alcohol content of 5 to 5.5 percent by volume. Like many Belgian beers, it is a blend of young and old brews and reaches its peak after about 2 years of storage.

The Great American Beer Festival guidelines for Belgian Specialty Flanders Brown Ale are 11–14/1.044–1.056 OG, resulting in a strong alcohol content of 4.8–5.2 percent by volume; a final gravity in the 2–4 range; medium bitterness (15–25 IBU); and a red, copper, or brown color (12–18 SRM) from the use of caramel malt and dark candy sugar. These beers have a faintly spicy-sour to sweet-sour palate.

See BEER IN THE WOOD, BOTTLE-CONDITIONED BEER, LAMBIC, and LOUIS PASTEUR.

Today the fruit remains in the beer for about 6 weeks. The fruit-to-beer ratio varies. The beer's original gravity is 10–17.4/1.040–1.071/4–7.1 Belge. Final gravity ranges from dry (0.6) to sweet (8.5). Alcohol content is 3.7–6 percent by volume, and bitterness is 15–21 IBU. Color is 8–13 SRM or higher. The Great American Beer Festival guidelines for Lambic Fruit Ales are 10–17.5/1.040–1.072 OG, 5–7 percent alcohol by volume, and 15–21 IBU, with appropriate color.

Another type of Belgian fruit ale is Liefmans Frambozen. This fruit ale has a Flanders brown ale base. The beer is a lovely sweet-sour delight, made by methods similar to those outlined for lambic fruit beer production.

See BELGIAN BROWN AND RED ALES; FRUIT, VEGETABLE, HERBAL, AND SPECIALTY BEERS; and LAMBIC.

BELGIAN FRUIT ALE

Belgian fruit ales are usually made from a base of lambic beer. The fruits used are cherries (Kriek), raspberries (Framboise), black currents (Cassis), peaches (Pêche), and muscat grapes (Druiven). Kriek is the original Belgian fruit ale.

Traditional Kriek and Framboise are dry like champagne and sometimes drunk with mulled sugar. The ones exported to this country are often sweetened with sugar in their finish. Originally, the cherries used in Kriek were sour black cherries (*Schaarbeek*), usually dried on the tree. They were added to 18-month-old lambic.

BELGIAN GOLDEN ALE

A very brilliant, golden to straw-colored, strong ale. The style is quite popular in Belgium and was invented by the Moortgat Brewery, near Mechelen. Their Duvel (Devil) is a very strong pale ale (14.9/1.061 OG, 6.4 percent alcohol by volume) made from very pale Pilsner malt. This beer's final gravity is 2.8, its bitterness about 30 IBU, and its color around 3.5 SRM. The beer is brewed in two batches, one at 14/1.057 and the other at 17/1.070 (from added sugar), using two different yeast strains. The end product is a blend of the two brews. This is a bottle-conditioned ale. A number of other Belgian brewers have copied the Duvel style.

See BOTTLE-CONDITIONED BEER.

BELGIAN PALE ALE

See SAISON BEER.

BELGIAN STRONG ALE

The Belgians are particularly noted for the strong ales they produce. They often classify such beers as *bière spéciale* (special beer), and almost anything goes. These "special beers" are usually produced with the addition of dark candy sugar. They are fermented under very warm temperatures (86°F, or 30°C) with two or three yeast strains, including an additional, final ferment in the bottle.

Augustijn Ale is a strong amber ale (7.4 percent alcohol by volume) with a refreshing dry finish and a slightly bitter aftertaste. From the Van Steenbergen brewery, this is a "real ale," fermented in the bottle. It is at its prime 3 to 5 months after bottling.

Pauwel Kwak is a Flanders beer (from the village of Buggenhout) with a wine-tinted amber color. Malty and dry to the taste, it is a very strong beer (6.3 percent alcohol by volume) with an original gravity of 15/1.061.

The Great American Beer Festival guidelines for Belgian Strong Beers are 16–24/1.064–1.096 OG, 7–11 percent alcohol by volume, 20–50 IBU, and 3.5–20 SRM.

See ABBEY BEER and BELGIAN GOLDEN ALE.

BELGIAN WHITE BEER

A large number of Belgian beers are made up of significant amounts of wheat, notably the lambic group. Another "white," called *wit* (pronounced "vit") is similar in some ways to the Berliner *weisse* style. This beer type is rapidly gaining popularity. Louvain White, an old style, had 5 percent oats, 45 percent wheat, and 50 percent green (air dried rather than kiln dried) barley malt and rolled wheat. The mash is held for an especially long protein rest. This results in a very cloudy (white) beer.

The city of Hoegaarden has a long history of brewing white beer. At one time, 50 breweries were making this style, but the last one closed in the mid-1950s. In the 1960s, Pierre Celis, who had lived near Hoegaarden's last white beer brewery, decided to revive the style. His brewery, DeKluis (cloister), started brewing Hoegaarden White in the old way in 1966.

Hoegaarden White is a very pale beer, lightly tart, mellow, with a sweet-sour overlay. The beer contains coriander and Curaçao orange zest (peels). Its original gravity is 12/1.048/4.8 Belge, and its alcohol content is 4.85 percent.

By the 1980s, the style had become quite popular. Other brewers introduced Interbrew S.A. white beers. In 1989, Celis sold his company to the Belgian Interbrew S.A. which continued to make the beer, and moved to Austin, Texas. In 1992, he opened a brewery in Austin to brew a slightly different version of his beer. Celis White is 12/1.048 OG, 4.8 Belge, 2.7 final gravity, 4.9 percent alcohol by volume, 13.5 IBU, and about 1.5 SRM. Ingredients include 50 percent high dried 6-row American barley malt, 50 percent raw Texas winter wheat, Willamette and Cascade hops, orange peel, coriander, and a natural *Lactobacillus* ferment, along with the regular yeast. The beer is pasteurized and refermented with another yeast strain, which makes for a very complex taste profile.

The white beer style is beginning to be copied in many countries, especially in the Netherlands and the United States. Spring Street Wit is contract brewed in Minnesota for the New York Spring Street Brewery. This beer is very refreshing, with the following characteristics: 11.5/1.046 OG, 4.9 percent alcohol by volume, 10–15 IBU, and about 3 SRM. It is flavored with coriander and orange peel. Another example of this style is Sunshine Wheat, brewed by the New Belgium Brewing Co. in Fort Collins, Colorado.

The Great American Beer Festival guidelines for Belgian White are 11–12.5/1.044–1.050 OG, 4.8–5.2 percent alcohol by volume, 15–25 IBU, and 2–4 SRM. It can be cloudy, but it should have unmalted wheat in the makeup. It also can be spiced, as noted above.

Dark White

A dark white style called Amber Wit was probably brewed in the distant past. Some Dutch brewers, including Heineken, are experimenting with the style Tarwebok (wheat bock). The Spring Street Brewery is also experimenting with an Amber Wit that is 12.5/1.050 OG, 5.2 percent alcohol by volume, and amber in color.

See LAMBIC.

BELHAVEN BREWERY LTD.
DUNBAR, EAST LOTHIAN
SCOTLAND

Belhaven is a relatively small Scottish brewery (capacity 55,000 barrels) that traces its roots to the early 18th century. The company exports its Belhaven ale and lager to the United States through Inter-Floridana of Casselberry, Florida. Belhaven also bottles Traquair House Ale (imported into the United States by Merchant Du Vin of Seattle, Washington) for the tiny Traquair House Brewery of Peebleshire.

See SCOTTISH ALE.

BELLE-VUE BREWERY
BRUSSELS, BELGIUM

Belle-Vue is the largest of Belgium's lambic brewers, with its flagship brewery located beside a canal on the edge of Brussels. The company was acquired by Interbrew a few years ago and now produces lambics at three different plants.

The company sells several variations on its classic lambic, including Belle-Vue Frambozen, Kriek, Gueuze, Kriek Primeur, and Selection Lambic Gueuze. Belle-Vue's

Gueuze, Kriek, and Frambozen are now imported to the United States by Paulaner North America of Englewood, Colorado. Belle-Vue beers are also available in Canada.

See LAMBIC.

BENTONITE

A natural aluminum silicate clay capable of absorbing ten times its weight in water. When added to wine or beer, it acts as a clarifier by coagulating proteins. Twenty-four hours before addition to the beer, it is mixed with water to form a slurry at a rate of 0.25 ounce (8g) of bentonite to 3 ounces (91 ml) of preboiled and cooled water. Sources indicate varying amounts of bentonite (1 to 5 ounces [30 to 148 g] per 5 gallons [19 L] of liquid), so check package instructions. Bentonite is used mostly in wines.

See CLARIFICATION.

BERLINER WEISSE

The Berliner style of white *(Weisse)* beer. It has been called the champagne of the north. Berliner Weisse can be brewed only in Berlin, since it is an appellation.

Traditional Berliner Weisse was made from a mixture of 75 percent wheat malt and 25 percent barley malt, with an original gravity of 7–10/1.028–1.040, 3–4.5 percent alcohol by volume, 5–10 IBU, and 2–4 SRM. The beer is brewed almost as it was in the 18th century. The yeast used is seeded with about 20 percent *Lactobacillus delbreucki*. This *Lactobacillus* is very similar to the *L. bulgaris* and other strains used in health food drinks and yogurt production in the United States.

This type of beer was quite popular in pre-Prohibition America. Today, however, there are no American tart white beers being made. Several brewers have attempted this style (among them Minnesota's August Schell), but the public has not been receptive.

The real Berliner Weisse is drunk from a large, widemouthed, stemmed glass, after it is mixed with *schuss* (a dash of raspberry syrup), green waldmeister (essence of woodruff), or even grenadine. The combination of Berliner Kindl Weisse and raspberry syrup is quite luxurious as a cooler on a hot afternoon. The taste is like that of raspberry champagne.

The Great American Beer Festival guidelines for Berliner Weisse are an original gravity of 7–8/1.028–1.032 OG, 2.8–3.4 percent alcohol by volume, 10–22 IBU, and 3–6 SRM.

Original Gravity	Final Gravity	Alcohol by Volume	IBU	SRM
Berliner Kindl Weisse 1980				
7.5/1.030	1.5	3.1%	4	≈4
Berliner Weiss 1895				
10.3/1.041	1.9	4.4%	≈5	≈4

BERRIES

See FRUIT.

BES

An ancient Egyptian god/goddess. This deity originated in the Sudan and is represented as a grotesque, bearded dwarf with a crown and sword. There is no clear gender distinction for Bes, but, as primary god/goddess of women in labor, his/her fondness for beer established a spiritual association with brewing second only to that of the goddess Hathor.

The likeness of Bes, the god/goddess of childbirth and beer, can be found in artifacts from antiquity, such as this ancient mask.

BEST BITTER

See BITTER.

BETA AMYLASE

An enzyme that breaks down starch into maltose. Beta amylase works best at a temperature of 140° to 149°F (60° to 65°C) and will stop working at temperatures much higher than that. A mash at 158°F (70°C) will have little or no beta amylase activity but considerable alpha amylase activity, resulting in a more dextrinous (less fermentable) wort.

See ENZYMES.

BETA GLUCAN

A gum present in the cell walls of barley and malt that causes various problems, such as slow runoff, by increasing the thickness of the mash and wort. Beta glucan can be broken down by the enzyme beta glucanase.

BETA GLUCANASE

An enzyme that breaks down beta glucan. Beta glucanase acts at the temperature used for an acid rest — about 122°F (50°C).

BEVER DAYS

From *bever*, a snack (originally a drink) between meals. From Latin *bibere*, to drink. Beverage has the same origin.

Bever days were days in Anglo-Saxon Britain when extra beer and bread were served at Eton College during the afternoon in the college hall to scholars and their friends.

BICARBONATE

A salt that contributes much to the alkalinity of water. Bicarbonates can cause problems for the brewer if the level exceeds 25 ppm during the mash for lighter beers. At this level, the bicarbonates will remove calcium and raise the pH, resulting in lower yields. Excessive bicarbonate levels also will extract tannins from the grain husks. Bicarbonates can be removed by boiling the water. The boiling process drives off carbon dioxide (CO_2) from calcium bicarbonate ($Ca[HCO_3]_2$), leaving behind water (H_2O) and calcium carbonate ($CaCO_3$), in the form of a precipitate.

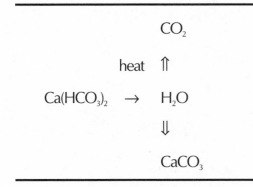

$$Ca(HCO_3)_2 \quad \rightarrow \quad \begin{array}{c} CO_2 \\ \text{heat} \Uparrow \\ H_2O \\ \Downarrow \\ CaCO_3 \end{array}$$

The water is then decanted off the sediment, and the brewing can begin. Bicarbonates also can be removed by adding calcium hydroxide ($Ca[OH]_2$), or slaked lime, which will cause the calcium carbonate to settle out.

$$Ca(OH)_2 + Ca(CHO_3)_2 \rightarrow 2CaCO_3 + 2H_2O$$

Calcium sulfate or magnesium sulfate may be added to neutralize the bicarbonates, or the brewer may simply use dark roasted malts and brew darker beer.

JOHN BICKERDYKE

The author of *The Curiosities of Ale and Beer,* one of the two most significant anthologies of beer lore ever written. This benchmark work was first published in 1889.

Bickerdyke was, in fact, the pen name of three individuals who assembled a staggering collection of songs, poems, literature, and lore of beer. Charles Cook, J. G. Fennel, and an unknown English cleric collaborated to produce this work, last reprinted in 1965. "John Bickerdyke" has become known today as a 19th-century beer historian, despite being the creation of three separate writers.

BIDALE

A charitable gathering where ale was sold to the guests and the profits were given to some needy person to relieve a financial crisis. The bidale, or bidder ale (from the Saxon word meaning "to pray"), eventually fell from favor as the guest of honor tended to squander the money on drinks for the other guests.

BIÈRE DE GARDE (FRENCH COUNTRY BEER)

The northwest area of France has always been noted for its brewers and beers. The Calais-Dunkerque area; the Flanders, Artois, and Picardy regions; and the flat *houtland* (wood country) harbor major brewing enclaves. Hazebrouck in northwest France is a hop-growing area, and Picardy hops may have been used in beer as early as the ninth century. The barley grown in the Flanders, Champagne, and Burgundy regions was good malting barley. Before World War I, each village in the region had one or two brewers (now only about 20 total), and there was a single tavern for every 50 people. The beers were mostly of ordinary strength. However, ordinary brews could not survive past the onset of warm weather. Brewers took to brewing *bière de garde* (beer to be cared for, or for laying away) so that beer would be available during the summer months. To survive such laying away, the beer had to be brewed strong and bottle-conditioned.

This style has changed over the years, as brewers have modified the process. After World War II, many brewers started using bottom-fermenting yeast instead of top-fermenting yeast. In the 1970s, a few of the bottom-fermenting brewers returned to top fermentation and started using cold-conditioning after a warm ferment with top or bottom yeast, similar to that used by German altbier brewers.

Such beer was brewed from pale malts, plus some dried — in the Vienna style — to dark amber. Sometimes candy sugar or dextrose or glucose chips are added, resulting in 14.6–18.5/1.060–1.076 OG, 6.5–8.5 percent alcohol by volume, and about 25–28 IBU. Color ranges from rich gold to reddish brown (12–14 SRM). Fermentation, after an infusion mash, is with top or bottom yeast at temperatures near 60° to 65°F (15.5° to 18°C). The beer is unfiltered and sometimes bottle-conditioned in cork-finished champagne bottles. The taste of *bière de garde* is similar to that of Belgian ales.

Original Gravity	Final Gravity	Alcohol by Volume	IBU	SRM
Brasseurs Bière de Paris 1982				
12.3/1.049	2.8	5%	≈22	≈12
Jenlain 1985				
15.6/1.064	3.4	6.6%	25	9.8
Pelforth Brune (Lille) 1992 (brown ale, double malt)				
17.3/1.070	5	6.5%	Unknown	25
Septante 5 1985				
18.3/1.075	5.5	6.9%	≈25	9

BI-KAL

The top-shelf full-strength beer of ancient Sumer.

See SUMERIAN BEER.

BILBIL

A type of beer once brewed in Upper Egypt from Indian millet, called durra. The grain was germinated between leaves of Onna Oskur *(Calotropis procera),* sun-dried, and milled into a fine flour. The flour was added to water in a large earthenware pot, then boiled over on open fire for 6 to 8 hours. After the wort had cooled, yeast was added. This first brew was called Merissa. If it was boiled again, filtered, and refermented, it was called bilbil. This word comes from *bülbül,* or mother of nightingale, because it was said to cause drinking men to sing.

See EGYPTIAN BEER.

BIRCH BEER

A nonmalt, slow-fermenting potent brew originally made from black birch sap, twigs, and honey. Birch beer was light and sweet and eventually evolved into a soft drink.

BITTER

The most popular beer style in England. British bitter ale and pale ale are similar, except that pale ale is bottled and bitter (which is usually weaker in alcohol content) is dispensed on draft (often cask-conditioned). Bitter ale is a step up from mild ale and just a little hoppier and paler in color.

A British brewing text quotes the following guidelines for "British fined beer" (i.e., cast-conditioned beer) or bitter: 7.5–11.3/1.030–1.045 OG, 2.8–4.4 percent alcohol by volume, 28–38 IBU, and 6.1–23 SRM. The same source lists 1960 draft bitter (cask-conditioned) at 7.7–

A cask-conditioned bitter ale label from Whitbread

11.3/1.031–1.045 OG, 3–4.6 percent alcohol by volume, and 20–40 IBU. The British consume most of their beer in public houses (pubs), and the alcohol content is necessarily lower because of this fact.

Ordinary Bitter (Traditional)

The Great American Beer Festival guidelines for ordinary bitter are 8.0–9.5/1.033–1.038 OG, 3–3.7 percent alcohol by volume, 20–35 IBU, and 8–12 SRM.

Traditional bitter is brewed from very hard water to full attenuation (dry), with low carbon dioxide and some diacetyl and fruitiness allowed. Ordinary bitter is a little higher in body, with minimal diacetyl and fruitiness.

Strong Bitter

This is not a particular style but a higher-quality and stronger version of Traditional Ordinary Bitter described above. It is also called special bitter or extra special bitter (ESB).

The Great American Beer Festival guidelines for English Special Bitter indicate more original gravity and fullness than those for ordinary bitter: 9.5–11/ 1.038–1.045 OG, 4.1–4.8 percent alcohol by volume, 28–46 IBU, and 12–14 SRM. English Extra Special Bitter is a little stronger and maltier at 11.5–15/ 1.046–1.060 OG and 4.8–5.8 percent alcohol by volume. English Extra Special Bitter is also a bit hoppier at 30–55 IBU.

Original Gravity	Final Gravity	Alcohol by Volume	IBU	SRM
Hale's Pale American Ale (Washington) 1980				
9/1.036	2	3.6%	36	≈16
Red Hook ESB (Washington) 1987				
13.1/1.052	2.7	5.3%	32	≈8
Young's RamRod (England) 1985 (special bitter)				
11.5/1.046	2.4	4.8%	38	≈16

See CASK-CONDITIONED BEER, LIGHT ALE, and PALE ALE.

BITTERING HOPS

Hops with high concentrations of any of the three major hop acids — humulone, cohumulone, and adhumulone — also called alpha acids. Bittering hops, used to add bitterness, are usually added early in the boiling of the wort but also can be added at specific stages during the boil. Common bittering hops used include Brewer's Gold, Bullion, Cluster, Eroica, Galena, Pride of Ringwood, and Super Styrians. Generally, bittering hops range from 4.5 percent to more than 13 percent total alpha acid for the super alpha strains. Bittering hops are not usually noted for aromatic qualities, but there are a few exceptions. Exceptions include Centennial, Chinook, Hallertau Northern Brewer, Northern Brewer, Nugget, and Perle.

See HOPS.

BITTERNESS UNIT

An internationally agreed upon unit that indicates the amount of bitterness a beer contains. One bitterness unit (BU) is defined as 0.0001335 ounce avoirdupois of iso-alpha acid per gallon of beer. This converts to metric very nicely: 1 mg of iso-alpha acid per 1 L of beer, which is 1 ppm.

See HOPS and INTERNATIONAL BITTERNESS UNIT (IBU).

BLACK AND TAN

Traditionally, an equal mixture of dark and pale beers such as stout and mild ale or porter and Pilsner. Although the name is considered objectionable by some people because of its use in reference to British forces in Ireland during the 1920s, the drink actually predated the political troubles.

BLACK BEER

The darkest of dark beers. Stouts and porters have been called black beers, and Dublin, Ireland, is known as the "Black Beer Capital of the World."

A group of German black beers, popular in what was once East Germany, are simply called *schwarzbier* (literally, black beer). These are described in an East German brewing text as 12/1.048 OG, with Pilzen-type hops at 25–45 IBU and colored malts to darken the color above 35 SRM. The most famous of these beers is Kostritzer Schwarzbier, a sweet beer from Kostritz, Thuringia, a brewery now owned by Bitburger. Kulmbacher Monchshof Kloster Schwarz is also referred to as a *schwarzbier,* although at 21 SRM it is not all that black. It is actually more like a *dunkel.*

The Japanese also are famous for their Germanic–style black beers. The most famous and oldest of these is Sapporo Black Beer, which is available in the United States in the winter.

One Brazilian black beer is Xingu, from Cascador. Xingu is a bottom-fermented brew with a sweet taste. It has some characteristics of dark lager, as well as sweet stout.

The Great American Beer Festival has no black beer style, but the Association of Brewers lists standards for Bavarian Dark Schwarzbier as 11–13P/1.044–1.052 OG, 3.8–5 percent alcohol by volume, 22–30 IBU, and 25–30 SRM (dark brown to black).

Original Gravity	Final Gravity	Alcohol by Volume	IBU	SRM
Kostritzer (East Germany) 1950				
12/1.048	5.3	3.6%	40	38
Kostritzer (Germany) 1993				
12.5/1.050	3.2	5%	35	34
Sapporo Black Beer (1992)				
13/1.052	3.5	5%	25	38

See AMAZON BLACK BEER, PORTER, SAPPORO BREWERIES, and STOUT.

BLACK CHAMPAGNE

The name given to imported English stout by French courtiers under Louis XIV. The ale was provided by Lord Humphrey Parsons, a rich London brewer whose horse accidentally overran King Louis's mount during a steeplechase. Lord Humphrey Parsons offered his horse to the king, but when the king learned that the Englishman was a brewer, the king asked him to supply the court with beer.

BLACK VELVET

A cocktail made with equal amounts of champagne and stout. It is usually prepared in a champagne glass. The stout is carefully poured along the inside of the champagne glass so that it does not mix with the champagne.

BLIND PIG

A term used during Prohibition for a beer hall or a saloon. Enterprising saloon keepers would charge admission to view some curiosity, such as a blind pig. Admission to the sideshow included, of course, a complimentary drink.

BLOND OR GOLDEN ALE

Americans once called blond or golden ale "cream ale," but that has come to be something quite different (a bottled lager ale). Today's golden ales are straw (blond) to pale amber in color (2.5–8 SRM) with a medium alcohol content (3.8–5.7 percent by volume). These golden ales are related to the pale ales, with assertive to intense hop levels. Original gravity is 10–13.9/ 1.040–1.061, final gravity 2.2–3.7, and bitterness 20–40 IBU. Blond ales differ from bottled American lager ales in that they are not lagered—they are brewed entirely as ales.

This style incorporates ale-type ingredients but is designed around malts that are paler than the typical British ale malt. In the United States, where the style is becoming popular, brewers use 2-row barley malt, dextrin malt, and sometimes a little caramel or Munich malt for extra color. American specialty hops from Oregon and Washington (Fuggle, Brewer's Gold, Northern Brewer, Cascade, Willamette, and Perle) are used.

The Great American Beer Festival guidelines for blond or golden ale are 11–14/1.045–1.056 OG, 4–5 percent alcohol by volume, 15–30 IBU, and 3–10 SRM.

ORIGINAL GRAVITY	FINAL GRAVITY	ALCOHOL BY VOLUME	IBU	SRM
Full Sail Golden Ale (Oregon) 1990				
12/1.048	2.9	4.8%	23	≈5
Summit Extra Pale Ale (Minnesota) 1992				
12/1.048	2.7	4.9%	28	5
U.S. cream ale 1901				
13.6/1.054	2.2	5.9%	40	Unknown

See LAGER ALE.

BLOW-OFF TUBE

A one-inch plastic tube used in homebrewing fermentation that fits into the mouth of a carboy. This method of fermentation, sometimes called the blow-by method, allows the primary fermentation to blow off all the froth and carbon dioxide without allowing air to come in contact with the fermenting beer. This air could cause contamination of the fermenting beer.

See CARBOY.

BOCK BEER

A style of beer developed in Bavaria that was originally brewed in the late fall from the first malt and hops of the harvest. It was aged in deep caves throughout the winter and drunk in the spring. It was traditionally sold beginning on the first day of spring, which came to be known as Bock Beer Day. Bock beer season lasts for 6 weeks.

There are many stories concerning the origins of this style. A picture of a billy goat almost always appears on the label because those who drank the beer acted like youthful billy goats. (The German word for goat is *bock*.) Another story concerns a medieval drinking bout between a brewer and a knight. The contestants were supposed to

The goat is a symbol for bock beer, perhaps because those who drank it behaved like youthful billy goats. The jester on this label might indicate another type of behavior.

drink, stein for stein, until one of them was judged to be drunk (when he could no longer thread a needle while standing on one leg). The combatants drank, stein after stein, until at last the knight dropped his needle and stooped to pick it up. While he was in that vulnerable position, a nearby goat knocked him to the ground. The knight was unable to get up, so the mayor awarded the victory to the brewer. This may be how the goat became the symbol for strong beer served at spring festivities. The contest reportedly took place in the village of Einbeck. Today Einbecker is one of the more famous dark beers produced in Germany.

Einbeck (in Lower Saxony, northern Germany) was once the most famous brewing city in Europe. Einbecker beer was strong in alcohol and high in gravity, which made it possible to export the beer to much of northern Europe. Munich and other Bavarian cities soon adopted the style.

Today bock beer is lager beer and is required by German law to have an original gravity of 16/1.066 and an alcohol content of 6.6 percent by volume. It also must be brewed only from malted barley. The style originally included a fair percentage of roasted or dark malts, but today there are many pale bocks. The dark malts generally used include dark Munich malt, dark caramel malt, and dextrin malt, resulting in a fairly dark color (26–40 SRM). Bitterness is 20–35 IBU. The beer has 250 ppm hardness and a sweet, malty palate.

The Great American Beer Festival guidelines for Traditional Bock are 16.5–18.5/1.066–1.074 OG, 6–7.5 percent alcohol by volume, 20–30 IBU, and 20–30 SRM. Guidelines for Helles (pale) Bock are 16.5–17/1.066–1.068 OG, 6–7.5 percent alcohol by volume, 20–35 IBU, and 4–10 SRM.

Original Gravity	Final Gravity	Alcohol by Volume	IBU	SRM
Kulmbacher Schweizerhofbräu Bock 1987 (a pale bock)				
16.1/1.066	2.4	5.2%	Unknown	8
Einbecker Bock 1878				
18.1/1.074	5.2	6.8%	30	Unknown

American Bock Beer

European bock beer is generally similar to German bocks, but not always heavier than 16/1.066 OG. American bock beer, also known as Wisconsin bock, has a long and rather spotty history. It is similar to American dark beer, but it may be a bit paler in color (4.5 to 12 SRM). Today's American bocks may be brewed with dark malts such as Munich, caramel, and even black malt, and with Washington hops. Alcohol content is around 5 percent by volume. American bocks are seasonally issued in early February.

Original Gravity	Final Gravity	Alcohol by Volume	IBU	SRM
Lucky Bock 1985				
11.6/1.046	3	4.5%	16	18
Milwaukee bocks 1908 (average)				
13/1.052	4.7	4.3%	Unknown	Unknown

See AMERICAN LAGER, BAVARIAN BEER, and DOPPELBOCK.

BODY

A quality of beer that reflects its ending density and the way that it feels in your mouth. Proteins make up the bulk of a beer's body, but unfermented sugars contribute as well. Body tends to refer to the amount of thickness and mouth-filling properties a given sample contains. This sensation of palate fullness in the mouth helps define the body of the beer. Filtered beers sometimes have problems achieving adequate body.

BOHEMIAN BEER

A very pale (almost straw-colored), medium-alcohol (4.5 to 5.5 percent alcohol by volume) lager beer with a dry, crisp taste, mellow bitterness, and highly aromatic bouquet. Also called Plzen, Pilsner, Pils, Classic Pilsner, and German Pils. One of the world's greatest breweries is located in Plzen, Czech Republic (Bohemia). The beer brewed in Plzen, Bohemia is Pilsner Urquell. *Urquell* means "original." This "original Pilsner" has been copied in all parts of the world. Until recently, the beer had been brewed in almost identical fashion for well over a hundred years.

In 13th-century Bohemia (now part of the Czech Republic), householders were granted the royal privilege of brewing beer for their own use. In 1842, a number of householders united to form a "citizen's brewery" in Plzen. The beer they brewed was very much like the present-day product. This was possible because of the malting methods developed in the latter part of the 18th century. New and better kilning controls had made very pale barley malt a possibility. Until then, most beers had been relatively dark in color, even when called pale.

More important was a new yeast strain brought to Plzen from Munich in 1840. This special yeast had the ability to ferment beer at very low temperatures, down to about 33°F (0.5°C). At that time in Munich, beer was brewed with a cold ferment that was carried on in the winter in deep caves. Temperatures below 40°F (4°C) were achieved by using ice harvested from frozen lakes. The beer was stored until summer. It was called lagered, or stored, beer, from the German *lagern,* "to store."

The cold temperatures allowed an infection-free ferment to produce a fairly low alcohol content, with no souring or bacterial contamination to ruin the taste. This cold ferment was much slower than a warm ferment, resulting in a smoother, mellower product. The very pale, brilliantly clear beer looked great in the fine Bohemian crystal that was just then becoming popular in Europe and the United States. This combination of very pale Bohemian malts; lovely Saaz hops; a long, slow cold ferment; and the beauty of the product brought about a revolution in the brewing industry. With the possible exception of the invention of mechanical refrigeration (1860s), this was the most important development in brewing history.

Ingredients in the Original

In keeping with ancient traditions, this beer contained only four ingredients: malted barley, hops, water, and yeast. The Czech Zatec region produces Saaz hops, which are among the world's finest. The malts are from native barley grown in the Moravian region of old Bohemia.

This 14th-century Bohemian brewery was connected to a convent.

The water of Plzen is softer (51 ppm hardness) than most famous brewing waters, and this requires a mashing cycle that is three times longer than usual to ensure proper acidity for protein and starch conversion.

Brewing Method

The brewery in Plzen has recently been modernized, but until that happened, Pilsner Urquell was brewed with equipment and methods almost identical to those used in the mid–19th century, despite the fact that the brewery had to be rebuilt after World War II. The brewery does have some modern space-saving and timesaving innovations, but tradition is still of utmost importance.

The Plzen brewery made its beer by a unique method of blending four different batches brewed from four different yeast strains. (Lager beers are produced using "pure" yeasts, and such blending is necessary to match a particular taste profile.) The beer was brewed in 20 small copper brew kettles (4,700 gallons, or 178 hl, each), over a gas flame. The Plzen brew had 12 degrees Plato fermentable sugars (which has an original gravity of 1.048 and nearly three times the hops (35 IBU until recently; now 27) used by the average American brewery. The alcohol content was around 4.8 percent by volume. The initial, or primary, ferment was carried out in 1,500 775-gallon (29 hl) open wooden fermenters. The 12- to 14-day ferment was followed by a 3-week secondary ferment and aging in wooden tanks (1,000 to 1,500 gallons, or 38 to 57 hl, each) stored underground. Finally, the casks were bunged (closed), and the beer was aged for 9 weeks more. Total production time was about 14 weeks. Modern brewers complete the process in 14 to 20 days.

Until recently, modern Pilsner Urquell was similar to the original, and the only "export" treatment it received was pasteurization. An 1897 export sample (Actien Brauhaus) was listed as 12.2/1.049 OG, 4.8 percent alcohol by volume, and about 42 IBU. An 1887 Pilsner from the Czech Budweis brewery was described as 11.34/1.046 OG, 4.5 percent alcohol by volume, and about 34 IBU, which (except for the hops and rice) is very similar to Budweiser. All that may be changing, as the brewery must compete in the modern world. Anheuser-Busch (maker of Budweiser) is trying to buy the financially troubled Budweis brewery, and the future of its products, and those of other Czech brewers, is uncertain.

Bohemian, or Pilsner, beer is the most popular beer style in the world. Most modern Pilsners are an insult to the name, but many do meet that great standard. Some, such as Pilsner Urquell, are available in the United States. Other Czech beers found in the United States include Gambrinus (also from Plzen) and Starobruno (from Bruno).

Classic Pilsner Style

These pale-colored beers have a medium alcohol content (4.8 to 5.7 percent alcohol by volume) and a rich, assertive flavor. Only the original four ingredients are used: malted barley (very pale European 2-row Moravian malt produced in the traditional style of Bohemia), hops (Saaz), water, and yeast. Bouquet and taste are impressive. Characteristics are as follows: 11–14/1.044–1.056 OG, 2.2–4.5 final gravity, 25–45 IBU, and 2.5–4.5 SRM.

Original Gravity	Final Gravity	Alcohol by Volume	IBU	SRM
Anton Dreher Michelob (Austro-Hungarian Empire/Bohemia) 1896				
11.3/1.045	3.1	4.3%	≈35	≈5.5
Anton Dreher Pilsner (Austro-Hungarian Empire/Bohemia) 1901				
10.8/1.043	2.4	4.4%	≈40	≈5
Bohemian 1906 (average six samples)				
11.3/1.045	3	4.3%	≈43	≈5
Pilsner Urquell 1981				
12.1/1.048	3.7	4.3%	43	4.2
Pilsner Urquell 1993				
12.1/1.048	3.7	4.3%	27	4.2

Bohemian Style (Classic) Pilsner Lager

The Great American Beer Festival guidelines for this style indicate a maltier fullness: 11–14/1.044–1.056 OG, 4–5 percent alcohol by volume, 35–45 IBU, and 3–5 SRM.

North German Pilsner

The North German Pilsner lager style differs from that of the Czech Republic. It has a slightly lower original gravity (11–12/1.044–1.048), a low final gravity, a paler color, a dry taste, a somewhat lower alcohol content, and a more pronounced hop nose, coupled with slightly less actual IBU from Hallertauer, Spalt, Tettnanger, and Northern Brewer hops. Incidentally, Pinkus Ur-Pils, profiled in the following table, uses organic malt.

The Great American Beer Festival guidelines are 11–12.5/1.044–1.050 OG, 4–5 percent alcohol by volume, 30–40 IBU, and 3–4 SRM.

Original Gravity	Final Gravity	Alcohol by Volume	IBU	SRM
Bitburger Pils (Germany) 1981 (as found in United States)				
11.3/1.045	1.9	4.9%	≈27	≈3.5
Hacker-Pschorr Braumeister Pils (Germany) 1989				
12.0/1.048	2.1	5.2%	34	2.9
Pinkus Ur-Pils (Germany) 1985				
11.1/1.044	2	4.8%	≈28	≈3.5

See Bavarian beer, fermentation, lager, and Pilsner Urquell.

BOILING

One of the most critical steps in the brewing process. Boiling extracts the bitterness from the hops, sanitizes the wort by killing microorganisms, and causes proteins to fall out of the beer in the form of hot break. A vigorous boil is necessary for a good hot break.

The length of the boil varies from batch to batch and brewer to brewer depending on the processes used. An all-grain brewer typically does longer boils (90 minutes or longer) because he or she is trying to reduce the volume of liquid and concentrate the sugars. In contrast, an extract brewer is typically worried most about getting the flavor right, so hop bitterness extraction is the most critical aspect. Hop bitterness is extracted within 50 minutes. Boiling longer than that will not appreciably affect the bitterness, so most extract brewers boil for about 1 hour.

See BREWING PROCESS and HOT BREAK.

BOILING HOPS

Hops added for bittering purposes. Also called bittering hops or kettle hops. The amount of bitterness extracted from the hops during the boil is a function of time, wort density, and hop form (utilization rates — or the percentage of alpha acids that is isomerized and remains in the finished beer — are lower for whole hops than for pellets). Hop utilization can be as low as 10 percent and seldom exceeds 40 percent.

See HOPS.

THE BOOK AND THE COOK

As part of the annual event called "The Book and the Cook," which brings cookbook authors to more than 45 Philadelphia restaurants, the University of Pennsylvania Museum of Archaeology and Anthropology has turned its attention to beer each March since 1991.

For five years running, the museum has presented beer book author Michael Jackson in a weekend of tasting events open to the public. In March 1995, for example,

Jackson presided at a Friday evening dinner served in the museum's Upper Egyptian Gallery. Traditional Pennsylvania foods were matched with beers from the state's specialty brewers, with Jackson commenting on the beers between courses. Attendees received a key chain developed by the museum featuring a reproduction of an ancient Mesopotamian clay cuneiform tablet with Akkadian inscriptions of a beer recipe, circa 1400 B.C.

The following evening, Jackson took tasters through a tour of American microbrewed beers, with the provocative title "East versus West: Who Brews Best?" More than 100 beers were available for sampling in the museum's Chinese Rotunda. A buffet of regional foods was provided, and Jackson made himself available for book signings. Participants also were invited to take a self-guided gallery tour.

The event is not mere folderol: The museum has a large collection of food and drink artifacts from around the world, including a variety of beer-related materials from ancient Mesopotamia, some dated as early as 2600 B.C. Soloman Katz, a professor at the museum, made headlines some years back by suggesting that early humans turned to agriculture not because they were so enamored of growing grain for bread, but because they could grow grain for beer.

Another take on ancient brewing is that bread was used instead of barley. At the museum program in 1993, Fritz Maytag of Anchor Brewing unveiled a Ninkasi, his second attempt at brewing this ancient Sumerian beer. He based his recipe on one he found in a hymn to Ninkasi, the Sumerian goddess of beer and brewing. Maytag eschewed barley in the brewing process and instead used bread made of an ancient strain of wheat called emmer. The brewery produced about 2,000 magnum bottles of this ancient Sumerian beer. Jackson said the experience of drinking the beer was "like stepping into a time machine."

See NINKASI.

BROUWERIJ FRANK BOON NV HALLE, BELGIUM

Frank Boon did not come to lambic brewing as scion of an old lambic family. He began by blending lambics, then turned his skills to brewing these medieval beers. Boon runs a small revivalist brewery founded in 1975, and his products are very highly regarded. Output is minuscule — around 3,000 hl (79,254 gallons) per year.

Although a newcomer to the field, Boon values tradition highly. His lambics are all 100 percent spontaneously fermented, and he uses only whole fruit, without the addition of syrups or extracts.

Boon produces a gueuze, a Kriek, a framboise, and a faro. His Mariage Parfait vintage lambics are blended from the best casks of outstanding years. In the United States, Boon lambics are handled by Vanberg & DeWulf of Cooperstown, New York.

See BELGIAN FRUIT ALE; FARO; FRAMBOISE; FRUIT, VEGETABLE, HERBAL, AND SPECIALTY BEERS; GUEUZE; KRIEK; and LAMBIC.

BOSTON BEER CO. BOSTON, MASSACHUSETTS

Jim Koch, founder of Boston Beer Co. and brewer of Samuel Adams Boston Lager, boasts an impressive brewing lineage. His great-great-grandfather Louis Koch ran a brewery in St. Louis back when Anheuser-Busch was just a fledgling company. Louis Koch's brewery failed, but his descendant's Boston Beer Co. is running rings around Anheuser-Busch in the specialty beer market. Boston Beer Co. is the preeminent United States contract brewing company. Founded in 1984, it is now the eleventh-largest United States brewing company in terms of volume, with 700,000 barrels sold in 1994. It also operates a microbrewery in Boston, where brews are tested and some draught beer is produced for the Boston market.

Jim Koch is the founder, president, and brewer of Boston Beer Co.

Jim Koch's father worked as a brewer for several regional breweries during the 1950s and 1960s. Koch says that many of his current recipes have been inspired by those passed down by his father, grandfather, great-grandfather, and great-great-grandfather.

Koch founded Boston Beer Co. in 1984. A brash but charming entrepreneur with a varied résumé, Koch is a graduate of the Harvard Law/MBA program. He worked as an instructor for the British Columbia Outward Bound School before joining the business world as a manufacturing consultant. In the mid-1980s, he struck off on his own, returning to his ancestral craft with Boston Beer Co.

Koch brought his manufacturing savvy to the brewing world by pioneering the practice of contract brewing, in which a company contracts the brewing of its beer to another brewery. By using the brew kettles at big, underutilized breweries such as Pittsburgh Brewing Co., Blitz-Weinhard Brewing Co., and Stroh Brewery Co., Koch has been able to efficiently turn out a technically impeccable specialty beer with admirable savings in cost and labor.

His company has been among the fastest-growing specialty brewers and is now the eleventh-largest United States brewer in terms of volume, producing 700,000 barrels in 1994. Although the company maintains a small research and development brewery in Boston, 99 percent of its beer is brewed at other breweries.

An unabashed self-promoter, Koch has drawn equal measures of approbation and

Samuel Adams Boston Lager

Samuel Adams Boston Lager won several early medals at the Great American Beer Festival and has received extensive promotion as the "Best Beer in America." One of the early standard-bearers among craft beer brands, it is a beer of character and consistency. A robust lager brewed to an original gravity of 1.050 with 4.4 percent alcohol by volume, it is crisp and malty, with a nice balance from Hallertauer Mittelfrüh hops. The practice of dry hopping lends an enticing floral aroma. It may not be the best beer in America, but it is certainly one of the better ones.

admiration from fellow craft brewers. But few can deny that he has brought extraordinary visibility and credibility to the craft beer segment of the industry.

Boston Beer Co. has served as a model for would-be brewing entrepreneurs and has even drawn admiring attention from the industry giants. By working in partner-

In 1994, the Boston Beer Co. ranked eleventh among United States brewing companies, with 700,000 barrels sold.

ship with beer wholesalers and striving to educate consumers about traditional beer styles, the company has helped build the specialty beer niche into a rapidly growing segment of the market.

The company now produces around a dozen brands, including Samuel Adams Boston Lager, Boston Stock Ale, Lightship, Cream Stout, Honey Porter, Double Bock, Triple Bock, Cranberry Lambic, Weizen, Dunkelweizen, Wheat, Winter Lager, and Octoberfest.

See ALE, BOCK BEER, CONTRACT BREW-ING, LAGER ALE, MARKET SHARE, MICRO-BREWERY, PORTER, SEASONAL BEER, STOUT, and WHEAT BEER.

BOSTON BREWERS FESTIVAL

An East Coast festival entering its fourth year in 1995, the Boston Brewers Festival (BBF) is one of the larger gatherings of microbrewers and their fans in the country. A one-day event usually held in May at the World Trade Center in Boston, the BBF is held in two 4-hour sessions to accommodate 10,000 samplers of the more than 250 craft brews from about 85 microbrewers.

The 1994 festival was sold out, and attendees plowed through 150 barrels of beer — close to 5,000 gallons (18,950 L). According to Jonathan Trembley, the copro-ducer of the festival. "Many of the beers

More than 250 craft brews can be sampled at the Boston Brewers Festival.

from other parts of the country are very hard to find locally, and receive a special exemption from the state of Massachusetts to be sold here for one day only."

There are no competitions, as the BBF tries to put the focus on the beers themselves. The festival features homebrewing displays by clubs and suppliers, food available for purchase, and live blues and rhythm and blues music.

Although the selection of beers may hint at a Northeast bias, there are no regional limits. At the 1994 festival, beers were available from some of the largest craft brewers in California (including Anchor, Anderson Valley, and Sierra Nevada), Montana (Spanish Peaks), Oregon (Rogue), Texas (Celis), and Louisiana (Abita).

Even though the BBF takes up a whole floor of Boston's cavernous World Trade Center, the crowds in front of brewery booths can get fairly thick. The pourers staffing the booths are practiced and speedy hands, however. Attendees are

given a tasting glass, beer sampling tickets, and a slick program listing all the participating breweries and beers in generous detail.

The event is sponsored by BB Festivals, which also produces the Great Southern Brewers Festival in Atlanta.

See GREAT SOUTHERN BREWERS FESTIVAL.

BOTTLE-AGED BEER

A synonym for bottle-conditioned, meaning that the beer continues to ferment while in the bottle.

See BOTTLE-CONDITIONED BEER.

BOTTLE CAP

Round metal closure with a plastic or cork gasket, used to seal bottles after filling. The predominant type is the "crown" style cap, in versions that either twist off by hand or require a bottle opener to remove. Most bottles larger than 12 ounces now use a resealable aluminum twist-off bottle cap, the other major style of closure.

The crown bottle cap was patented in 1892 by William Painter, an investor who dubbed the new style a "crown" because of its resemblance to a king's crown. The crown was the most successful of many attempts to find a cheap, reliable, and sanitary bottle cap, and by 1910 it had displaced nearly all other caps of the era. The crown design endures virtually unchanged since its inception. Painter founded the Crown Cork and Seal Company, which

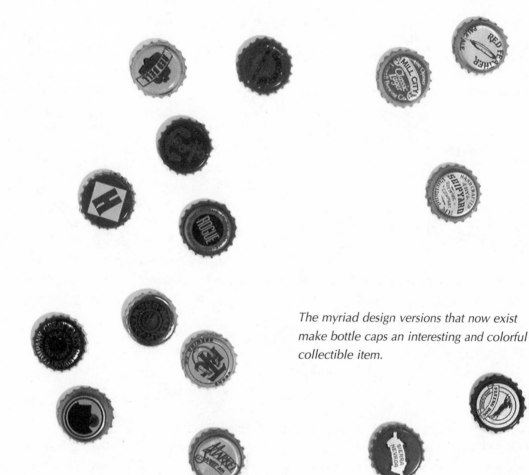

The myriad design versions that now exist make bottle caps an interesting and colorful collectible item.

remains one of the largest crown manufacturers.

Painter's original caps had a cork liner, which was eventually replaced by a soft, pliable plastic one. Recently, a liner was created that absorbs oxygen, extending the beer's shelf life.

The first caps were simply laquered to prevent the steel from rusting, but it didn't take long for breweries to request litho-

graphed artwork on their crowns to distinguish their products from the rest.

BOTTLE CAPPER

A piece of equipment that caps filled beer bottles. This unit is generally located within the same framework as the bottle filler. It has a top hopper, which contains the caps (crowns) and a feed chute that feeds the caps to the receiving throats. Generally, air is used to assist the feed or to remove any debris within the chute. The filled beer bottles enter the crowner and are raised to the throat, where a controlled preset pressure is applied and the crown liner is sealed and crimped onto the bottle.

See BOTTLE FILLER.

BOTTLE-CONDITIONED BEER

Beer produced in a manner similar to that used to make champagne. Alexander Nowell discovered the use of glass bottles for storing beer late in the 16th century. The procedure used in that era is described in a recipe for a beer from Münster, called Koet (a sour beer with a tart, winelike flavor). After the ferment has started and is well under way, the recipe directs, "remove the yeast foam, and fill in jars which will stand open for two more days before corking. Before corking the jars add a nail of nutmeg and a little sugar, then cork and pack in sand" (presumably to protect against bottle explosions or to keep the cork intact in the bottle).

This method is not that different from the method used by American homebrewers during Prohibition, when a teaspoon of sugar was added to a quart of beer before capping. Of course, modern bottle-conditioning methods are a bit more sophisticated, but the principal difference is in the method of adding the sugar.

Modern brewers frequently add a "dosage" of sugar (priming) and yeast, or fresh beer newly fermenting with active yeast, to the entire brew rather than to each bottle. This ensures that the amount of additional extract is uniformly distributed throughout the batch of beer being bottled. The beer is then allowed to condition (carbonate) slowly over a period of a month or more before being shipped to market.

Bottle-conditioned beers are disappearing from the market, but a few brewers still use the system. Such beers are prized by knowledgeable consumers because they continue to improve in the bottle for up to 5 years, depending on the strength of the beer and storage conditions.

See CASK-CONDITIONED BEER and REAL ALE.

BOTTLED BEER

Beer packaged in glass bottles. It is said in Fuller's *Worthies of England* that bottled beer was invented by chance by Alexander Newell, dean of St. Paul's, a master of Westminster School, and an avid angler, during the reign of Queen Mary (1553–1558).

As Fuller put it, "Whilst Newell was catching of fishes, Bishop Bonner was catching of Newell, and would certainly have sent him to the shambles, had not a good London merchant conveyed him away upon the seas." Newell had been fishing from the banks of the Thames when he received word that the bishop was after him, and he had to take flight immediately.

After Queen Mary's death, Newell

returned to England. One day while fishing, he remembered that on the day of his flight, he had stashed his favorite repast, beer he had put in a bottle, in a safe place along the bank. He searched for and found his long-abandoned bottle. He "found it no bottle, but a gun, such was the sound of the opening thereof; and this is believed (casualty is the mother of more invention than industry) the original of bottled ale in England."

Although others surely must have put beer in bottles before Newell, the bottle was thought to be merely a container, not a means of conditioning beer. The revelation that ale, even after many years in a bottle, acquired an unusual and delicious flavor led to the fairly rapid spread of the use of bottles. Many Elizabethan writers mention this custom. In *Bartholomew Fair,* by Ben Johnson, Ursula calls to the drawer to bring "a bottle of Ale to quench me, rascal!"

See GLASSWARE.

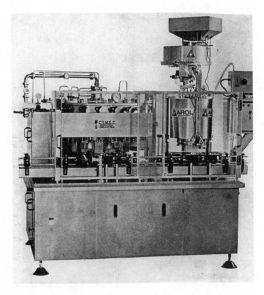

Bottle fillers have become increasingly sophisticated, as this 24-spout filler with 4-head rotary crowner illustrates.

BOTTLE FILLER

A machine that fills bottles. Bottle fillers are very complex and fill at varying speeds, depending on the model type. A small microbrewery might run around 40 to 60 bottles per minute, whereas a large brewery might run up to 2,000 per minute.

Beer to be bottled comes from bright beer tanks and is carbonated anywhere from 2.7 to 3.2 volumes of carbon dioxide. Bottle fillers have a beer receiving bowl, which in turn feeds the bottle filling heads, which are arranged in a circle and revolve around the beer bowl. The normal sequence of events is as follows: The bottle enters the filling machine via conveyors and star wheel guides. The bottle is positioned under a filling head and sealed against it. Prevacuation occurs, removing the air in the bottle. This is followed by a carbon dioxide counterpressure equal to that in the bowl above. The beer bowl pressure is kept between 2 and 3 bar, depending on the machine and the beer's carbonation level. A float control ensures that a constant amount of beer is kept in the bowl. Once the bottle is counterpressured, beer is delivered via the filling tube. Filling tubes can be short or long depending on the overall structure and operating mechanisms of the filling head. When a predetermined beer height in the bottle is reached, a valve in the filling head shuts off the flow. Once the bottle is filled, it is released from the head, then knocked or water-jetted to make the beer fob with a thick creamy foam to the top of the bottle and slightly over. This helps minimize oxygen content.

When aseptic filling is called for, sterile bottles are conveyed in sterile tunnels to the filler, which is located in a sterile capsulelike room. Generally, only very large breweries have this capability.

After the bottles are filled and fobbed, the bottle is directed to the crowner, which is generally located within the same framework as the filling machine.

See BOTTLE CAPPER and BREWING PROCESS.

BOTTLE RINSER

A piece of equipment used in bottling lines where clean, sterile nonreturnable bottles are being used. The rinser generally consists of a twist contained within an enclosed stainless steel chamber. The bottles are guided in on the bottling lines from a feed table. They are then twisted upside down, jetted inside and outside with filtered water and a sanitizer (12 ppm iodophore is a commonly used sanitizer), drained, and twisted upright before heading toward the bottle filler.

Bottles are moved via conveyors under the filling head in a typical bottling line.

BOTTLES AND BOTTLING

One of the most common packages for beer worldwide. Bottling can be done by hand or by expensive, automated bottling lines. Automated bottling lines can be enormous, sometimes taking up complete buildings. Commercial brewers such as Anheuser-Busch, Miller, and Coors have many bottling sites and own the largest, most automated bottling lines in the world.

Bottle and label design are important components in beer marketing and often become trademarks. Grölsch beer is known for its distinctive ceramic-capped 16-ounce (473 ml) bottle, a particular favorite of homebrewers. The Carlsberg Brewery bottle is so well designed that it has a permanent place in the Museum of Modern Art, in New York City.

Brewers are also innovative with bottle labels. Some place front, back, and neck labels on the bottles. Others paint the label directly on the glass. Japanese brewers use beautiful label art. Others wrap the crown with different colored foil.

Bottle color is important to the preservation of beer. Three colors of glass are commonly used to bottle beer: brown, green, and clear. Green glass and clear glass are not useful in preventing off-flavors caused by light-struck beer, which is beer that has been spoiled by light and temperature. Light-colored beer is particularly prone to being light-struck because light passes through it more easily than it does through dark beer. Brown glass does offer protection from light.

Clear glass is preferred by some brewers because it allows the consumer to see the beer's color —particularly important to breweries marketing light beers, which they hope consumers will associate with fewer calories.

Brewers who choose to use green or clear glass try to encase the bottles in thick paper products, ensuring that no sunlight reaches the glass. The Miller Brewing Company adapts their clear-bottled beer in order to impede the process of spoilage caused by overexposure to light. However, they use brown bottles in their new all-malt beers. Samuel Smith of The Old Brewery in Yorkshire, England, takes a unique approach by adding a substance to their clear glass bottles which blocks or deflects most of the harmful ultraviolet light.

BOTTLE WASHER

A large piece of equipment used to clean returnable bottles that require a complete sequence of soaking and jetting using cleaning compounds (since soap residues can adversely affect the taste of beer). The bottles are washed inside and out at temperatures rising stepwise from 70°F to 160°F (21°C to 71°C). The typical wash cycle is as follows:

- First hot-water rinse: 70°–75°F (21°–24°C))
- Second hot-water rinse: 120°–125°F (49°–52°C)
- Caustic soak: 160°F (71°C)
- Caustic spray: 160°F (71°C)
- Third hot-water rinse: 120°F (49°C)

- First cold-water rinse: 70°–75°F (21°–24°C)
- Second cold-water rinse (sterile filtered water): 60°F (15.5°C)

During this process, the label is removed from the bottle. The bottle washer includes an efficient system for disposing of removed labels and broken glass. Washing times and temperatures vary from brewery to brewery.

BOTTOM-FERMENTING YEAST

A lager yeast that ferments best at temperatures of 40° to 55°F (4° to 13°C). Lager yeast *(Saccharomyces uvarum,* also known as *Saccharomyces carlsbergensis)* ferments more slowly than ale yeast but can produce a cleaner-tasting beer. Bottom-fermenting yeast produces very low levels of diacetyl, esters, and other yeast by-products in the finished beer.

See YEAST.

BOUQUET

The aroma of a beer. The consideration of bouquet is an important part of beer evaluation and enjoyment.

See AROMA.

BREW

The quantity of wort in the preparation of beer.

BREWER

Traditionally, a man who brews beer. A woman who brewed beer was distinguished by the term *brewster*. In recent decades, however, brewster has fallen from use, and brewer has come to be used to define either a woman or a man who brews beer.

See WOMEN, BEER, AND BREWING.

BREWERESS

A synonym for brewster.

See BREWSTER.

BREWERIANA

The collecting of beer artifacts and paraphernalia by beer enthusiasts. Bottle caps, coasters, old beer signs, and cans are among the many things collected and exhibited.

See AMERICAN BREWERIANA ASSOCIATION.

BREWERS AND LICENSED RETAILERS ASSOCIATION

R. W. Simpson, Director
42 Portman Square, London
W1H 0BB United Kingdom
011-44-171-486-4831
Fax 011-44-171-935-3991

This London-based organization is a clearing house for information on brewing and selling beer in the United Kingdom.

BREWERS' ASSOCIATION OF AMERICA

Henry King, Executive Director
P.O. Box 876
Belmar, NJ 07719
908-280-9153

The Brewers' Association of America (BAA) was founded in 1941 and since that time has been the unified voice of America's smaller brewers. It currently has a strong representation of the country's microbrewers and brewpubs but is dedicated to the resolution of problems and issues for brewers of all sizes. The BAA holds an annual convention dedicated to the improvement of the brewing industry. The organization publishes its newsletter, called *Bulletin,* 16 times per year.

BREWERS ASSOCIATION OF CANADA

R. A. Morrison, President
155 Queen Street, Suite 1200
Ottawa, Ontario, Canada K1P 6L1
613-232-9601

The Brewers Association of Canada is the national trade organization of the Canadian brewing industry. It was founded in 1943 to give a voice to Canadian brewers. Twenty-four breweries currently are members. The association publishes 5 newsletters each year, as well as monthly sales bulletins and an annual statistical bulletin. It also maintains programs promoting responsible consumption of alcohol.

BREWERS' GUILD

P. J. Ogie, President
8 Ely Place, Holburn
London, EC1N 6SD United Kingdom
44-171-405-4565
Fax 44-171-831-4995

The Brewers' Guild was established in London in 1906 by brewers who saw a need for a professional organization in order to create a forum for development, training, and quality brewing. The organization today has international chapters in Africa and Ireland, and publishes a monthly journal with a circulation of 3,000. The Guild also publishes *The Brewers' Guild Directory,* a worldwide brewery directory, and *The Grist,* a technical microbrewing magazine. The Brewers' Guild also offers educational courses ranging from one-day seminars to week-long programs.

BREWERY

A facility for the production of beer. Today there are many different classifications of breweries, ranging from homebrewers, who brew beer at home using small-scale equipment and generally produce 5- or 10-gallon batches of specialty-style beers, all the way up to large, international conglomerate breweries such as Anheuser-Busch and Guinness PLC. In between, there are microbreweries, which by definition produce fewer than 15,000 barrels of beer per year and tend to distribute them locally; brewpubs, which brew and sell their wares on-premise in varying quantities; contract brewers, who develop a recipe and marketing concept but allow another brewery to actually brew and bottle the beer; and regional brewers, who produce over 15,000 barrels of beer annually and distribute those products in a regional, rather than national, area.

See ANHEUSER-BUSCH, BREWPUB, CONTRACT BREWING, GUINNESS PLC, HOMEBREWING, MICROBREWERY, and REGIONAL BREWERY.

BREWING ASSOCIATIONS

Brewing associations are located throughout the world and have been created for a variety of reasons. Some began as legislative groups that lobby for the industry within the government, some for marketing reasons, and some simply for support and the exchange of information about brewing.

Brewers associations, also called guilds, no longer have the power to regulate as they did in the past. Alcohol is a huge source of governmental income (via tax) and consequently has fallen victim to laws and regulations.

Brewing associations today are limited to lobbying on their own behalf, and acting as information centers, where brewers can exchange ideas and discuss brewing technology, market trends, and environmental and other matters that affect them.

Companions of the associations are the

A 16th-century print of a brewery

commercial brewing schools, such as the Doemans Schule in Germany.

BREWING LIBRARIES

Brewing libraries are located throughout the world. Many are associated with large brewing companies. These libraries offer books, journals, and other resources not generally available elsewhere.

BREWING PROCESS

The steps a brewer follows to make beer.

See BOILING, BOTTLE FILLER, CARBONATION, CHILLING, CRUSHING, FERMENTATION, MASHING, SPARGING, WATER, and YEAST.

The Brewing Process

1. Malt is fed into the mill.

2. The mill grinds the malt into grist.

3. The grist is fed into the mash tun, where it is mixed with warm or hot water. If the infusion method is used, only the mash tun is utilized.

4. If infusion is not used, it is during the decoction phase of the brewing process that the mash is sent through the lauter tun, where the mash is clarified and becomes the refined wort.

5. Hops are added to the wort in the brew kettle, where the actual brewing of the mixture occurs.

6. The hops are removed from the mixture, and the wort passes through the hop back and is flavored by the hops.

7. The whirlpool removes the undesirable proteins by centrifugal force.

8. The wort moves through a cooling area, the heat exchanger, where it is brought down to a temperature suitable for fermentation.

9. The yeast is added to the wort in the fermentation tank or vessel.

10. Following fermentation, the wort moves along to the conditioning tanks, where it sits undisturbed until it reaches its finished, aged state, again variable depending upon the style.

11. The finished beer is filtered here. Note that in order to impart some unique characteristic, some styles are not filtered at all.

12. The beer passes to a holding tank, where it remains until it is bottled or kegged for transport, sale, and consumption.

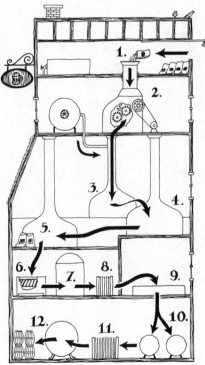

BREW KETTLE

The vessel where wort extracted from a mash tun is heated and boiled with hops. Also called a copper because brew kettles used to be made from copper, which has high heat-transfer properties. Today these kettles are mainly made from stainless steel because it is easier to clean and lasts longer. These vessels can be heated in a variety of ways, including a steam jacket, a direct gas fire, gas coil/jacket, an electric immersion heater, or an external heater (electric, steam, and so on). The brew kettle often features a copper dome and is the visual centerpiece of many breweries.

BREWMASTER

A master brewer, by degree, and also the individual who supervises the day-to-day operations at a brewery.

BREWPUB

A small brewery that serves most of its beer on the premises, often through an associated restaurant or taproom.

Brewpubs were common in 17th- and early-18th-century America, where on-premises production and sale of beer was the rule rather than the exception. This

The brew kettle is standard brewing equipment, whether for a homebrewer or a large national brewer.

The brewing equipment of the Oliver Breweries, Camden Yard, Baltimore, Maryland

practice of on-premises production and sale of beer continued until Prohibition. After Prohibition, the practice of on-premises brewing was made illegal in many states. Fortunately, these laws have been repealed in most states, and there are now over 360 brewpubs in the United States, most of which have opened within the past 10 years. Early United States brewpubs included Buffalo Bill's in Hayward, California; Yakima Brewing & Malting in Yakima, Washington; and Mendocino Brewing Co. in Hopland, California.

Brewpubs usually run a number of their own brews on house taps, interchanging year-round and seasonal specialty beers. Some brewpubs also serve beers that are brewed at microbreweries or other small breweries. Some brewpubs also offer other alcoholic beverages as well, especially single-malt Scotch whiskeys, which share a malty kinship with beer.

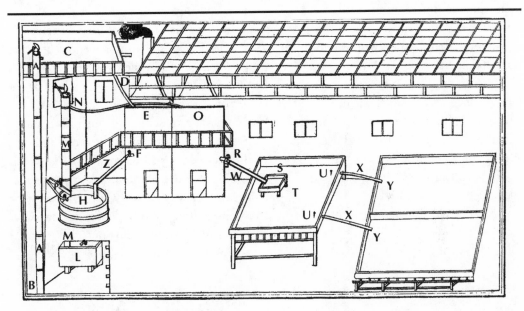

Brewmasters have a variety of brewhouse setups to work with, all of which vary from brewery to brewery. This is a view of the interior of an early 19th-century brewhouse, featuring the following parts: AA—cold liquor pumps, B—well, C—cistern or reservoir, D—water outlet into copper, E—liquor copper, F—outlet of copper, H—mash tubs, L—underback, MM—wort pumps, N—inlet to wort copper, O—wort copper, P—mill spout, R—wort lock, S—hop drainer, T and Y—hopbearer and coolers, U—plugs, W—copper outlet for wort, X—cold water inlet for mashing, and Z—inlet into copper conducting liquor to bottom of mash tub between bottom and false bottom. At the far right, below the cooler are the fermenting tubs, below which are the casks for filling.

Brewpubs usually incorporate a restaurant. Early brewpubs served typical pub fare, but many now offer extensive menus of beer-related foods. Some brewpub restaurants are actually quite elegant. The aesthetic appeal of copper brew kettles has led many brewpub architects to place the brewhouse prominently adjacent to the dining room (and in some cases directly in the dining room), offering diners a view of the kettles.

Brewpubs are the fastest-growing segment of the burgeoning United States microbrewery movement. There are currently more than 360 brewpubs and more than 205 microbreweries, for a total of over 570 small, craft breweries operating in the United States. Outside the United States and Canada, brewpubs are found in Great Britain, Germany, and the Czech Republic, among other countries.

See MICROBREWERY, MICROBREWING, and MICROBREWERY MOVEMENT.

BREWSTER

See BREWER and WOMEN, BEER, AND BREWING.

BREWSTER SESSIONS

Justice of the peace sessions in England established by law in 1729 and continuing until very recent times in which brewers' licenses were granted or denied. The name reflects women's historical control of the beer industry. (A brewster is a female brewer.)

BRIDE ALE

In Old England, a special ale prepared and sold by a bride on her wedding day, for which she received contributions from friends. Also known as bride-bush, bride wain, and bride-stake. The *Christian State of Matrimony* (1545) relates, "When they come home from the church, then beginneth excess of eatyng and drynking, and as much is waisted in one daye as were sufficient for the two newe-married folkes halfe a yeare to lyve upon."

In some places, regulations were enacted to restrain excesses in the keeping of bride ales, as an entry in the Court Roll of Hales Owen shows: "A payne ye made that no person or persons that shall brewe any weddyn ale to sell, shall not brewe aboue twelve stryke of mault at the most, and that the said persons so marryed shall not keep nor have above efght messe of persons at hys dinner within the burrowe, and before hys brydall daye ho shall keep no unlawful games in hys house, nor out of hys house on payne of 20s."

BRIGHT BEER TANKS

See CONDITIONING/BRIGHT BEER STORAGE TANKS.

BRITISH BEER

British-style beer encompasses the ale beer styles developed in the British Isles since the fifth century, when ale seems to have replaced metheglin (spiced mead) as the national drink. In general, the British have developed a wide range of what we now call ale styles. These include bitters and pale ales, India Pale Ale, mild ale, brown and dark ales, old and strong ales, porters, stouts, and barley wines.

Originally, the British brew was unhopped, and it was called "ale." In 1524, Flemish immigrants settled in East Kent and began to cultivate hops. They continued to make hopped "beer" as they had on the continent. That was the original distinction between beer and ale: Beer had hops; ale did not. For some time, ale and beer existed side by side in Britain, but by the beginning of the 17th century, the hopped beer had won out, although unhopped ale lingered on into the 19th century. Today we know ale as a form of beer, although in Britain beer is still considered the weaker product and ale the stronger.

The British brew their ale by a method quite unlike that used to make lager ale. The basic ingredient of pale ale is British 2-row barley malt. Two-row barley is different from the American 6-row variety in that it has 2 rows of barleycorns on the stalk instead of 6 and a lower protein content. The 2-row variety is a little less suited to brewing with other grains, although this is certainly done. The British sometimes use American corn as a grain adjunct (they call it maize), and they also add sugar to their ales. This is a remnant of the heyday of the British Empire, when cheap Caribbean sugar was widely available. Modern English brewers are returning to all-grain brews with little, if any, sugar.

British barley malt may be brewed by a simpler starch-sugar conversion method: the single-step infusion mash. The grains are infused with warm water to reach the starch-conversion temperature almost immediately and steeped at 150° to 158°F (65.5° to 70°C) to encourage conversion of the starches to fermentable sugars. British ales are typically brewed in 7 to 10 days and, at least in the case of mild and bitter ales, are consumed as quickly, without any aging. Bottled beers and stronger ales are often aged. The former may even be cold-conditioned in the nature of German altbiers.

See BARLEY WINE, BELGIAN BEER, BITTER, PALE ALE, PORTER, and STOUT.

BRITISH BEST BITTER

See BITTER.

BRITISH BROWN ALE

See BROWN ALE.

BRITISH GUILD OF BEER WRITERS

Barrie Pepper, Chairman
P.O. Box 900
Hemel Hempstead
Herts HP3 0RJ
England
011-44-1442-834-900
Fax 011-44-1442-934901

The British Guild of Beer Writers was founded in 1988 by Roger Protz, editor of *What's Brewing,* a publication of the Campaign for Real Ale.

The guild's membership stands at over 110, with a handful of North American and European members.

Its objective is to secure a wider reading and listening public for the beer industry through positive media coverage.

BRITISH STANDARD ALE

See BITTER.

BROWN ALE

Brown ales come in all shades and flavors. The style is quite eclectic.

The old brewing texts do not recognize brown ale as a type of beer. The term *brown ale* has been used to describe a particular type of beer only in the past 30 years or so. In some ways, brown ales are a little like porters, yet paler, sweeter, mellower, not as dry, and usually lower in alcohol.

In England, where the style was invented, there are two main varieties of brown ale: southern and northern, known as English mild ale and English brown ale, respectively.

English Mild Ale

The southern style of brown ale is dark brown (about 50 SRM), almost opaque, sweet, low in original gravity (9 to 10.5 or even lower), low in alcohol (3 to 3.5 percent

by volume), and low in bitterness (20 IBU), with malty, almost fruity undertones. This type of brown ale is called mild ale in Britain when served on tap, often real ale (cask-conditioned) style. British beer writer Michael Jackson calls brown ale England's dessert beer. Crystal (or caramel) malt is a major ingredient, so the beer has a smooth, sweetish mellowness, with an almost butterscotch flavor from the presence of diacetyl (below 0.06 ppm). This type of beer does not sell well in the United States. Americans prefer a less sweet, heavier brown ale. A modern English brewing text defines "draught mild" as 7.7–9.1/1.031–1.037 OG, 2.5–3.6 percent alcohol by volume, and 14–37 IBU; and "brown ale" (usually bottled) as 7.5–10.2/1.030–1.041 OG, 2.5–3.6 percent alcohol by volume, 16–28 IBU, and color up to 34 SRM.

The Great American Beer Festival guidelines for English Mild Ale are 8–9/1.032–1.036 OG, 2.5–3.6 percent alcohol by volume, 14–20 IBU, and 17–34 SRM.

Original Gravity	Final Gravity	Alcohol by Volume	IBU	SRM
Grant's Celtic Ale (Washington) 1992				
7.6/1.030	2.4	2.7%	26.4	35
Highgate Mild (England) 1992				
8.9/1.035.5	2.6	3.3%	22	24

English Brown Ale

The northern type of brown ale is typified in the famous Newcastle Brown. This type of beer has a reddish brown color (16 SRM), is drier than the mild ale, has a higher alcohol content (4–4.5 percent alcohol by volume), and is somewhere around 20 IBU. The light roasted malty taste is mellow and smooth. No American brewer seems to be making this type of beer today.

The Great American Beer Festival guidelines for English Brown Ale are 10–12/1.040–1.050 OG, 4–5.5 percent alcohol by volume, 15–25 IBU, and 15–22 SRM.

Original Gravity	Final Gravity	Alcohol by Volume	IBU	SRM
Samuel Smith Nut Brown Ale (England) 1983				
12.3/1.049	1.7	5.4%	≈22	≈35

American Brown Ale

American brown ales are no less novel and distinctive. They are sometimes called California brown or Texas brown, both of which may be hoppier than what is becoming known as American brown, which is itself hoppier than the English variety and has little or no diacetyl.

The Great American Beer Festival guidelines for American Brown Ale are 10–14/1.040–1.055 OG, 4–5.5 percent alcohol by volume, 25–60 IBU, and 15–22 SRM.

Original Gravity	Final Gravity	Alcohol by Volume	IBU	SRM
Pete's Wicked Ale 1993				
13.1/1.053	3.1	5.3%	21	36
Pyramid Best Brown 1993				
13/1.052	3.8	4.9%	25	22

See BELGIAN BROWN AND RED ALES.

BUDEJOVIVKY BUDVAR, CESKE BUDEJOVICE

Budvar, is located in Bohemia. Known in German as Budweis and in Czech as Ceske Budejovice, Budvar is about the size of a regional brewery in United States standards, with production hovering around 500,000 hl (13,208,923 gallons). The fall of the Iron Curtain has made Budvar a pawn in the game of international trade. Budvar owns the Budweiser name in parts of Europe, which has blocked the United States giant Anheuser-Busch from using the name in some markets.

Anheuser-Busch has been working with the Czech government to purchase a minority stake in Budvar. As a result, there is a growing St. Louis influence in Ceske Budejovice, including the construction of a community center and the introduction of various cultural aid programs.

See ANHEUSER-BUSCH.

BUDWEISER

See ANHEUSER-BUSCH.

BUFFALO BEER FESTIVAL

The 1994 Buffalo Beer Festival was the fourth annual and drew more than 5,000 people. In 1995, the sponsors changed the venue for this late-January festival to the Buffalo Convention Center in downtown Buffalo to accommodate more people. More than 100 beers were featured.

BUFFER TANK

A stainless steel tank that is often used in line from a bright beer tank to a filtration system. Its effect is mainly to guard against pressure shock prior to the beer's entering the filtration system.

See CONDITIONING/BRIGHT BEER STORAGE TANKS.

BUREAU OF ALCOHOL, TOBACCO AND FIREARMS

National Laboratory Center Library
1401 Research Boulevard
Rockville, MD 20850
301-294-0410

The governing body of the beer industry in the United States This organization oversees label laws, alcohol content laws, and advertising policy for the United States government.

BURNER

See GAS BURNER.

BURTON ALE

Burton ale, the original pale ale type, was named after the small town of Burton-on-Trent (on the Trent River in the English Midlands). As many as 46 operating breweries were located there at one time. Water from the deep wells of Burton was the major factor in production of high-quality ales, especially pale ales. That water was very high in calcium, magnesium, and sulfate (1,200 ppm) hardness, which had a beneficial effect on the utilization of hop acids in the production of beer. Modern brewers sometimes harden their water by adding those chemicals, which they call Burton salts. The water, and the brewers who used it, made Burton the brewing capital of England, a title it claims even today.

By the 13th century, the monks at nearby abbey were brewing beer, and the town's reputation as a brewing center was well established. The Alsopp family was the first to brew commercially there, during the reign of Charles II, but Bass is the most famous in history. The brewery holds England's first registered trademark on its logo. In general, the beers called Burton ales are heavy-gravity beers, the most famous of which is India Pale Ale (IPA).

Original Gravity	Final Gravity	Alcohol by Volume	IBU	SRM
Alsopp Burton Ale 1879				
17/1.070	3.6	8%	≈75	≈20
Worthington Burton Ale 1889				
24.2	7.5	10.1%	≈75	≈20

See BASS PLC, INDIA PALE ALE (IPA), and PALE ALE.

BURTON UNION SYSTEM

A method of fermentation that was, and to a much lesser extent still is, used in Burton-on-Trent, England. It comprises several lines of oak casks (up to 180 gallons, or 6.8

hl, each) containing internal attemperation coils and a swan-necked pipe at the top of each cask. Fermenting wort is passed into these collecting vessels during the height of fermentation. The pipe at

The Burton Union System is made up of linked cases and troughs. This system affords the brewer the unique opportunity to produce large quantities of yeast, due to the inherent trough design. Only one brewery in the world today — Marston's of Burton-on-Trent — uses this system.

the top of the cask discharges yeast into a collecting trough positioned at a slant below the casks. The yeast settles out there while the barm is collected at one end of the trough and returned to the cask. At the end of fermentation, most of the yeast will have been collected in the trough. This system is obviously space prohibitive, but it does add certain characteristic flavors to beer. Stainless steel versions of the oak casks also are used.

BUTTERFLY VALVE

A manual or automated valve that has a vertical stainless steel plate seated within its body. It can be used for flow control, although it generally has less fine-tuning than a ball valve.

See BALL VALVE.

CALANDRIA

An external chamber through which wort from a brew kettle might be circulated and heated. A calandria might be heated by an electric immersion heater, steam coils, or gas-fired coils. Circulating and heating the wort outside the brew kettle has the advantage of easy cleaning and high efficiency.

CALCIUM

A metallic element. As an ion, calcium provides most of the hardness found in water. It is a very important element to brewers in that it lowers mash and wort pH. It does not affect the flavor of beer, but if water used to top off fermenters and such is high in calcium, it can promote haze.

A calandria circulates wort from a brew in order to heat it.

Normally, a range of 50 to 100 ppm is optimum for brewing water, depending on the malt used and the amount of bicarbonates in the water.

See WATER.

CALCIUM CARBONATE

A nearly insoluble precipitate formed when heating water that has a high concentration of bicarbonates. Calcium carbonate will redissolve into the acidic wort, raising the pH, unless it is removed before the wort is added. Normally, boiling water for 15 minutes, allowing it to cool, and carefully decanting the water off the white precipitate is the simplest method for dealing with calcium carbonate.

CALIFORNIA BEER FESTIVAL

By far the largest beer festival in San Diego was held at the San Diego Sports Arena for its first go-round in April 1995. The event is expected to be held annually at about the same time each year.

Featuring handcrafted, microbrewed beers from around the world, the festival principals report upward of 22,000 visitors. Coproducer John Thomas said, "The purpose is to promote handcrafted beer and the chance for the public to try such unusual beers as Lemon Lager from the Saxer Brewing Company and Buffalo Gold Ale brewed by the Rockies Brewing Company. There will be some foreign micros here, but no one brewery will be allowed to dominate."

Going somewhat against the grain of recent festivals, the California Beer Festival holds two beer-tasting competitions, one judged by professional taster, and the other by attendees. "We're taking great care to ensure all brewery participants that the contest will be fair, consistent, and professional," Thomas said. "Any technique used to attract votes during the People's Choice Contest will automatically disqualify that entry. And restrictions will apply to the use of the California Beer Festival name and logo by all contest participants. We want the awards to mean something."

The professional judging panel considers beers in a variety of styles, and a select panel judges a "Best of Show" to be announced toward the end of the festival. Music, food, a variety of speakers, and 50 breweries with well over 100 beers were on tap.

CALIFORNIA COMMON BEER/CALIFORNIA STEAM BEER

See COMMON BEER.

CALIFORNIA SMALL BREWERS ASSOCIATION

Bob Judd
1330 21st Street, Suite 201
Sacramento, CA 95814
916-444-8333

This association prides itself on the support it provides to smaller brewers in the state. It also sponsors an annual beer festival, now in its eighth year.

CAMPAIGN FOR REAL ALE (CAMRA)

Richard Smith, Secretary
230 Hatfield Road
St. Albans, Hertfordshire
AL1 4LW United Kingdom
011-44-1727-867201
Fax 011-44-1727-867670

The Campaign for Real Ale (CAMRA), based in Britain, has the enviable reputation of being the world's largest and most effective consumer organization. It was founded in 1971 by four people who were concerned about protecting non-pasteurized, cask-conditioned "real ale." They publicized their cause whenever a small cask-conditioned brewery closed by staging protest marches lamenting the passing, complete with open caskets filled with bottles of the brewery's offering. The result was increased public awareness of the difference between cask-conditioned ale and the ale being sold by the big breweries. A new appreciation for "real ale" took hold and has continued to grow.

Current membership exceeds 45,000 people in over 150 chapters across Great Britain. CAMRA was founded as the Society for the Preservation of Beers from the Wood, and was later called the Campaign for the Revitalization of Ale.

The name CAMRA was adopted in 1973. CAMRA sponsors the Great British Beer Festival, which is held annually in the summer. It has open membership and publishes various periodicals dealing with the brewing industry, including the monthly *What's Brewing*.

See REAL ALE.

CAMPAIGN FOR REAL ALE (CAMRA) CANADA

P.O. Box 2036
Station D
Ottawa, Ontario
Canada K1P 5W3
613-837-7155

This organization has modeled itself on the work of CAMRA in the United Kingdom and, similarly, works as an effective consumer group for the beer industry.

CAMPDEN

A commercial name for a sterilizing agent consisting of potassium metabisulfite compressed into tablets. When added to water, the tablets dissolve, releasing sulfur dioxide into the water. Sulfur dioxide will not kill all yeasts or bacteria as chlorine will, but it will impede the growth of those yeasts and bacteria left alive. When using potassium or sodium metabisulfite, the brewer must allow at least 24 hours for all gases to vent out prior to pitching yeast or bottling.

CANADIAN INDEPENDENT BREWERS ASSOCIATION

Stewart Petrie, President
35 Chatfield Lane
Mississauga, Ontario
Canada L4Z 1K8
416-897-2422

This nonprofit organization represents the business interests of Canadian microbreweries, brewpubs, and suppliers.

CANE SUGAR

Table sugar or sucrose. Cane sugar is used in brewing some Belgian styles (such as tripel) or for priming. Certain forms of cane sugar, such as Demerara sugar or treacle, are also used in brewing British ales but never in lagers.

CAN FILLER

A machine that fills cans in a rotating manner. Can fillers are normally large machines capable of filling 500 to 2,000 cans per minute via filling tubes. The flow stops when the beer reaches a predetermined height in the can. Any remaining air in the can is ejected to a separate bowl in the filler. The cans are then sent to a seamer. Prior to reaching this mechanism, carbon dioxide is blown over the top of the beer to minimize air pickup.

See BOTTLE FILLER.

Most large can fillers are capable of filling 500 to 2,000 cans per minute.

CANNSTATTER WASEN

Perhaps with an eye on the partying going on in Munich, Germany, each autumn, the king of Württemberg established a harvest festival in 1818 in Stuttgart. This festival is still held each fall. There, in the Cannstatt district, the Cannstatter Wasen Volksfest is held at roughly the same time as Munich's Oktoberfest, and the celebratory ethos is just as vigorous. This festival is less crowded and offers a more generous selection of beers than the Oktoberfest. Dinkelacker, Schwaben Brau, and Stuttgarter Hofbrau are the three locals, making a Volksfestbier similar to Märzen though slightly lower in gravity.

See OKTOBERFEST.

BRASSERIE CANTILLON BRUSSELS, BELGIUM

A small lambic brewery run by a family that has been brewing since the early 18th century. The current brewery was built in the 1930s by Paul Cantillon and is now operated by another member of the Cantillon family, Jean-Pierre Van Roy. The company's products are much valued by purists, but the brewery's production is circumscribed by the fact that beer is brewed only from late fall to early spring. The rest of the year, Van Roy runs an on-site lambic museum, a "living" exhibit intended to educate the public on the wonders of lambic.

See LAMBIC.

CARAMELIZATION

The darkening and thickening of sugars when cooked. Caramelization occurs during the boiling stage (although malts are caramelized during the malting process as well). Caramelized sugars have a sharp flavor and darken the wort. Caramelization occurs most often in high-gravity brewing, so extract brewers who boil only 6 quarts (5.7 L) or so of water are unlikely to achieve very light colors.

CARBOHYDRATE

A chemical compound consisting of carbon, hydrogen, and oxygen. This class of compounds includes all sugars.

CARBONATING STONE

A ceramic or stainless steel seal-sintered tube that is installed in the final bright beer tank. Carbon dioxide is injected through the stone when the tank is filled with beer. The carbon dioxide percolates through the stone and into the beer, creating the carbonation. The level of carbon dioxide injected is monitored so as to control the final carbonation.

CARBONATION

The process of allowing carbon dioxide to dissolve into the beer under pressure. After the fermentation process is complete, beer

Carbonation Chart

Pounds per Square Inch

Temperature of Beer (°F.)	1	2	3	4	5	6	7	8	9	10	11	12	13	14	15
30	1.82	1.92	2.03	2.14	2.23	2.36	2.48	2.60	2.70	2.82	2.93	3.02			
31	1.78	1.88	2.00	2.10	2.20	2.31	2.42	2.54	2.65	2.76	2.86	2.96			
32	1.75	1.85	1.95	2.05	2.16	2.27	2.38	2.48	2.59	2.70	2.80	2.90	3.01		
33		1.81	1.91	2.01	2.12	2.23	2.33	2.43	2.53	2.63	2.74	2.84	2.96		
34		1.78	1.86	1.97	2.07	2.18	2.28	2.38	2.48	2.58	2.68	2.79	2.89	3.00	
35			1.83	1.93	2.03	2.14	2.24	2.34	2.43	2.52	2.62	2.73	2.83	2.93	3.02
36			1.79	1.88	1.99	2.09	2.20	2.29	2.39	2.47	2.57	2.67	2.77	2.86	2.96
37				1.84	1.94	2.04	2.15	2.24	2.34	2.42	2.52	2.62	2.72	2.80	2.90
38				1.80	1.90	2.00	2.10	2.20	2.29	2.38	2.47	2.57	2.67	2.75	2.85
39					1.86	1.96	2.05	2.15	2.25	2.34	2.43	2.52	2.61	2.70	2.80
40					1.82	1.92	2.01	2.10	2.20	2.30	2.39	2.47	2.56	2.65	2.75
41						1.87	1.97	2.06	2.16	2.25	2.35	2.43	2.52	2.60	2.70
42						1.83	1.93	2.02	2.12	2.21	2.30	2.39	2.47	2.56	2.65
43						1.80	1.90	1.99	2.08	2.17	2.25	2.34	2.43	2.52	2.60
44							1.86	1.95	2.04	2.13	2.21	2.30	2.39	2.47	2.56
45							1.82	1.91	2.00	2.08	2.17	2.26	2.34	2.42	2.51
46								1.88	1.96	2.04	2.13	2.22	2.30	2.38	2.47
47								1.84	1.92	2.00	2.09	2.18	2.25	2.34	2.42
48								1.80	1.88	1.96	2.05	2.14	2.21	2.30	2.38
49									1.85	1.93	2.01	2.10	2.18	2.25	2.34
50									1.82	1.90	1.98	2.06	2.14	2.21	2.30
51										1.87	1.95	2.02	2.10	2.18	2.25
52										1.84	1.91	1.99	2.06	2.14	2.22
53										1.80	1.88	1.96	2.03	2.10	2.18
54											1.85	1.93	2.00	2.07	2.15
55											1.82	1.89	1.97	2.04	2.11
56												1.86	1.93	2.00	2.07
57												1.83	1.90	1.97	2.04
58												1.80	1.86	1.94	2.00
59													1.83	1.90	1.97
60													1.80	1.87	1.94

To Use This Chart: First find the temperature of your beer in the outside columns. Look across until you reach the carbonation level desired. Then look up to the top of that column to find the required pressure, and set your regulator accordingly.

Carbonation Chart

Pounds per Square Inch

16	17	18	19	20	21	22	23	24	25	26	27	28	29	30	Temperature of Beer (°F.)
															30
															31
															32
															33
															34
															35
															36
3.00															37
2.94															38
2.89	2.98														39
2.84	2.93	3.01													40
2.79	2.87	2.96													41
2.74	2.82	2.91	3.00												42
2.69	2.78	2.86	2.95												43
2.64	2.73	2.81	2.90	2.99											44
2.60	2.68	2.77	2.85	2.94	3.02										45
2.55	2.63	2.72	2.80	2.89	2.98										46
2.50	2.59	2.67	2.75	2.84	2.93	3.02									47
2.46	2.55	2.62	2.70	2.79	2.87	2.96									48
2.42	2.50	2.58	2.66	2.75	2.83	2.91	2.99								49
2.38	2.45	2.54	2.62	2.70	2.78	2.86	2.94	3.02							50
2.34	2.41	2.49	2.57	2.65	2.73	2.81	2.89	2.97							51
2.30	2.37	2.45	2.54	2.61	2.69	2.76	2.84	2.93	3.00						52
2.26	2.33	2.41	2.48	2.57	2.64	2.72	2.80	2.88	2.95	3.03					53
2.22	2.29	2.37	2.44	2.52	2.60	2.67	2.75	2.83	2.90	2.98					54
2.19	2.25	2.33	2.40	2.47	2.55	2.63	2.70	2.78	2.85	2.93	3.01				55
2.15	2.21	2.29	2.36	2.43	2.50	2.58	2.65	2.73	2.80	2.88	2.96				56
2.11	2.18	2.25	2.33	2.40	2.47	2.54	2.61	2.69	2.76	2.84	2.91	2.99			57
2.07	2.14	2.21	2.29	2.36	2.43	2.50	2.57	2.64	2.72	2.80	2.86	2.94	3.01		58
2.04	2.11	2.18	2.25	2.32	2.39	2.46	2.53	2.60	2.67	2.75	2.81	2.89	2.96	3.03	59
2.01	2.08	2.14	2.21	2.28	2.35	2.42	2.49	2.56	2.63	2.70	2.77	2.84	2.91	2.98	60

The numbers in the grid express the volumes of carbon dioxide (CO_2); a liter of beer containing three liters of CO_2 (at standard temperature and pressure) is said to contain 3 volumes of CO_2.

has very little carbonation (typically 1 to 1.5 volumes). It requires additional carbonation to provide the sparkle, head, and additional flavor. Two methods are normally used to carbonate beer: natural carbonation and artificial carbonation. The method used usually depends on the brewer, the beer, and how the beer is handled.

Artificial Carbonation

Large commercial breweries use this method, as their beers have been filtered and pasteurized and no longer have living yeast in them. A carbonating stone is used to bubble carbon dioxide through the beer, achieving precise carbonation levels. After the beer has reached the desired carbonation level, it is ready for kegging or bottling.

Natural Carbonation

Natural carbonation is a bit more complex. First the beer is removed from the settled yeast, usually by transferring it to another vessel. This beer still contains active yeast in suspension. Some type of fermentable sugar is then added as a priming agent, and the beer is mixed well. Then it is bottled or kegged and allowed to carbonate by letting the yeast consume the newly added sugar. This takes 1 to 3 weeks. The brewer must be careful to use the right amount and type of priming sugar. If too much priming sugar is used, over-carbonation will occur, possibly even resulting in exploding bottles.

Another way of naturally carbonating beer is kraeusening. Instead of adding sugar to the beer, unfermented wort is added to the fermented wort, inducing a small second fermentation.

Natural Carbonation

Priming Agent	Amount per 5 Gallons (19 L)
Dextrose (corn sugar)	¾ cup (170 g)
Honey	1 cup (226.8 g)
Maple syrup	1¼ cups (340.2 g)
Molasses	1 cup (226.8 g)
Brown sugar	⅔ cup (151 g)
Beet or cane sugar	⅔ cup (151 g)
Dried malt extract	1¼ cups (340.2 g)

Note: The amounts given should be considered the upper limits to avoid over-carbonation.

In some lager breweries, toward the end of fermentation, the tank is sealed, allowing carbon dioxide to dissolve naturally into the beer.

See BREWING PROCESS.

CARBON DIOXIDE RECOVERY PLANT

A complex series of equipment designed to take carbon dioxide from the fermentation vessels, purify it, and render it usable for other brewing functions. The equipment in a recovery plant includes the following:

- Fob tank
- CO_2 balloon tank
- Booster compressor

- Water scrubber
- Activated carbon purifiers
- Water cooler
- Activated aluminum dryers
- Ammonia compressor and cooler
- Liquid CO_2 tank
- CO_2 evaporator

Once the carbon dioxide has passed through this complex series of equipment, the gas will be purified.

CARBON DIOXIDE TESTER

A piece of equipment designed for measuring the carbonation of beer. This is done by taking a sample from a tank or a bottle and then using the tester by shaking the beer within in order to knock the carbon dioxide out of the solution and into a sealed chamber. The user then takes a temperature and pressure reading from the tester and refers to a chart to determine the volume of carbon dioxide dissolved in the sample.

Testers are designed for tank samples and bottle/can samples. The accuracy of the testing procedure is vital to achieve a consistent product suitable for either draft dispensing or packaging in bottles or cans.

CARBOY

A large vessel (usually 5–7 gallons) used in homebrewing. A carboy is usually a

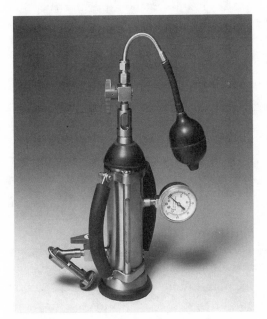 

To determine the volume of carbon dioxide in a sample of beer being brewed, carbon dioxide volume meters such as these are used.

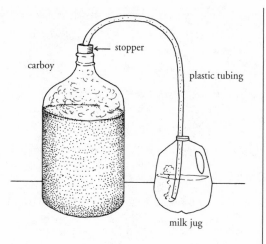

A simple homebrewing set-up

narrow-necked glass or plastic container and is commonly used in conjunction with a blow-off tube.

See BLOW-OFF TUBE and FRUIT.

CARLSBERG BREWERY COPENHAGEN, DENMARK

Brewer Jacob Christian Jacobsen started Carlsberg in 1874. The first half of the brewery name came from his son, Carl. The second part is the Danish word *berg* (hill) for the promontory on which the brewery was built. Even before Jacobsen founded the Carlsberg Brewery, his family had made great strides in the world of brewing.

In the late 1700s, Christian Jacobsen, a farmer's son, went to Copenhagen and began brewing. Starting what was to become a family tradition, he looked to technology to help him brew better beers by being one of the first to use a thermometer, an enormous advance in brewing.

Christian Jacobsen's son, Jacob Christian Jacobsen, further examined the ways science could help brewing. In 1854 he set off on a journey from Copenhagen to Munich to obtain lager yeast from a former mentor, Gabriel Sedlmyer. To keep the small containers of the yeast that Sedlmyr gave him from drying out, he kept his stovepipe hat over them, and at every stagecoach he poured water over the yeast. In this manner he successfully completed his return journey. He used the yeast to brew the first good-quality lager beer in Denmark.

Jacob Christian Jacobsen was relentless in his pursuit of scientific excellence. Among his friends and colleagues were Anton Dreher, Louis Pasteur, Gabriel Sedlmyer, and Eugene Velten of Marseilles, also a brewer. In 1875 Jacobsen set up the Carlsberg Laboratories, which in addition to its obvious interest in brewing sciences was an endowment that pursued research of benefit to Denmark. The next year, the Carlsberg Foundation began operations to "benefit science and honor the country."

One of the single most important discoveries at the laboratory was made by Emil Christian Hansen, a scientist who had worked at the Carlsberg Brewery. He isolated the first single-cell yeast culture. Once the trick of isolating different yeast species was known, it became a matter of experimenting to find which ones made acceptable beers. His experimenting was successful in 1883, an accomplishment that went a long way toward ensuring brand consistency by eliminating bad yeast strains.

A view of the mash tuns and tanks at the Carlsberg Brewery in Copenhagen, Denmark. Founded in 1874, Carlsberg has grown to become one of the great international brewers.

Today Carlsberg is one of the five breweries that make up the huge Carlsberg A/S (formerly United Breweries Ltd.) group, the others being Frederika, Neptune, Wiibroes, and Tuborg. Carlsberg A/S controls about 80 percent of the Danish national beer market. Recently Carlsberg A/S merged with Allied-Tetley of Britain to form one of the largest commercial breweries in Denmark.

Perhaps the most famous part of the Carlsberg Brewery is its elephant gate, inspired by Rome's Minerva Square. The four great elephants have become the brewery's symbol and have appeared on Carlsberg beer labels since the beginning.

Carlsberg has become one of the great international breweries, with brewing investments in 9 countries, licensed production in 14, and export to more than 100. In the United States, Anheuser-Busch handles importation of Carlsberg beer, including Carlsberg Lager, Light, and Elephant Malt Liquor. Anheuser-Busch also contracts an Elephant Red, which is produced under license in Canada for the American market. Though Carlsberg A/S is known for its high quality lagers, it also produces quite a few ales, including an Imperial Stout.

See ANHEUSER-BUSCH, LIGHT BEER, and MALT LIQUOR.

CARLSON'S BREWERY RESEARCH

Randy Carlson
P.O. Box 758
Walker, MN 56484
218-547-1907

An independent research group dedicated to research projects related to the brewery industry. Carlson's produces old-time brewery calendars that have become industry favorites, featuring 19th century brewery lithographs and brand trademarks.

CARLTON & UNITED BREWERIES, CARLTON, VICTORIA, AUSTRALIA

A subsidiary of the Foster's Brewing Group. Producers of the Abbots, Brisbane, Carlton, Fiji, Foster's, Redback, Resch's and Sheaf labels. The company also brews Guinness brands under license.

CASE PACKER

A piece of equipment that automatically packs bottled beer into cardboard cases with six-packs or into plastic crates. The case packer is located at the end of a bottling line. Labeled bottles are guided into separate channels, arranged, and then automatically dropped into the cases or crates. If cardboard cases are used, the cases are sealed and conveyed for loading onto an automatic or manual palletizer.

CASK

A stainless steel, aluminum, or wooden container used for holding naturally conditioned, unfiltered beer. Mainly used for draft beer dispensing in England, where the consumption of naturally conditioned, hand-pumped beer represents up to 50 percent of total beer sales.

Barrels were originally made by highly skilled craftsmen called coopers. Casks came in three varieties: dry, wet, and white. Wet cooperage deals with the manufacturing of water-tight barrels, such as those used in brewing.

Cask-conditioning cellar at the Samuel Smith Brewery in Tadcaster, England

Casks are filled at the brewery with fermented wort straight from the fermentation vessels. Approximately one million cells per ml (29,600,000 cells per ounce) of yeast are present, enabling a secondary fermentation to take place in the cask. Isinglass finings are added to the cask, which enables the yeast to settle when the cask is finally situated in the pub cellar. After 72 hours of settling, the cask can be tapped and vented. If the beer is now bright and well-conditioned, it can be served in its natural state at the bar (ideal temperature is 55°F, or 13°C).

CASK-CONDITIONED BEER

Beer or ale conditioned in the cask or keg. It is produced by adding sugar syrup and a fining, or clarifiying, agent to the finished cask as it leaves the brewery. (A handful of hops is added at the same time if the brew is to be "dry hopped.") The fining is usually isinglass, an extract of the swim bladders of some kinds of fish. The purpose is to cause the yeast to settle after it stops working, to form trub at the bottom of the vessel. A second ferment in the cask follows, taking place in the cellar of the tavern or pub where the beer will be served. The bunghole is partially closed by means of a shive, a bung (plug) that has a small hole for a smaller plug, called a spile. These plugs allow the pub manager to control the escape of carbon dioxide from the second ferment in the cask.

When the beer is ready (conditioned and settled), it may be drawn from the cask by means of a beer engine, a small suction or vacuum hand pump. Such a pump moves the beer into the glass through a dispenser tap, which may have a restricted opening (by means of a device called a sparkler to allow the beer to be drawn with a magnificent head sitting above the glass (which will be full, almost to the brim). This restricted opening has the more important effect of further reducing the modest amount of carbon dioxide in the beer at that time.

The second ferment allows the carbon dioxide to escape slowly, preventing saturation of the finished beer. It allows some carbon dioxide to stay in the beer, resulting in a soft, velvety mouthfeel.

In the days before the invention of the beer engine, the cask would be set horizontally on the counter in its cradle, with the bunghole at the top. A spigot would be pounded into a stoppered hole previously prepared for that purpose at the end of the cask. The spigot would force the stopper into the keg, allowing the free flow of beer through the spigot.

The continental equivalent of cask-conditioned beer is rare today and is produced by an entirely different method. Instead of adding sugar syrup, the lager brewer adds

Wooden casks are among the oldest types of containers for storing and serving beer.

new, freshly fermenting beer to the aged beer, encouraging a new ferment in the old beer. The cask used in this system must be much sturdier, to allow for a possible 50 psi (345 kPa) pressure buildup, because these brewers want carbon dioxide in their beer (but only about 10 psi, or 69 kPa). The brewer then bungs the vessel to allow for carbon dioxide buildup. This procedure results in natural carbonation. This style of cask-conditioning is called *gekräust* in Vienna, where the method was first used.

When the beer is served, the cask is set upright on the serving counter (the opposite of the British horizontal setting), and a spigot is pounded into a stoppered hole (located on the side of the cask near the bottom of the container). The carbon dioxide pressure in the keg ensures prompt movement of the beer into the glass. Later, as the pressure wanes, the top bunghole is opened to allow air and gravity to dispense beer from the barrel. German brewers do not allow the wood to touch their beer in this process, as the casks are lined with pitch or resin, which imparts little or no taste to the beer. This also was standard American practice in pre-Prohibition days. Nineteenth-century American beer writers all spoke kindly of the flavor nuances from the pitch lining of the dispensing casks.

British-style cask-conditioning may find favor in the United States and elsewhere in the world. However, it is unlikely ever to be accepted in Germany, Austria, or the Czech Republic.

See BEER IN THE WOOD, BOTTLE-CONDITIONED BEER, and REAL ALE.

CASK/KEG WASHER

A piece of equipment that cleans and sterilizes casks or kegs both inside and out. The machine may be relatively manual to fully automated. The washing cycle generally comprises a water prerinse, a hot caustic wash (or steam sterilization), and a

Older cask washers, such as the one in this 1891 illustration, were crude in comparison with the machines used to clean and sterilize casks today.

cold-water final rinse. More automated machines often are attached to a beer-racking machine.

CATAMOUNT BREWING CO. WHITE RIVER JUNCTION, VERMONT

Stephen Mason (with partners Alan Davis and Steve Israel) was one of the first to bring British-style microbrewed ale to New

Catamount Porter

Emblazoned with the leonine head of the rare Yankee catamount (as the mountain lion is called in New England, from cat-a-mountain), Catamount Porter is one of the few porters produced by New England breweries. It is a deliciously chocolaty brew, with a creamy head the color of coffee ice cream and a fine malty aroma. It has a smooth, roasty body, with some coffeeish bitter notes and hints of licorice.

Brewed and Bottled by Catamount Brewing Company
White River Junction, Vermont

England. Catamount started operations in 1986, starting as a small-scale brewery serving only Vermont. The state's relatively low year-round population made it necsary to expand the brewery's horizons, and

Catamount was soon shipping beer throughout the region. Expanded horizons have brought expanded volume, and in 1994 the brewery sold 16,500 barrels of beer throughout New England.

The company's mainstay products remain ales (Catamount Gold and Amber), and beer critic Michael Jackson has called the brewery's porter "the finest produced in the Northeast." Catamount's hoppy Christmas Ale is much anticipated each year. In recent years, the company has branched out stylistically with several German-style brews, including its Bock and Octoberfest.

See ALE BEER.

CELEBRATOR

See AYINGER, BRAÜEREI.

CELIS BREWING CO. AUSTIN, TEXAS

When Pierre Celis, noted Belgian wheat beer brewer, arrived in Texas in 1992 announcing his intention to build a state-of-the-art wheat beer brewery, not a few eyebrows were raised in the beer industry. Texas, while a large beer market, was not known for adventuresome consumers. The first microbrewery in Texas, Reinheitsgebot Brewing Co., had failed after trying valiantly to interest Texans in German-style all-malt lagers. Celis's trademark Belgian white beers were a step higher on the esoteric scale and out of the main-

Celis White

A top-fermented beer with notes of fruit and yeast in the aroma and flavor. Delicately spiced with orange peel and coriander, this beer is smooth and refreshing, with a crispy cleansing palate. It won gold medals at the 1992 and 1993 Great American Beer Festivals in the Herb and Spice Beer category.

stream at best. In addition, given traditional small brewery marketing models, it usually takes some years for a small brewery to expand its market beyond the local area. Located in Texas, Celis might never reach the growing numbers of beer enthusiasts on the coasts.

As it turned out, Celis was a visionary, not a fool. Miller Brewing Co. purchased a majority stake in the company in March 1995, vindicating his vision. Celis is staying on to run the operation and now has the deep pockets to expand capacity and build distribution throughout the United States.

Celis, of course, has done it all before. When the last wheat beer brewery closed in his native Hoegaarden, Belgium, in 1957, Celis changed career, from milkman to brewer to save a vanishing beer style. His small Hoegaarden brewery grew and grew, until he was selling 300,000 barrels a year in 1989. A large Belgian brewing firm, Interbrew S.A., brewer of Stella Artois, bought him out and

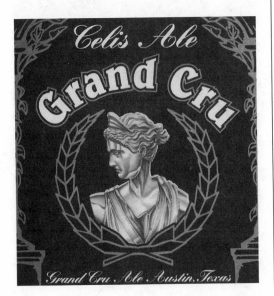

still produces the beer today.

Celis produces his trademark Celis White, a top-fermented spiced wheat beer (4.8 percent alcohol by volume); Celis Pale Bock, a top-fermented amber-colored pale ale (4.8 percent alcohol by volume); Celis Golden, described as a "Czech-style" Pilsner (4.8 percent alcohol by volume); Celis Grand Cru, a Belgian-style strong ale (8.7 percent alcohol by volume); and Celis Raspberry, a fruit beer using raspberry juice (4.9 percent alcohol by volume).

See FRUIT, VEGETABLE, HERBAL, AND SPECIALTY BEERS and WHEAT BEER.

CEREVISIA

The Latin name for a strong beerlike drink mentioned in Pliny the Elder's *Natural History.* In this book by Pliny (23-79 A.D.), cerevisia is mentioned as the popular national drink of the Gauls, who are credited by some historians as inventing the wooden cask to store this beer, apparently prepared around 400 B.C. Cerevisa was prepared by boiling barley and then adding another grain that was readily available during the harvest, such as wheat, rye, or maize. The Gauls would be considered specialty brewers by today's standards, since their cerevisia is also said to contain spices such as cumin, cinnamon, or coriander, used today by homebrewers, microbrewers, and specialty brewers alike. After fermentation, the Gauls stored their cerevisia in wooden casks until it was ready to drink. The term *cerevisia* has been adapted throughout brewing history and is present today in *Saccharomyces cerevisiae,* the scientific name for top-fermenting yeasts used by brewers around the world.

See CASK, CASK-CONDITIONED BEER, and *SACCHAROMYCES.*

CERVESARIIS FELICITER

An ancient Roman blessing meaning "long life to the brewsters."

CERVOISE

An old French term for ale brewed without hops.

CHALK

See CALCIUM CARBONATE.

CHERRIES

See FRUIT.

CHICAGO BREWING CO. CHICAGO, ILLINOIS

Chicago Brewing Co., founded in 1989, prides itself on being "the only commercial brewery in Chicago." Although the distinction may be fleeting, it currently makes the only beer brewed and bottled in Chicago proper (there are brewpubs and

other microbreweries on the outskirts of town). The brewery has a capacity of 30,000 barrels and is the first brewery to open in Chicago since Peter Hand Brewing Co. shut down in 1976.

Chicago Brewing Co. is a family-run operation. The company's owners include Stephen Dinehart, who has a background in strategic planning and market development; Craig Dinehart, with experience in chemical analysis; and Jennifer Dinehart, who had a career in direct marketing and communications. A few other Dineharts also are underfoot.

The company has attached the word "Legacy" to all its brands (Legacy Lager, for example), and the Dineharts are very conscious of the history implicit in their enterprise. The Chicago Brewing Co. name dates back to 1847, when the city's first lager brewery was started. The brewery had 2 miles of subterranean vaults, with enormous

brewhouses and malthouses. The brewery burned in the Great Chicago Fire of 1871 and was never rebuilt.

Today's Dinehart operation is substantial as small breweries go. The brewery

Chicago Brewing Company's award-winning Legacy Lager

includes a two-stage copper brewhouse that was once used by Pohlmann Brewing Co. of Kulmbach, Germany; vessels that can accommodate its 30,000-barrel-per-year capacity; and two packaging lines, one for bottles and one for kegs.

The Dineharts have been aggressive in opening markets for their beers and now ship to 30 states and several foreign countries (including England and Germany). The company brews Legacy Lager, the flagship brand; Legacy Red Ale, an Irish-style amber ale; Heartland Weiss, a Bavarian-style filtered wheat beer and Big Shoulders Porter, an English-style dark ale.

See AMBER AND RED BEERS, LAGER ALE, PORTER, and WHEAT BEER.

CHICHA

The most common corn-based beer brewed by Native American women from the American Southwest through Latin America. A sacred brew, chicha is made in small, village breweries and served in quart glasses, traditionally along with roast guinea pig. Ranging in color from pale yellow to deep red or purple, most chicha is fermented for 48 hours before undergoing a secondary fermentation in clay pots buried in the ground. Inca custom dictated spilling the first few drops on the ground as an offering to the goddess Mama Sara.

Among the many varieties of chicha are chicha morada, an unfermented, nonalcoholic beer; chicha picante, served with a squeeze of lemon and hot pepper sauce; and chicha de jora, a very strong brew at 38

Chicha is the name given to aca, the maize beer of the Incas, by the Spanish. Chicha has been produced commercially since the 19th century.

CHILDREN AND BEER

Until the past half century, beer, particularly small, or weak, table beer, was routinely served to children in Western cultures. Throughout Latin America, for example, beer was an important component of some peoples' diets, and children always received their share. As recently as the early 19th century, some British boarding schools were expected to provide students with appropriate brews, often produced on the premises. In the collective medical wisdom of 15th- through 19th-century America and Europe, dark beers were commonly prescribed to very young patients as a tonic and restorer.

Until this century children were routinely given weak beer, sometimes called small beer, as a beverage and as a tonic. Here, women and children pick buds from hop vines.

percent alcohol by volume. The rarest chicha is *fruitilada*, an extraordinary fruit beer brewed from corn and strawberries. This bright pink brew, with its thick head of foam, is served sprinkled with cinnamon, mace, and cilantro.

See ACA CHICHA, FRUITILADA and LATIN AMERICAN BREWERIES.

CHILLED LIQUOR TANK

A stainless steel tank that holds a reservoir of chilled water at 33° to 35°F (0.5° to 2°C). This water is used for cooling the wort moving from the brew kettle to the fermenting vessel and for cooling the fermenting vessels and bright beer tanks. This is particularly important in hot climates where the ambient temperature of city water may be above 60°F (15.5°C) and hence not provide adequate cooling. The chilled water used for cooling wort via a heat exchanger is heated up in the process and passed to the hot liquor back (tank), where it can be used for the next day's brewing.

CHILL HAZE

Cloudiness in beer caused by proteins and polyphenols in solution. Chill haze can be reduced in the following ways: chilling to force a cold break, brewing with 2-row malt or American 6-row malt, filtering, or lagering. Chill haze is made up of protein (15 to 65 percent); polyphenols, especially tannins (10 to 35 percent); and carbohydrates.

See HAZE and TRUB.

CHILLING

The process of getting the temperature of the wort to drop as quick-ly as possible to reduce the possibility of infection by organisms. Water boils at 212°F (100°C), but yeasts work only at temperatures below 80°F (27°C). A brewer must, therefore, have a way to reduce the temperature of the wort quickly to prevent the growth of organisms that thrive at temperatures from 80° to 120°F (27° to 49°C). Professional brewers use heat exchangers to cool the wort rapidly. Extract homebrewers often boil only 6 quarts or so of liquid, then dilute that with cold water to get close to the desired fermentation temperature. More advanced homebrewers use wort chillers, which are like small heat exchangers that use cold water running through copper tubing to cool the beer.

Various types of wort chillers are available. Some are inserted into the brew pot, then cold water is pumped through them. These are called immersion chillers. With other wort chillers, the hot wort is siphoned or pumped through a tube, and cold water

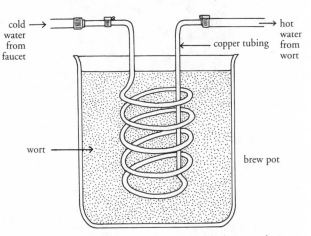

cold water from faucet → copper tubing ← hot water from wort

wort → brew pot

A wort chiller cools the hot wort quickly by circulating cold water through it.

is circulated on the outside of the tube. These are called counterflow chillers.

One advantage of using a wort chiller is that it promotes a good cold break, the process by which proteins and other suspended matter (called trub) settle out of the beer when it is cooled rapidly.

See BREWING PROCESS and COLD BREAK.

CHIMAY, ABBAYE DE NOTRE-DAME DE SCOURMONT, FORGES, BELGIUM

Chimay is the best-seller among the Trappist beers of Belgium. The abbey was one of the first to market its beer, which is now sold around the world.

Chimay Blue

A powerful ale that is almost impenetrably complex. Brewed to an original gravity of 1.081, it is a potent 9 percent alcohol by volume. Critics accord this ale "world classic" status and with good reason. It has great depth of flavor and a smooth, fruity palate.

The abbey was built around 1850, and the brewery was added about a decade later. Noted Belgian brewing chemist Jean DeClerk had a hand in reformulating the abbey's beers after World War II. He was buried at the abbey after his death in 1978.

The company produces a line of ales, the best known of which are Chimay Peres Trappistes Rouge (Red), Chimay Peres Trappistes Blanc (White), and Chimay Peres Trappistes Bleu (Blue). The brewery also makes Chimay Bouchonnee, Chimay Grand Reserve (a larger corked bottle of Chimay Blue), and Chimay Cinq Cents (a commemorative version of Chimay White). The Chimay beers are imported into the United States by Manneken-Brussels Imports, Inc., of Austin, Texas. Chimay Rouge is available in Canada.

See ABBAYE.

CHINA ALE

A homebrewed Old English ale bittered with China root and coriander. Aged in wood for 14 days, it is then put up in stone bottles with lemon peel and raisins.

CHINESE BEER

China is the number one brewing country in Asia. Per person consumption of annual domestic production is 7.0 L (2 gallons).

China has a long beer-brewing history. Mongolians and other ethnic groups within this huge and diverse country have been brewing beer for thousands of years.

Western lager was first introduced to China through 19th-century traders. The Germans established the first lager brewery in China at Tsingtao in 1897. As the Western governments increased their "concessions" in China, the number of breweries also increased. The breweries supplied the colonists and colonial military forces stationed there to protect the colonies.

Christian missionaries in China took up their antialcohol banners as prohibitionists did in the West. The Western brewers struck back with advertising such as "American Alcohol Cures Opium" and "Sanitary Alcohol."

When China eventually regained possession of the European colonies, it nationalized the breweries. During this period China also increased the number of hop farms. All ingredients for Chinese beers are internally produced.

As the communist government of China relaxes its grip on the economic sector, more entrepreneurs are seizing the chance by opening microbreweries to service small communities and towns. With the Chinese population around one billion, there is plenty of opportunity for such microbreweries.

Virtually every Chinese eating establishment, from the simplest noodle stall on up, serves beer. Beer is cheaper than bottled water and soda, and is easier to find.

The quality of Chinese beer is often inconsistent. A superior example, however, is Peking Beer. Evidently, it is much sought after, and therefore the stock turnover is high, keeping the product fresh for consumers.

Beer is inexpensive in China: 640-ml (22-ounce) bottles cost from $0.20–0.35, American.

Tsingtao beer is probably the most recognized Chinese brand in the United States. The brewery has been exporting it since 1954, but it is hard to find inside the country. Because China is interested in acquiring hard currency, the country exports most of this beer.

As the Chinese gain more Western expertise, expect to see them become more of a force in international brewing.

See JIU/CHIU and T'IEN TSIOU.

CHINESE POET-SAGES AND STRONG DRINK

In the group of poets collectively known as the Seven Sages of the Bamboo Grove (from the third century A.D.), drunkenness became a way of life. Chief among those sages was Liu Ling, who drowned, smashed on sake, while leaning out of a boat in an effort to embrace the moon's reflection in the water.

So strong was the tendency of Chinese writers to overindulge in drinking that K'ung-Fu-tzu, known to us as Confucius, devoted an entire chapter of his collected wisdom (a work dating to the 12th century B.C.) to the dangers of strong drink. In many ancient societies, drunkenness was believed to allow the human spirit to expand its boundaries to a higher state of thinking and feeling. The Chinese no doubt also held this belief.

CHLORDANE

A chlorine compound added to municipal water supplies as a source of chlorine for the purpose of preventing bacterial contamination. Brewers using a water source that contains chlordane may rid the water of chlordane to prevent off-flavors.

See CHLORINE.

CHLORIDE

A chlorine ion that is a very weak base and is easily neutralized. It will enhance the bitterness and stability of beer. Chloride levels should be less than 100 ppm for light beers and around 350 ppm for darker beers. Any salty taste can be reduced by the addition of calcium or magnesium.

CHLORINE

A greenish yellow gas that is never found in its natural state on earth. Chlorine is very reactive and quickly combines with other elements to form compounds. It is added to municipal water supplies to kill bacteria in the treatment plant or in supply lines between the plant and the final destination. If chlorine is added to water that has not had organic matter filtered out, chlorophenols may form. This is highly undesirable, as chlorophenols produce off-flavors in beer and can be noticeable at a concentration level as low as a few parts per billion.

Chlorine may be used as a sanitizing agent by adding 1 tablespoon (14.75 ml) of regular household bleach (sodium hypochlorite) to 1 gallon (3.75 L) of water. This sanitizing solution effectively cleans anything that will come in contact with the beer. Twenty minutes of contact with the solution is required for the full sanitizing effect, then the equipment should be rinsed with hot water. Normally, no bacteria will survive in a water heater if the temperature is set high enough. Doubling the amount of bleach will not reduce the amount of time required, but it may leave a chlorine residue that will not be rinsed away, leading to a problem with chlorophenols.

CHRISTIAN TRADITION, BEER AND ALE IN

Although beer was present in biblical times both before and after Christ, most references of the period reflect a wine-drinking populace. During the pre-Christian era, beer was routinely shipped from Egypt to all parts of the Middle East, where it was marketed for drinking and a host of other purposes. Pre-Christian Greeks, for example, regarded beer with suspicion, believing it to be the direct cause of leprosy. Mediterranean peoples, however, bought shiploads of brew to use in softening ivory to make jewelry.

As Christian beliefs spread to Europe and, later, to the New World, beer commonly replaced sacramental wine in the Mass. In about 690, Pope Gregory I, acting on suggestions from missionary priests, changed Christ's traditional birthday in October to December 25, when Germanic tribes celebrated the winter solstice. By offering free beer to the tribes, the pope was able to convert them to Christianity.

In the New World, Spanish conquistadors found beer-making everywhere they went. Biblical line references soon gave way to anecdotal sagas of Christian celebrations replete with beery tales. Thus, in two 17th-century paintings of the Last Supper found in Lima and Cuzco, Peru, Jesus Christ is offering his disciples not bread and wine, but *cuy* (roast guinea pig) and aca chicha (corn beer). These paintings reflect the efforts of the Christian church to create familiar and understandable objects illustrating Western religious beliefs.

The major Christian denominations have a significant number of saints associated with beer and beer drinking. Ancient European stories of the lives of saints abound with references to beer. For example, Saint Brigid changed bathwater into beer to satisfy a colony of lepers.

Both testaments of the Bible contain a bewildering number of contradictory attitudes toward drink in general and drunkenness in particular. King Solomon counsels, "A man hath no better thing to do under the sun than to eat, drink, and be merry." Elsewhere, the Bible refers to the drunken as those "who hath sorrow, who hath woe."

This uncertain dogma posed problems when missionaries ran into beer-swilling pagans. The church tended to advise the use of beery excess to convert pagans. Once they were baptized, however, the priests called for abstinence, and local beer production ground to a halt.

During the golden age of temperance (1840–1933), hundreds of volumes were penned and published by clerics trying to decide whether beer was all right for Christian souls. But the church, for centuries engaged in brewing and selling beer, soon became embroiled in disputes over the knotty problem. Was the wine at the Last Supper fermented or unfermented?

In the modern world, church teachings generally tend to regard beer as "the good-man weakness." Nonetheless, events such as Cincinnati, Ohio's blessing of the bock (where high church officials bless the brew of spring) offer hope that beer may again return to its rightful place as a joyful gift from God.

CHRISTMAS BEER

See FESTBIER.

CHURCH ALE

A beer-drinking party or gathering held by clerics to raise money, especially for church buildings and maintenance. The medieval church, never at a loss for creative methods of fund-raising, used public thirst to inspire generosity. These drunken revels, which were held on consecrated ground, became so popular that reformers were scandalized. Despite the opposition, the practice of conducting church ales continued for centuries.

CIDER

A drink made from apple juice. Hard cider is made from apple juice that is fermented. The fermentation process for hard cider is similar to beer, in that sugar and yeast are added and the liquid is left in a closed container to ferment. The quality of cider is affected by variables such as the type of apples used, what bacteria are present, or which sweeteners or additives are used. Even weather can be a factor.

Freshly picked apples as well as windfall or rotten apples can be used to make cider. They are stored for about a week to soften, then washed thoroughly and crushed in an apple press, from which the juice is collected. A bushel of apples will produce about 3 gallons of liquid. Many cider makers add sulfur dioxide at this stage to kill unwanted bacteria. The juice must sit for 24 hours, after which its natural sugar level should be determined

Operating a screw-type apple press

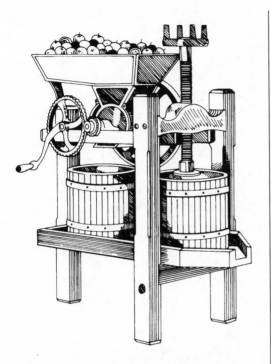

A grinder-type apple press is a reliable method to extract juice for cider.

with a hydrometer. The amount of sweetener, such as honey, added will depend on the hydrometer reading, since excess sugar will increase the alchol level of the final product. The sugar or other sweetener, such as honey, is then added with the yeast to promote fermentation. (Some cider makers recommend using champagne yeast or adding acids, such as tannic acid, to enhance the character.) Once the yeast is added, the cider is placed in a container, and sealed over, with a watertrap air lock on the barrel. This allows the gases created during fermentation to escape, while preventing bacteria and wild yeasts to enter the liquid.

The fermentation process can take several weeks or even months depending on the temperature, with some cider-lovers saying the slower the fermentation, the better the cider.

Once the primary fermentation is complete, the cider is siphoned off, leaving behind the dregs that developed during fermentation. If a clearer cider is desired, it is filtered for a more sparkling end product, although soe people prefer the natural haze. From there it is transferred into sterile bottles. More sweetener can be added at this stage for secondary fermentation in the bottle as well as for effervescence. Once placed in bottles, it is left there for months.

A sweet cider is one in which the fermentation is interrupted so not all the sugar is converted to alcohol and the final brew will have a sweeter, less dry, taste.

Applejack is the alcoholic core of hard cider, traditionally taken from a barrel of hard cider in which the water content has frozen. Because of its high alcohol content, a federal license is required to make applejack legally.

C.I.P. TANK

A stainless steel "cleaning in place" tank containing heated chemical solution that is pumped to beer vessels via spray balls for automated cleaning. The cleaning liquid is recirculated back to the C.I.P. tank for continual heating and further circulation. A C.I.P. tank may be heated with steam, gas, or electricity.

CLARIFICATION

The process of removing suspended proteins, as well as yeast and other large molecules, that can lead to a cloudy or hazy appearance in lighter beers. There are three main reasons for wanting to remove these particles: to improve aesthetics, to make the beer ready for consumption sooner, and to help stabilize certain styles. The proteins and yeast are removed after the fermentation by a long cold storage, addition of a clarifying agent, or filtration. Another technique is to avoid excessive levels of proteins in the beer before fermentation by ensuring that you get a good hot and cold break.

Additives used to encourage the settling out of proteins, yeast, and other large molecules are known as clarifiers or finings. Typically, these additives are added after the fermentation is complete; they react with the proteins and yeast in the beer to form a precipitate that will settle to the bottom of the vessel. One clarifier in particular, Irish moss, is added during the boil, which helps coagulate and settle out the haze-causing material.

Clarifying filters have porous membranes that allow the beer to pass through but prevent the yeast and other particles from doing so. Filtration does change the character of beer, and since the yeast is being removed, more yeast may have to be added at priming to produce carbonation. Otherwise, the beer will have to be artificially carbonated during the bottling process.

See CHILL HAZE, FININGS, GELATIN, and LAGERING.

CLARIFIER

An agent added to beer to encourage the settling out of proteins, yeast, and other large molecules that can cloud beer. Several different types of clarifying agents are available, including bentonite, gelatin, Irish moss, isinglass, and Polyclar. Wood chips are occasionally used but require more effort and care, as they must be soaked, boiled, and rinsed before being added to the lagering vessel. For the most part, wood chips help settle out only the yeast and do not affect the proteins.

See BENTONITE, FININGS, GELATIN, IRISH MOSS, ISINGLASS, and POLYCLAR.

CLASSIC PILSNER

See BOHEMIAN BEER.

COCK ALE

A favorite drink in England in the early part of the 18th century. Cock ale was believed to be a strengthening and restorative compound and was prepared according to the following recipe:

Take a cock a half a year old, kill him and truss him well, and put into a cask of 12 gallons of Ale to which, add four pounds of raisins of the sun well picked and stoned, washed and dried; sliced Dates, half a pound; nutmegs and mace two ounces: Infuse the dates and spices in a quart of canary twenty-four hours, then boil the cock in a manner to a jelly, till a gallon of water is reduced to two quarts; then press the body of him extremely well, and put the liquor into the cask where the Ale is, with the spices and fruit, adding a few blades of mace; then put to it a pint of new Ale yeast, and let it work well for a day, and, in two days, you may broach it for use or, in hot weather, the second day; and if it proves too strong you may add more plain table ale to palliate this restorative drink, which contributes much to the invigoration of nature.

COIRM

An ancient Gaelic term for ale.

COLD BREAK

The process by which rapid cooling of boiled wort causes proteins and other material to drop out of suspension. A cold break is more effective when a small amount of wort is cooled quickly (such as with a counterflow chiller) than when a large amount is cooled more gradually (as with an immersion chiller).

The precipitate from a cold break is often called cold trub and consists of proteins (about 50 percent), polyphenols (12 to 25 percent) and carbohydrates (21 to 33 percent). The amounts of polyphenols and carbohydrates vary depending on how finely the grist is crushed. Lager beers tend to be cleaner tasting when the precipitate from the cold break is removed, but in no case is all of it removed. The presence of

cold trub does not necessarily mean that haze will form.

COLD SPRING BREWING CO. COLD SPRING, MINNESOTA

Cold Spring Brewing Co. has had half a dozen owners since its founding in 1874. Since World War II, the company has been run by the Johnson family, persevering in a period that was inhospitable to smaller regional breweries.

The company is best known for its Cold Spring beer. The Cold Spring Export brand was marketed nationally as a specialty beer in the 1980s, based partly on the appeal of its classic 19th-century-style label. The label still incorporates the brewer's Star of David motif, which was once stamped on barrels of beer to connote freshness.

The brewery has a capacity of 350,000 barrels and produces several labels besides Cold Spring, including North Star, Kegle Brau, White Label, and Fox Deluxe (the last two are low- or no-alcohol brews).

COLD TRUB

Sediment that gathers as the result of quickly cooling hot wort.

See COLD BREAK and TRUB.

COLLEGE ALES

A drinking custom practiced at schools in England, Germany, the United States, and

Ale was the preferred breakfast drink for the British before coffee and tea became widely available and popular. Children as well as adults were expected to consume a quantity of ale to start the day.

elsewhere. Beer drinking played an important role in the traditions and rituals of many colleges. Some universities, such as Queen's College, Oxford, even brewed their own ales. One such ale, called Chancelor's ale, was brewed using sixteen bushels of malt per barrel. Two wine glassfuls would intoxicate most people. It was kept in oak bell-shaped casks and was never tapped until it was two years old. Some of the casks have been in use for half a century, but Chancelor's ale is used only at high table, when a man takes very high honours. On such or other special occasions the dean will grant an order for a pint of this liquor, the largest quantity ever allowed at a time.

At the beginning of the 18th century,

bread and ale were served at breakfast at some universities. Toward the middle of that century, tea was introduced at both Oxford and Cambridge, which altered the character of the meal.

In colonial America, Harvard College continued the practice of college ales, but these seem to have disappeared.

In Germany, beer drinking has been more closely associated with student life than in any other country. Both students and alumni take these customs most seriously and punctiliously uphold them.

The social life of German university students centers on the dining hall of each fraternity or club, called a *Kneipe.* All manner of drinking games and bouts occur. Once or twice a week, club members gather to honor Bacchus. At those meetings, challenges and purposeful insults are made, accepted, and settled by drinking large amounts of beer.

COLONIAL BEER

Early colonial American farmers were a very thirsty lot. Their work was hard and constant. Their diet was heavy, consisting of a great deal of starch and foods preserved by drying, smoking, and salting. This led to a prodigious thirst. Since water was suspect from early on, and its quality decreased as the number of inhabitants grew, alcoholic beverages were in great demand.

The colonists praised the healthful benefits of beer. Indeed, the yeast in beer was a major contributor to good health. As their beers were unfiltered, its yeast — containing B vitamins and other nutrients — was consumed too.

Hops grew naturally in many areas of

The Pennsylvania home and brewery of William Penn, who was one of many prominent early Americans to brew beer. Others were John Adams, Thomas Jefferson, and George Washington.

the original colonies. Other native ingredients, particularly spruce and maple syrup, were also used.

Many of the leading citizens, including founding fathers John Adams, Thomas Jefferson, and George Washington, were brewers.

The log of the Pilgrims tells us that at least part of the reason the Mayflower landed at Plymouth Rock was that the victuals, including the beer, were spent. From that point forward, beer played a very important role in Colonial America. The colonial ale-house pictured here indicates the popularity of beer.

Prevailing attitudes of the time required tavern licenses be granted only when such drinking establishments would be located directly next door to the school or church. From the earliest times of the Puritans, drunkenness was forbidden, but beer consumption was considered vital to human survival.

On beer brewed in Virginia, Roger Beverly commented in 1705: "The poorer sort brew their beer from molasses and bran, with Indian corn malted and dried in a stove; with presimmons dried in cakes and baked; with potatoes; with the green stalks of Indian corn cut small and bruised; with squashes and with Jerusalem artichokes . . . planted for that use. . . ."

English ale brewing continued in the United States until it was rapidly displaced by lager beer, which was brewed in ever-increasing amounts by German immigrants. This displacement began in the 1840s and was complete by the end of the century.

COLOR

Color is measured at two steps of the brewing process: The color of the malt is graded after kilning, and the color of the finished beer is assessed when it is ready for consumption. The two are inextricably linked because the color of the malt determines the color of the beer. Three color scales are commonly used in the brewing literature: SRM, Lovibond, and EBC. SRM, or Standard Reference Method, and Lovibond are the same scale, but brewers tend to describe their malts in degrees Lovibond and their

finished beers in SRM. Although these scales are used in the beer community as color scales, they are actually measurements of light. The color of a beer is affected by ambient lighting and by the width of the glass in which it is served. A darker beer will be perceived as lighter if it is served in a thin glass. Other factors, such as bubbles in the beer and background color, also affect perception of the beer's color.

Color Definitions

SRM (Standard Research Method)

Color	SRM NUMBER
Water	0.0
Light straw	1–2.5
Pale straw	2.5–3.5
Dark straw	3.5–5.5
Light amber	5.5–10
Pale amber	10–18
Dark amber or copper	18–26
Very dark amber	26–40
Black	40+

Note: Some sources use the European system, called EBC (European Brewing Convention scale). To convert from EBC to SRM, multiply the EBC number by 0.375, then add 0.46.

Malt purchased at most homebrew shops usually comes with a Lovibond number on the package. This information is essential for homebrewers to duplicate recipes or produce correctly colored beers. The Lovibond rating determines how dark the beer will be. Pale malts have a very low Lovibond number, typically less than 2.

Crystal malts range in color from 10 through about 100 degrees Lovibond. Chocolate malts are about 300 degrees Lovibond. Black patent malts are very darkly roasted and have a Lovibond number of 500 or higher.

A beer with a low SRM number is very pale. Budweiser is about a 2. Bass Ale is a 10, Michelob Dark a 17, and Salvator a 21. Stouts are very dark, perhaps 50 to 70 SRM. Beers in the 0–5 SRM range are generally referred to as "very pale," those in the 5–10 range as "straw" or "gold," those in the 10–15 range as "light amber," those in the 15–20 range as "copper" or "dark amber," those in the 20s as "brown," and those above 30 as "black."

The EBC (European Brewery Convention) is an entirely different scale that does not easily map to the SRM. A rough approximation (reliable only for SRM values below 4) is given by the following equation (described by George Fix):

$$EBC = 2.65 \times SRM - 1.2$$

COLORADO BREWERS' FESTIVAL

In 1993, 27 brewers participated in this Fort Collins festival. Nearly double that number were expected in 1995. The festival is held the last weekend in June, when the weather is hot but the air dry and the sky usually a brilliant blue. The beer is usually at the proper serving temperatures.

The 2-day festival offers food and merchandise booths galore, music and other entertainment, and beer from most of the native Colorado brewers. It is limited to Colorado brewers, but that's not much of a limit. There are a growing number of brewers in the state, and the behemoths Coors and Anheuser-Busch also qualify.

COMMON BEER

The name given to a number of American beers that do not fit the usual fermenting styles. The most famous of these is California common beer, originally known as California steam beer. Other less-widely known examples include Kentucky common beer and Pennsylvania swankey.

Steam beer originated at the time of the California Gold Rush and is close to being an ale — warm-fermented, but with bottom-working (lager) yeast instead of the usual top-working (ale) yeast used for that beverage. Mid-19th-century German immigrant brewers finished their beer in warm California as they had been taught in their homeland — by lagering it (but not for as long and not at such cold temperatures).

This new beer was kraeusened in the German (lager) style rather than primed in the English (ale) fashion. Priming is the addition of sugar to the finished beer, which then causes a ferment in the container, resulting in a small increase in alcohol content and carbonation. German brewers felt obligated, even in their adopted country, to follow the ancient Reinheitsgebot (pledge of purity). Sugar was forbidden, so a small amount of kraeusen (new fermenting beer) was added to the casks before bunging and delivery. This additional ferment gave the product a rich, creamy head, especially so because the beer was served warmer, and therefore under much heavier pressure (carbonation), than we are accustomed to seeing these days. Steam beer appears to have been first made in about 1851.

Even though ice machines had become available by the 1870s, steam beer remained popular in San Francisco and other parts of California. John Buchner, writing in the *Western Brewer* in 1898, noted, "[Steam beer] is bottom fermenting [like lager], and the fermentation proceeds at the high temperatures of 60–68F/15–20C) . . . steam beer is allowed from ten to twelve days from the mash tub to glass."

He continued, "The 'steam' refers to the strong carbonation, 'a pressure of fifty to sixty pounds per square inch,' caused by the introduction into the beer, when it is already in the barrel, of a portion of new wort at the early stage of fermentation ('green beer') — a process called 'kräusening.' This is a priming operation, also used by some lager brewers, which leads to afterfermentation in the barrel, thus building up the 'steam.' Generally speaking, steam beer is not a connoisseurs drink." Buchner had nothing better to say for it than that "it is a pretty fair drink. . . . At any rate, it tastes better than the raw hopped, bitter and turbid ales."

The production of steam beer flourished, and by the end of the 19th century, there were more than a hundred steam beer breweries in California, with others in Oregon, Washington, Idaho, and Wisconsin. At one time, there were 27 steam beer breweries in San Francisco alone. By Prohibition (1919), however, only seven remained.

When Prohibition was repealed in early 1933, only one steam brewery, the Anchor Brewing Co. (founded in 1896), was revived. Anchor was the smallest United States post-Prohibition brewery, and it was always lowest in production during those years. Moreover, production continued to drop from around 1,500 barrels (46,500 gallons, or 1,760 hl) in the early years to fewer than 700 by 1965.

Bankruptcy seemed inevitable for the faltering brewery. It was only by a twist of fate that young Fritz Maytag heard of the brewery's plight. Maytag, 27, was just out of Stanford graduate school. He had come to enjoy the special qualities of steam beer at San Francisco's Old Spaghetti Factory. He went to the brewery to offer his condolences to the owners and ended up buying a major interest.

California common beer is a darker version of cream ale, a paler top-fermented beer with similar characteristics. It was fermented warm, not too well aged, and served young as "present use" beer. The old wooden beer kegs were kraeusened with fresh beer wort.

Modern cream ales are bottled American lagered ales, and modern steam beer is a trademark of the Anchor Brewing Co. Ingredients include 2- or 6-row American barley malt, up to 10 percent caramel malt, and maybe some darker malts for extra color. Washington Northern Brewer hops are preferred.

California common beer is lagered cold but may be stored at cellar temperatures (about 55°F, or 13°C). It has the following characteristics: 11–14/1.044–1.056 OG, 4.6–5.6 percent alcohol by volume, 30–45 IBU, and 8–17 SRM. A turn-of-the-century recipe for California steam beer called for 11–12.5/1.044–1.050 OG (including 33 percent adjuncts and sugars), 35 IBU, and 10–20 SRM (as amber as Munich beer).

Pre-Prohibition breweries made several kinds of tart beers, including a Berliner Weisse style and Kentucky common beer, a dark beer from sour-mash ferment popular in Louisville in the late 1800s. A recipe for Kentucky common beer calls for 10–12.5/ 1.040–1.050 OG, 27 IBU, and 2 percent *Lactobacilli* in the yeast. This was a dark beer (20–40 SRM).

Pennsylvania swankey, another American common beer from that era, was flavored with aniseed or a similar flavoring, boiled 30 minutes in the wort. Its original gravity was 7/1.028 and its bitterness 22 IBU. "Swankey" came from the German *schank-bier,* or beer of lower gravity, as compared to *vollbier,* beer of regular gravity.

Original Gravity	Final Gravity	Alcohol by Volume	IBU	SRM
Anchor San Francisco Steam Beer 1989				
11.9/1.047	3	4.6%	33	14
San Francisco Steam Beer 1948 (with corn)				
11.5/1.046	4	3.9%	40	≈14
Kentucky Common Beer 1907 (two samples)				
12.2/1.049	4.7	3.8%	27	≈22

See ANCHOR BREWING CO. AND LAGER ALE.

CONDITIONING/BRIGHT BEER STORAGE TANKS

Stainless steel tanks designed especially for conditioning, carbonating, and storing beer. The tanks can be either vertical or horizontal, are normally pressure rated to 30 psi (207 kPa), and are insulated and clad. They usually have the following fittings:

- Glycol cooling jacket
- Swing-in/swing-out door
- Carbonation facility
- Sample port
- Thermometer
- Pressure relief/antivacuum valve
- C.I.P. facility

The tanks are often located in a temperature-controlled room near the bottling and kegging lines.

Conditioning (bright) beer tanks can be either vertical or horizontal.

CONTINENTAL LAGER

See INTERNATIONAL LAGER.

CONTRACT BREWING

The practice of contracting the production of beer to a brewery owned by another party. This method of production is often used by entrepreneurs who want to produce a brand of beer but are unwilling or unable to make the capital outlay to construct their own brewery.

The most successful specialty brewer in the country, Boston Beer Co. of Boston, Massachusetts (of Samuel Adams fame), is primarily a contract brewer. Other well-known contract brewers include Pete's Brewing Co. of Palo Alto, California, and New Amsterdam Brewing Co. of New York City.

Many small breweries also contract part of their production to larger breweries. Small breweries without bottling lines sometimes find it more cost-efficient to contract their bottled beer production to a larger plant, at least in the short term.

As the United States beer market evolves, it is likely that contract beer production will increase. Many second-tier American brewers still have substantial excess capacity that can be used by contract producers. For small breweries that want to expand their geographic presence, contract production can be preferable to building another brewery.

Purists in the microbrewing community often cast aspersions on contract brewing, arguing that contract brewers escape the costs of the labor-intensive brewing process while advertising themselves as microbrewers. Despite its detractors, contract brewing is economically attractive. Since contract brewers can use their capital for advertising rather than brewhouse construction, their beers can get high visibility in the market very quickly. Given industry excess capacity, their volume is almost unlimited. In addition, if sales decline, contract brewers are not saddled with a useless brewery.

Contract brewing, under the name licensed for production, has a long history in the international sphere. Even Guinness Stout was once produced by a brewery in Long Island City, New York, for the American market. Today's American consumer seems to prefer international labels that are imported, but consumers in other countries are not as picky.

Brewers who want to sell their products in foreign countries often use contract production. Since beer is a perishable product, it often makes sense to license production to a foreign plant rather than ship beer great distances. American brands such as Budweiser, Miller, and Coors are produced by brewers in Europe and Asia for those regional markets. The Guinness and Heineken brands are ubiquitous throughout the world due to a network of licensed producers and joint ventures. Although Guinness is no longer brewed in New York, it is produced in Canada (though not for the American market).

Several big-name imported beers are brewed in Canada for United States consumers, a practice that allows them to be called "imports" even though they are not imported from very far away. Since brewers must include point-of-origin information on their packaging, it is easy for beer consumers to find out actually where the beer is made.

In the final analysis, contract brewing probably does not deserve the bad rap it has received. Modern breweries use the same methods and equipment the world over and brew to careful specifications, making geographic location less important than it once was. Given the available capacity, contract, or licensed, production is a practical method for producing beer.

Pictured here, the cooling tank in Hell Gate Brewery, New York, ca. 1891

CONVEYOR

Stainless steel or nylon chains used for delivering bottles or cans through a bottling or canning line. The chains are pulled through by motors and are set up with guide rails.

COOLING PLANT

A building or location within a building that provides a refrigerated medium for cooling beer in holding and fermentation tanks and/or provides temperature-controlled rooms. Equipment used in cooling plants includes condensers and compressors charged with ammonia or Freon R12 or R22. Both ammonia and Freon cool a medium such as water, brine, or a propylene glycol solution, which is circulated in tubing through the beer to cool it.

COOPERAGE

The art of barrel or cask making. One who made them was called a cooper. The craft of cooperage has declined as fewer brewers cask-condition their beer.

A cooper at work in the Samuel Smith brewery in Yorkshire, England

COORS BREWING CO. GOLDEN, COLORADO

The Coors Brewing Co. is notable for operating the largest single brewery in the world. Its Golden, Colorado, brewery has a capacity of approximately 20 million 31-gallon(117-L) barrels per annum, and the great brewery has sprawled to fill an entire valley in a small town just north of Denver.

PREMIUM BEER
Brewed in Golden, Colorado with Rocky Mountain Water.

Coors Light

The archetypal American "light" or reduced-calorie beer. When quaffed ice cold, Coors Light has all the flavor of an especially robust mineral water. Consumed at a slightly more civilized temperature, a little of the Coors house character comes out: a clean malty freshness that is not to be despised. This malty character is to be found in greater measure as one ascends the Coors flavor ladder, particularly in the company's excellent Winterfest, a seasonal offering in the Vienna style.

From the outside, Coors' Golden brewery looks like a depressingly modern beer factory. Inside the brewhouse, tradition reasserts itself, with serried ranks of copper kettles in vast tiled halls and an exquisite little pilot brewery, all burnished copper and brass, on a balcony above the brewhouse floor.

Today the company operates three plants in the United States: the Golden brewery, a Memphis, Tennessee, brewery purchased from Stroh, and a packaging plant in the Shenandoah Valley.

Coors is a family-owned company, founded in 1873 by Adolph Coors and Jacob Schueler. The latter left the business after a few years, and the company became the Adolph Coors Golden Brewery.

Coors endured a longer period of Prohibition than most, since Colorado went dry in 1916, 3 years earlier than the rest of the country. Coors survived that long, dark night by making malted milk and near-beer.

For most of its history, Coors was one of many midsized regional breweries around the country. In the 1970s, however, Coors beers developed a degree of cult popularity, and people from all over the country engaged in illicit transport of Coors Banquet beer to the East and West.

Coors enthusiasts no longer have to transport the beer great distances, however, since Coors gradually built up its nationwide distribution system in the late 1970s and early 1980s.

Coors Banquet (the original Coors) has lost its cult cachet now that it has become so widely available, and like

The original Adolph Coors Company, Golden, Colorado, 1893

many other older beer brands, it is in decline. Coors Light has replaced it as the brewery's flagship product (coming in as the number four brand in the country in 1994, behind Budweiser, Budweiser Light, and Miller Lite).

Coors has also made a splash in the malt beverage market with Zima, a clear malt-based "cooler" with little resemblance to beer.

Like its diversification into Zima, the Coors company has made business forays into varied fields, including high-quality ceramics and packaging. But beer is what built Coors, and lately the company has refocused on its core beer business.

Like the other big family breweries of the United States (Anheuser-Busch and Stroh), the Coors family has passed on specific ideas of what makes a good beer. The company does a proportion of its own barley malting, and most notably, refuses to pasteurize its beer. Many cranky

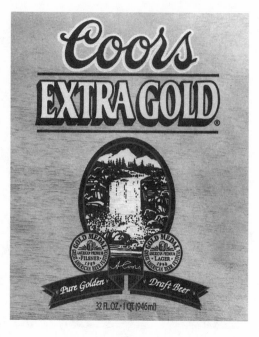

old brewmasters (along with microbrewing's young Turks) feel that pasteurization can subtly alter beer, and today quite a few brands are micro-filtered (whence packaged "draft-style" beers). But Coors went to all this trouble before it was fashionable: pumping the icy cold finished beer through great tubular cellulose filters, packaging it cold, and then shipping it out in super-insulated railcars and tractor-trailers (and keeping an eye on it when it's en route. If a super-insulated Coors railcar is delayed in a siding, the company dispatches tasters to point-of-arrival, to ensure that the beer has not been damaged). Coors distributors also had to keep their beer cold, before this became general practice.

The Coors Brewing Co. suffered censure in the 1970s and early 1980s from various activist groups for a supposed "anti-union" bias and conservative political philosophy. The current generation of corporate leadership, personified by Peter Coors (who appears as a company spokesperson in occasional TV commercials) has bent over backwards to dispel any lingering image problems, with large-scale corporate initiatives for literacy and clean water.

COORS BREWING CO. TECHNICAL LIBRARY

Mail BC 520
Golden, CO 80401
303-277-3506

Coors is currently the third largest brewery in the United States and has a plethora of information in its technical library, not only on its own history, but also on technical matters of brewing chemistry.

COPPER

A vessel used in the brewing process. *See* BREW KETTLE.

The sight of grouped coppers, or brew kettles, is a formidable one, and one that draws the public to visit microbreweries and brewpubs.

COPPER AS AN ELEMENT IN BREWING

A common metallic element that is present in trace amounts as a yeast nutrient. If levels exceed 10 ppm, however, copper can be toxic to yeast. It is not easily dissolved in water and thus is a good material for brewing equipment. Copper also has greater heat-transfer properties than stainless steel

Copper tanks are the most expensive kind used in today's growing microbrewery and brewpub movement.

and is used at many breweries for boiling and mash tuns. Since wort is acidic, it will react with copper. Before its initial use or after a scrubbing, a copper tun should be boiled with a mild acid-water (vinegar and water) solution of around 4 to 5 pH. This will ensure that the copper will not affect the wort that is boiled in it.

CORN

A grain that is usually used as an adjunct in United States commercial brewing. It is also used in some indigenous beers of Africa, where it is often mixed with sorghum.

In United States commercial practice, unmalted corn (or rice) is mixed with 6-row pale malt to form a grist of about 25 to 50 percent corn and 50 to 75 percent pale malt. The 6-row malt is used because it has high enzyme levels and can convert the unmalted grains. Used by itself without adjuncts, 6-row malt tends to produce beer with haze problems. Homebrewers interested in brewing American-style lagers may want to try mashing with flaked maize.

See SORGHUM BEER.

CORN SUGAR

Dextrose, a fermentable sugar often used in homebrewing for priming (carbonation). Corn sugar also is occasionally used to produce lighter beers with higher alcohol content without adding body. When used as a source of fermentable sugar, 1 pound per gallon (120g per L) will yield a specific gravity of about 1.035 (9 degrees Plato).

COUCH

In traditional floor malting, the couch is the layer of germinating barley spread on the malt floor.

COURAGE LTD. MIDDLESEX, ENGLAND

A subsidiary of Scottish and Newcastle, who purchased it from Fosters Brewing Group of Australia, Courage is one of Britain's largest brewing combines. The company operates Berkshire Brewery of Reading, Berkshire; John Smith's Tadcaster Brewery of Tadcaster, Yorkshire; Bristol Brewery of Bristol; Stag Brewery of Mortlake, London; and Webster's Fountainhead Brewery of Halifax, Yorkshire. Courage also brews numerous brands under license for the United Kingdom market, including Foster's, Kronenbourg, Holsten, Molson, and Miller beers.

See CONTRACT BREWING.

CREAM ALE

See LAGER ALE.

CROWN CAP

A metal cap with a cork or plastic lining and a crown-shaped skirt that is crimped around the mouth of a beer bottle to form an airtight seal. It was developed in 1892.

See BOTTLE CAP.

CROWN CORK

A synonym for crown cap.

CRUSHING

The process of reducing the whole kernels of malted barley to grist by grinding them in a malt mill. Also referred to as grinding or milling. The purpose of crushing is to maintain the shape and integrity of the original husks while at the same time pulverizing the creamy white starchy endosperm of the malt so that it can be mixed with the water in the mash.

See BREWING PROCESS.

CERVECERIA CUAUHTEMOC MONTERREY, MEXICO

Cuauhtemoc is a name with powerful resonance in Mexican history, borne by an Aztec hero martyred by the conquistadors. Today it is a name carried on by Mexico's largest brewing combine, Cerveceria Cuauhtemoc.

Cuauhtemoc and a smaller subsidiary, Cerveceria Moctezuma, are owned by FEMSA, a large Mexican holding company with diverse business interests. Cuauhtemoc operates nine breweries, producing the Carta Blanca, Indio, Bohemia, Chihuahua, and Tecate brands. Moctezuma brews Dos Equis, Tres Equis, Superior, and Sol.

Other large North American brewing entities have shown great interest in the Cuauhtemoc/Moctezuma operations. Miller Brewing Co. bought a stake in 1993, and John Labatt, Ltd., purchased an even larger chunk in 1994.

Cerveceria Cuauhtemoc was founded in 1890 by six partners — Isaac Garza, Jose Calderon, Jr., Francisco Sado, Jose A. Maguerza, Francisco Sada, and Jose M. Schnaider. The brewery remains a family company, operated by descendants of the original founders.

Dos Equis XX

Moctezuma brews several beers with the Equis name, with Dos Equis XX certainly the most interesting of them. The amber-colored Dos Equis XX has received nationwide distribution in the United States, primarily in Mexican restaurants. It is usually classified as a Vienna-style lager, a geographically anomalous classification that requires a historical footnote. It is thought that Vienna-style beers may have accompanied the emperor Maxmilian to Mexico in the 1860s, and the style could have become entrenched during his brief imperial reign. The misguided Maxmilian, of course, was reviled by the Mexican people and quickly deposed and executed. If Vienna-style lagers live on, perhaps it is because their firm, malty character suits the national cuisine so well. Dos Equis XX has a clean, malty aroma; a firm, malty flavor; and an attenuated hop finish.

Today, in addition to its strong domestic position, Cuauhtemoc exports substantial quantities of beer. Although the bulk of the company's exports are destined for the United States, in recent years Cuauhtemoc has also opened markets in Europe and Asia. In Great Britain, the nascent lager beer market has proved especially receptive to Mexican lagers.

In the main, Cuauhtemoc/Moctezuma beers are typical of North American lagers — light-bodied and light-flavored golden beers. Peripatetic German brewmasters had a hand in many brewery start-ups in the Americas (Cuauhtemoc included), and the Cuauhtemoc/Moctezuma brands bear a German imprint, especially notable in the companies' more robust offerings, such as their Christmas brands — Cuauhtemoc Commemorativa and Moctezuma Noche Buena. Noche Buena in particular is a dark, well-balanced brew. Although Mexican brewers have been somewhat dismissive of these seasonal efforts in the past, the worldwide "specialty" beer resurgence may yet save them from extinction. Noche Buena, which had made sporadic appearances in the United States market, was the beneficiary of a stronger marketing campaign in 1994.

See LAGER ALE and VIENNA BEER.

CUCKOO-ALE

In old England, a local celebration in honor of the return of the first cuckoo in spring. In Shropshire (Salop), the advent of the first cuckoo was celebrated by general feasting among the working classes. As soon as the first note was heard, even if it was early in the day, men would leave their places of work and spend the rest of the day partying and carrying on.

CULLEN ACT

An amendment to the Volstead Act, passed by the United States Congress in March 1933 authorizing the production and sale of beer that did not exceed 3.2 percent alcohol by volume.

CULTURING YEAST

The purpose of culturing yeast is to isolate a single pure strain of yeast from other possible contaminants such as bacteria and wild yeast. Culturing must be done under sterile conditions; otherwise, the contaminants will dominate the yeast, and the effort to isolate a pure strain will be in vain.

Clean Environment

The first requirement is a "clean room." This can range from a scrupulously cleaned and sanitized counter to an entire room outfitted with high-efficiency particle filters that blow sterile air into the room, generating a positive pressure that keeps out contaminants. Other methods require a glove box or laminar flow hood. A glove box is an enclosed, sanitized box with hand holes in the sides and usually a pair of gloves fitted to the opening, through which items are manipulated. A laminar flow hood is a hood over a work space that relies on high-efficiency particle filters to blow sterile air across the work space to prevent contaminants from landing on the work surface. Whichever method is used, work surfaces should be sanitized by either high-temperature steam or a chemical solution.

Isolation of a Culture

An inoculation loop is heat sterilized, cooled on a sterile surface (often the medium) containing the sample of desired yeast, and then dipped into the medium. The loop is then passed back and forth across a petri dish containing a medium of malt extract and agar. This petri dish sample is allowed to grow for 3 to 5 days. If only white or cream-colored streaks or spots smaller than ¼ inch (6 mm) across appear in the area that was streaked, the dish will contain only colonies of yeast. If anything else appears, the dish must be discarded, as it is contaminated.

Stepping Up

Once a dish contains isolated yeast colonies, the yeast must be grown out to an acceptable number of colonies for the final starter. First, a wort with a specific gravity of not more than 1.040 is made from water and malt extract, and is heat sterilized. An inoculation loop is sterilized in a flame and cooled on a sterile surface. One of the small colonies of yeast is transferred from the petri dish with the inoculation loop to .5 teaspoon (2 ml) of sterile wort and allowed to cool for 2 to 3 days. Then this is stepped up to 3 tablespoons (50 ml) of wort and allowed to grow for 2 to 3 days. It is then stepped up to 15 ounces (500ml) of wort.

Final Starter

When the initial starter has grown out, it is made into a larger starter. This time 1 quart (about 1 L) of wort with a specific gravity of not over 1.040 is made and poured into a large 2-quart (about 2 L) container and heat sterilized. When the starter wort is cooled, the initial starter is poured into the new, larger starter. When the larger starter has reached high kraeusen, it is ready to be pitched into a 5-gallon (19 L) batch of wort or made into subsequently larger starters to be used for making a large volume of beer. Generally, a larger starter is preferred. Many home-brewers use small starters but should really double or triple the size of their starters to ensure quick-starting fermentation.

See YEAST.

DARK ALE

See BROWN ALE.

DARK BEER

See BAVARIAN BEER.

DECOCTION MASH

A method of mashing that breaks down proteins and starches in the boiling phase. Decoction mashing is the most complex of the major mashing methods, but it is the one most commonly used by European lager brewers and is often credited with producing smoother, maltier beers. The principle of decoction mashing is that part of the mash is removed from the tun at the end of each rest, boiled (typically for about 15 minutes), and then returned to the brew pot, bringing its temperature up to the next step (or close to that temperature). The process of removing part of the mash and boiling it is referred to as decoction. After the first decoction, the decocted portion is held at the saccharification temperature, which is 149° to 158°F (65° to 70°C).

Typical schedules call for either one, two, or three decoctions. The two-decoction process is probably most common and consists of a protein rest at about 122°F (50°C), followed by a decoction that brings the temperature to the saccharification rest at about 150°F (65.5°C). The second decoction brings the mash temperature to the lauter rest temperature of about 170°F (77°C). The lauter rest step stops enzymatic activity. When a three-decoction mash is used, the process begins with an acid rest at about 97°F (36°C). The acid rest corrects the pH but is often skipped, with the pH being balanced through the addition of gypsum. When a brewer describes a decoction as boiling the "thick part of the mash," he or she means boiling mostly grain; boiling the "thin part of the mash" means boiling mostly liquid.

DEGREE

A unit of measurement that measures the concentration of solids or alcohol in a solution, equivalent to a percentage.

DE KONINCK BREWERY ANTWERP, BELGIUM

The original De Koninck Brewery was a pub, located just outside Antwerp's city walls. The current De Koninck was founded in 1833.

The Van den Bogaert family, with a long history of brewing, carries on the De Koninck tradition. The brewery produces two products: De Koninck, an amber, top-fermented beer (5 percent alcohol by volume) and De Koninck Cuvee (8 percent alcohol by volume). Production is approximately 150,000 hl a year.

DEMERARA

A very coarse, very dark brown sugar that is less refined and has a higher molasses content than the brown sugars typically found on a grocer's shelves. Demerara sugar is noted for having large crystals and takes its name from a place in Guyana, from which it originates. Demerara is generally unavailable in the United States, but it is an ingredient in some recipes, particularly those in older recipe books from England. A reasonable substitute for Demerara is brown sugar mixed with molasses.

DENSITY

A measurement of the amount of sugar dissolved into solution in the wort. Density readings are taken with a hydrometer, which is calibrated to plain water. Various scales are

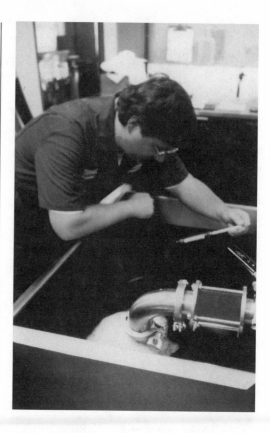

The brewmaster of the Full Sail Brewing Company measures the gravity of the wort used in Full Sail's Wassail Winter Ale.

used. The most common one in homebrewing is specific gravity, also referred to as original gravity or starting gravity, which measures the difference between wort density and water density as a percentage where water has a gravity reading of 1.000. For example, wort with a gravity reading of 1.050 is 5 percent more dense than water. Professional brewers more often use the Plato scale (functionally equivalent to the Balling scale), which reflects the weight of sugar per 100 g of water. Belgian brewers use a short form of the original gravity scale called Belge. For example, a homebrewer's reading of 1.060 would become 6 degrees Belge. In Belgium, the density of the wort is derived from the value of the original gravity by subtracting one (1) and moving the decimal point two digits to the right. An original gravity of 1.072 therefore equals 7.2 Belge or Belgian degrees. Additionally 1 percent Belgian equals approximately 2.5 Plato.

See ORIGINAL GRAVITY.

DENTERGEMS

See RIVA.

DEPALLETIZER

A machine used for unwrapping pallets of glass bottles and cases for feeding into a bottling line.

DEXTRIN

A polysaccharide produced as an intermediary step in the conversion between starches and sugars. Dextrin provides body and calories, but it does not ferment when combined with commonly used brewing yeasts. Dextrins are essential to the particular taste of beer.

DEXTRINASE

See ENZYMES.

DEXTROSE

Glucose.

See CORN SUGAR.

DIACETYL

A by-product of fermentation that is usually an indicator of too short a fermentation. Diacetyl is a powerful aromatic compound that imparts a buttery or butterscotch flavor to beer. Normally, allowing the beer to remain on the yeast for a few days after the vigorous fermentation has subsided is sufficient to reduce the diacetyl level in the finished product.

Different strains of yeast produce different diacetyl levels and have different diacetyl reduction qualities. Some diacetyl qualities are desirable in some styles of beer. For example, some diacetyl contributes a smoothness or roundness to the character of some beer syles.

DIASTASE

A group of enzymes in malt that are capable of converting starches to sugars. Diastase is a combination of alpha amylase and beta amylase. The amount and effectiveness of the diastase is measured in degrees Lintner and is referred to as the diastatic power of a malt. The higher the number, the more effective the conversion of starches will be. More diastase can be mashed in with adjunct grains.

See ENZYMES.

DIASTATIC POWER

The measure of a malt's amylase enzyme content. This number reflects the malt's ability to convert starches to sugars. Diastatic power is measured in degrees Lintner; the higher the value, the greater the ability of the malt to convert starches to sugars. A typical 2-row Klages malt may have a diastatic power of 130 degrees Lintner, while a wheat malt may have a power of 160 degrees Lintner and a German Pilsner malt a power of 80 degrees Lintner. Occasionally, one may find malts with diastatic power measured in degrees Windisch-Kolbach; if so, divide by 3.5 to get degrees Lintner.

DIATOMACEOUS EARTH FILTER

A filtration system employing diatomaceous earth powder (kieselguhr) as the filtration medium. Diatomaceous earth is made from silicified skeletons of diatoms and is blended in such a way as to form different grades and micron levels of purity. The filtration unit must include permeable septa arranged vertically or horizontally. There are three main types of filters: horizontal leaf, vertical leaf, and candle.

Leaf filters have a series of stainless-steel leaves. In vertical leaf filters, both sides of the filter are covered with diatomaceous earth powder, whereas in horizontal leaf filters, just the upper surface is covered. Candle filters are vertical and comprise vertical disks or tubes coated with powder.

Generally, two or three different powders are used to coat the septa prior to beer filtration. A coarse precoat comes first, followed by one or more finer coats to achieve the desired filtration level. The filter design, as well as the actual filtration chamber, includes interlinking pipework, valves, a dosing tank, and integral pumps.

DIAT-PILS

See DRY BEER.

DIMETHYL SULFIDE (DMS)

A compound present in beer that gives it a cooked corn aroma and a maltier taste. In higher concentrations, dimethyl sulfide (DMS) will impart a flavor of cooked vegetables to beer. It can be an indicator that the bacterium *Hafnia protea* is present and has converted some of the nitrates to nitrites. It is usually present in wort that has not been cooled rapidly enough or is allowed to sit too long after cooling. More often it is caused by malt characteristics and improper brewhouse procedures, such as inadequate boils. In successful batches, DMS is eliminated during quick cooling.

DINKELACKER BRÄUEREI A.G. STUTTGART, GERMANY

Founded in 1888, this large Stuttgart brewer is a stakeholder in several other regional German breweries. This brewer produces Dinkelacker CD-Pils, Privat,

Pilsner, Diat-Pilsner, Dinkel-Leicht, and Dinkelacker Alkohofrei. Several of the Dinkelacker brands are imported into the United States by Grolsch Importers of Atlanta, Georgia. Dinkelacker is available in Canada on a limited basis.

DISTILLATION

The process of heating water inside a still to the boiling point to produce steam, then running the steam through a condenser to cool it, returning it to its liquid state. All mineral and chemical ions dissolved in the water are left in the still, and the water produced is pure distilled water.

The main reason to distill water in brewing is to remove impurities from less-than-desirable brewing water. Distilling lowers the levels of offending ions to tolerable levels so that the water can be used for brewing. If a brewer decides to use nothing but

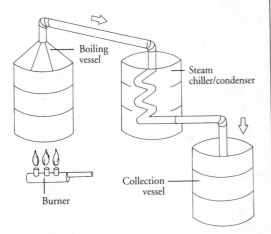

Distilled water is used in brewing to remove impurities from less-than-desirable brewing water.

distilled water, gypsum and other agents must be added to provide certain ions that will ultimately provide character to the beer. Distilled water should be used only if all local sources of water are undesirable for brewing.

See WATER.

Dixie

The hothouse climate of New Orleans is made for quaffing light lager beers, and Dixie is just the ticket. It is a pale beer, lightly aromatic with a firm, malty body. When chilled, it is very crisp and restorative.

DIXIE BREWING CO. NEW ORLEANS, LOUISIANA

Dixie Brewing Co. was fading away when Kendra Bruno and her husband purchased it in the mid-1980s. Housed in a handsome (if somewhat down-at-the-heels) turn-of-the-century building, the brewery still boasts a few cypress vessels. When the Brunos acquired Dixie, it was an act of faith more than anything else, for the brewery's obsolescent brewhouse and prohibitive

Dixie Blackened Voodoo Lager

Deep mahogany in the glass, contrasted by a creamy white head, this beer has a sweet, malty aroma. Its lighter-than-expected body makes for a refreshing, quaffable beer.

The Dixie Brewing Co. offering includes Dixie Lager, Jazz Amber Light, and Blackened Voodoo Lager.

debt made its survival unlikely. Even the water bills had not been paid.

Through canny business sense or pure good fortune, Dixie embraced off-beat specialty beers just as they were becoming a market force and struck upon a winning brand in Dixie Blackened Voodoo Lager. The brand was soon distributed widely (bolstered by a brief but widely publicized ban in Texas, due to the use of the word *Voodoo* on the label).

The brewery has now stabilized and is brewing a steady stream of rather unusual beers (including White Moose, a chocolate beer that is very tasty) as well as several beers with particular New Orleans evocations, such as Jazz Amber Light and Nite Life. The company also still produces its onetime flagship brand, Dixie.

See LAGER ALE.

DOPPELBOCK

A strong beer originally brewed by monks of the order of St. Francis of Paula, who named their beer Salvator (Savior). Paulaner Salvator was soon copied, and now there are about 120 of those beers in Germany. They all have an *-ator* suffix. Paulaner Salvator is available in the United States in bottles and on draught. It has an original gravity of 19/1.079, with 7.4 percent alcohol by volume. Other German doppelbocks available in the United States include Ayinger Celebrator (Fortunator in Europe) and Doppelspaten Optimator (also found on draught).

Doppelbock (double bock) is just as strong today as it was in the past. An 1853 sample of Salvator had an original gravity of 19.5/1.081 and 5.8 percent alcohol by volume. An 1878 sample had an original gravity of 18.4/1.076 and 6 percent alcohol by volume. German law defines doppelbock as having an original gravity above 18/1.074, with more than 7 percent alcohol by volume, and 23–40 IBU. These are good standards for this beer type, which has some sweetness, as evidenced by the hefty final gravity of some doppelbocks (of 4 to 6 degrees Plato). Malt flavors predominate, and hop levels are relatively unassertive, although they are noticeable. The high alcohol content lends a barley wine flavor to some doppelbocks. Indeed, doppelbocks do fit the barley wine profile, except that they are bottom-fermented. Bitterness is 25–40 IBU, and color is 18–35 SRM. Doppelbocks contain pale Munich and dark Munich caramel malts, dextrin malt, and black malt. They also contain Hallertauer hops.

Some American craft brewers brew doppelbocks, notably Samuel Adams of Boston and the Widmer Brewing Co. of Portland, Oregon. The Widmer Brewing Co. uses top-fermenting yeast in the German altbier style.

The Great American Beer Festival has guidelines for Doppelbock Lager. Those guidelines are 18.5–20/1.074–1.080 OG, 6.5–8 percent alcohol by volume, 17–27 IBU (moderate bitterness), and 12–30 SRM.

Original Gravity	Final Gravity	Alcohol by Volume	IBU	SRM
Ayinger Celebrator/Fortunator (Germany) 1983				
18.2/1.075	5	6.9%	≈26	≈16
Paulaner Salvator (Germany) 1887				
18.8/1.077	7.7	5.8%	≈28	≈16
Paulaner Salvator (Germany) 1986				
18.3/1.075	3.3	7.7%	≈26.5	≈12

See BOCK BEER.

DORTMUNDER ACTIEN BRÄUEREI DORTMUND, GERMANY

First incorporated in 1868 as Dortmunder Bierbrauerei, Dortmunder Actien Bräuerei (DAB) has an annual production of more than 3,000,000 hectoliters. The brewery's United States agent is DAB Importers of Moorestown, New Jersey. Guinness International imports Dortmunder into Canada.

DORTMUNDER BEER

The Dortmund brewers developed Dortmunder, one of the four great continental beer styles (the others being Bohemian [Pilzen], Bavarian [Munich], and Vienna [Wien]).

Dortmund, Nord Rhein, Westphalen, is the largest brewing city in Germany, with 9 breweries (down from 121 at the turn of the century) accounting for more than one-quarter of the total German beer production. The city was given brewing rights in 1293, and the beer produced there has always been high in quality, so much so that other towns tried to keep Dortmunder beer out of their territory by force. Dortmund brewers were compelled to defend their beer shipments.

Originally, the beer of Dortmund was brewed with wheat, but it has been pale and bottom-fermented since 1843, the beginning of the great "pale" beer revolution, when the pale Pilzen, or Bohemian, beer came to be so popular. In the 1870s, the Dortmunder Union Brewery brewed the original Dortmunder style, which became a favorite of Otto von Bismarck, the great German chancelor. In Germany, only beers brewed in Dortmund may be called *Dortmund Bier.*

The original Dortmunder beer's major component was its famous malt. This was from a special malting process based on a long steep similar to that used for Munich malt (over a 2-day period, rather than the 1-day process favored at Plzen and Vienna), but at lower temperatures, preserving the pale color necessary to the beer's construction. The popular 2-row Moravian barley had, by that time, come to replace the traditional 4-row varieties used previously in most European beers.

Dortmunder beer has more body and more taste than Bohemian Pilzen, yet is lighter, milder, and drier than Munich or Vienna beer. It is hopped less than Pilzen and more than Munich beer.

The original Dortmunder Lager had a relatively high original gravity of 15/1.061,

with a strong 5.6 percent alcohol by volume, and a moderate (compared to Pilzen) bitterness of 32–37 IBU. Brewed with an especially long lagering cycle, the beer was just slightly darker than the Pilzen of that era. Dortmund water is quite hard (750 ppm); only that of England's famous Burton-on-Trent is harder (1,200 ppm). Such hard water begs for strong, well-hopped beers. Today's beer may be as low as 12.5/1.050 OG. In Dortmund, the beer is called "export" because of the extraordinary preparation required, including filtering and pasteurization. It also is called "blond" because of its pale color. Dortmunder may very well have been the first beer prepared to export standards. Elsewhere in Europe, the beer is called "Dort."

Dortmunder, as a beer style, was quite popular in the United States before Prohibition, having been brewed by such greats as Schlitz and Pabst during that era. The last American old-line Dortmunder was brewed at Leisy Brewing in Cleveland before it closed in 1960. Many old American brewing texts provide information on the special malting and brewing methods required for its production. Several microbreweries are now reviving the style.

An old analysis of an 1884 Dortmunder Victoria shows 15.97/1.065.4 OG, 5.5 percent alcohol by volume, 30–40 IBU, and light tartness (0.075 lactic acid).

Dortmund is also famous for its fine altbiers, which are the regular drink of that city, according to beer critic Michael Jackson. None is as strong as an 1889 Dortmunder Adambier: 18.1/1.075 OG, a whopping 9.3 percent alcohol by volume,

40 IBU, and extreme dryness and tartness (0.6 lactic acid).

The Dortmunder export style is expected to have the following characteristics: a 12–14/1.048–1.056 OG, 4.8–6 percent alcohol by volume, 4.2–4.5 final gravity, medium bitterness (23–29 IBU), very pale color (4–6 SRM), and 750 ppm hardness.

The Great American Beer Festival guidelines call for 12–14/1.048–1.056 OG, 5–6 percent alcohol by volume, 23–29 IBU, and 3–5 SRM.

Original Gravity	Final Gravity	Alcohol by Volume	IBU	SRM
Capital Gartenbräu Special (Wisconsin) 1989				
11.7/1.046	2.5	4.8%	22.5	≈4
Gordon Biersch Export (California) 1989				
13.2/1.053	2.7	5.5%	≈23	≈3.5
Dortmunder beer 1968				
12.9/1.052	1.9	5.8%	24	≈3

DOS EQUIS XX

See Cerveceria Cuauhtemoc.

DOUBLE BOCK

See DOPPELBOCK.

DOUBLE STOUT

See STOUT.

DOUBLE, TRIPLE, AND QUADRUPLE BEERS AND ALES

The terms *double, triple,* and *quadruple* refer to gravity or density. The old brewers often drew off the earliest wort (the heaviest) to make a double- or triple-strength brew. The later draw (near the end of the wort run) might have been used to produce a "single," or simple (small), beer. This is similar to English and American brewers' use of *XX* and *XXX.* British brewers sometimes call this method *parti-gyle* brewing — drawing off a portion of the mash to make a strong beer and using the remainder as the basis for brewing a lighter beer.

In the case of bock beers, the terms *double* and *triple* have similar meanings, referring to a particular strength.

See ABBEY BEER and DOPPELBOCK.

DRAUGHT/DRAFT BEER

Beer that is in casks or kegs rather than bottles or cans. Also spelled *draft,* although *draught* is the spelling used throughout this text. Draught beer, or beer on tap, is widely considered by

At one time most all beer was drawn directly from casks or kegs.

the consumer to be a fresher product than bottled beer. Usually stored under pressure in metal kegs, it is often not pasteurized and not filtered to the extent that many bottled beers are. These general characteristics contribute to the freshness of the beer, as does the fact that draught beer is preferably consumed within 7 to 30 days of brewing.

DRAYMEN

A term for men who drove low, sturdy carts called drays.

Draymen, who carried beer casks or kegs, worked up a formidable thirst.

Beer was typically delivered to pubs and other retail outlets in stout drays, and some breweries use them still as a means of carrying on tradition. Since the invention of motor vehicles, drays have become less prominent, although they still exist. The Youngs Ram Brewery at Wandsworth, London, is a well-known example of a brewery that still uses drays.

Delivering heavy casks of ale is a hard job, and draymen worked up quite a thirst. Breweries provided for that thirst by giving daily allotments of ale to their workers, a tradition that continues to this day.

DRY BEER

A low-alcohol-content malt liquor that is force fermented, often with the help of enzymes to change the normally unfermentable dextrins into fermentable sugars. This process has the effect of reducing the beer's final gravity and flavor. "Dry" means not as sweet as regular beers.

Dry beer was introduced by the Asahi Brewing Company of Tokyo, Japan, in 1987. Using a variety of yeasts, Asahi created Asahi Super Dry with a slightly higher alcohol content and reduced beer extract: a clean finish with little or no aftertaste. The beer became so popular in Japan, during 1987, that the brewery's sales increased by 33 percent. Other Japanese brewers quickly came out with their own dry beers. Dry beer— a low-alcohol-content malt liquor—was introduced in the United States in 1988. American dry beers are not up to Japanese standards in flavor or quality. American brewers have even produced dry light beers — not only are these beers low in alcohol content, they are also low in calories.

The alcohol content of dry beer is usually about the same as that of regular beer (5 percent). The original gravity is around 10.5/1.042. A bitterness level of 15 to 23 IBU seems likely, since the reduced sweetness enhances the existing hop elements. Color is within the normal pale lager range. The final gravity is necessarily low, in the 0.8 to 1.4 range, depending on original gravity.

The reduced sweetness of dry beer makes it more compatible than regular beer with some kinds of food. Dry beer goes especially well with broiled or steamed fish and with Japanese or Chinese cuisine. It also has 8.5 percent fewer calories than regular beer.

The Europeans, especially the Germans, have developed their own "dry" beer for diabetics. It is called diat-Pils, and it predated the Japanese style by nearly 20 years. Some of these beers have been exported to the United States and labeled "dry beer." Diat-Pils is not meant to be low in calories, just low in carbohydrates.

The Great American Beer Festival guidelines for American Dry Lager call for 10–12.5/1.040–1.050 OG, 4.3–5.5 percent alcohol by volume, 15–23 IBU, and 2–4 SRM.

Original Gravity	Final Gravity	Alcohol by Volume	IBU	SRM
Asahi Super Dry Draught 1988				
10.7/1.043	1.2	5%	≈18	≈3
Bud Dry 1989				
10/1.040	1.15	4.7%	10	2
Holsten Dry Beer 1990 (diat-Pils in Europe)				
11.2/1.045	0.077	5.9%	24	3.5
German diat-Pils 1971 (low-carbohydrate prototype)				
10.8/1.043	0.5	5.3%	Unknown	4.9

DRY HOPPING

See HOPS.

DRY STOUT

See STOUT.

DUBBEL

See ABBEY BEER.

BRASSERIE DUPONT LEUZE-EN-HAINAUT, BELGIUM

Brasserie Dupont is one of a handful of Belgian breweries that produce saison, a top-fermented summer seasonal beer that is a tradition in the French-speaking region of Belgium. Brasserie Dupont is a farm/brewery, a combination that is still found in Belgium, though hardly anywhere else.

The brewers sell eggs out of the brewery office as a sideline.

The brewery is run by Marc Rosier, who is the brewer, and his sister serves as microbiologist. Their interest in sustainable agriculture has led them to organic farming, and one of their beers, Foret, is a certified organic saison. Foret, brewed to 5 percent alcohol by volume, uses only organically grown hops and barley, with filtered artesian well water.

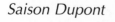

Saison Dupont

In keeping with the saison style, Saison Dupont is an orange-colored beer, with a full, creamy head and palate-cleansing hop edge. It is a peppery, fruity beer and is bottle-conditioned, which gives it a yeasty, restorative quality. One can picture Belgian farm workers in the old days uncorking bottles of Saison Dupont during their lunch break in the hayfield.

The brewery's best-known beer is Saison Dupont, which has received "world classic" status from noted beer critic Michael Jackson. At 7 percent alcohol by volume, it is more potent than Foret, with a fruity, lively character. It is bottle-conditioned to bolster its longevity, as saisons were traditionally brewed in the winter for summer consumption.

Brasserie Dupont beers are imported to the United States by Vanberg & DeWulf, a small firm in Cooperstown, New York. Dupont beers are available as a specialty in Canada.

See SAISON BEER.

DÜSSELDORFER ALT

See ALTBIER.

DUTCHMAN'S DRAUGHT

A "big swig" or copious draught. One of many allusions to the Dutchman's reputed fondness for drinking.

DUVEL

See MOORT GAT, BRASSERIE.

BRASSERIE DUYCK
JENLAIN, FRANCE

Brasserie Duyck is one of the best-known producers of the bière de garde style, a strong ale traditionally produced by the farm/breweries of northern France. Bière de garde, translated as "beer to keep," is a reference to its suitability for aging. The style dates from a time when farmers brewed this beer during the winter while the fields were fallow, then laid it away in the cellar to be drawn on for the rest of the year.

Brasserie Duyck was founded in 1922 by Felix Duyck and is currently operated by his son and grandson. The brewery has had to add capacity to meet the demand for its Jenlain, which is now exported to the United States.

See BIÈRE DE GARDE.

Jenlain French Country Ale

Jenlain is packaged in a corked 375 ml (11-ounce) bottle. It has a lovely malty flavor, with little of the citric bite of some of its Belgian ale cousins. This is a sweet, full-bodied beer with some licorice notes in the aftertaste.

ALAN EAMES HISTORICAL LIBRARY

75 Pine Street
Brattleboro, VT 05302
802-254-6100

An extensive collection of beer-related books, the Alan Eames Historical library consists of more than 1,000 volumes in 18 languages dating as far back as 1620 A.D. This library also includes 11 file cabinets of documents and clippings related to United States breweries dating to 1950. Rare illustrations, postcards, posters, and prints that are not available elsewhere are part of this enviable collection of beer ephemera.

EAST INDIA PALE ALE

See INDIA PALE ALE.

EBC

See COLOR and EUROPEAN BREWERY CONVENTION.

EBERS PAPYRUS

The greatest surviving work on ancient Egyptian medicine. It contains more than 600 prescriptions, many of which rely on beer as a major component. For example, sweet, beer-soaked dates were prescribed to relieve constipation, and powdered olives and beer to cure indigestion.

EGG ALE

A highly nutritious beer. A recipe for egg ale calls for the gravy of 8 pounds of beer, 12 eggs, a pound of raisins, oranges, and spices to be placed in a linen bag and left in a 12-gallon barrel of ale until the ale has ceased fermenting. Then 2 quarts of Malaga sack were added. After 3 weeks in the cask, the ale was bottled with a little sugar for priming.

EGYPTIAN BEER

Beer was so important to the ancient Egyptians that the hieroglyphic symbol for food was a pitcher of beer and a loaf of bread.

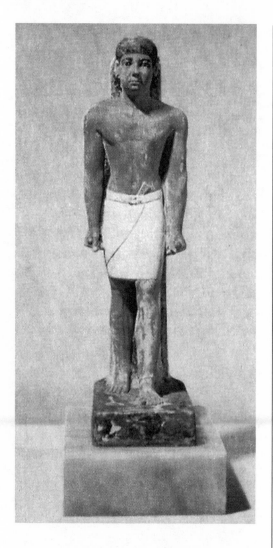

This statue of Neter-Her-Plah is thought to be related to the brewing of beer in ancient times.

hermes, or old, beer; beer of truth; beer of the goddess Maat; and *setoherit,* a narcotic beer used as a sleeping agent.

The basis of all Egyptian beers was barley bread. The ancient chemist Zosimus described the brewing process as follows:

"Take fine, clean barley and moisten it for one day; draw it off and lay it up on a windless place until morning; again wet it and dry it (until shredded) and rub it until it falls apart. Next, grind it and make it into two loaves just like bread and cook it rather raw, and when the loaves rise, dissolve in sweet water and strain through a sieve."

These half-baked loaves were mashed and crumbled over a large fermenting vessel, then forced through the bottom of a woven reed basket, falling into the clay vessel below. Clay fermenting jars, many larger than an average man, were covered with pitch on the outside to make them airtight. When filled with beer, the jar was stoppered with a plug of Nile mud, and lagering began.

Every household, rich or poor, brewed beer. There were also huge commercial breweries throughout the country. Toward the end of the pharaonic period, the Paison and Senthous brewery paid a fortune in excise taxes on the thousands of gallons of beer it brewed.

For the average family, the brewery was located in the kitchen. Most often, women were responsible for brewing and selling beer, both in the home and in Egypt's thousands of beer shops. The palace of the pharaoh provided the royal household with regal brews, with the chief beer inspector

They enjoyed a bewildering variety of beers, including brown beer; iron beer; sweet beer (lagered with dates); *neter,* or strong, beer; white, black, and red beers; and Nubian styles. Among the top-shelf beers that appear to have been brewed for religious purposes were "friend's" beer; beer of the protector;

Pictograms from pharaonic Egypt illustrate the brewing of beer.

Egypt of the pharaohs were paid with a daily ration of four loaves of bread and two jugs of beer, and it was customary for mothers to bring beer to school for their sons.

In religious life, beer was attributed to Isis, the goddess of nature. Ramses III (1300 B.C.) had a temple inscription to show that he had consecrated 466,303 jugs of beer to the pantheon of gods.

Each year a 47-day feast was held in Thebes, during which the people took out the mummies of their pharaoh-gods for parades and celebrations. During the feast, sacramental beer was liberally dispensed, free, to celebrants.

The tomb-makers in the Valley of the Kings worked solely for rations of beer and grain brought from Thebes across the river Nile. The surpluses were used to hire servants and to pay for services rendered.

The Egyptian art of brewing remained hidden in the tomb paintings of the Egyptians and the clay tablets of the

being responsible for quality control. Pharaohs also received thousands of jars of beer each year in the form of taxes and tributes from cities, provinces, and territories. Beer was money, and the minimum wage was two pitchers, each several gallons in size, for a day's work.

Hops were unknown to the ancient Egyptians, although bitter herbs such as lupine and skirret often were added to the brew or served as an appetizer with the beer itself.

Peasantry and farmers in the

An Egyptian granary and male grain carrier are shown in this ancient drawing.

Babylonians, until discovered by archeologists, enabling historians to date the beginnings of beer back 8,000 years.

See TOMBS and BEER.

EISBOCK

A type of beer in which the alcohol has been concentrated by freezing the beer and removing the ice. Such beer is much stronger and usually more flavorful than regular beer. The Reichelbräu Brewery in Kulmbach, Bavaria, Germany, has registered the name Eisbock for its seasonal doppelbock, brewed annually in August and September for consumption at the town's Eisbock Festival at the end of March. Reichelbräu Eisbock Bayrisch G'frorns (Bavarian Frozen) can be called a doppelbock as defined by Bavarian law in that its original gravity is over 18/1.074. According to London beer writer Michael Jackson, Eisbock is very dark (50 SRM), of barley-wine strength (10 percent alcohol by volume), with an original gravity of 24/1.098 and a bitterness of 27 IBU. Jackson says that Eisbock has a "hint of a whisky-and-coffee liquor in its warming."

This type of beer may not be made legally in the United States, but a number of brewers have accidentally produced an ice bock. One Canadian brewer (Niagara Falls Brewing) has made an Eisbock since 1989, using the technique to concentrate its flavors rather than simply brew a strong beer. This beer starts at 15.3/1.061 OG and 6 percent alcohol by volume, then is frozen at 30°F (-1°C) for 2 weeks, resulting in a beer that is 8 percent alcohol by volume and has a theoretical original gravity of 24/1.084.

Original Gravity	Final Gravity	Alcohol by Volume	IBU	SRM
Reichelbräu Eisbock Bayrisch G'frorns (Germany) 1992				
24/1.098	6	10%	27	50

See DOPPELBOCK and ICE BEER.

ELDRIDGE POPE, LTD. DORCHESTER, DORSET ENGLAND

A brewery founded in 1837 by Charles Eldridge, a tavern keeper and spirits merchant. In the early days, it was called the Dragon Brewery. When Charles died in 1846, the brewery passed on to his wife Sarah. An ambitious businesswoman, she built a network of tied houses, and expanded the brewery's business, with an eye towards the newly laid railroad networks then reaching Dorchester. Unfortunately, the Eldridges' only son died at age 16 after breaking a toe in the brewery and contracting lockjaw. After her son's death, Sarah took on a partner named Alfred Mason, a "brewer's clerk" who took a one-third share of the business. In 1852, her daughter Emily married a lawyer named John Tizard, who also took an interest in the business. When Sarah died in 1856, Tizard and Mason became partners in the expanding brewery. The two men rapidly acquired

The beers of Dorchester had been known throughout the world since the 17th century, but it was Thomas Hardy, a good friend of Alfred Pope, who immortalized them in prose. In his detailed description of the fine ale poured at a Dorset wedding feast in the *Trumpet Major*, Hardy wrote: "It was of the most beautiful colour that the eye of an artist in beer could desire; full in body, yet brisk as a volcano; piquant, yet without a twang; luminous as an autumn sunset; free from streakiness of taste; but finally, rather heady. The masses worshiped it, the minor gentry loved it more than wine, and by the most illustrious county families it was not despised."

It is said that Pope had a hand in editing Hardy's description of the beer, and the passage might be considered one of the earliest testimonial advertments.

Under the Pope family, which controls the brewery to this day, Eldridge Pope, Ltd. became a prosperous regional brewery, with current capacity of 150,000 barrels. Its beers have become well-known in the United States due to the efforts of a firm called Phoenix Imports, of Ellicott City, Maryland, which makes the company's Thomas Hardy's Ale available to consumers in the United States.

The company also brews Thomas Hardy Country Bitter, Royal Oak, Dorchester Bitter, and Goldie Barley Wine.

tied house properties in Dorchester and in the burgeoning port of Southampton.

When Mason retired in 1870, two young brothers, Edwin and Alfred Pope, bought his one-third stake in the company, then comprised of two breweries and seven malt houses. In 1873, Tizard died an untimely death, and the Popes were able to buy his two-thirds share.

ENGLISH BITTER

See BITTER.

ENGLISH BROWN ALE

See BROWN ALE.

ENGLISH MILD ALE

See BROWN ALE.

ENGLISH OLD ALE

See ENGLISH STRONG ALE.

ENGLISH SPECIAL BITTER AND EXTRA SPECIAL BITTER

See BITTER.

ENGLISH STANDARD ALE

See BITTER.

ENGLISH STRONG ALE (OLD ALE, STOCK ALE, AMERICAN STOCK ALE)

Strong ales have always been popular with the British, who have a long history of brewing strong old ales.

English Old Ale

In general, the original gravity of English strong ales, also known as old ales, is similar to that of the German *starkbier* (strong beer): an original gravity of 15–18/1.062–1.073. This is a very loosely defined style, however, and gravities both over and under this range are common. Some reach barley wine strength — that is, above 18/1.074. The style goes by many names, including celebration ale and strong country ale.

Old ales are often stronger or special versions of a brewer's regular product. They are bottom-conditioned, laying-away (hence the name "old") beers and benefit from aging. Most are fairly dark (12 to 25 SRM), and the alcohol content may be high (6.5 to 8.5 percent alcohol by volume). Old ales are assertively to aggressively hopped (30 to 50 IBU, or even higher), with the hops, alcohol intensity, and fermentation esters all contributing to a well-rounded, malty taste.

A Campaign for Real Ale (CAMRA) beer style seminar held in London in August 1994 settled on three categories of English Old Ales, each with three strengths (low gravity — 10.8–14.1/1.043–1.058; medium gravity — 10.8–12.3/1.043–1.049; and strong gravity — above 17/1.070. The categories are Mild Old (low and medium strengths only); Bitter Old; and Stock, or Blended, Old. A few English old ales are found in export versions in the United States.

American Stock Ale

American stock ales are similar to English old ales, but they are rarely bottle-conditioned, and they are rarely suitable for laying away.

Modern American brewers are more likely to brew a barleywine-style ale, which has taken the place of stock ale in the United States.

The Great American Beer Festival guidelines for English Old/Strong Ale are 15–19/1.060–1.075 OG, 6.5–8.5 percent alcohol by volume, 30–40 IBU, and 10–16 SRM. They call for "full-bodied malty sweetness" and "fruity-estery flavors."

Original Gravity	Final Gravity	Alcohol by Volume	IBU	SRM
George Gale Prize Old Ale (England) 1994 (Stock Old)				
22.9/1.094	6.2	9.5%	47	36
Theakston's Old Peculier (England) 1994 (Bitter Old)				
14.1/1.058	3.7	5.6%	29	36
Rogue Olde Crustacean (Oregon) 1993 (barleywine-style)				
24/1.098	4.5	10.4%	80	≈22
Samuel Adams Boston Stock Ale (Massachusetts) 1990 (modern stock)				
13.9/1.057	3.9	5.3%	33	17
Strong Burton Ale 1805				
26.2/1.110	3.2	13.1%	≈83	Unknown

See BELGIAN STRONG ALE, GERMAN BEER STRENGTHS, INDIA PALE ALE (IPA), KULMINATOR (EKU KULMINATOR) AND THE WORLD'S STRONGEST BEERS, and SCOTCH ALE.

ENTIRE

The original English name for porter. Also called Entire Butt. This brew was called Entire because the beer was a blend of several ales. To be properly conditioned, the beer required long maturing times — much longer than alehouse brewers could afford. Entire was directly responsible for the establishment and growth of large commercial brewers who could afford to wait for their stocks of Entire to mature. Large commercial brewers also could ensure consistency, something that alehouse brewers could not guarantee. As a result, the latter soon went out of business, and the commercial brewers filled the void.

See PORTER.

ENZYMES

Proteins produced by plants and animals that act as catalysts for biochemical actions. In brewing, enzymes are responsible for the conversion of complex carbohydrates in grains to fermentable sugars. These enzymes are referred to collectively as diastase, a group of enzymes including alpha amylase, beta amylase, dextrinase, and beta glucanase.

Some of the enzymes used in brewing or potentially related to brewing include those shown in the following table. An important point that many brewers miss is that enzyme actions affect most steps of the brewing process, not just the mash or the malting process. Beta-glucanase used to speed filtration and papain used to chill-proof a beer are examples of enzyme action outside the mash tun.

The most widely known enzymes in brewing are the diastatic enzymes alpha and beta amylase. Alpha amylase occurs naturally in malted barley; it is responsible for hydrolyzing the starches in malt (and any adjunct grains that may be added to the grist) to form the fermentable sugars glucose and maltose. Beta amylase produces only maltose.

Glucoamylase is used to speed fermentation, especially in the production of diet (light) beers and malt liquors. Dextrins are usually unfermentable, but by adding glucoamylase, the dextrins break down and become fermentable, yielding higher alcohol content and minimizing body (attributes that are desired in malt liquors). Glucoamylase also is used to produce diet beers that have a low alcohol content. Normal fermentation is allowed to proceed, then heat is applied to drive off the alcohol, glucoamylase is added, and fermentation is resumed.

Beta glucanase breaks down beta glucan, a gummy substance derived from the husk walls that causes poor mash efficiency and slow sparges.

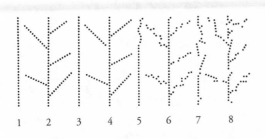

Malt starches and enzyme action.

1. Straight-chain starch (amylose).
2. Branched starch (amylopectin).
3. Beta glucans (looks like amylose but contains both 1-3 and 1-4 links).
4. Amylopectin under attack by dextrinase.
5. Amylose being attacked by beta amylase.
6. Amylopectin attacked by beta amylase.
7. Amylose attacked by alpha amylase.
8. Amylopectin attacked by alpha amylase.

Brewing Enzymes

Enzyme	Actions
Alpha amylase	Liquifies starches in grain, converting them to sugars, providing sugars for yeast. Primary enzyme in mashing process.
Amyloglucosidase	Converts thinned starches to glucose. Used in the production of diet beers.
Beta amylase	Provides sugars for yeast; attenuates wort.
Beta glucanase	Degums mash; speeds filtration; affects ethanol production in fermenter.
Cellulase	Supplements amylase action; increases beer body.
Cytase	Makes starches available to amylases.
Diastase	Alpha amylase and beta amylase combined.
Glucoamylase	Attenuates wort for producing dry beers.
Hemicellulase	Facilitates mashing.
Papain	Chillproofs beer, maintaining clarity at low temperature; enhances diastatic activity.
Pectinase (polygalacturonase)	Prevents gel formation in fruits (useful in the production of fruit beers).
Phytase/phytin	Lowers pH.
Protease	Provides nitrogen for yeast.
Pullalanase	Attenuates wort.

Proteinase enzymes assist in the modification of barley to malt and are critical to fermentation because they provide nitrogen for yeast growth. Proteinase also is added to commercial beers to eliminate haze. Naturally occurring proteinase is not an option for haze prevention because any proteinase in the wort is eliminated by the high temperatures of the boil. Therefore, papain is often added.

See ALPHA AMYLASE, BETA AMYLASE, and HAZE.

ERLANGER BEER

See BAVARIAN BEER.

ESTERS

Organic compounds comprising an alcohol and an acid that tend to have strong, often fruity aromas. The predominant ester found in beer is ethyl acetate, which smells like a solvent; it is the product of ethanol reacting with acetic acid. Excessive esters are undesirable in any beer, but certain types of esters at certain levels can enhance beer. Ales typically have a fruitier aroma than lagers. This is a result of the ale yeast strain and the fact that fermentation is done at higher temperatures for ales than for lagers. Certain strains of ale yeast are highly prized for the ester levels they normally produce.

Most of the esters found in beer are produced during the growth phase of the yeast, so an inadequate pitching rate can cause elevated levels of esters. If there is inadequate oxygen or the fermentation takes place at too high a temperature, ester levels also will rise. For example, with high-gravity beer, less oxygen dissolves into the wort, so a higher pitching rate is required to prevent excessive esters. Finally, some yeast strains tend to generate more esters than others.

EUROPEAN BREWERY CONVENTION (EBC)

Secretariat General
2380 BB Zoeterwoude
P.O. Box 510
Netherlands
011-31-71-456047

The European Brewery Convention (EBC) was founded in 1946 and is dedicated to the promotion of scientific cooperation within the malting and brewing industries.

See COLOR.

EUROPEAN BREWING AND THE EUROPEAN UNION

The European Union (EU), to which most Western European countries belong, is an organization based in Brussels that works to increase competition by removing inter-European barriers to trade and competition. Based on the 1987 mandates of the EU, Germany was forced to admit beers for sale in Germany that did not conform to the Reinheitsgebot, the German law of purity.

The establishment of the EU is causing the European brewing industry to undergo dramatic changes. The United Kingdom's tied-house system, in which breweries are allowed to own pubs and restaurants that serve only their products, is being looked at with an eye toward abolishing the practice. Some argue that large breweries with more cash to spend can control the outlets to the detriment of small brewers. After all, a brewer needs to sell the product to pubs, but if the vast majority of pubs are owned by the mega–brewers, how easily can the small brewer sell the beer? On the other hand, some small brewers and consumer organizations, such as CAMRA, feel the abolition of the tied estate will bring the ruination of small brewers because the large brewers will simply cut their prices to the point where small brewers will no longer be able to compete, because they have higher costs per unit.

The recent social revolution in Europe and the subsequent fall of communism has opened many doors to renewed commercial efforts in which the brewing industry has been quick to respond. One of the first items western Germany sent to her rejoined land to the east was beer. In the West, breweries quickly formed links with ones in the newly freed parts of Europe or laid plans to establish new breweries in those depressed lands. The countries of Eastern Europe are seen as fertile grounds for renewed investments by brewing companies.

As modern Western equipment is installed in these breweries, the standards of the beers they produce will continue to improve.

There have been some serious discussions within the EU of establishing a two-level tax structure to help brewpubs and microbreweries remain competitive with the larger breweries.

Even pubs are slowly coming under the regulating influence of the European Community. Regulations concerning method of dispense, the measure, sanitation and other ways of pub life are coming under scrutiny. There even was a move to replace the venerable pint with metric standards of measure.

Europe, taken in totality, is the biggest beer producing continent. It is just ahead of the Americas, producing 445,687,000 hl per year versus American production of 437,453,000 hl.

EVANSVILLE BREWING CO. EVANSVILLE, INDIANA

A former G. Heileman brewery, Evansville Brewing Co. in Indiana is now employee owned and operated. It has a large plant with a capacity of 1,000,000 barrels, and the company still produces a substantial volume of popularly priced midwestern brands with famous regional brewery names like Weidemann, Cook's, Falls City, and Lemp. Other brands include Drummond Brothers, Gerst Amber, and the peripatetic Harley Davidson beer.

EXPORT

Any beer that is produced with the intent of being exported to another country. At various times certain United States brewers have produced special beers for this purpose, calling them "export" style beers. In Canada, for example, brewers such as Molson and Labatt have one version of their beer for consumption in Canada, and another version for sale and consumption in the United States.

EXTRACT

A measure of the amount of sugar dissolved in water. Extract is usually expressed as wort density per pound of sugar source material per gallon of water. For example, 1 pound of pale ale malt will yield an extract of approximately 1.028 per pound per gallon.

Hancocks, a leading Welsh brewery, produced this export ale.

FALSE BOTTOM

A removable base of a mash tun or lauter tun that has holes or open slots in it to allow wort runoff, grain removal, and cleaning. Normally, there is a 1- to 1½-inch space between the false bottom and the real bottom, allowing for easy runoff. In small mash tuns, the false bottom can be removed, whereas in large tuns they are mechanically lifted up off the real bottom.

FAN

See FREE AMINO NITROGEN.

FARO

A highly carbonated Belgian beer made up of equal parts of high- and low-gravity lambic beer and usually aged less than 1 year. The mix is then sweetened with candy sugar and sometimes colored with caramel. This nearly extinct style is also called faro-lambic.

See LAMBIC.

FELINFOEL BREWERY COMPANY, LTD. LLANELLI, DYFED, WALES

This Welsh brewery was founded on its present site in 1878 and was the first brewery in the United Kingdom to can beer, in 1935. The company produces a range of ales that are exported to North America. Thames America of San Rafael, CA, is the United States agent.

> *Felinfoel*
> *Welsh Bitter*
>
> A handsome golden beer with a big, malty body, rich hop character, and hint of licorice in the finish.

See BITTER.

FERMENTATION

The process whereby yeast manufactures certain enzymes to break down sugar molecules into simpler molecules, namely glucose.

The overall chemical equation of fermentation is as follows:

$$C_6H_{12}O_6 \rightarrow 2C_2H_6O + 2CO_2$$

(glucose)   (ethyl alcohol)   (carbon dioxide)

Fermentation occurs in three general phases: lag, aerobic or respiration, and anaerobic.

Lag Phase

Yeast cells absorb various nutrients through the cell wall, but before they can do this, they must have the right enzymes to transport the different molecules. Each yeast cell readily absorbs glucose and processes such molecules directly whenever encountered. Other sugars and amino acids require different enzymes before they can be taken into the cell.

After the yeast has been pitched into the wort, it begins building up food reserves before the cells can reproduce and ferment the sugars. The yeast stores these reserves as glycogen, a starchy material rendered from glucose. During this time, the yeast cells also take up amino acids, converting them to proteins, and absorb oxygen and other trace materials needed for the creation of new cells. Reproduction is the first great priority upon pitching, and the yeast will not do anything else until food reserves are built up.

Aerobic Phase

Once the reserves are built up within the yeast cell, it will start its reproduction cycle of budding. The mother cell starts to build a new cell from a lateral protrusion, manufactures the required cell elements from its reserves, and passes the elements through its cell wall to the new bud. During this process of synthesizing new material, oxygen is required to synthesize sterols and other fatty substances that will make up the cell wall and internal structures. The yeast absorbs all the oxygen within the wort during this process. That is why adequate aeration is so important. Once all the available

A healthy fermentation of ale yeast

oxygen or amino acids are gone, reproduction will stop.

If the wort is not racked off the trub, which contains sterols and unsaturated fatty material, the yeast may use some of these materials and reproduce to some degree, even without dissolved oxygen. This may contribute to higher alcohol levels (fusel alcohols) being formed. Although racking wort off the trub is believed to produce cleaner beers, it is not always necessary when brewing ales. It should, however, always be done with lagers to ensure a crisp character.

During the respiration phase, the yeast reduces glucose to pyruvic acid, which lowers the pH of the wort. Then the pyruvic acid is reduced to activated acetic acid (acetyl coenzyme A), which in turn goes through a series of chemical reactions to create adenosine triphosphate (ATP). The ATP molecule is an easily consumed energy source for the yeast cell.

Anaerobic Phase

Once all the dissolved oxygen has been removed from the wort, the relatively simple process of fermentation begins. The yeast continues to break down glucose, but it also breaks down larger sugars to glucose through enzyme reactions. Glucose is still broken down to pyruvic acid, but the pyruvic acid is now broken down into carbon dioxide and acetaldehyde. Then acetaldehyde is reduced to ethyl alcohol. The chemical process is as follows:

$$C_6H_{12}O_6 \rightarrow 2C_3H_4O_3 \rightarrow 2CO_2 +$$
(glucose)　　　　(pyruvic acid)　　(carbon dioxide)

$$2C_2H_4O \rightarrow 2C_2H_6O$$
(acetaldehyde)　　(ethyl alcohol)

See YEAST.

FERMENTATION METHOD

The method used to convert fermentable sugars into carbon dioxide and alcohol. The fermentation method is a major determinant of a beer's character and the most important variable in beer production. It involves the yeast type used, the temperature at which the ferment is carried out, and the size and shape of the fermenting vessels. The higher the temperature, the faster the ferment (and its effects) will be, because the speed of all chemical changes doubles (or halves) for each temperature change of 18°F (10°C). Thus, a warm ferment (above 58°F, or 14°C) will produce a beer with ale characteristics regardless of the type of yeast used. A cold ferment (usually in the 40° to 50°F, or 4° to 10°C, range) and/or aging at even colder temperatures (30° to 40°F, or -1° to 4°C) will produce a beer with lager characteristics.

The ferment is usually divided into two stages. In the primary stage, most of the fermentable sugars are converted to alcohol and carbon dioxide. In the secondary stage, the final fermentation activity takes place. Sometimes warm and cold fermentation are used with the same yeast and beer. For example, ale brewers will cold-condition their beer before bottling or shipping. There are also hybrid styles, which are manufactured with both ale and lager methods.

See ALTBIER, BAVARIAN BEER, COMMON BEER, FERMENTATION, KÖLSCH, and LAGER ALE.

FERMENTING VESSEL

A stainless steel, glass, or plastic vessel in which yeast is added to cooled wort from the brew kettle and the fermentable sugars are converted to alcohol and carbon dioxide. Two main designs are used: open-top fermenting vessels and enclosed, conical-bottom fermenting vessels.

Open-top fermenting vessel design is very simple — a cylindrical or square vessel with an open top. The ratio of surface area to depth is determined by the yeast type, but it is normally between a 2:1 to 1:1 to 1:2 ratio. Cooling is achieved with attemperation coils.

Enclosed, conical-bottom fermenting vessels are tall and cylindrical, and have a 60- to 70-degree bottom cone for yeast collection. They are glycol jacketed and can be pressurized up to 30 psi. These vessels are normally at least three to four times taller than their diameter.

See ATTEMPERATION COIL.

A stainless steel fermenting vessel at the manufacturing facility of the Paul Mueller Co.

FESTBIER

Many German brewers brew a special beer for the winter holidays called festbier. This beer is often made in the Märzenbier style, although a bock bier or doppelbock style is sometimes employed. In England, Germany, and indeed all of northern Europe, the traditional holiday drink is strong ale or dark beers. These roots have spawned annual seasonal beers, which are specially made and have become a tradition with many breweries.

From World War II until 1975, that tradition had gradually been lost in the United States. On some occasions a brewery would put a special label on its regular beer, but that was about it. Then in 1975 the Anchor Brewing Co. of San Francisco (at the time the nation's smallest brewery) brought out its first Our Special Ale, owner Fritz Maytag's Christmas present to the American brewing tradition. There's been an Anchor Christmas Ale every year since. Many other brewers and breweries have also reinstituted that fine tradition. In this country most brewers introduce a winter beer instead of a Christmas beer, this in keeping with our rich and diverse cultural heritage.

The new craft brewers have been especially quick to pick up on this tradition, and most of these small brewers have produced special holiday beers. The best of these, and certainly the most widely distributed, is the Sierra Nevada Celebration Ale, first brewed in 1981. At this point only one megabrewer, Coors, has picked up on this opportunity by brewing a Winterfest beer in the Märzen style of Germany.

During the winter holiday season, a number of German and Bristish brewers send their beers to the United States market, and in 1994, there were even Belgian Christmas beers available in the United States.

See ANCHOR BREWING CO., OCTOBERFEST, VIENNA BEER, and SEASONAL BEER.

FILTERING

A synonym for filtration.

FILTRATION

The passage of liquid through a permeable substance to remove solid matter. Specific to brewing, it is the separation of the wort from the spent grains.

There are many different types of filtration equipment available, ranging from plate or pad-type filters to cartridge filters to pleated cartridge filters, which are the most expensive of the group.

See PAD FILTER.

FINAL GRAVITY

The specific gravity of beer as measured when the fermentation stage is complete.

See DENSITY and SPECIFIC GRAVITY.

FINAL SPECIFIC GRAVITY

A synonym for final gravity.

FININGS

Various substances, usually organic, that brewers use to clarify beer. Finings cause suspended matter to coagulate and fall to the bottom of the fermentation vessel. Isinglass, which comes from the bladders of tropical fish, and Irish moss, a seaweed, are two common examples of finings. Gelatin is sometimes used by homebrewers.

See CLARIFIER.

FINISHED BEER

Beer that is ready to be racked and served.

FINISHING HOPS

Hops added at the very end of the boil. Normally, finishing hops are added in the last minutes of the boil or after the boiling is complete but before cooling begins (unlike boiling hops or flavoring hops, both of which are added earlier in the boil). They impart little or no bitterness to the beer, but their essential oils, which contain the aromatic and other flavor compounds, dissolve into the beer and impart aroma to the beer.

Since these essential oils are quite volatile, they must be added late in the boil; otherwise, the heat will drive them off. Exactly when they are added depends on beer style, hop type, and brewer's preference.

See FLAVORING HOPS and HOPS.

FIRE BREWING

A traditional brewing method that uses a direct flame to heat the brew kettle. In the United States, the Stroh Brewery Company still uses this method. Many other brewers use steam or hot water to heat the brew kettle.

FLAKED MAIZE

Partly gelatinized corn, the grain of which has been cracked, cooked, and then flaked between rollers. It is used in some British ales and United States lagers.

FLAVORING HOPS

Hops added in the last 30 minutes of a boil. Flavoring hops contribute a bitter, hoppy flavor to the beer. They contribute little to the aroma, since their volatile oils are generally destroyed, even by a short boil. Finishing hops, conversely, contribute to beer's aroma and hop character, but not to bitterness.

See AROMATIC HOPS, BOILING HOPS, FINISHING HOPS, and HOPS.

FLOCCULATION

The process whereby yeast cells aggregate into masses at the end of fermentation and sink to the bottom in irregularly shaped blobs or a thick layer of foam, contributing to clarified beer. Some yeast strains flocculate more efficiently and effectively than others. A strain of yeast that tends to form thick layers of yeast foam is said to be highly flocculent.

See FLOCCULENT YEAST.

FLOCCULENT YEAST

A generic yeast strain that causes cells to clump together and leads to clarification of beer.

See FLOCCULATION and YEAST.

FLOOR MALTING

A traditional germination method whereby steeped barley is spread over a flat surface or floor until germination is complete.

Floor malting is a traditional germination method whereby the steeped barley is spread over a flat surface in layers, where it germinates for up to 13 days. This illustration from the late 1800s shows the process.

FOREIGN EXTRA STOUT

See STOUT.

FRAMBOISE/FRAMBOZEN

See BELGIAN FRUIT ALE.

FREE AMINO NITROGEN (FAN)

A measure of nitrogen in amino acids in the wort. This nitrogen is usable by yeast and should be at a minimum level of 150 ppm, although the normal range is 240 to 275 ppm (some malts may be higher). Low FAN levels contribute to off-flavors such as that caused by diacetyl.

FREE HOUSE

In Britain, a pub that is not owned by a brewery but instead by a proprietor or even as part of a chain. A free house sells whatever beers and spirits the owner wants rather than what a brewer dictates.

Because most pubs are tied houses (tied to a larger brewery), free houses are essential to the establishment and growth of small breweries in Britain because small brewers face the almost impossible task of getting their beers into tied houses. Without outlets for their products, small brewers quickly close. Many of the smallest breweries have but a handful of free houses (sometimes only one) in their trading area to which to sell their beers.

FRENCH BEER

See BIÈRE DE GARDE (FRENCH COUNTRY BEER).

FRUCTOSE

A crystalline sugar ($C_6H_{12}O_6$) that is found with glucose in fruit juices and honey.
See SUGARS.

FRÜHJAHRS STARKBIERFEST

A Munich (Germany) festival held in the spring beginning on St. Joseph's Day (March 19). The emphasis is on doppelbocks. The Paulaner brewery, established by Pauline monks in the 17th century, made the first doppelbock and called it Salvator (Savior). German brewers since then have given the suffix *-ator* to their doppelbocks, but Paulaner still has the honor of tapping the first kegs of doppel at this festival.

Starkbier means "strong beer," and the lore of Munich holds that strong beer at this time of year is especially beneficial to the health, so a celebratory drink or two is known as the springtime beer cure. The first glass of the season is presented to the prime Minister of Bavaria at a VIP-only inauguration ceremony which, with its comic political roasts, does wind up on local television. The festival then rolls on for seventeen days, time enough for many a cure.

See OKTOBERFEST.

FRUIT

Fruit is often added to beers — usually lighter-colored, lighter-bodied beers — to impart flavor and color. Berries and cherries work well in this regard. In commercial practice, Belgian lambic ales are often available in fruit flavors; for example, Lindemans' Framboise is a raspberry-flavored beer. Lindemans also produces Kriek (cherry-flavored beer) and Pêche (peach-flavored beer). A wide range of fruit recipes are available to homebrewers. Excellent beers have been made with fruits such as apples, cranberries, kiwifruit, plums, grapes, pears, and apricots.

Fruit can be added to almost any style of beer, although strongly flavored or dark beers often dominate the subtler flavors and aromas of the fruit. Nevertheless, the darker styles often work well with some types of fruit. For example, raspberry dunkel weizens and raspberry porters have won kudos for quite a few brewers. Most often, though, a pale ale or wheat beer is used as the basis for a fruit beer.

Fruit can be added to the beer at any of three stages: in the primary ferment, in the secondary ferment, or at bottling. Adding fruit during the boil is generally not a good idea because fruit contains pectin, which is what causes jelly to gel. Gel in fermenters is undesirable and can be alleviated by using the enzyme pectinase. Adding fruit to the primary ferment is probably the most common approach for most homebrewers, but the secondary ferment may be a better choice because the yeast will have had a chance to build up a large number of cells and to begin to produce alcohol. The risk of infection is probably lower, and the brewer is less likely to get a vigorous yeast fermentation that could clog the airlock or blow-off tube. Brewers may want to use an open fermenter or a larger blow-off tube when working with fruit beers because even when fruit is added to the secondary ferment, it can produce vigorous fermentation.

Several forms of fruit are used, from fresh-picked produce to artificial extracts. Some of the more commonly used forms include fresh fruit, frozen fruit, fruit juices, fruit preserves, prepackaged crushed fruit, fruit wine base, fruit liqueurs, natural fruit flavors, and artificial fruit flavors.

Fresh fruit added at the primary stage must be crushed or macerated and then pasteurized by turning off the heat from the brew pot, adding the fruit to the pot, and steeping the fruit for 20 to 30 minutes. Berries can be frozen and then added to the wort; freezing helps break down the cell barriers, making the sugars more accessible to the yeast.

Bacteria that live on fruit usually inhabit the skin, so peeling fruits such as apples before adding them to the brew can help, although pasteurizing the fruit will kill most bacteria. Wine makers often treat the fruit or its juice with sulfites, usually by adding Campden tablets. This takes a bit of planning, as fruit juices treated with sulfites should sit for a day or so before being added to the ferment. Several homebrew supply stores sell fruit-flavored extracts and natural or artificial flavors. These are easy to use but often do not give a true fruit flavor.

Adding juices and pureed fruits to the secondary ferment works well. Many experienced brewers feel that it is best to add fruit at this stage. Fruit is seldom added at bottling, although some brewers like to leave a few raspberries or other pieces of fruit in the bottle.

As mentioned previously, adding fruit to the secondary ferment often results in a vigorous fermentation, especially when it is added in the form of fruit extract or wine base. In addition, many fruits will float on the beer and clog small blow-off tubes, creating a large amount of thick blow-off. Homebrewers may want to use larger carboys when brewing fruit beers.

The amount of fruit added to a beer depends on the style of beer, the type of fruit, and the intensity of flavor desired. Subtle fruit flavors are often preferred. For most types of fruit, the rule of thumb is 1 pound (0.45 kg) per gallon (3.79 L). The brewer should use a bit of common sense and keep in mind the flavor intensity of various fruits. Cranberries produce a very tart flavor, and if they are used excessively, that tartness will become acidic and biting. Using 1 pound (0.45 kg) of cranberries for a 5-gallon (19 L) batch is a reasonable starting point. Similarly, strawberries have a very light flavor, and 2 pounds (0.9 kg) or more per gallon (3.79 L) are usually needed.

Fruit beers require a longer secondary ferment than usual. The yeast and enzymes need time to break down the sugars fully to avoid potential over-carbonation problems. In addition, it takes time for the fruit flavors to integrate with the beer. Randy Mosher, in *The Brewer's Companion,* suggests a minimum of 2 weeks and preferably up to 2 months for this stage. Mosher also suggests using liqueurs for both flavoring and priming, since liqueurs are usually made with added sugars.

See BLOW-OFF TUBE; CARBOY; CIDER; ENZYMES; FRUIT, VEGETABLE, HERBAL, AND SPECIALTY BEERS; and PERRY.

FRUITILADA

An ancient brew made from corn and Andean strawberries by the Quechuan women of what is now Peru. This extraordinary spontaneously fermented beer is produced only for the 10-day Pauchua Mama Festival.

Fruitilada is traditionally served in quart glasses with a 2-inch head of foam. The head of the beer is sprinkled with cinnamon, mace, and other herbs and spices. The first drops of every glass are spilled on the ground in memory of the goddess Pauchua Mama.

FRUIT, VEGETABLE, HERBAL, AND SPECIALTY BEERS

Any beer or beer style that is changed by the addition of fruits, vegetables, herbs, spices, or unusual fermentables such as potatoes, chocolate, maple syrup, honey, and molasses. The key element that a brewer must consider in making this type of beer is that the specialty element must not dominate the taste, but it must have some effect on the flavor. A chocolate beer will not be successful if it is too chocolaty; a raspberry beer should have a restrained raspberry flavor. What role does honey, maple syrup, or molasses play? If an element's character remains intact in the finished beer, it is a specialty beer. If the character is hidden, as in the use of molasses in stout, then the end product is just stout, not molasses stout.

Harmony and balance must be the primary focus in brewing such beers. Specialty elements might be added directly to the brew kettle (hot extraction), during the primary ferment (cold extraction), or even at the end of the process (via flavored extracts or essences). Hot extraction may alter the character of fruits, vegetables, and spices, but cold extraction, while retaining more of the flavor, may introduce bacteria. Fruit extracts and concentrates may be preferable for some beer types (for instance, cranberry-apple concentrate, as opposed to fresh cranberries and apples). Essences may have an artificiality that the brewer might not wish to introduce, but they may be used to add a flavor (such as chocolate, amaretto, or hazelnut) that will enhance a particular brew.

In general, hops are used sparingly (5–20 IBU) in fruit, herbal, and specialty beers, so as not to destroy the delicate flavor balance of such brews. These beers are usually of modest original gravity (10–12/1.040–1.048), although some beers, particularly spiced winter ales, have much higher gravities. The grains used are mostly pale 2-row malt, but wheat is quite compatible with many fruit ale formulations, so a base of 50 percent wheat is not uncommon.

Fruit Beer

Any beer in which the fruit is a major element of the character. The base beer is usually pale, but the color of the beer might be darkened considerably by the addition of some fruits (such as blackberries and blueberries). Some fruit beers might have even higher gravities, especially in the case of a raspberry barley wine or a raspberry stout, and in that case a darker, hoppier beer base might be used.

Vegetable Beer

Many different vegetables are used in beer. Chili beer is becoming popular. It is usually pale in color, and the chilies range from mild to hot. One popular brand, Cave Creek Chili Beer, is regular beer in a clear glass bottle with one or two jalapeño peppers added during bottling time. Rogue Mexicali Chili Beer is much milder.

Pumpkins are another preferred vegetable. Pumpkin ale also is pale, with its character enhanced by spices (pumpkin pie spices, for example). Pumpkin beers have low hopping rates (about 15 IBU). Potatoes have been used, but the potato character is very difficult to impart to beer.

Herbal Beer

Ginger and root beers are typical herbal specialty beers. Although most folks expect these two beers to be nonalcoholic, these ingredients also make good specialty brews. Ginseng root is another herbal additive that is attaining some popularity in the market. Coffee beer is usually presented in the form of coffee porter or stout.

Spiced Beer

The spiced beers of winter are possibly the best examples of spiced beer. These beers (cinnamon, nutmeg, and so on) are usually dark amber (20–30 SRM), but not black, and mostly strong, often at barley wine strength. Seattle Pike Place Brewery offers an oregano-flavored ale, Birra Prefetto, to accompany Italian food. Old American lager brewers sometimes made spiced lagers using juniper berries (occasionally spruce tips), anise, and even orange zest (peels).

Belgian white beers may contain spices such as coriander as well as orange zest, but this flavoring is normal for the style and these are not considered "spiced ales" per se. Careful and judicious use of spices might well enhance pale ales, as in the case of some Belgian ales, but these would probably not be marketed as "spiced ales."

The Great American Beer Festival guidelines for fruit, vegetable, herbal, and spiced beers are 7.5–27.5/1.030–1.110 OG, 2.5–12 percent alcohol by volume, 5–70 IBU, and 5–50 SRM.

Specialty Beers

The Great American beer festival guidelines define specialty beers as "beers . . . brewed using unusual or unique fermentables other than, or in addition to, malted barley. For example maple syrup, potatoes or honey would be considered unique. Rice, corn or wheat are not considered unique." The same guidelines designate these characteristics: 7.5–27.5/1.030–1.110 OG, 2.5–12 percent alcohol by volume, 0–100 IBU (legally, beer must have *some* hops in it), and 1–100 SRM. To be specific, anything goes!

Original Gravity	Final Gravity	Alcohol by Volume	IBU	SRM
Grant's Spiced Ale (Washington) 1990				
14.5/1.059	3	6.1%	30	≈12

Original Gravity	Final Gravity	Alcohol by Volume	IBU	SRM
Hamms flavored malt liquors (Minnesota) ca. 1970 (lemon-lime, strawberry, raspberry)				
16.6/1.068	6.7	5.2%	5	2.3
McMenamin's Ruby Raspberry (Oregon) 1987				
9.8/1.039	2.6	3.8%	≈20	Pink
Portage Bay Raspberry Pale Ale (Canada) ca. 1980 (regular beer flavored with fruit essence at bottling)				
11.5/1.046	2.9	4.6%	12	≈6
Rogue Mexicali Chili Beer (Oregon) 1991				
12.2/1.049	3.2	4.7%	26	≈8

See BELGIAN FRUIT ALE and FRUIT.

FULL BEER

See VOLLBIER.

FULL-BODIED

A description of beer that is rich and mouth-filling, as opposed to thin and watery.

See MOUTHFEEL.

FULL SAIL BREWING CO. HOOD RIVER, OREGON

Formerly known as Hood River Brewing Co., Full Sail is one of the fastest-growing western microbreweries, having sold 52,484 barrels in 1994. The company's Full Sail ales have a strong following on the West Coast of the United States. The brewery also operates an on-site brewpub, called the Whitecap, where Full Sail beers are poured on draft and pub fare is served.

See AMBER AND RED BEERS, BREWPUB, and MICROBREWERY.

Full Sail's executive brewmaster, James Emmerson, stands in front of the company's new bottling line, which has a 300-bottle-per-minute capacity.

Full Sail Amber Ale

"Amber" is one of the most overused stylistic tags by the new generation of breweries, but the Full Sail version is not just another cookie-cutter amber. It is malty and full-bodied, with a great hoppy aroma and a rich flavor that is almost toffeeish. Full Sail Amber Ale is more complex than an upstart microbrewery beer has any right to be.

The stainless steel fermenting vessel at the original Full Sail Brewing Co. brewhouse was made by J.V. Northwest.

GAL.

An abbreviation for gallon.

GALLON

A liquid measure with a capacity of 231 cubic inches equal to 128 fluid ounces (3.7853 L). A common unit of measurement in the United States. One American gallon is equal to ⅚ imperial gallon.

GAMBRINUS

See PRIMUS, JAN.

GAS BURNER

Either a ring-type burner located directly under the stainless steel base of the vessel being heated or a tubular burner situated inside the tank being heated and through which a flame is directed.

GAY-LUSSAC

A piece of equipment devised by Joseph Louis Gay-Lussac that is used to determine the percentage of alcohol in a solution.

D. L. GEARY BREWING CO. PORTLAND, MAINE

It is safe to say that David Geary is the only American brewer to learn his trade in an earth-floored Scottish brewery. In the early 1980s, Geary met the Laird of Traquair, the scion of an ancient Scottish brewing family, who was visiting Portland, Maine, on business. The Laird invited Geary to work at his brewery, located in a room beneath Traquair Manor, in Peebleshire, Scotland. Geary soon chucked a sales career and headed off to Scotland.

It was there that Geary became familiar with the brewer's craft, learning his trade using oak vessels and 17th-century brewing accoutrements. Following his stint at Traquair, Geary worked in a series of small

English breweries under the tutelage of Peter Austin, a gentleman who is often considered the father of the British small brewery movement.

Geary was eager to bring his newfound knowledge back to the United States, where the microbrewery movement was in its infancy. He invited Alan Pugsley, a protégé of Peter Austin, to return with him to the United States and start a small brewery. Pugsley agreed, and D. L. Geary Brewing Co. was born. Ground was broken in 1985, and the enterprise began selling beer commercially in 1986.

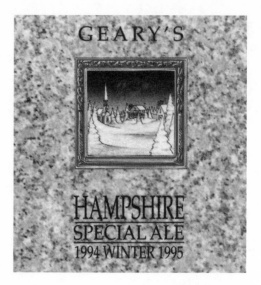

D. L. Geary brews a pale ale as its seasonal offering.

This is a utilitarian brewery, located in a slab-sided warehouse in a wooded industrial park on the outskirts of Portland, Maine. The brewery has a Peter Austin–designed brewhouse, a plant especially well suited for ale brewing.

D. L. Geary produces three brands: Geary's London Porter, Pale Ale, and Hampshire Ale. The first is the company's flagship product, the second a winter beer. Hampshire Ale is a big, malty brew, styled after an English extra special bitter. As might be expected, it is potently hopped.

See ALE BEER and MICROBREWERY.

Geary's Pale Ale

A classic Yankee ale, from its lobster label to its Anglo-Saxon pedigree. This crisply drinkable beer has a firm body and a nice hop edge. "It's a beer for drinking," Geary says. "It's got flavor, body, and beauty, but best of all you can drink it — and that's the key to success."

GELATIN

A fining agent used to clarify beer. When added to beer, gelatin combines with tannic acid, proteins, and yeast to form a precipitate that falls out of suspension, leaving a clearer beer. Brewer's gelatin or ordinary unflavored gelatin may be used. One tablespoon (14.79 ml) is enough to clarify 5 gallons (19 L) of beer.

See CLARIFICATION and FININGS.

GENESEE BREWING CO. ROCHESTER, NEW YORK

Genesee is the largest independent regional brewery in the United States, with a capacity of 4,000,000 barrels. Although it does not use anything near its full capacity, "Genny" still sells a substantial amount of beer in its upstate New York and Penn-

Genesee 12-Horse Ale

Somewhat less robust than the name suggests, but quite typical of the distinctly American-style light, golden ale. Genesee 12-Horse Ale is a fairly light-bodied beer with a smooth, malty creaminess.

sylvania markets. The company's beers are de rigueur in taverns throughout the region, and this loyal customer base has much to do with the company's endurance.

The original Genesee Brewing Co. was founded in 1878 but went under during Prohibition. After the repeal of Prohibition, Louis A. Wehle opened a new firm, using Genesee's brewing plant. The Wehle family still operates the company, which has become something of an anomaly on the American brewing scene: the largest single-plant brewing operation still in existence.

The company is one of the largest ale brewers in the United States, with a substantial part of its sales coming from Genesee Cream Ale and Genesee 12-Horse Ale. Commendably, it was one of the few breweries to persist in producing a seasonal bock beer during the 1970s and 1980s. Though available only sporadically, Genny Bock (billy goat on the label and all) is symbolic of the brewery's commitment to tradition.

The company's other brands include Genesee Beer, Genesee Light, and Genesee Ice. The company also owns the labels of the Fred Koch Brewery of Dunkirk, New York, and produces Koch's Golden Anniversary Beer.

Recently, Genesee has embraced specialty beers, with products such as J. W. Dundee's Honey Brown Lager. Most sound more special than they are, but the company has recognized the existence of the trend, and more such products are said to be in the works.

See ALE, ICE BEER, LIGHT BEER, and REGIONAL BREWERY.

GERMAN BREW STRENGTHS

German law defines *starkbier* (strong beer) as 15–18/1.062–1.073 OG, 5.8–7.3 percent alcohol by volume, and 20–40 IBU. *Schenkbier* is weaker than *vollbier* (regular beer), under 10.5/1.042 OG or so. *Spezialbier* (special or seasonal beer) is between starkbier and vollbier, at 12.5–14.9/ 1.050–1.061 OG, 5–6 percent alcohol by volume, and 5–40 IBU.

See VOLLBIER.

GERMAN PILSNER

Pils falls within the German *vollbier* (full beer) category. Most people assume there is but one pilsner style. That is not the case in Germany, where beer definitions are strictly adhered to. There are four German classes of pilsner: *Klassische Pilsner* (Classic Pilsner); *Süddeutschen Pilsner* (South German Pilsner); Sauerländer Pilstypus (Sauerland Pilsner-type); and the *Hanseatische Pilsenertyp* (Hanseatic Pilsner-type). Pils is the only style that is brewed in every German state.

Classic Pilsner has more emphasis on hops, and is precisely crafted to be robust, have a full mouthfeel, and be well-rounded. A good German example of a Classic Pilsner is König Pilsner.

South German Pilsner is more robust and has more aromatic malt aroma than the German norm for the style. An example is Bräumeister Pils from Hacker-Pschorr in München.

Sauerland Pilsner-type is particularly light and delicate, but not very bitter at all. It is, often enough, easily identified because of its particularly light colour. Warsteiner Pils is a good example of this style.

Han is particularly bitter, dry and sharp-tasting from the hops. This North German style is mostly found around Jever. An example of this style is Jever Pilsener from Friesiches Bräuhaus zu Jever, which is owned by Hamburg's St. Pauli Brewery.

GERMINATION

The second step in producing malt from raw barley. After the barley is soaked in water, it is spread out in piles and allowed to sprout, or germinate, which modifies the malt.

See MALTING.

GERMINATION SYSTEMS FOR BARLEY

There are three types of barley germination systems.

The first is manual floor malting, the original method of germinating barley. Here grain is turned manually, allowing for air to circulate throughout and encouraging germination.

The second system is compartment malting. This is done in a Saladin box, a rectangular open-top container with a base of removable slotted plates. Grain depth may be 3 to 5 feet. The grain is turned by means of helical screws. The slotted bottom

Germinating floors at the Anton Dreher Brewery in Budapest, Austria

allows for conditioned air to be forced through the bed, controlling moisture and carbon dioxide content.

The third system, *Wanderhaufen,* is essentially an open-ended compartment. Steeped grain is discharged into one end of the rectangular box while the grain on the "street" is moved slot by slot downward in a controlled fashion toward the awaiting kiln. Specialized turners pick up the grain and move it farther down the street, with minimum mixing of different grain lots. This system is automated, controlling temperature, airflow, and spray steeping, to provide optimum malting conditions for each type of grain.

GINGER BEER

A traditional beer made with ginger, which imparts a distinct taste and aroma. Ginger was among the many herbs and spices used by brewers to balance the sweetness of malt before the advent of hops. Commercial examples of ginger beer are almost nonexistent, although ginger is used in some holiday or Christmas ales.

GLASS

See GLASSWARE.

GLASSWARE

The preferred vessel from which to drink beer. Much as with food, appreciating a good beer involves relishing its aroma, appearance, and taste. Glassware allows for a fuller sensory enjoyment. Unlike pottery or pewter, glass allows the drinker to see the beer's color, observe the bubbles rising, and view the depth of the head. (It should be noted that beer tasters in breweries drink from opaque vessels so they can concentrate on the taste and not be distracted by the appearance.) Different shaped glasses offer different presentations of the beer's aroma. Some glasses have wide openings that allow the drinker to place his or her nose inside the glass to better breathe in the beer's perfume.

Since glassware does not retain flavors or odors, the drinker can better appreciate the aroma of the beer.

For Americans, the glasses of choice are the hour-glass tumblers, which have a heavy

Dimple mug   Orval's distinctive goblet.

base and narrow center that flares out to a bell at the top. Also popular are straight tumblers and tall Pilsners — footed glasses that resemble narrow inverted cones.

The Pilsner glass is a popular specialty glass in Germany because it allows for a good display of the Pilsner beers. Germans also favor glass steins; one-liter tumblers that flare at the top; wide, shallow goblets; and wheat-beer glasses, which have slender, outward curving sides and a bell-shaped top. The English prefer a straight-sided pint glass for their substantial beer, as do the Irish for their stout.

The prize for glassware variety, however, must go to the Belgians, who seem to have a different-shaped glass for each beer. (Visitors to Belgian public houses are sometimes taken aback when they order a beer and are told that all the glasses for that style are in use.) The Belgians serve tart

Glassware is named for the beer style or the brewer. Left to right: Alt, Willibecker, Pescara Pilsner, Riedel Vinum Beer, and Weizea.

Glasses for (left to right) Gueuze, Duvel, Riedel Vinum Gourmet, Nonic "bulge", and Standard

beers in tall, narrow flutes, so the aroma rises to the nose; abbey-brewed beers in wide, goblet-style glasses that allow the beer to breathe; and Duvel beers in glasses with tulip-shaped bowls that allow the foam and beer to be consumed simultaneously. A footed tumbler with a wide bulge in the center called a Thistle glass is used for heavy, aromatic beers, and a cordial glass is used for strong ales.

The crystal clearness of good glasses enhances the presentation of good beer, but the user should take caution with the care of the glassware. Beer glasses should not be washed with soap but cleaned with a sterilizing solution, since soap residue can flatten the head on a good beer. Soap residues inside bottles, as most homebrewers know, can turn the taste of the beer.

See MUG and STEIN.

GLEN EYRE BEER FESTIVAL

Every November the bar manager and bar treasurer of the Glen Eyre Halls of Residence Club (GEHORC), a nonprofit bar run by students for the benefit of undergraduates at Southampton University, England, put on a two-day beer festival. No one seems to know how long the festival has been going on, though the Glen has been a residence hall for over 30 years. In 1995 there were over 50 real ales to sample, as well as a selection of fruit wines, four different hard ciders, and a sing-along piano player to keep things moving.

GLYCOL CHILLER

A unit in which a concentrated food-grade propylene glycol mix (40 percent propylene-glycol and 60 percent water) is chilled for circulation through cooling vessel jackets and for cold filtration. Normally fitted with a small reservoir, these units depend on a high glycol concentration and the efficiency of associated condensing units to maintain low reservoir temperatures. They may circulate glycol at 15° to 26°F (-9° to -3°C).

See CHILLING.

GLYCOL JACKET

A multipass jacket that is wrapped around an enclosed fermenting vessel or bright beer tank to cool beer. The jacket is often located on the angled cone of a fermenting vessel or the dished bottom of a bright beer tank. It is designed for overall cooling of 20°F (6.6°C) per hour.

See CHILLING.

GOBLET

A drinking glass that has a deep bowl on a short stem and does not have a handle. A goblet usually holds 9 to 12 ounces (266 to 355 ml) of liquid.

See GLASSWARE.

GOD IS GOOD

An early English term for yeast, whose ability to change water into intoxicants inspired giving thanks to God.

GODDESSES OF BREWING

In light of recent archaeological fieldwork, it appears that beer making is at least 8,000 years old. Written records go back about 5,000 to 6,000 years.

The birthplace of beer is likely to lie in Africa, although recent findings show that the peoples of the Amazon River basin of South America have been engaged in large-scale farming of fermentable grains and tubers for 8,000 years. The earliest written evidence of beer is from the ancient Middle Eastern kingdoms of Assyria, Sumer, Mesopotamia, and Babylon. Beer production is evident throughout ancient Middle Eastern society, extending through Egypt and Africa and all the way to the indigenous peoples of Latin America.

Beer was usually believed to be a gift from a goddess, rather than from a male god. This divine generosity was thought to have been prompted by pity for the plight of human beings — the only animals doomed to a life plagued by the knowledge that one day we must die.

The major goddesses responsible for giving the world its first beer were Ninkasi (the lady who fills the mouth) of Sumer and Hathor of Egypt. Menquet was another Egyptian goddess of beer. Some confusion exists over the gender of Bes, a grotesque dwarf deity from the Sudan, adopted by the Egyptians as a beer god/goddess and the protector of children and women in labor. The ancient goddess Ishtar had many beer associations, particularly among the Assyrians.

The goddesses of brewing survive to this day among isolated tribal groups in Africa and India. All brewing is accompanied by prayers and offerings to the earth goddesses Mama Sara and Pauchua Mama, both of whom date back long before the rise of Incan civilization.

Just as goddesses are universally believed to have given humans the gift of beer, women historically have been the

Supernatural beings were often associated with beer and wine, as this 16th-century print of an angel holding a goblet indicates.

brewers of beer. It is obvious that women used their brewing skills to maintain power and status in male-dominated hunter-gatherer societies. In remote corners of the modern world, women continue their domination of beer making.

Wherever female spirits influenced their daughters in the making of beer, brewsters returned the favor by offering as a sacrifice small quantities of every brew. South American Indians continue to pour a small amount of beer to the ground before tasting it, in acknowledgment of these spirits.

See AZTEC BEER GODS, BES, and NINKASI.

BROUWERIJ DE GOUDEN BOOM
BRUGES, BELGIUM

The Vanneste family has brewed beer in Bruges, Belgium, for more than 200 years. Paul Vanneste, the current brewmaster, has devoted his efforts to maintaining his family's and city's brewing traditions. As a result, Brouwerij de Gouden Boom is part museum and part brewery.

In its capacity as a brewery, Gouden Boom produces several noted wheat beers, including Blanche de Bruges, a spicy, fruity beer that is bottle-conditioned. The brewery exports to North America, where its beers are handled by Vanberg & DeWulf of Cooperstown, New York.

See WHEAT BEER.

Gouden Carolus

A rich, dark ale made from pale and dark malts and a proportion of wheat. Brewer's Gold and Saaz hops (grown in Belgium) are used, together with orange peel and coriander. The beer is brewed to an original gravity of 1.076, with an alcohol content of 7.0 to 7.8 percent by volume. It is a rich, powerful beer with a delicious malty aroma. Hints of prune and peach are evident in the flavor, which is very smooth and sweet. Gouden Carolus is bottle-conditioned and is said to benefit from several months' storage.

BROUWERIJ GOUDEN CAROLUS
MECHELEN, BELGIUM

The current Gouden Carolus was founded in 1905, although the beers it produces have much longer histories. This brewery's best-known product is Gouden Carolus, known in its home market as Carolus D'Or (Golden Charles), a name that refers to Emperor Charles V, who grew up in Mechelen. This beer has been brewed since 1369. The company also brews Mechelschen Bruynen and Triple Toison D'Or. Gouden Carolus is imported to the United States by Phoenix Imports of Ellicott City, Maryland.

See ALE and BOTTLE-CONDITIONED BEER.

GRAIN PRECLEANER AND CLEANER

The precleaner is a piece of equipment set up to remove both coarse impurities and fine impurities from barley being received at the malthouse from the farm. Grain passes through a coarse sieve to remove impurities such as straw, earth, and stones. It then passes through a fine screen that removes fine particles such as sand and seeds. The grain flow is accompanied by an airflow, to help remove dust and very light particles.

The cleaner is a piece of equipment generally comprising a rotating metal cylinder with indentations on the inner face, sized to catch particulate matters smaller than

Grain must be cleaned of impurities such as straw, stones, and sand before it can be used.

whole grain kernels, which automatically drop out. Half kernels, seeds, and the like are caught here and rejected. The barley is then graded to size, with the machine generally sieving out grains less than 2.2 mm (0.09 inch) in width. Grading screens oscillate to and fro, separating the different grain sizes.

GRAND CRU AND CUVÉE

Superior Belgian beers. Grand Cru, meaning "special vintage," is really the brewer's favorite or "best" beer. It is most often used for special occasions, such as weddings, victory celebrations, grand openings, and such. It is used much the way champagne is used in other countries. Grand Cru is brewed in smaller quantities than other brands of the same brewery.

Tim Webb, in the *Good Beer Guide to Belgium and Holland* (CAMRA Books) says this about Grand Cru/Cuvée:

"The terms 'cuvée' and 'grand cru' are frequently applied to a wide variety of beers in Belgium and the Netherlands. However, the terms . . . say nothing about the beer in the bottle except to imply that it will be expensive.

"The term 'Cuvée' is commonly used in the names of label beers, regular brewery ales, which are masquerading under a false name for a particular distributor. One Dutch bar owner told the Guide that 'grand cru' means 'big crutch,' and is used either to suggest machismo or else because the beer is so puny that it needs extra support!

"The Guide uses neither term in classifying a beer's style."

It would be very easy to simply toss these into the strong ale category, but there is a problem: the labeling. It is preferable to retain this category but point out that these beers are, indeed, strong ales. Since many Grand Crus are aged for prolonged periods, it wouldn't do them justice to simply toss them into the general "strong ale" category, where, perhaps, they might get lost or marginalized.

GRANT

A small vessel or trough to which wort is directed from the mash tun for visual and hydrometer inspection. Wort may be recycled back to the mash bed for clarification. This is known as *Vorlaufvehrfahren.*

GRANT'S CELTIC ALE

See Yakima Brewing & Malting Co.

GRAVITY

See density.

GREAT AMERICAN BEER FESTIVAL

The Great American Beer Festival (GABF) is North America's largest beer festival, a smorgasbord of suds that is the *ne plus ultra* for beer fans, the Super Bowl of brew fests — which may be why it is now promoted with Roman numerals attached. At the 13th (or XIIIth) festival in 1994, about 20,000 visitors to the 2-night gala in Denver's Currigan Exhibition Hall encountered the staggering tally of more than 1,100 beers from 263 American breweries.

A 2-day blind tasting of beers by a professional panel is held prior to the public tasting. In 1994, the seventh year of the professional panel, 50 judges tasted beers from 42 states in 34 style categories. No best of show is selected, but gold, silver, and bronze medals are awarded for the top three finishers in each category.

The GABF is put on by the Association of Brewers, a nonprofit association that grew out of the American Homebrewers Association. The association serves as a resource for anyone wishing to get involved in smaller-scale brewing, which is virtually the only way anyone starts brewing these days, and the GABF is its blowout extravaganza. It is also great fun, but founder Charlie Papazian cautions that the association "goes to great lengths to make sure people do a responsible job. It's not a drunken spree at all. People go there to taste and talk about the beer and discover new favorites."

Papazian has been known to go so far as to call the festival "educational," and there are numerous displays of brewing techniques, cooking demonstrations, book signings, and the like. It helps to bring an empty knapsack, as there are piles of literature to cart away, as well as beer coasters, labels, buttons, and crowns. But the wondrous profusion of beers is the real draw. The bulging menu includes a lot of splendidly obscure names of distinctively flavored beers: El Toro Oro Golden Ale, Mirror Pond Pale Ale, Untouchable Scotch Ale, Pyramid Apricot Ale, Harvest Moon Pumpkin Ale, Sea Dog Oktoberfest, Heavenly Hefe Weizen, Whitewater Wheat Ale, and Big Nose Blond.

The early festivals were smaller and funkier, which may be true of the entire microbrewery industry. Dan Bradford, now publisher of *All About Beer* magazine, directed the GABF for 10 years. "When I began, the festival had twenty-two breweries and a couple hundred of my close friends attended," he said. "Beer, right now, is one of the most exciting things going on for those

interested in quality, in food, and in a certain lifestyle. It's intriguing to learn about the various components, the stylistic variety, the difference between an ale and a lager, and the like. But it's easy to learn about and discuss without being a snob, the way talking about wine puts off many people, or single malt whiskeys, which are so obscure there isn't anyone you can talk with about them. Hence the draw."

The professional panel was instituted alongside of, and then in place of, a consumer preference poll of the early years. The poll was rarely free of controversy, especially when critics claimed Samuel Adams kept winning the best beer award

Each year the GABF attracts crowds of as many as 20,000 beer lovers.

because it gave away more free beer paraphernalia than any other brewery.

Back then, it was no great difficulty to sample all the new beers one had never tried. Now there are logistical problems: One-ounce servings of 1,200 beers comes to 1,200 ounces, or 9.375 gallons of beer — a hard night's work. Even over the 2 nights of the festival, 9-plus gallons would be stretching all sorts of gustatory, legal, and biological limits.

It helps to have a tasting plan. One might drink only porters, pale ales, beers with fruit in them, or beers named after animals. Beers with goofy names might work. In addition to the brands listed above, in 1994 the goofy name list would

have included What the Gentleman on the Floor Is Having, Moose Juice Stout, Three Blind Monks, Doggie Style, Duck's Breath Bitter, and Chicken Killer Barley Wine.

See ASSOCIATION OF BREWERS and GREAT BRITISH BEER FESTIVAL (GBBF).

GREAT BRITISH BEER FESTIVAL

For the lovers of fine real ale, the 5-day Great British Beer Festival (GBBF) is Mecca. Despite a national rail strike in 1994, 45,000 pilgrims braved hot and muggy weather to find that the English know how to keep beer in its best condition

GABF beer-style guidelines, established yearly, are the industry standard.

no matter what the circumstances.

This was the 17th annual festival sponsored by the Campaign for Real Ale (CAMRA), offering up to 300 cask-conditioned ales at the Grand Hall Olympia in Kensington (England), poured into roughly 182,000 pints. (Visitors buy pints or half-pints at the GBBF, as opposed to the normal American practice of pouring 2-ounce samples for tasters.)

Despite justifiable pride in the English ales, the festival is not chauvinistic. More than 100 imports, mostly specialty beers, were poured at the Foreign Beer Bar, and hard ciders and perries also were available.

A good deal of the excitement of the festival takes place before the doors are opened to the public. A panel of beer judges picks the Champion Beers of Britain. Beers from breweries at least two years old are nominated by CAMRA members and then grouped into eight categories (six beers to a group): Mild, Bitter, Best Bitter, Strong Bitter, Porter/Stout, Old/Strong Ale, Barley Wine, bottle-conditioned Beer. From the winners in these categories, a Best of Show is chosen (the bottle-conditioned beer is not eligible). As might be expected, the winning beer makes full use of the marketing advantages for the following year.

The winners are announced at the beginning of the festival, so festival-goers are quick to swarm around them before going on to pick their own best of show.

Attendance at the GBBF has been steadily growing. The 1994 figures showed an increase of 8,000 visitors, with a concomitant growth in the volunteer staff to 750. Organizer Christine Cryne does not expect those numbers to shrink. "Real ale is growing in popularity, and a wider range of people are drinking it," she says. "The 1994 event demonstrated this very clearly. In particular, we saw dramatic proof that more women are turning to good beer."

The GBBF is but one of several festivals organized by CAMRA throughout England. Contact CAMRA for current information about other upcoming festivals.

See CAMPAIGN FOR REAL ALE (CAMRA) and SCOTTISH BEER FESTIVALS.

GREAT CANADIAN BEER FESTIVAL

Formerly the Victoria Microbrewery Festival, sponsored by the Campaign for Real Ale (CAMRA) Victoria, the Great Canadian Beer Festival is the north country's largest tasting of microbrewed beers. The 1994 festival attracted more than 3,200 visitors. According to festival chairman John Rowling, "We are taking advantage of the increasing interest in new beer products offered by the numerous microbreweries in western Canada and the northwest United States, and of Victoria's growing reputation as a beer tourist destination. Victoria is listed in Jack Erickson's *Brewery Adventures in the Wild West* as one of the ten western North America 'brewery adventure' cities."

The 2-day annual festival showcases Victoria as the British Columbia beer capital, but plenty of other Canadian brewers are represented as well. United States beers also are not neglected. CAMRA Victoria asks each brewery to send at least one representative to tend its festival booth.

The festival offers the usual food booths, T-shirts and promotional materials, and musical entertainment. Exhibitors include maltsters, hop growers, glassware companies, and even the Royal British Columbia Museum. CAMRA Victoria is a 200-member offshoot of the 45,000-member CAMRA of the United Kingdom.

See CAMPAIGN FOR REAL ALE (CAMRA).

GREAT EASTERN INVITATIONAL MICROBREWERY FESTIVAL

The inaugural Great Eastern Invitational Microbrewery Festival, held at and sponsored by the Stoudt Brewing Company in Adamstown, Pennsylvania, took place in 1992. Only 14 breweries were present for the two-session festival, but even so traffic was a problem. The wrinkles have now been ironed out, and the Great Eastern has become one of the more popular beer events east of the Mississippi for attendees and brewers alike.

Carol and Ed Stoudt send brewers invitations to the festival, which is now broken up into three 4-hour sessions (one session on Friday night and two on Saturday). About 1,000 beer fans attend each session. Every attendee receives a souvenir glass and as many 2-ounce pours as he or she desires. A ticket also entitles the bearer to indulge in "The Best of the Wurst," a meal consisting of wurst, German potato salad, and beer bread.

Naturally, the Stoudt brewery store remains open for souvenirs and champagne-size bottles of Stoudt beers.

Adamstown is located midway between Lancaster and Reading, and the Stoudt sprawl is now a magnet for antique hunters, country dancers, and beer aficionados. Ed Stoudt says that the brewery complex "is all just a natural progression of our interests." The progression began with a small steak house opened in 1962 and evolved into a virtual amusement park of gemütlichkeit and breweriana. The festival is held in a genuine beer garden — a roofed but open-air brewery hall — where the Stoudts hold their own smaller-scale brew fests throughout the summer. The couple can often be found presiding at a massive wooden table in the traditionally private *Stammtisch* area of the brewery hall, fenced off for the family but basically open to the festivities.

Carol runs the brewery end of the operation. "We want brewers to like the event," she says, "so we don't want to make it cost-prohibitive." The Stoudts put the brewing reps up at a local hotel and feed them between festival sessions. Well over 50 beers from top East Coast microbreweries are served. The festival's success led the Stoudts to create the annual Great Eastern Oktoberfest as well.

GREATER NEW YORK BEER EXPO

Sponsored by the Little Shop of Hops and the *Beer & Tavern Chronicle,* the Greater

New York Beer Expo debuted at the Jacob Javits Center in 1993 and has since moved to the New York Coliseum.

GREAT NORTHERN PORTER

See SUMMIT BREWING CO.

GREAT NORTHWEST MICROBREWERY INVITATIONAL

This invitational festival brought 40 brewers with 400 kegs to Seattle's Exhibition Hall in 1994 and was produced by Festivals Inc. The festival's beer sale proceeds went to the nonprofit Culinary Arts Promotions Association, whose members acted as volunteer pourers.

See NORTHWEST MICROBREW EXPO.

GREAT SOUTHERN BREWERS FESTIVAL

From the producers of the Boston Brewers Festival, the first Great Southern Brewers Festival was held in 1995 at the North Atlantic Trade Center in Gwinnett County, Georgia, just outside Atlanta. As at the Boston festival, the promoters planned two 4-hour sessions at the Lakewood Exhibition Center, with 40 craft brewers supplying 100 different beers to an estimated attendance of 10,000, each given a souvenir tasting glass, an event and tasting program,

and musical entertainment. No beer competition was planned.

See BOSTON BREWERS FESTIVAL.

GREAT TASTE OF THE MIDWEST

Mitch Gelly, 1995 president of the Madison Homebrewers and Tasters Guild in Wisconsin, said, "For the ninth year of the Great Taste of the Midwest festival we got close to 50 brewers from throughout the Midwest. It's a nice, usually a small, crowd, and 95 percent of the breweries that attend are staffed by the brewmasters or the immediate staff. So it's the people who are actually making the beer, not just representatives doing the pouring. That's nice for a public tasting."

The annual 1-day event is held early each August, at the Olin-Turville Park in Madison. In 1994 there were 1,500 attendees and 35 breweries serving about 100 different beers. A crowd of 2,000 people and samplings of 130 to 140 beers were expected for 1995.

GRIST

Coarsely ground grain used to brew beer. Can also refer to (1) the amount ground at one time, (2) sieved and ground barley or wheat malt that is ready for mashing, or (3) a quantity of barley (or barley and wheat malt) sufficient for one mashing.

Grain needs to be coarsely ground before it can be used to brew beer. The grain is not, however, as finely ground as flour.

GRIST CASE

A mild steel case that holds crushed grist from the mill prior to mashing. A control slide at the base of the chute controls the flow in situations where milling and mashing occur simultaneously (desirable in microbrewing). When milling and mashing occur at the same time, the mill hopper serves as a grist case, holding uncrushed grains.

GROANING BEER

A potent brew made in anticipation of and preparation for the birth of a child. In Europe and the American colonies, groaning beer and groaning cake were served to midwives and mothers in labor. The sustaining benefits of ale were considered essential to the health and survival of both infant and mother, who was encouraged to drink copiously during childbirth.

GROWLER

An American slang term for a pitcher or pail in which beer was carried home from the saloon. "Rushing the growler" referred to repeated trips back to the saloon for refills. Children were most often sent on these beery errands.

GRUIT

A mixture of herbs and spices used as flavoring and bittering agents before being replaced by hops. Gruit (also known as grut, gruyt, grug, and gruz) was made from aniseed, wild rosemary, caraway seeds, coriander, cinnamon, ginger, juniper berries, milfoil, nutmeg, sweet gale, and yarrow.

GUEUZE AND GUEUZE-LAMBIC

See LAMBIC.

GUINNESS PLC DUBLIN, IRELAND

Arthur Guinness acquired the St. James's Gate Brewery in Dublin, Ireland, in 1759. Guinness's genius and brewing skill refined the sweetish dark beer style known as porter into the classic example of bitter, roasted malt stout.

Somewhat more than 200 years later, the Guinness Brewing Group continues to operate St. James's Gate and has 13 other plants. Guinness brands also are brewed under license in 23 countries.

The principal product of the Guinness Brewing Group is, of course, Guinness Stout. The origins of the drink date back to the early 19th century, when Guinness was a porter brewery. The company named one of its stronger porters Guinness Extra Stout Porter. Eventually, the porter appellation was dropped, and the rest is history.

In the years since its creation, Guinness Stout has been mentioned more often than any other beer in poems, songs, novels, and short stories by authors great and small. The cocktail Black Velvet, a wondrous drink made of champagne and Guinness, was a favorite of the German statesman Otto von Bismarck. Black Velvet was first served in observance of the death of Prince Albert, Queen Victoria's husband, in 1861. The champagne portion stood for the nobility, and the Guinness represented the commoners, who adored Albert.

The famous black beer makes for a curious world beer, but that is what it has become, carving a niche for itself from the pubs of Dublin to the sweltering tropics half a world away. Guinness Stout is now the most cosmopolitan of beers, sold in 120 world markets.

The Guinness Stout served in the Caribbean is not precisely the same as that served in Ireland, as the Dublin brewery makes half a dozen formulations, including pasteurized and unpasteurized draught; pasteurized and unpasteurized bottled; a strong bottled Guinness for European markets; and a somewhat different strong bottled product for tropical climes (the famous Foreign Extra Stout). In the United States, consumers get a pasteurized draught, served using a proprietary nitrogen–carbon dioxide system, and a bottled product brewed using some proportion of adjunct grains. The various stouts range in original gravity from 1.039 for draught to 1.073 for the strongest bottled versions.

During and after World War II, Guinness Stout was brewed in the United States at the Burke Brewery in Long Island City, New York. The arrangement, begun in 1939, was made so that the supply would not be interrupted by U-boats. After the war, it turned out that Guinness drinkers were chauvinistic enough to want their stout from the source — St. James's Gate — not Long Island City. The licensing agreement was terminated in 1954. Today Guinness

Guinness Stout

Guinness used a "Guinness Is Good for You" ad campaign for years. Prominent in their advertisements were testimonials from physicians singing the praises of Guinness as a healthful tonic. Given current medical evidence, these doctors may not have been far off the mark. Whether Guinness is therapeutic or not, draught Guinness is one of the most aesthetically pleasing beers around: black in the glass, topped with a stark white head. Easy on the eyes, Guinness is also easy on the palate: roasty, smooth, and creamy almost to a fault.

Stout is imported into the United States by the Guinness Import Co. of Stamford, Connecticut, and Guinness PLC operates a corporate office in London, England.

See STOUT.

GYLE

Unfermented wort. The term is usually used in conjunction with the kraeusening process. Before adding yeast and fermenting the wort, a small amount of wort is reserved as a priming agent. This reserved wort, or gyle, is carefully stored in a sanitized container and usually refrigerated to prevent it from being spoiled by wild yeasts or bacteria. Once the fermentation is complete, the gyle is added back into the beer, and it is bottled. It is used at the rate of about 1 quart (0.95 L) per 5 gallons (19 L) of beer, but this varies with the style of beer. To reduce the risk of contamination during storage, it is a good idea to can the wort.

See PARTI-GYLE BREWING.

GYPSUM

The common name for calcium sulfate ($CaSO_4$). When added to a mash with a high pH, it becomes a source of calcium, which will help lower the pH. One gram of calcium sulfate added to water will add 62 ppm calcium ions and 148 ppm sulfate ions.

HACKER-PSCHORR BRAU MUNICH, GERMANY

One of Munich's top brewers, now owned by Paulaner. The company was founded in 1417.

Producer of Munchner Hell, Hacker-Bräu Edelhell, Munchner Dunkel, Pschorr-Bräu Weisse, and Hubertus Bock, among others.

HALF-AND-HALF

In Britain, a blend of two styles of beer — for instance, bitter and porter, bitter and stout, or bitter and mild ale. It is analogous to a Black and Tan.

See BLACK AND TAN.

HARPOON ALE

See MASS. BAY BREWING CO.

HART BREWING INC. KALAMA, WASHINGTON

Hart Brewing Inc. was founded as the Hart Brewing Co. in 1984, one of the first generation of northwestern micro-breweries. The company was started by Beth Hartwell and her husband, Tom

Baune, in a turn-of-the-century general store in Kalama. They later sold the company to a group of five beer enthusiasts, and it has expanded rapidly in the years since.

One thing that has stayed the same is the Baune-Hartwell Pyramid trademark, chosen because of the ancient Egyptians' role in the development of beer and brewing. The Pyramid logo, which appears on the Pyramid labels,

Daily tours of Hart Brewing Inc.'s new facilities in downtown Seattle are offered to the public.

Hart Brewing Inc. produces both Pyramid Ales and Thomas Kemper Lagers.

represents great pyramids rising from the coniferous forest of the Northwest, an apt symbol of the impact new small brewers have had on the beer market in the region. The Pyramid product line includes Pyramid Best Brown, Pale Ale, Wheaten Ale, Hefeweizen, Amber Wheat, Snow Cap, Wheaten Bock, Porter, and Kälsch.

Hart now owns another small northwestern brewer, Thomas Kemper Brewing Co. of Poulsbo, Washington. Hart acquired Kemper in 1992 and expanded the operation substantially. Kemper is a lager craft brewery,

Pyramid Apricot Ale

A light-bodied ale with a powerful apricot aroma. There is fruit in the flavor as well, and drinking this beer might be likened to consuming an intoxicatingly fruity potable perfume. Though not a session beer, Pyramid Apricot ale is delicious for dessert.

Espresso Stout

A clean, strong brew brimming with a rich, nutty flavor. Smooth but powerful, it has chocolate and fruit notes. With the gourmet coffee boom in full swing, the tie-in with stout is a natural.

with products that include WeizenBerry, Rolling Bay Bock, Winterbräu, Pale Lager, Amber Lager, Dark Lager, Oktoberfest, Hefeweizen, and White (a Belgian-style wheat beer).

Hart continues to brew the Pyramid and Hart brands in Kalama, and Thomas Kemper remains a distinct brewery. The company has built a brand-new brewery in Seattle near the Kingdome. This brewery will make beers from both product lines.

Hart has been especially bold in introducing new specialty beers, including Espresso Stout and Pyramid Apricot Ale. Both brands, in their style and substance, appeal to people who might not ordinarily drink beer. While the Apricot Ale is made with the natural essence of apricots, the

Pyramid Ales' new Kälsch, a refreshing golden ale inspired by the local "Kölsch" beers of Cologne, Germany, arrives in bottles and barrels just in time for summer.

Espresso Stout gets its rich flavor not from coffee beans but from dark specialty malts.

See MARKET SHARE, MICROBREWERY, and STOUT.

RALPH HARWOOD

Perhaps the only individual who can claim responsibility for a beer style, Entire. Harwood operated the Blue Last Brewery in London. His clientele were cobblers, who were fond of a beer cocktail drawn from three casks. Tiring of hand-mixing three varieties of beer into one portion, Harwood ordered this mixture, called Entire or Entire Butts, to be brewed locally.

The Entire style was the precursor to porter. It relied on an odd collection of ingredients, including a particular kind of bean and stale or soured ale. Dark porter was the precursor of stout, and Harwood's brainchild soon spawned the porterhouse, where London porter and a cheap cut of meat, called a porterhouse steak, were the bill of fare.

See PORTER.

HATHOR

An Egyptian goddess of beer, queen of dance, and queen of drunkenness. Usually depicted as a voluptuous woman with the head of a cow, Hathor appears with a human face in most references.

When Ra, the sun god, lost his patience with the human race, he decided to punish the people by turning Hathor loose. She did her job well, as the streets were flooded with blood, and the survival of the species was very much in doubt. Once started on her gruesome work, Hathor was not easily stopped. To slow her down, Ra took the human blood flooding the towns and added barley and fruit. The resulting mixture became the world's first beer. The next morning, when the goddess returned to finish her job, she was stopped cold by an ocean of beer. Tasting the beer and liking it, she quickly became drunk, forgot about finishing off humankind, and went on her merry way. Since then, Hathor has remained the chief Egyptian goddess of beer and drunkenness.

HAZE

A condition in which beer appears to be cloudy. Brewers refer to two types of haze, *temporary haze* (usually called *chill haze*) and *permanent haze*. Both types of haze are caused by proteins bonding with tannins, but the bond formed in a chill haze is weaker than that formed in a permanent haze. A chill haze forms at temperatures near freezing but disappears when the beer warms to near 50°F (10°C).

Haze problems can be reduced by careful mashing, sparging, and boiling; by filtering the beer to remove protein particles; or by using proteolytic enzymes, gelatin, isinglass, or other additives.

See CHILL HAZE.

HBU

See HOMEBREW BITTERING UNIT (HBU).

HEAD

The foam at the top of a glass of beer, present after decanting. The term can also refer to the froth that forms on top of the wort during the primary fermentation. Head retention is often a characteristic used to rate or judge a particular beer sample and is measured by the time required for a 3-cm (0.39 inch) foam collar to disappear from the top of a decanted beer sample.

HEAT EXCHANGER

A piece of equipment, generally of stainless steel plate and frame construction, that is used in wort cooling, cold filtration, and hot liquor heating. All types of heat exchangers depend on the counterflow across plates (occasionally tubes) of different-temperature liquids. For example, chilled water or naturally cold city water is used in wort cooling, with maybe a second glycol pass for low-temperature fermentation. In cold filtration, propylene glycol or brine at 26°F (-3°C) or lower is used to chill beer. In hot liquor heating, steam might be used in the exchange process.

See CHILLING, GLYCOL CHILLER, and GLYCOL JACKETS.

HEAVY BREWING

A brewing method that calls for using less water than usual at the beginning of the process, then adding the remaining water later. Heavy brewing, an invention of the United States brewing industry, is based on the fact that a particular amount of grist and water will produce a particular wort, which when fermented will produce a particular beer. Typically, a wort with a density of 11 degrees Plato will produce a beer of about 4.8 percent alcohol by volume, to which hops are added to a bitterness level of 15 IBU. This will occupy a particular volume in brewing, fermenting, and aging vessels. In heavy brewing, a brew of 11 degrees Plato is made by using, say, 70 percent of the water used normally, resulting in a beer with an original gravity of 15.7 degrees Plato, 6.9 percent alcohol by volume, 21.4 IBU, and a dark color. The remaining water is then added (carbonated), at the end of the process, to produce the final product. In this way, the brewery can increase its capacity by 30 percent — the same number of vessels hold 30 percent more wort. Most authorities agree that there is no difference in the quality of a heavy-brewed beer compared to a beer produced by the standard method.

HECTOLITER (HL)

A unit of measurement equivalent to 100 liters. Hectoliters are the standard metric unit of measurement for beer.

G. HEILEMAN BREWING COMPANY, INC.
LA CROSSE, WISCONSIN

G. Heileman, once an obscure regional brewery, rose to prominence in the 1980s when its regional brewery acquisitions made it one of the largest United States brewers. The company operates several well-known regional breweries, including Blitz-Weinhard Brewing Co. of Portland, Oregon (brewers of Henry Weinhard's Private Reserve); Rainier Brewing Co. of Seattle, Washington (Rainier Ale); The Lone Star Brewing Co. of San Antonio, Texas (Lone Star); Carling National in Baltimore, Maryland (National Bohemian); and the Old Style Brewery in La Crosse, Wisconsin (Old Style).

Purchased by Australian financier Alan Bond in the mid-1980s in a leveraged buyout, G. Heileman could not overcome a debt burden that plunged it into Chapter 11 bankruptcy in 1991. It remains the fifth-largest United States brewing company, but declining sales have forced a substantially downsizing. After the company hit the skids, several breweries broke off to

Called the world's largest six-pack, the tanks at the G. Heileman Brewing Co., Inc., in La Crosse, Wisconsin, hold 22,200 barrels of beer — enough to fill 7,340,796 cans.

do business on their own, including Pittsburgh Brewing Co. of Pittsburgh, Pennsylvania; Evansville Brewing Co. of Evansville, Indiana; and Minnesota Brewing Co. of St. Paul, Minnesota.

In early 1994, the Hicks, Muse investment group purchased G. Heileman and installed new management. Hicks, Muse has had a good track record in turning damaged companies around.

Most of the company's beers are available in the regions surrounding each brewery. G. Heileman does not have a national brand, one reason, according to analysts, that the company has had difficulty building market share.

See REGIONAL BREWERY.

HEINEKEN N.V. AMSTERDAM, NETHERLANDS

Fittingly, Heineken, one of the world's truly international brewers, originated in Amsterdam, one of the world's great shipping ports. The brewery got its name from Gerard Adriaan Heineken, who acquired the De Hooiberg brewery in 1864. De Hooiberg was a small brewery that had been founded in 1592 and was serving a small regional market. Soon after the Heineken takeover, the market expanded to the entire country and abroad.

Heineken produces its beers at more than 90 breweries in some 50 countries around the world. Heineken beers are exported to another 60 countries. The company has brewery interests, licensing agreements, and export deals on every

Henry Weinhard's Private Reserve

Henry Weinhard, a German immigrant, was the founder of the Henry Weinhard Brewery in Portland, Oregon, in the mid–19th century. Following Prohibition, the company merged with a competitor to form Blitz-Weinhard. This new company introduced Henry Weinhard's Private Reserve in the late 1970s, before the brewery was acquired by G. Heileman. By the early 1980s, this product had developed something approaching a cult following in certain markets. Weinhard's, with a dash more hop character than the archetypal American lager, is only marginally more characterful than its mainstream competition; the enthusiastic reception it was accorded is an indication of just how thirsty people are for beer with character. G. Heileman has big plans for Weinhard's and hopes to build it into a quasi-national brand.

Heineken Special Dark

A rich, roasty brew that starts with a velvety maltiness that carries through to a sweet aftertaste. It has a strong malt aroma with a kiss of hop character.

continent. In Europe, Heineken has breweries in the Netherlands, France, Spain, Italy, Greece, Ireland, Hungary, and Switzerland. The combine's primary international brands are Heineken, Amstel, Buckler, and Murphy's Irish Stout.

Heineken exports its beer to the United States. Although the company has operated a brewery in Canada, it has never brewed in the United States, believing that the beer's import status provides it with cachet. The Heineken brand is currently the best-selling import in the United States.

Heineken's United States franchise got its start when an enterprising Holland America cruise line steward began importing the beer after the repeal of Prohibition. This canny steward, named Leo Van Munching, Sr., soon built a profitable trade selling Heineken in New York and farther afield. His son, Leo Van Munching,

Jr., built the business into the most powerful beer-importing franchise in the country. The company was recently bought by its Dutch parent and is now known as Heineken, U.S.A.

See STOUT.

HEKT

The pharaonic Egyptian term for beer. Also called hequ.

See EGYPTIAN BEER.

HERBAL BEERS

See FRUIT, VEGETABLE, HERBAL, AND SPECIALTY BEERS.

HERBS AND SPICES

A wide range of herbs and spices, from cinnamon to Szechuan peppers, are added to beer. Most recipes use only whole spices or fresh herbs. There are several ways to use herbs and spices in brewing. The spices may be added to the boiling wort; they may be added at the end of a boil, just as finishing hops are; a tea may be made by steeping the herbs and spices in water before adding them to the wort; or a spice extract may be made by soaking the spices in vodka or another alcohol to extract as much of their essence as possible. In the last case, the alcohol acts as a solvent.

One of the most common uses of spices is in fest beer — beer specially brewed for the winter holidays. A mixture of spices normally used in traditional Christmas baking — such as cinnamon, ginger, nutmeg, and cloves — is often used. A commercial example of this type of beer is Anchor's Our Special Ale.

Spices Used in Beers

Spice	Amount per 5 Gallons (19 L)
Anise	½ to 1 teaspoon (2.5 to 5 ml)
Cardamom	½ to 1 teaspoon (2.5 to 5 ml)
Cinnamon	1 stick for light flavor, 3 to 4 sticks for sharper flavor
Cloves	2 cloves for light flavor, 5 or more for sharper flavor
Coriander	½ to ¾ ounce (14 to 21 g), pulverized
Fennel	½ to 1 teaspoon (2.5 to 5 ml)
Ginger	2 to 6 ounces (57 to 170 g), shredded
Nutmeg	½ to 1 teaspoon (2.5 to 5 ml)

Flowers also are used for flavoring. For example, lavender, heather, and rose petals have been used in beers. Mint has been used in some beers, with good success in meads. Similarly, spruce, juniper berries, and other unusual ingredients have been used to flavor beers.

Some spiced or herb-flavored beers are brewed fairly often. Quite a few homebrewers have experimented with ginger beers, and some commercial beers are brewed with chili peppers — for example, Ed's Original Cave Creek Chili Beer — although these are often viewed as curiosity items. Different varieties of chili peppers will produce sharply different flavors and levels of heat. The heat of a pepper is produced by a chemical called capsaicin. Most brewers would not want anything hotter than a jalapeño. Most chili pepper beers are based on a light pale ale or a light lager. The pepper can be added at various stages, either in the boil, the primary ferment, the secondary ferment, or the bottling.

See FRUIT, VEGETABLE, HERBAL, AND SPECIALTY BEERS.

HICCUP

A spasmodic inhalation, with closure of the glottis, accompanied by a peculiar sound. Believed by some to derive from the *hekt* (beer) cup of the ancient Egyptians. A commonly observed sign of overindulgence.

HISTORY OF BEER AND BREWING

Beer brewing is an art first developed in Mesopotamia (present-day Iraq) more than 8,000 years ago. Residual materials found in ceramic pottery identified by archeologists as the remnants of the beer makers' craft give us reason to believe beer's origins go back 10,000 years. But without written or archeological evidence, a birth date for beer beyond 8,000 years ago must remain speculative.

Evidence of brewing activity from 5,000 years ago is in the form of clay tablets with cuneiform (wedge-shaped) inscriptions

A bakery and brewery from the tomb at Meket-Re at Thebes, Egyptian Dynasty XI, ca. 2000 B.C.

Pictograms such as this of Norman conquerors enjoying beer help us to determine just how old beer is.

that were discovered around 1840 at Nineveh and Nimrud by Austen Henry Layard, an Englishman who chanced upon Assyrian ruins while journeying overland to Ceylon. He had hoped to find some sort of inscriptions in stone, but what he discovered was a buried library of over 25,000 broken tablets which he removed to the British Museum for translation. The translations were begun by Henry Rawlinson, a British officer who had discovered the key to deciphering cuneiform — the "Record of Darius" — on the Behistun rock near the city of Kermanshah in Iran.

Many of the cuneiform tablets were commercial ledgers, which show us how beer, or kash, was used as currency or an instrument of barter. Records describe how the stonemasons who built the great structures of the pharaohs were paid with vessels of beer. Beer was used as a dietary staple before bread-baking was discovered.

According to Shin T. Kang, translator of cuneiform tablets:

"Together with bread, onions, fish, and seed-seasoning, beer was one of the more important items in the ancient Mesopotamian diet. The Sumerians seemed to have made a fermented beer by combining barley and water, and adding flavorings such as malt. Beer was used as part of the rations of government officials, and messengers, and was widely expended in offerings to gods and goddesses, such as for the goddess Angina, at the field-offering for deceased persons, and much was consumed at the palace. For all these purposes, beer was collected from the people, either as a form of taxation or as a religious gift."

From the following translations of cuneiform tablets by Mr. Kang, one can see that beer was an important commodity.

Hieroglyphics such as this one suggest that beer drinking was a part of early Egyptian life.

Tablet Nr 191

1 ordinary beer, royal (quality)
—inspected by the constable of the
*   king: for the sheep-shearing.*
Receipted by the governor.
The year when the city Simurum was
*   destroyed for the 9th time.*

Tablet Nr 293

550 sila of fine beer
31 gu, 190 sila of ordinary beer for the meal
*   offering: from Lú*
Receipted by Ur-sa
The month of the goddess Lisin
The year when the city of Sassurum was
*   destroyed.*

Tablet Nr 300

18 sira of fine beer,
70 ordinary beer,
60 weaker beer, 15 sila,
for the offering of prayer to the goddess
*   Inanna at Uruk,*
*   on the 28th day.*
From Ur-mes.
Receipted by the governor.

The month of the divider.
Year that in which the city Simanum was
*   destroyed.*

Tablet Nr 313

15 sila of fine beer,
55 sila of ordinary beer,
*   on the 16th day;*
15 sila of fine beer,
50 sila of ordinary beer,
*   on the 17th day;*
10 sila of fine beer,
40 sila of ordinary beer,
*   on the 18th day;*
40 sila of beer,
*   on the 19th day;*
15 sila of fine beer, 40 sila of ordinary beer
*   for queens and priestesses.*
From A'alli.
Receipted by the governor.
The month of the 6-month temple.

Translations also reveal laws and religious prayers and hymns that refer to beer or its ingredients.

"The waitress, who gives free beer or barley, can not ask for anything in return."

"When certain criminals and political dissidents gather at the tavern, and the waitress will not turn them over to the Palace (authorities) — she will be killed."

Life was tough for nuns, too:

"Should a nun open a beer-house, or even so much as step into a tavern (beer bar) for a beer — this citizen will be burned."

The allure of beer must have been strong, even for the religious. Here is a prayer to (or about) Ninkasa, the great goddess:

Ninkasa, the smart gem of her mother,
Her mash tun is of greenish Lapis lazuli,
Her beer stein is made of hammered silver
and gold.
Her presence by the beer makes it seem magnificent,
She brings joy when she sits by the beer.
With a special mug she pours the beer, and
goes about untiring, having the mug
tied around her waist.
May the wine I serve be especially good.
The bird who drank the beer is sitting here
and is happy,
He is supposed to help me find the troops
of Uruk.

Another prayer:
The gods cried over the land.
She was not hungry because of her distress,
but was thirsty (longing) for a beer.

In 1933, the ancient city of Mari, on the Middle Euphrates in eastern Syria, was excavated by French archaeologists. Some 13,000 tablets were discovered, as well as the ruins of a palace. Mari was pillaged by Hammurabi of Babylon around 1760 B.C. The important point is that the tablets shed light not only on international relations, but also on the public and the private lives of the inhabitants.

The people at court lived and ate well. The tablets reveal that the people ate beef, mutton, wild game, and fish, as well as vegetables such as peas, beans, and cucumbers. Garlic was available. Dates, figs and grapes were commonly mentioned in the tablets, along with herbs and spices. According to the tablets, bread was made in several forms. One was thin crisp disks made from barley flour (for baking bread, wheat flour is vastly superior to barley flour). There was also leavened bread. So, the basic ingredients for making beer were at hand — barley, and yeast in leavened bread. Indeed, beer was locally produced, but wines had to be imported from other countries.

In Babylon, under Nebuchadnezzar, beer was the main drink. It was brewed in many different styles that determined which herbs and spices were used to flavor it.

So, before we had the Great Pyramids, and the Sphinx, and Cleopatra's needles, before the mighty Greek and Roman empires, there was beer.

Sadly, brewing and the brewing culture in Mesopotamia were destroyed by the Mohammedan conquests of the Middle East in the 8th century A.D. The Koran, the holy book of the people, forbids the consumption of alcohol. (Some secular Middle Eastern states do, now, brew beer: Iraq, Iran, Israel, Lebanon, Syria, and Turkey. Most of the breweries are state owned.)

Phoenicia was the ancient Greek name for the long and narrow coastal strip of Palestine-Syria extending from Mount Carmel north to the Eleutherus River in Syria. Phoenicia developed into a manufacturing and trading center early in the history of the Near East. By the second millennium B.C., a number of Phoenician and Syrian cities, including Arvad, Berytus, Byblos, Sidon, Tyre and Ugarit, achieved preeminence as seaports. They vigorously traded in purple dyes and dyestuffs, glass, grain, cedar wood, wine, weapons, and metal and ivory artifacts. Since the beer culture passed from Mesopotamia into Egypt, it is conceivable that Phoenician ships made beer runs along the North African coasts.

Early in the first millennium B.C., Phoenicians explored the Mediterranean as far as Spain and into the Atlantic, establishing colonies on the Tunisian coast at Carthage (ca. 800 B.C.), beyond the Strait of Gibraltar at Cadiz, and elsewhere along the Atlantic coast. Phoenician enterprise turned the Mediterranean, from the Levant to Gibraltar, into a great maritime trading arena. The Phoenicians were merchants and sailors. They only participated in domestic homebrewing and therefore their contribution to the beer culture was localized.

HL

See HECTOLITER.

HOEGAARDEN BREWERY, INTERBREW N.V. HOEGAARDEN, BELGIUM

The village of Hoegaarden has a history of brewing dating back to 1318. Monks settled in the area in 1445, and by 1770 were producing more than 25,000 hl of beer each year. By 1880, this village of 2,000 had 35 breweries.

The major product of the Hoegaarden breweries was a white (wheat) beer, but this style declined in popularity during the post–World War II era, and the last brewery closed in 1957. The tradition was revived by a milkman named Pierre Celis, who had worked in one of the local breweries as a youth. Celis's Hoegaarden Brewery single-handedly resuscitated the white beer style. Interbrew, S.A., brewer of Artois, one of Belgium's major brewers, eventually bought him out. After selling Hoegaarden, Celis emigrated to Austin, Texas, where he started a successful microbrewery.

The flagship white beer is made from a mix of malted barley and wheat. Hops, coriander, and curaçao are then added to the boil. The wort is cooled, and fermentation begins in large (1,400 hl) fermenters. At a certain point, small amounts of sugar and yeast are added to the beer. Once it is bottled or kegged, it is kept in warm storage to allow a secondary fermentation to take place.

Today Hoegaarden's white beer is popular throughout Europe, where it is highly regarded for its healthful properties. The brewery produces more than 800,000 hl per year. Hoegaarden white beer is imported into the United States by Paulaner North America of Englewood, Colorado.

See CELIS BREWING CO. and WHEAT BEER.

HOEGAARDEN WHITE

See BELGIAN WHITE BEER.

HOFBRÄU MUNCHEN MUNICH, GERMANY

Founded in 1589 as the Bavarian court brewery of Wilhelm V, Hofbräu moved to its current location in 1828. As Germany's political institutions evolved, Hofbräu passed from royal hands to those of the state government. To this day, the company is operated by the government of Bavaria.

The brewery produces beer for its world-renowned beer hall, the Hofbräuhaus. The Hofbräuhaus was renovated in the late 19th century, became a favorite of the Nazi party during its rise to power (Adolf Hitler delivered speeches there on occasion), and today is the premier international gasthaus in Munich. On any given day, the Hofbräuhaus is mobbed with tourists. It can accommodate 2,500 people within its cavernous halls. An outdoor beer garden offers a somewhat less raucous environment in which to sample Hofbräu's beers, which are uniformly excellent.

The brewery is said to be one of the originators of the bock beer style, and its Maibock and Delicator doppelbock are not to be missed. Hofbräu produces numerous brands, including Altmunchner Hellgold, Altmunchner Dunkelgold, Munchner Kindl Weissbier, Pils, Urbräu Hell, Weizen Hefefrei, Delicator, Maibock, Octoberfestbier, Octberfest Märzen, and Festbier.

In the past, the company's beers have been imported by Hudepohl-Schoenling of Cincinnati, Ohio, a regional brewery and sometime beer importer with German roots.

See BOCK BEER and OKTOBERFEST BEER.

HOLSTEN BRÄUEREI A.G. HAMBURG, GERMANY

Holsten is an aggressively international German brewer, producing beer at seven German breweries and eight foreign plants.

Holsten Diat Pils

In 1952, Holsten developed an extended fermentation process intended to convert a greater amount of the wort sugar to alcohol. The beer that was created using this process was originally aimed at diabetics but became Great Britain's most popular German import. Holsten Diat Pils was introduced in the United States in 1989 as Holsten Dry. It is a crisp, highly attenuated beer with an assertive hop character.

The company proudly states that foreign markets account for 40 percent of its sales, and Holsten Premium is now sold in more than 40 countries. In the United States, Holsten brands are imported by Holsten USA in Tarrytown, New York.

See DRY BEER.

HOMEBREW BITTERING UNIT (HBU)

A formula devised by Charlie Papazian to estimate the bitterness of hopped malt extract. It is also called the alpha acid unit (AAU). The HBU is determined by multiplying the equivalent number of ounces of hops by the alpha acid percentage of the hops used. For example, 2 ounces of 5 percent alpha acid hops in a 3.3-pound can of hopped malt extract would yield 10 HBU.

See ALPHA ACID UNIT and INTERNATIONAL BITTERNESS UNIT (IBU).

HOMEBREWING

The craft of brewing beer at home rather than in a brewery setting. Homebrewers in the United States look to the American Homebrewers Association (AHA) as their primary support organization. In many cities and towns across the United States there are homebrewing

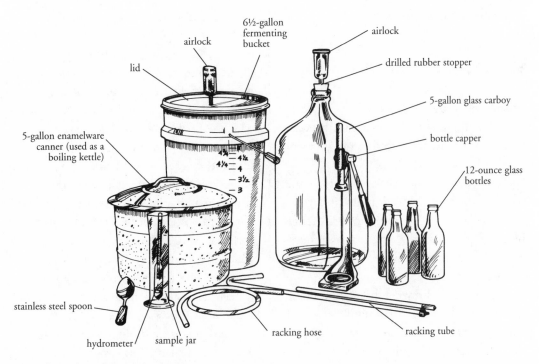

Basic homebrewing equipment

Homebrewers are often so involved in their craft that they design and print their own labels.

clubs that provide technical support, recipe sharing and troubleshooting information to homebrewers.

See AMERICAN HOMEBREWERS ASSOCIATION and ASSOCIATION OF BREWERS.

HONEY

Honey is most often used in making meads, although commercial craft brewers also use it to make interesting variations of standard styles.

The type of honey used will affect the flavor of the beer or mead. Light honey flavors are provided by sage flower, orange blossom, clover, alfalfa, and mixed honeys. Stronger flavors are provided by buckwheat and heather honeys.

When used in brewing, honey should be pasteurized, because it contains yeast and bacteria. Many homebrewers and mead makers prefer to boil their honey, but doing so may drive off volatile aromatic compounds.

To pasteurize the honey while preserving its delicate flavor, it may be heated in a pressure cooker to 176°F (80°C) for 2½ hours. The honey is then added to the beer in the primary ferment when the yeast reaches high kraeusen (a large head of foam). The amount of honey added will depend on the type of honey and the intensity of flavor desired. Subtle honey flavors are achieved with 1 pound (0.45 kg) or less per 5-gallon (19 L) batch, noticeable honey notes with about 2 pounds (0.9 kg), and very pronounced honey characteristics with more than 3 pounds (1.35 kg). When honey constitutes a significant percentage of the fermentables in a malt-based beer, it is often referred to as a bragget. The character of meads is dominated by honey, which constitutes up to 100 percent of the fermentables (some variations include significant fermentables from apple cider, grape juice, and other fruits). Honey is approximately 25 to 35 percent water, leaving 65 to 75 percent fermentable sugars — and that is 100 percent fermentable sugar, which is why meads often have a final gravity of less than 1.000 (alcohol is lighter than water). The sugars in honey are primarily the simple sugars (monosaccharides) fructose and glucose, although trace amounts of maltose and sucrose are present.

HOP BACK

A stainless steel vessel into which wort from the brew kettle is cast in a brewery using whole hops in the boil. The vessel has a removable slotted or drilled base that acts as a strainer. The kettle is cast, and the hops are allowed to settle over the strainer. Normally, a cone-shaped bottom is used in a hop back, which enables the hops to build a deep, packed base. This further aids filtration of the wort, as precipitated proteins remain on top of the hops during runoff to the fermenting vessel.

Fresh whole hops can be added into the hop back prior to casting the brew kettle to help impart some hop fragrance. When running off from a hop back, the first few gallons are normally recirculated until bright wort is achieved.

HOP BINE

A twisting, leafy stem of the hop plant. The leaves and hop cones sprout from the bine. Each plant has several bines.

Hop bines are trained along strings either up a central pole or to overhead wires to which the strings are attached. They may grow to more than 20 feet, although some new varieties of hops grow to a more manageable length of 8 to 10 feet. The new varieties produce the same yield as their much taller relatives.

Hop flower

Trained hop bines

HOPS

The vining plant *Humulus lupulus,* a member of the Cannabinaceae Family. This is a native perennial plant found in the temperate zones of Europe, North America, and Asia and is used almost exclusively for brewing purposes. Hops are believed to have many medicinal properties, such as aiding sleep, stimulating appetite, and aiding digestion. Hops also are used as a preservative. A related annual species, *Humulus japonicus,* grows in Japan and is used mainly as a quick-growing garden screen.

The grooming of hop plants is the subject of this illustration.

The common hop originated in Europe and is a long-lived perennial with rough, climbing stems that wind clockwise around a support or trellis. The plant can grow up to 25 feet (7.5 m) in a single season. Under favorable conditions, hops have been recorded growing 6 inches (23 cm) in a single day. The stem produces strong, hooked hairs that help the plant cling to its support. The leaves are dark green, hairy, and heart-shaped. They are serrated and deeply lobed, with three to five lobes each.

Hops are dioecious — that is, they have separate male and female plants. Identification of the sex of the plant is possible only when the plant blooms. The male flowers form pyramid-shaped, loosely branched flower clusters that are 2 to 6 inches (5 to 23 cm) long. The male plant is usually not used except in breeding new hop strains or in improving crop yields. Wind carries the pollen to the

Weighing hops at the Samuel Smith Brewery in Yorkshire, England

The female hop plant is the one used in brewing.

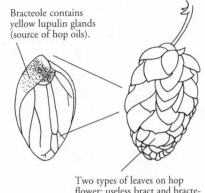

Bracteole contains yellow lupulin glands (source of hop oils).

Two types of leaves on hop flower: useless bract and bracteole with seed and lupulin

The hop flower

Located at the inside base of the bracts are many tiny yellowish glandular sacs called lupulin glands. These sacs contain resins and essential oils, along with nitrogen, sugars, pectin lipids, and wax. They can make up as much as 15 percent of the flower's weight. The resins and essential oils contained in the lupulin glands provide the distinct bitterness, flavor, and aroma in beer, as well as its reputed medicinal attributes.

How Hops Are Grown and Processed

Hops grow well over a wide range of climatic and soil conditions but thrive best in deep, well-drained soil. Soil that is shallow, contains an abundance of clay, or does not drain well should be avoided. Hops require plenty of water during spring and summer but none in autumn. They need direct sunlight and should not be grown in regions that are subject to long, severe winters. They prefer warm, windless summers and should be harvested before the first

female flowers — short spikes or catkins that hang in clusters. During their development, the stem elongates and the petals, or bracts, expand, forming the scales of the mature cones, or strobiles. The mature strobiles are yellowish green and oblong or ovoid in shape. They can be up to 4 inches long and feel papery. The mature, dried strobiles constitute the commercial hop.

The bracteole leaves of the female plant are the source of hop oils.

frost. In autumn, winter, and early spring, the soil should be prepared for the upcoming season by weeding and adding manure before the shoots appear.

Propagation is done by taking root cuttings in the winter after the plant has withered and gone dormant. This is done by uncovering the root of the plant and locating a large shoot with numerous buds, also known as a rhizome. The rhizome is cut off and planted sometime before the spring growing season. This method ensures the continuation of a particular strain, as each new plant will be genetically identical to its parent.

At a typical commercial farm in the United States, hops are planted in rows of hills spaced 6 to 8 feet (2 to 2.5 m) apart, with the rows 7 to 8 feet (2 to 2.5 m) apart, yielding 680 to 1,000+ hills per acre. In England, hops are planted 3 to 7½ feet (1 to 2 m) apart, with the rows 6 to 9 feet (2 to 3 m) apart, depending on the trellis system used, yielding 774 to 2,420 hills per acre.

Growing methods vary from country to country, but in all cases some support for the vines must be provided. Generally in the United States and England, the vines are trained to climb strings suspended from wire trellises and attached to a stake at each hill. In other countries, the vines climb poles located at the hills. In the United States, two strings are used per hill, whereas in England two or four strings are used. As a rule, two vines usually share a string. The height of the trellises ranges from 8 to 25 feet (2.5 to 8 m) depending on the country. In the United States, almost all trellises are 16 to 18 feet (5 to 5.5 m) high to facilitate the use of harvesting machines.

Hops are heavy feeders, needing a lot of calcium, nitrogen, phosphorus, and potassium. These are added in either organic or inorganic form. In the United States, the common source is farmyard manure or green manure, onto which a cover crop of a nitrogen-fixing plant is sown in the fall and plowed under in the spring. In England, large amounts of manure, fishmeal, and other materials are added in the fall and plowed under in the spring.

When the hops are ripe, they become bright yellowish green, sticky, crisp, and papery. At this time, they contain the maximum number of lupulin glands. Overripe cones turn a darker yellow, shatter easily,

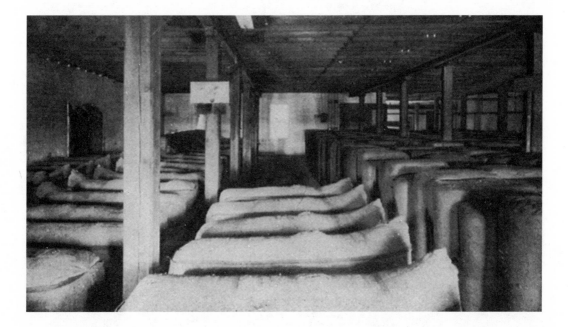

Dried hops are aged in bins for 1 to 12 days.

and have lost some lupulin glands. For the most part, hops mature fairly consistently from year to year, depending on the variety and the environmental conditions. When harvesttime arrives, hops are picked by hand or by machine. In the United States, they are picked almost entirely by machine. In England, they are picked by both methods. Some people consider handpicking to be the superior method, as fewer lupulin glands are lost during the harvest.

The typical procedure in the United States is to cut the vines and take them to a mechanical harvester housed in a shed. A typical large-scale picker, or harvester, has wire picking fingers or loops mounted on bars that travel over the vines, plucking the cones as they pass. Portable machines and other picking designs are also used.

Once the hops are picked, they are gathered and taken to a hop kiln, or oasthouse, as it is called in England. There they are loosely and evenly scattered on a slatted floor covered with burlap or wire mesh. The bed of hops may be up to 40 inches in depth. Hot air is then allowed to pass through the hops by natural convection or by forced air for deeper beds. Fresh hops have a moisture content of around 80 percent, which is reduced to about 8 percent by drying. Temperatures are usually 140° to 150°F (60° to 65.5°C) for bittering hops and 130°F (54°C) or less for aromatic hops. The drying time ranges from 6 to 20 hours depending on the depth of the hop bed, humidity, air temperature and velocity, and original moisture content of the hops.

HOP PICKING IN NEW YORK

Hops are being harvested in this illustration from Twenty-five Years of Brewing, *published in 1891.*

pressed into "pockets" that weigh about 160 pounds (72 kg).

Most hop bales are sold to a hop broker. The broker inspects the hops and accepts or rejects them based on their quality. After they are accepted, they are analyzed for alpha acid content and many other characteristics, then placed in storage in a refrigerated warehouse. Without direct sunlight and under low temperature (around 32°F, or 0°C) and low moisture conditions, they suffer little oxidation and will keep for up to 2 years.

Typically, a buyer from a brewery will purchase a year's supply of hops. The brewery will then take shipments from the broker who is storing the hops on-site. The broker will take samples and test the alpha acids throughout the storage stage.

Forms: Whole, Plugs, Pellets, and Oils

The dried hops are moved to bins, where they will cure for 1 to 12 days, depending on the capacity of the bins. Curing allows the moisture left in the hops to equalize. It also improves the aroma and makes the hops more pliable to withstand the baling process.

The cured hops are then compressed into bales. In the United States, a hop bale is approximately 18 cubic feet (0.5 cubic meters) and weighs around 200 pounds (90 kg). The hop bale is then wrapped in plastic or burlap. Some growers vacuum seal the bales under nitrogen or carbon dioxide in an oxygen barrier–type material such as a foil-Mylar laminate. In England, bales are com-

Whole hops are also called leaf hops or whole-leaf hops. These terms are somewhat misleading because the flower, not the leaf, is used for brewing. Whole hops are the hops taken directly from the bales and repackaged into smaller containers. These hops will expand to near their original size and look the same as before baling, though a bit flattened, and most of the lupulin glands will be intact. Poor storage and packaging materials may cause whole hops to lose their alpha acids and essential oils faster

Three of the four kinds of hops used in brewing are pellets (top left), plugs (bottom), and whole flowers (upper right). The fourth form is hop extracts or oils.

than other forms of processed hops. With today's oxygen barrier packaging and cold storage, however, their quality is usually ensured.

Hop plugs are whole hops that have been compressed into approximately .5-ounce (14 g) plugs that measure 1 inch (2.5 cm) across and are 5 inch (1.3 cm) thick. These are also known as Type 100 pellets. They take up one-third the space of whole hops.

Hop pellets are made by running the hop bale through a hammer mill to reduce them to a fine powder. The powder is then compressed and extruded through a pellet die to make a final product that looks much like rabbit food. Great care is taken to generate as little heat as possible to prevent the loss of too much of the hop resin. Typically, the pellets are vacuum sealed in foil bags weighing 44 pounds (20 kg). Hop pellets take up about one-quarter the space

of whole hops. They are also known as Type 90 pellets.

Hop extracts and oils fall into one of three main categories: iso-alpha extracts, hop oil extracts, and total extracts containing all the hop elements. Iso-alpha extracts add bitterness to beer but do not add flavor or aroma. Hop oils add aroma but no bitterness. Total extracts provide bitterness, flavor, and aroma. The process used to make these extracts varies, but solvent extraction is the most common method for making iso-alpha extracts and total extracts. Steam distillation is used to make hop oil extracts directly from whole hops or from a total extract.

Measuring Hops: Oils and Acids

The amount of essential oils in hops is about 0.5 to 2 percent of the total weight. It is rare to find the oil content listed on a package of hops, but some suppliers have started listing it. The oil is very volatile and is lost quickly during storage and in the boiling of beer. Thus, aromatic hops are added late in the boil or at the end. They also may be added after the first stage of fermentation, which is called dry hopping. Less than 2 ppm of hop oil is normally used. Typically, 1 to 4 ounces (28 to 113.5 g) of whole hops or pellets are used in a 5-gallon (19 L) batch of homebrew. The amount and variety of hops used depend on the style of beer being made.

251

Hop oil contains more than 200 different compounds, and it has been extremely difficult, if not impossible, to identify all the compounds that provide the aroma and flavor in beer. Humulene, myrcene, and caryophyllene make up 80 to 90 percent of all hop oils. However, they do not provide all the aroma and flavor. Research has shown that a combination of the three major compounds along with some of the many minor compounds accounts for a beer's aroma and flavor.

The amount of the three major compounds is used as a metering device in the breeding of new hop strains. Most aromatic hops have a higher percentage of humulene than of myrcene and caryophyllene. Only new hop strains containing higher concentrations of humulene will be tested as potential aromatic strains.

This greatly reduces the number of test brews needed and significantly reduces the amount of time required to develop a new strain.

Hops also are measured for the amount of alpha acid they contain. This is expressed as a percentage, found by dividing alpha acid weight by the total hop weight. This percentage is important to brewers because they are trying to maintain a consistent product, and the alpha acid content of hops varies from harvest to harvest and may be affected by prolonged or improper storage. By knowing the alpha acid content of the hops, brewers can calculate exactly how much hops to add to their brew.

The exact amount of bitterness of a beer is measured in International Bitterness Units (IBU). One IBU is approximately equal to about 1 mg of iso-alpha acid per 1 L (1.06 quarts). To obtain the exact IBU, a sample of beer is shaken with a solvent of iso-octane, which extracts the iso-alpha acids from the beer. This mixture of solvent and iso-alpha acids is then placed in a spectrophotometer and exposed to ultraviolet light. The spectrophotometer measures the amount of light that is absorbed by the mixture, which is proportional to the amount of

Native Americans in western Washington State picking hops in the 1880s. American hops were in great demand then because of the hop blight in Europe.

Hop Variety Comparison

Variety	(%) Alpha Acid	Class	Storage	(%) Humulene	(%) Oil	Aroma	Origin
B.C. Goldings	5.0	A	P	45	0.7	Mild, slightly flowery	Canada
Brewer's Gold	7.0	B	P	12	1.5	Neutral	England
Bullion	7.5	B	P	12	3.2	Neutral	England
Cascade	5.8	A/B	P	13	1.2	Floral, spicy, citrusy notes	USA
Centennial	10.5	A/B	G	14	1.9	Medium, floral, citrusy	USA
Chinook	13.0	A/B	G	23	2.0	Mild to medium, spicy	USA
Cluster	7.0	B	VG	17	0.6	Medium, spicy	USA
Crystal	3.3	A	P	25	1.3	Mild, noblelike	USA
East Kent Goldings	4.8	A	P	45	0.7	Mild, slightly flowery	England
Eroica	12.0	B	P	0.5	1.0	Minimal	USA
Fuggle (English)	5.0	A/B	F	38	1.4	Mild, superior to domestic	England
Fuggle (domestic)	4.8	A/B	F	23	0.9	Mild	USA
Galena	13.0	B	VG	13	1.1	Medium	USA
Hallertau Hersbrucker	4.3	A	F	20	1.0	Mild to strong, noble	Germany
Hallertau Northern Brewer	8.5	A/B	VG	28	1.9	Medium to strong, distinctive	Germany
Hallertauer (domestic)	4.0	A	P	34	0.8	Mild, slightly flowery	USA/Germany
Hallertauer Mittelfrüh	4.5	A	P	40	1.0	Very fine, noble	Germany
Hallertauer Tradition	6.0	A	G	50	1.2	Very fine, noble	Germany
Hersbrucker (domestic)	4.5	A	F	25	0.9	Light, spicy	USA/Germany
Liberty	4.0	A	P	38	0.9	Mild, spicy notes, noble	USA
Lubelski or Lublin	4.0	A	F	30	1.0	Very mild, noble	Czech Republic/Poland
Mt. Hood	6.5	A	P	20	1.2	Mild, noble	USA
Northern Brewer (domestic)	9.0	A/B	G	25	1.9	Medium to strong	England/USA
Nugget	13.0	A/B	G	17	2.0	Heavy, herbal	USA
Perle	8.3	A/B	VG	31	0.8	Slightly spicy	USA/Germany
Pride of Ringwood	10.0	B	P	1.5	2.0	Medium	Australia
Saaz	3.8	A	P	43	0.6	Very mild, noble	Czech Republic
Saazer (domestic)	4.0	A	P	23	0.6	Medium, inferior to Saaz	USA
Spalt Spalter	4.3	A	P	19	0.8	Mild, slightly spicy, noble	Germany
Spalter (domestic)	4.5	A	P	15	0.8	Mild, inferior to Spalt Spalter	USA
Spalter Select	5.0	A	G	20	0.8	Mild, slightly spicy, noble	Germany/USA
Styrian Goldings	5.3	A/B	G	30	0.8	Mild	Slovenia
Super Styrians	9.0	B	F	12	0.9	Medium	Slovenia
Tettnang Tettnanger	4.5	A	P	23	0.8	Mild, slightly spicy, noble	Germany
Tettnanger (domestic)	4.5	A	P	21	0.6	Mild, slightly spicy, noble	USA
Willamette	5.0	A/B	F	25	1.3	Mild, spicy notes	USA
Wye Target	11.0	B	P	11	1.4	Medium	England

Storage Key:
P = Poor   G = Good
F = Fair   VG = Very Good

Class Key:
A = Aromatic   A/B = Aromatic or Bittering
B = Bittering

Keep in mind the following:

1. The average alpha acid content is based on whole hops and will vary from season to season. The average alpha acid content will be lower for hop pellets.
2. Storage is a rating designed to estimate how much alpha acid is lost during a 6-month storage period at 68°F (20°C). Poor indicates 41 percent or more alpha acid lost, Fair 31 to 40 percent, Good 20 to 30 percent, and Very Good less than 20 percent. Hops kept in an airtight container at temperatures below 32°F (0°C) can be stored for up to 2 years.
3. The Origin column is not necessarily where the strain originated but the country or countries of major production.

iso-alpha acids in the sample. From this data, the IBU number can be calculated.

Unfortunately, a spectrophotometer is too expensive for most microbreweries, brewpubs, and homebrewers. Thus, another method of measuring hops, the alpha acid unit (AAU). This is a measurement of the alpha acids or potential bitterness in 1 ounce of hops. For example, if 1 ounce of hops had an alpha acid content of 6.4 percent, the hops would be said to have 6.4 AAU; ½ ounce of these hops would have 3.2 AAU. The AAU is also known as the homebrew bittering unit (HBU). Both units are identical.

The major drawback of the AAU is that it is a measurement of the amount of hops being added to the beer, not the amount of bitterness in the final product. Only a fraction of the alpha acids in the hops will be used during the beer-making process. If a brewer starts out with 10 AAU of hops in the beer, the best he or she can hope for is 3 AAU of bitterness in the final product. The actual amount of alpha acids extracted depends on many factors, such as boiling time, how vigorous the boil is, the specific gravity of the beer, and the type of yeast used. The AAU is not the best unit of measurement when trying to maintain a consistent product.

Hop Varieties Available to Homebrewers

Many hop varieties are available to homebrewers. They are generally divided into two categories based on when they are used in the brewing process. Bittering

hops are added early, and all their essential oils are driven off during the boiling process, leaving the bitterness behind. Aromatic hops are added at the end of the boil to retain their essential oils, which impart flavor and aroma but little or no bitterness. A few varieties can be used for either bittering or aroma. See the table on the previous page for a comparison of hops by variety.

A small group of aromatic hops are called noble hops, so named by brewers for their superior ability to impart aroma and flavor. The definitive noble hops are Saaz, Hallertauer Mittelfrüh, Spalt Spalter, and Tettnang Tettnanger. Any other noble hop is measured against these four.

There are as many different beer recipes as there are brewers, and each brewer has a favorite hop to use. Following is a basic hop variety substitution chart. This can be helpful if a particular hop is not available. The substitutes listed are meant only as guidelines. Brewers should feel free to experiment.

Using Hops in Recipes: Utilization Rates and Times

When adding bittering hops to beer, it is important to know that not all the alpha acids will be extracted from the hops. It takes a minimum of 10 minutes of boiling to get any bitterness from the hops. This is because the alpha acids must first go through an isomerization process to form iso-alpha acids, which finally provide the bitterness. One would think that since it takes a long time to start extract-

Hop Substitutions

Variety	Substitutes
B.C. Goldings	Fuggle, East Kent Goldings, domestic Fuggle, Willamette
Brewer's Gold	Northern Brewer, Galena
Bullion	Northern Brewer, Galena
Cascade	Nothing equivalent, but it is widely available
Centennial	Cascade
Chinook	Galena, Nugget, Cluster
Cluster	Galena, Chinook
Crystal	Liberty, Mt. Hood
East Kent Goldings	Fuggle, B.C. Goldings, domestic Fuggle, Willamette
Eroica	Galena, Nugget, Chinook, Cluster
Fuggle (English)	Domestic Fuggle, Styrian Goldings, East Kent Goldings, B.C. Goldings
Fuggle (domestic)	English Fuggle, Styrian Goldings, East Kent Goldings, B.C. Goldings
Galena	Cluster, Nugget, Chinook
Hallertau Hersbrucker	Crystal, Liberty, Mt. Hood
Hallertau Northern Brewer	Domestic Northern Brewer, Perle
Hallertauer (domestic)	Crystal, Liberty, Mt. Hood, Hallertau Hersbrucker, Hallertauer Tradition
Hallertauer Mittelfrüh	Hallertauer Tradition, Crystal, Liberty, Mt. Hood
Hallertauer Tradition	Crystal, Liberty, Mt. Hood
Hersbrucker (domestic)	Crystal, Liberty, Mt. Hood
Liberty	Crystal, Mt. Hood
Lubelski or Lublin	Saaz, Spalt Select
Mt. Hood	Crystal, Liberty
Northern Brewer (domestic)	Perle, Hallertau Northern Brewer
Nugget	Galena, Chinook, Cluster
Perle	Northern Brewer, Cluster, Galena
Pride of Ringwood	Galena, Cluster
Saaz	Lubelski
Saazer (domestic)	Lubelski, Spalt Spalter, Spalter Select
Spalt Spalter	Spalter Select, Spalter, Saaz, Tettnanger
Spalter (domestic)	German Spalter, Spalter Select, Saaz, Tettnanger
Spalter Select	German Spalter, Saaz, Tettnanger
Styrian Goldings	English Fuggle, any of the Goldings, domestic Fuggle, Willamette
Super Styrians	Galena, Northern Brewer, Cluster
Tettnang Tettnanger	Domestic Tettnanger, Spalt Spalter, Spalter Select, Saaz
Tettnanger (domestic)	Tettnang Tettnanger, German Spalt, Spalter Select, Saaz
Willamette	East Kent Goldings, Fuggle, Styrian Goldings
Wye Target	Any bittering hop

ing the alpha acids, a longer boil will extract more — and maybe all — the alpha acids. The problem is that after a certain length of time, the iso-alpha acids start breaking down and are lost. The breakdown usually starts happening after about 2 hours of boiling. It is for this reason that most brewers boil only for 60 to 90 minutes.

How much of the alpha acids are retained at the end of the boil depends on how vigorously the wort is boiled, the specific gravity of the wort, the amount of alpha acids introduced, the form of the hops, the boiling time, the wort pH, the type of yeast used in the fermentation process, and quite a few other factors. What all this means is that many factors work against the brewer when he or she tries to calculate exactly how much bittering hops to use to produce a beer with a specific IBU level.

To calculate the amount of alpha acids that will actually make it into any given 5-gallon (19 L) batch of beer, the brewer must know several factors ahead of time. Some of these will not apply in all cases.

1. The concentration of the wort being boiled *(CW)*. If the wort is not diluted after the boil but is a full 5 gallons (19 L), *CW* = 1. Otherwise, calculate *CW*.

CW = Final Volume / Boil Volume

2. Use the original gravity *(OG)* from your recipe and the *CW* from factor 1 to calculate the gravity factor of the wort *(GFW)*. If *OG* is 1.050 or less, *GFW* = 1.

$$GFW = (((CW \times (OG - 1)) - 0.05) / 0.2) + 1$$

3. Calculate the hopping rate factor *(HRF)*. IBU is the desired IBU of the final beer.

$$HRF = ((CW \times IBU) / 260) + 1$$

4. Altitude affects the temperature at which the wort will boil. The higher the elevation, the lower the boiling temperature. If you live at sea level or very close to it, *AF* = 1. Otherwise, calculate *AF*.

$$AF = ((\text{Elevation in Feet} / 550) \times 0.02) + 1$$

Multiply all the factors together to achieve a combined factor *(CF)*.

$$CF = CW \times GFW \times HRF \times AF$$

Boiling time of the wort will have an effect on extraction efficiency, or utilization. Locate the length of your boil in the following chart:

Boil Time	% Utilization
30 minutes	11
45 minutes	18
60 minutes	20
75 minutes	22
90 minutes	23

Find the percentage of alpha acid *(%AA)* on your hop package. Plug in the numbers to calculate the amount of bittering hops you need:

$$\text{Hops in ounces} = \frac{\text{Volume in Gallons} \times CF \times IBU}{\text{Utilization} \times \%AA \times 0.749}$$

The volume is the volume at the end of the boil, normally 5 gallons (19 L), and *IBU* is the IBU of the final beer.

Example:

The recipe calls for an original gravity of 1.055. The altitude is 1,000 feet. The desired IBU is 32. A partial boil of 3.5 gallons (13 L) will be done, diluting to 5 gallons (19 L) after a 1-hour boil. The percentage of alpha acid on the hop package is 7.8%.

$$CW = 5.0 \text{ gallons} / 3.5 \text{ gallons} = 1.4$$

$$GFW = (((1.4 \times (1.055 - 1)) - 0.05) / 0.2) + 1 = 1.14$$

$$HRF = ((1.4 \times 32) / 260) + 1 = 1.17$$

$$AF = ((1000 / 550) \times 0.02) + 1 = 1.04$$

$$CF = CW \times GFW \times HRF \times AF = 1.4 \times 1.14 \times 1.17 \times 1.04 = 1.94$$

The amount of hops you'll need for a 1-hour boil:

$$\text{Hops} = \frac{5 \times 1.94 \times 32}{20 \times 7.8 \times 0.749} = 2.66 \text{ ounces}$$

Since some of the alpha acids will be lost to the yeast, the answer can be rounded up to 2 ounces.

Remember that the calculation above will give an estimate, and the only way to determine the exact IBU of the final product is to measure it with a spectrophotometer. The estimate is a good starting point, and your taste buds will tell you whether you need to adjust your bittering hops up or down the next time. Keep in mind that hop utilization rates differ by hop form: Rates for whole hops are significantly lower than those for pellet hops.

Choosing Hops: Matching to Recipes and Styles

There are many styles of beer and many varieties of hops. It is important to use the proper hop variety when trying to duplicate a particular beer style because each hop has a different combination of flavor and aroma attributes and intensity. The following chart lists the common hop varieties and their suggested beer styles.

Hops become the predominant bittering agent

We know beer was brewed over 8,000 years ago, but the earliest indications of hops being used as beer flavoring dates to between the 10th and the 7th centuries B.C. Hops were used in pharaonic Egypt by at least 600 B.C. Evidently, their use in ancient times was not remembered or passed along, or the information did not travel to Europe, because their use there as a bittering agent and as a preservative did not begin until around the 7th or 8th centuries. Some historians place the beginning

Hop Variety vs. Beer Style

Variety	Suggested Beer Style(s)
B.C. Goldings	English milds, pale ales, India Pale Ale, porters, stouts
Brewer's Gold	English ales, heavier German-style lagers
Bullion	English ales, heavier German-style lagers
Cascade	American pale ales, California common, stouts, porters American wheat
Centennial	American pale ales, American wheat, stouts, porters
Chinook	Pale ales to lagers, California common, India Pale Ale
Cluster	Any style
Crystal	American and German lagers
East Kent Goldings	English milds, pale ales, India Pale Ale, porters, stouts
Eroica	Wheat beers
Fuggle (English)	English milds, pale ales, India Pale Ale, porters, stouts
Fuggle (domestic)	English milds, pale ales, India Pale Ale, porters, stouts
Galena	Any style
Hallertau Hersbrucker	German lagers, ales, wheat beer
Hallertau Northern Brewer	California common, German lagers
Hallertauer (domestic)	German lagers, ales
Hallertauer Tradition	All lagers
Hersbrucker (domestic)	German lagers, ales
Liberty	All lagers
Lubelski or Lublin	Pilsners
Mt. Hood	American lagers, German lagers, ales
Northern Brewer (domestic)	California common, German lager
Nugget	Any style except light lagers
Perle	American pale ales, porters, German lagers and ales
Pride of Ringwood	Australian styles
Saaz	Pilsners
Saazer (domestic)	Pilsners
Spalt Spalter	German lagers, altbier
Spalter (domestic)	German lagers
Spalter Select	German lagers
Styrian Goldings	English milds, pale ales, India Pale Ale, porters, stouts
Super Styrians	Any style
Tettnang Tettnanger	German lagers, ales, American "premium lagers," wheat beer
Tettnanger (domestic)	German lagers, ales, American "premium lagers," wheat beer
Willamette	English milds, pale ales, India Pale Ale, porters, stouts, American ales
Wye Target	English ales and lagers

An illustration of hop cones from Twenty-five Years of Brewing

in the 11th century in the Czech Republic, where it became commonplace. However, references were made in 768 to "humlonaria" — or the name given to hop gardens — given to the Abbey St. Denis by King Pèpin le Bref. There were hop gardens at the Abbey St. Germain des Prés in 800, and at Corvey Abbey sur le Wesser in 822. In 855 and 875, there are references to humularium in the records of the Bishopric of

Cultivating the hops

Freising in Upper Bavaria. The presence of hop gardens suggests that hops were used in beer.

Before the 20th century, change took place very slowly. It only began to speed up with the spread of the Industrial Revolution and increased economic strength. The time between discovery and implementation is often measured in centuries. Part of this must surely be because time, and its most efficient use, is at the forefront of human consciousness. The plant itself is native to northern temperate zones in West-Central Asia, Northern Europe, and North America where it grew wild. Now hops are under human care as a cash crop, nurtured and looked after in much the same manner as grapes.

The use of hops spread out of Central Europe, carried along by the monks who were then the brewers in society. Their use was late arriving in England, where brewers stuck to other traditional means of spicing beer. As a bittering agent and as a preservative, which is what brewers were searching for all along, hops are superior to all other plants. Due to its qualities, it became the standard brewers settled on. Upon standardization, the uniformity of beer narrowed somewhat, though not completely, due to the vast varieties of hops available, diverse in their aromas and their bitterness.

HOPS CATEGORIES

There are three categories of hops from which brewers can choose. The choice is dictated by the use (and tradition) which they are intended. The three categories are copper hops, late hops and dry hops.

Copper hops are used in the boiler, i.e., the copper (the boilers of old were made of copper, hence the name). Copper hops are usually high in alpha acid, the bittering agent. When used in the boiling stage, fewer high–alpha acid hops than low–alpha acid hops are needed per brew volume, making them more economical.

Late hops are used just at the end of the boil, usually within the last 5–15 minutes, to restore much of the aromatic and flavor-giving elements that are driven off during the boil. These elements evaporate very quickly when heated. They are also called volatiles.

Dry hops are inserted in the primary ferment, the secondary ferment, or in the cask directly after filling. The purpose of dry hops is to add additional aromatic properties to the beer.

See HOPS.

HOT BREAK

The process of boiling wort so that proteins, carbohydrates, polyphenols, hop acids, and other substances coagulate in the wort and settle to the bottom of the brew kettle, contributing to the trub, which is the undesirable material that should be left in the brew pot when the brewer racks off the fermenter. The trub is approximately 40 to 65 percent proteins;

5 to 10 percent each carbohydrates, bittering substances, and polyphenols; and 1 to 2 percent fatty acids. Some brewers recommend skimming trub off the wort as it forms in the boil.

Decoction mashes break down the proteins to a greater extent, resulting in less trub. Additives such as Irish moss are often added to the kettle to encourage the coagulation of proteins and to force more material to drop out of suspension. The trub can be removed by filtering the wort through a hop back or by using a whirlpool.

See COLD BREAK and TRUB.

HOT LIQUOR BACK

A stainless steel tank in which the brewing liquor is treated (if necessary) and heated to the mash strike temperature. This tank can be heated using electricity, gas, or steam, and its temperature is thermostatically controlled.

HOT SIDE AERATION (HSA)

The addition of oxygen to the wort during its production. Aerating hot wort causes melanoidins and tannins in the wort to become oxidized, which can result in a stale flavor in the beer. Hot side aeration can be avoided by treating the wort gently during its production, especially when collecting sparge runoff from the mash and after boiling, when chilling the wort. Many brewers do not feel that hot side aeration is very significant.

JOSEPH HUBER BREWING CO., MONROE, WISCONSIN

A relatively large regional brewery (capacity 450,000 barrels) founded in the mid–19th century, Huber now produces a dizzying array of brands (many of them passed down from other now-defunct regionals). Among these are Alpine, Bavarian Club, Berghoff, Berghoff Dark, Berghoff Bock, Berghoff Light, Bohemian Club, Boxer Malt Liquor, Bräumeister, Bräumeister Light, Dempsey's Ale, Holiday, Huber, Huber Bock, Hi-Bräu, Regal Bräu, Van Merritt Light, Wisconsin Club, Wisconsin Gold Label Malt Liquor, Old Chicago, Rhinelander, and Rhinelander Bock.

Huber once produced Augsburger, a celebrated midwestern specialty beer. The company sold the label to Stroh, which now makes a full line of all-malt specialties and seasonals under the label.

See FRUIT, VEGETABLE, HERBAL, AND SPECIALTY BEERS and REGIONAL BREWERY.

HUDEPOHL-SCHOENLING BREWING CO. CINCINNATI, OHIO

Hudepohl-Schoenling is the ungainly name that resulted from the 1986 merger of two grand old Cincinnati breweries,

Hudepohl Brewing Co. and Schoenling Brewing Co. (Hudepohl Brewing Co. was founded in 1855 and Schoenling in 1934). Now fondly known as "Cincinnati's Brewery," the company brews a variety of local brands in a large utilitarian plant in the heart of the city.

Hudepohl-Schoenling was one of the first of the old-style regionals to brew a revivalist all-malt lager, a brand called Christian Moerlein (named after another historic Cincinnati brewer), and its darker cousin, Christian Moerlein Double Dark. The company also has made hay in the contract market, brewing a variety of beers and malt-based coolers for private labels. More recently, the brewery has turned to nonalcoholic beverages in a big way and has become

Christian Moerlein Double Dark

This dark, malty lager made its debut when characterful beers were few and far between in the Midwest. Today it has more competition in the specialty beer arena, but it remains a solid entry.

a substantial producer of packaged teas. This adaptable brewer also serves as an importer for a number of European labels, including Mackeson Stout.

See LAGER ALE and REGIONAL BREWERY.

BRÄUEREI HURLIMANN A.G. ZURICH, SWITZERLAND

Founded in 1836, Hurlimann has an annual capacity of 700,000 hl. The company's primary products are Hurlimann, a lager; and Sternbräu and Hexenbräu, dark lagers. The brewery may be best known for its Samichlaus, imported into America by Phoenix Importers, Ellicott City, MD.

See LAGER ALE.

Samichlaus

A contender for the title of strongest beer in the world. At 13 to 14 percent alcohol by volume, it is stronger than most wines. Samichlaus is a very sweet, malty, heavy-bodied beer. Rich and heady, it is best suited for sipping by a roaring fire after a long day of strenuous activity. More than just a beer, it could be marketed as a restorative tonic.

HYDROMETER/ SACCHAROMETER

A floating instrument used for determining the specific gravity of a liquid. Normally made of glass, it is weighted at one end. The stem of the instrument is graduated to indicate the gravity of the liquid in which it floats.

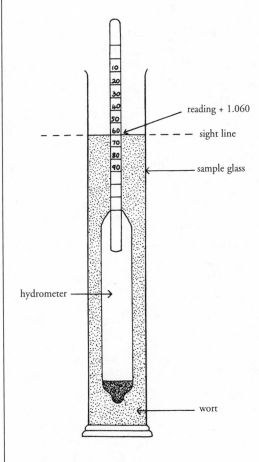

reading + 1.060

sight line

sample glass

hydrometer

wort

Reading the hydrometer

HYDROMETER/SACCHAROMETER

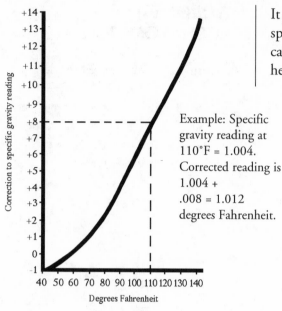

Temperature corrections for hydrometer readings

It is used in breweries for monitoring the specific gravity of wort and beer. In this case, the gravity is specific for sugar levels, hence the term *saccharometer*.

Example: Specific gravity reading at 110°F = 1.004. Corrected reading is 1.004 + .008 = 1.012 degrees Fahrenheit.

IBU

See INTERNATIONAL BITTERNESS UNIT (IBU).

ICE BEER

Beer whose alcohol content and flavor are concentrated by freezing the beer and then removing the ice, thus reducing its total volume and the density of all the ingredients. The Canadian brewer John Labatt introduced this beer in the winter of 1992–93, followed closely by Molson. The method of production is similar to that used to produce the Niagara Brewing Co.'s Eisbock in 1989. The idea is to concentrate flavor rather than increase alcohol content.

The beer, after fermentation, aging, and the addition of water, is brought down to about 25°F (-4°C) for about 2 days, long enough for ice crystals to form. The ice crystals are then filtered out, and the beer is bottled or kegged as usual. The alcohol content is slightly higher than usual (except Bud Ice, which has the same alcohol content as regular Bud because the ice crystals are left in). This is about 5.5–6.5 percent alcohol by volume, compared to about 4–5 percent in regular American and Canadian beers. There are even ice malt liquors (Colt Ice, Pabst Iceman) and light ice beers.

The concept of increasing alcohol content by freezing beer and removing the ice is patently illegal in the United States, as the Bureau of Alcohol, Tobacco and Firearms has declared such production to be "distillation." However, in this case, the process is perfectly legal because American (and Canadian) industrial brewers invariably brew their beers by the heavy brewing method. In that system, brewers start with less water and add the missing water at the end of the process. As a result, brewers can manufacture more beer with the same amount of equipment. As long as they do not concentrate the beer (by freezing) to less than they started with, the process is legal.

See EISBOCK and HEAVY BREWING.

ICE BUILDER

A type of chilling device that has a large liquid reservoir containing a multitude of cooling tubes. The reservoir can be set up for water, brine, or propylene glycol. The ice builder is hooked up to one or more condensers, which provide refrigeration via the tubes in the tank.

Liquid is cooled to a desired, preset temperature, then the coils start to build up ice (up to 2 inches) over their surface. This ice acts as stored BTUs and provides further cooling. The reservoirs (up to several thousand gallons) are well insulated and very efficient in providing consistent cooling. The liquid medium may then be used in heat exchangers or cooling coils or jackets.

IMPERIAL STOUT

See STOUT — IMPERIAL.

IMPORT

Beer produced in another country and brought in for merchandising purposes. Imported beer held a five percent share of the United States beer market in 1994. The substantial market for imported beer in the United States sets it apart from other societies. Although United States brewers have the capacity to meet demand easily with in-country production, American consumers find imported beer appealing.

Historically, the United States has been a very open market for beer, without the prohibitive tariffs that restrict the sale of imported beers in other countries. In most markets (Japan and the United Kingdom, for example) international beers are produced under license by domestic brewers.

Typically, this is the approach that United States brewers take when entering foreign markets — even in Canada (where Molson brews Miller and Coors beers and Labatt brews Budweiser).

American beer consumers seem to be finicky about where their beer comes from, and foreign beers brewed on these shores have not fared very well. Lowenbrau is the most visible example — a beer that went from being one of the top imports to a virtual nonentity in the years after Miller started brewing it in the United States.

Some foreign brewers have started producing their beer in Canada, so it can still be called "imported."

Import market share has varied somewhat from year to year, given vagaries of currency and demand, but analysts believe that imported beer will continue to play an important role in the United States market.

IMPORTER

A business that imports malt beverages produced in foreign countries into the United States. Federal law mandates that a company must have an importing license before it brings beer into this country. Importers must also submit their labels and packages for approval by the Bureau of Alcohol, Tobacco and Firearms before a given brand can be approved for importation. Each state also has its own labeling laws, which must be adhered to.

INCUBATOR

A piece of equipment used in the laboratory to store media, yeast slants, streaked growth plates, and beer bottles at ideal growth temperatures (generally 98.5°F, or 37°C). Incubators enable a fast, controlled growth of living microorganisms, which is important for yeast growth and quality control tests.

INDIA PALE ALE

A strong, paler variant of regular pale ale. George Hodgson, a London brewer, is credited with "inventing" India Pale Ale (IPA) near the end of the 18th century. At that time, the British were very busy consolidating their hold on the giant subcontinent of India. They had sent thousands of soldiers, seamen, merchants, bankers, and colonial administrators to that country. These folks all needed beer, and porter did not ship well. Beer was not so much a luxury as a necessity, as the purity of water supplies in India and elsewhere was unreliable.

Hodgson brewed his special India Pale Ale to be very high in alcohol content and highly hopped, both in the kettle and in the shipping cask. This provided excellent protection against souring. In addition, new malting methods coming into vogue allowed the production of paler malts than had been possible before. The nearly 5-month journey from England to India had a beneficial effect on the beer, as the continuous movement of the ship

India Pale Ale is the name derived from a very strong ale brewed in England and transported to the British troops stationed in India in the 18th century.

helped ensure maximum fermentation. The ship also crossed the equator twice during the journey, which resulted in two warm ferments. The attenuation (fermentation) rate was very high, and the beer finished out very dry, with a good amount of carbon dioxide in it.

India Pale Ale was very popular, and it soon gained a great reputation for brewer Hodgson. He had the trade to himself until about 1820, when other brewers, notably Alsopp and Bass (Burton-on-Trent brewers), joined in with their products. Alsopp developed even paler malts, allowing for an even paler product, and the sulfate-rich Burton water was much better for brewing the style than London's carbonate water.

Original IPAs may have been brewed as strong as 17–22/1.070–1.090 OG and hopped to an incredible 12.5 g/L. With Fuggle or Kent Goldings hops, this could amount to an overwhelming 150 IBU. Dry hopping at somewhere near 5.5 g/L (adding flavor and aroma, not bitterness) also was used. By the 1880s (the peak of the trade), the beer was being brewed to more modest gravities (about 15–17/1.060–1.070), a very dry final gravity of less than 2, 7–8.4 percent alcohol by volume, something above 55–70 IBU, and around 12–18 SRM. Although the beer was brewed and shipped in wood, that wood was probably English oak, which is harder and contains fewer tannins than other oaks and imparts less of its character on the beer.

The modern brewer's authentic IPA should be brewed with pale malts and perhaps some caramel malt to 14–17/1.057–1.070 OG, 6.4–8.1 percent alcohol by volume, 40–60 IBU (using English Fuggle or Kent Goldings hops plus dry hopping), and a pale 6–15 SRM. Some American craft brewers make this style too pale and much too mild; others inject oak chips for a wood flavor. This latter method is a definite flaw, as an IPA does not need a wood flavor to be authentic. Clearly the most famous American IPA is Ballantine Old India Pale Ale. The Ballantine Brewery closed the doors of its Newark, New Jersey, plant in 1972 after being acquired by Falstaff. The old Ballantine ale was, as the label declared, "aged in wood one year" (resin-lined wood in this case), then bottle-conditioned. The beer is still made (by Pabst–General Brewing), but, as the profiles below show, it is not at all the same product as the earlier Ballantine ale.

The Great American Beer Festival guidelines for India Pale Ale are 12.5–17.5/1.050–1.070 OG, 5–7.5 percent alcohol by volume, 40–60 IBU with a "full flowery hop aroma," and 8–14 SRM (deep copper color). It should be brewed from water with a "high mineral content."

Original Gravity	Final Gravity	Alcohol by Volume	IBU	SRM
Anchor Liberty Ale 1975				
14.8/1.061	3.3	6%	54	≈13
Alsopp India Pale Ale Red Hand 1901				
15.1/1.062	2.2	6.9%	≈75	≈16
Ballantine IPA 1960				
17.5/1.072	3.7	7.8%	60	≈13
Ballantine IPA 1994				
14/1.056	2.4	6.2%	37	≈5
Bass Pale Ale 1898				
17/1.070	2.75	7.7%	≈75	≈16
Grant's IPA 1983				
12/1.048	1.6	5.5%	55	≈10
United States IPA Rochester NY 1906				
16.6/1.068	2.6	7.6%	≈75	≈16

See BOTTLE-CONDITIONED BEER, BURTON ALE, PALE ALE, and WHITE HORSE IPA.

INDUSTRIAL BEER

See AMERICAN BEER and AMERICAN LAGER.

INFUSION MASH

A mashing method in which the malted barley and any other adjunct grains are soaked in water at hot, but not boiling, temperatures. This differs from the decoction mash in that no portion of the mash is ever heated to the boiling point.

The water and malted barley are mixed (usually referred to as "doughing-in" or "mashing-in") at a temperature of 146° to 158°F (63° to 70°C). Temperatures in the upper part of that range produce more dextrins (unfermentable sugars) and will yield a more robust body, while those near 148°F (64°C) produce more maltose (fermentable sugars) and a thinner body. This step of converting starches to sugars is called saccharification and is the single most important step in more complicated mashing methods. The infusion method assumes that the malts are well modified, and therefore it is most commonly associated with brewing ale. Most brewers use a pale ale malt with an infusion mash; however, most other malts today are fully modified and also will work with an infusion mash.

The grain is usually put into the mashing vessel (often a pot or a picnic cooler in a home brewery), and then hot water (about 170°F, or 77°C) is mixed with the grain until the desired temperature (about 150°F, or 65.5°C) is reached. The grain also can be added to the water. The mixture is then held as close to that temperature as possible for anywhere from 30 minutes to 2 hours. Shorter periods are used with mashes at higher temperatures, longer periods with lower temperatures. A typical mashing schedule might call for maintaining a temperature of 149°F (65°C) for 1 hour.

See DECOCTION MASH, MASHING, SACCHARIFICATION, and STEP MASH.

INFUSION MASH TUN

A circular stainless steel vessel, insulated to prevent heat loss, where crushed malted barley is mixed with heated brewing liquor to create the mash. In this simple system a one-step saccharification temperature (146° to 152°F, or 63° to 67°C) is achieved for conversion of starches to fermentable sugars. Well-modified malt is used in this process. The vessel has a false bottom standing 1 to 2 inches above the real bottom. The false bottom is either slotted or drilled with holes to allow drainage of clear wort from the vessel.

IN-LINE CARBONATOR/ AERATOR

A pinpoint mechanism using sintered tubing in pipework to provide gas injection of carbon dioxide or oxygen in-line to passing liquid. Many breweries use this mechanism to aerate wort moving from the brew kettle to the fermenting vessel and to carbonate beer flowing to the bright beer tank.

INSTITUTE FOR BREWING STUDIES

P.O. Box 1679
Boulder, CO 80306-1679
303-447-0816
Fax 303-447-2825

A branch of the Association of Brewers, the Institute for Brewing Studies compiles statistics on North American microbreweries and brewpubs and works within the framework of the Association of Brewers to educate microbrewers, homebrewers, and the community at large about brewing.

See ASSOCIATION OF BREWERS.

INSTITUTE OF BREWING

Major F. Bolton
33 Clarges Street
London
W1Y 8EE United Kingdom
001-44-171-499-8144
Fax 011-44-171-499-1156

A technical and educational organization that offers United Kingdom breweries programs to improve techniques.

INTERNATIONAL BITTERNESS UNIT (IBU)

An international system for measuring and expressing the bitterness in a given beer based on the parts per million content of alpha acid. The formula, where H = weight of hops in grams per liter, a% = alpha acid percent, b% = beta acid percent, 9 = a constant, and 0.3 = a 30% rate of efficiency in hop extraction, is:

$$IBU = H \times \frac{(a\% + \frac{b\%}{9})}{0.3}$$

The IBU is to some extent an estimate, since other factors such as wort gravity and boiling time significantly affect bitterness extraction.

INTERNATIONAL LAGER

The European version of American lager, brewed in the Bohemian or Pilsner style but with adjunct grains. Also called Euro-lagers, Euro-Pils, or Continental Pils.

International lager is a very pale beer with medium alcohol content (4.4–5.7 percent by volume), mild to slightly assertive taste (noticeable to moderate, or even impressive, hoppiness), and usually some hop bouquet. Original gravity is 10–13/1.040–1.052, final gravity 2.2–3.7, bitterness 22–30 IBU, and color 2.5–4.5 SRM. Ingredients are pale 2-row European barley malt and/or 6-row barley malt, with a minimal grain adjunct of not more than 25 to 30 percent rice or corn. Continental hops are used — Hallertauer, Northern Brewer, Saaz, Tettnang, Spalt, or Perle — along with medium-hard water (to 400 ppm hardness).

The Great American Beer Festival guidelines for Continental-Style Pilsners are 11–12.5/1.044–1.050 OG, 4–5 percent alcohol by volume, 17–30 IBU, and 3–4 SRM.

Original Gravity	Final Gravity	Alcohol by Volume	IBU	SRM

Becks (Germany) 1982 (for export only)

| 11/1.044 | 3.1 | 4.6% | 23 | 2.5 |

Harp Lager (Ireland) 1985

| 11.1/1.044 | 3.2 | 4.5% | 24.5 | 2.7 |

Heineken (Netherlands) 1982

| 12.2/1.049 | 2.7 | 5.2% | 17 | 4.3 |

Swiss Brewing Institute Standard (Switzerland) 1984

| 12/1.048 | 2 | 5.2% | Unknown | Unknown |

See AMERICAN LAGER and BOHEMIAN BEER.

INVERT SUGAR

A syrup of cane sugar (sucrose) and acid sometimes used as an adjunct. It is listed in some homebrewing texts, especially those from Great Britain. Invert sugar is sometimes sold under the name Lyle's Golden Syrup.

To make invert sugar, dissolve 1 pound (0.45 kg) of sugar in ¼ cup (59 ml) of water over low heat. When it forms a light syrup, add ⅛ teaspoon (0.6 ml) of tartaric acid and heat for a few minutes until golden brown. Do not boil.

ION

An atom that has either lost or gained one or more electrons and therefore has a net electrical charge. A *cation* is a positively charged ion (has lost one or more electrons), and an *anion* is a negatively charged ion (has gained one or more electrons).

Water can weaken the bonds that hold molecules together and dissolve the molecules. When a molecule is dissolved in water, it is *ionized* into its basic components. For example, sodium chloride will ionize into Na^+ and Cl^-.

See WATER.

IRISH ALE

A variation on pale ale, with caramel malt that gives the beer its reddish tinge and rounded flavor. Legend has it that the first king of Ireland was enveloped in a magic cloud while horseback riding. There he met a Celtic god with a beautiful young girl who handed him a glass of foaming red ale, and that may be where all the talk about Irish red ale began.

Irish ales are similar to Scottish ales but are a bit lighter and paler. Several Irish ales are brewed today, but they are not very distinctive. The most famous of bygone eras was that produced by G. H. Lett of Enniscorthy, County Wexford, which ceased production in 1956. Lett licensed its Ruby Ale to Pelforth in France and later to Coors in the United States. The beer, known in the United States as George Killian's Irish Red, is bottom-fermented and not particularly noteworthy, but with more taste than most other Coors products.

Lately, some other brewers have been making Irish reds and/or Irish ales. Typical of these is McGuire's Irish Red Ale (draught) from Pensacola, Florida. A bottled version, brewed in New Orleans, also is available. Vermont Burly Irish Ale is found only at the Vermont Pub and Brewery of Burlington, Vermont. Red ales and lagers seem to be the new wave, but not all are "Irish" and many are virtually tasteless.

Original Gravity	Final Gravity	Alcohol by Volume	IBU	SRM
George Killian's Irish Red (Colorado) 1987				
15.5/1.062	2.8	6.8%	17	≈16
McGuire's Irish Red Ale (Florida) 1993				
12/1.048	3.4	4.6	≈20	≈8
Smithwick's Export (Ireland) 1992				
12/1.048	≈2.6	≈5%	≈32	≈13
Vermont Burly Irish Ale (Vermont) 1989				
11/1.044	3.5	3.7%	18	≈25

See AMBER AND RED BEERS and SCOTTISH ALE.

IRISH MOSS

A type of seaweed used to settle out proteins that can lead to cloudy or hazy beer. It is added during the last 15 to 30 minutes of the boil at a rate of 1 tablespoon (14.79 ml) per 5 gallons (19 L) of wort.

See CLARIFICATION, CLARIFIER, and FININGS.

IRON

A metallic element that is not welcome in its ionized form in brewing water. The lower its concentration, the better, as it gives the beer an unpleasant, harsh taste. An acceptable limit for iron is fewer than 0.3 ppm. More than this amount will be noticeable and can interfere with normal yeast activity.

See WATER.

ISINGLASS

A substance made from shredded fish bladder that is used in brewing to help the yeast settle out of suspension in a finished beer. An electrostatic attraction pulls the yeast to the isinglass, which then settles to the bottom of the vessel. Isinglass is a must for cask-conditioned ales.

See CLARIFIER, FININGS, and HAZE.

MICHAEL JACKSON

Author Michael Jackson is widely known as the preeminent authority on beers from around the world. He is internationally recognized as the leading writer on beer, and his books on beer, travel, and spirits are available in 15 languages and have sold more than 3 million copies. The beer industry and beer connoisseurs from around the world owe a great debt to Michael Jackson, since without his desire to write about beer, its origins, its variations, and its appeal, the resurgence of the specialty beer segment might not have occurred, the microbrewery movement might never have been launched, home-brewing might have been left as a closet hobby, and beer might never have achieved the level of respect that it enjoys today.

Michael Jackson was born in the North of England and began his writing career by working

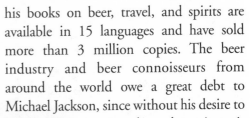

Michael Jackson is widely considered to be the pre-eminent authority on beer.

as a reporter on local newspapers. He began writing books on beer and whiskey in the 1970s because he felt that beer and whiskey deserved the same attention and respect that fine wines were receiving. His *World Guide to Beer, The Beer Companion,* and *The Pocket Guide to Beer* are still in print and continue to provide the backbone of information for those interested in beer. *The New World Guide to Beer,* a revised edition of his earlier book, was published in 1988.

Currently, Michael Jackson is a Director-at-Large of the North American Guild of Beer Writers and the first chairman of the British Guild of Beer Writers. Among Jackson's many awards is the Institute for Brewing Studies' first Achievement Award, and in 1994, Crown Prince Philippe of Belgium presented him with the Mercurius Award for Services to the Kingdom in recognition of his writings on Belgian beers. Additionally, he has lectured on Belgian beer at the Smithsonian Institution in Washington, D.C., and is a guest lecturer at Cornell University in New York. Jackson is currently involved in a television series called *The Beer Hunter,* which airs on PBS and the Discovery Channel, has been seen in 10 different countries, and is available on CD-ROM. He is also a professional beer judge at the Great American Beer Festival and a regular panelist at the Great British Beer Festival.

See BELGIAN BEER, GREAT AMERICAN BEER FESTIVAL, BRITISH BEER FESTIVAL, MICRO-BREWERY MOVEMENT, NORTH AMERICAN GUILD OF BEER WRITERS, SPECIALTY BEER, and INSTITUTE FOR BREWING STUDIES.

JEWISH TRADITION, BEER AND ALE IN

Jewish traditions about beer arose from Middle Eastern societies where wine drinking was usually the order of the day. However, the ancient Jews were not strangers to brewing. Shekar, the beer of the time, is mentioned in the Book of Isaiah. It comes from the Hebrew word for intoxication. Pre-Christian accounts of the Flood say that Noah was fond "not of the grape, but of beer," which he took aboard the ark. Noah's oldest son, Shem, took up beer making as an occupation, brewing from corn, dates, and honey.

During the Jews' captivity in Babylon, they brewed sicera, a highly potent beer thought to prevent leprosy. Several 19th-century scholars believed that the manna from heaven given to the wandering tribes of Israel was actually beer. This ancient bread-based beer, called boosa, is still made in the Sudan.

JIU/CHIU

A wheat beer made during the Han dynasty (200 B.C.) in China. Eventually, the character became the generic word for beer.

See CHINESE BEER.

JONES BREWING CO. SMITHTON, PENNSYLVANIA

A small regional brewery that produces the Stoney's and Esquire labels. The company also brews contract products, including Penn Pilsner for Pennsylvania Brewing Co. Jones has experimented with a number of other beers, including an amber nonalcoholic brew.

See CONTRACT BREWING, PENNSYLVANIA BREWING CO., and REGIONAL BREWERY.

JUDGING BEER

The evaluation of beer, usually for competitive purposes.

Beer judgings or competitions are generally by professional organizations, beer publications, or homebrew clubs. The venues of competitions vary widely, depending on the size of the event and the number of people expected to attend.

Professional Competitions

Professional and commercial competitions are usually held in spacious quarters because of the number of beers to be judged and then offered to the public.

Britain's CAMRA (Campaign for Real Ale), the world's largest beer drinkers' consumer group, conducts the GBBF (Great British Beer Festival). After competition results are announced, over 325 cask ales are available for sampling during the 5-day period of the festival. Judges at the GBBF are selected from among brewers, other beer consumer groups, the media (mostly print journalists), and others who are known to have a sound knowledge of British ales.

Some competitions restrict the kind of beers they judge; others take as many entries as they can. The GBBF is open only to cask-conditioned ales. The GABF (Great American Beer Festival) accepts almost all entries as long as they are brewed in North America.

Most professional panels have from three to eight members. A simple score sheet might include a list of criteria and the number of points to be assigned, while a complex score sheet might dictate the number of points to be awarded for each quality of the beer, with a ten-point category often called "overall impression."

Amateur competitions

Amateur competitions are often as well organized as the professional ones.

These competitions are usually run by homebrew clubs, county and state fairs, and beer publications.

Homebrew competitions often use the score sheet devised (and revised several times) by the American Homebrewers Association or the Home Wine and Beer Trade Association. Judging is often done by panels of two because of a lack of judges and the sheer number of styles and the number of entries. Tasting panels for beer publications often have more members and restrict themselves to a few beers (48) in one style. While homebrew and professional competitions take great care to conceal the identities of the beers from the judges, tasting panels for publications usually don't hide the beers being profiled. They are simply looking for feedback to pass on to their readers.

Criteria

First and foremost, beer judges need to examine how well a beer fits the style its brewer says it is and how it stacks up against its competition. Characteristics by which judges evaluate a beer include proper head retention and color for the style; aroma, bouquet, and taste within a style; carbonation and conditioning; mouthfeel and finish; hops and malt balance in both the nose and on the palate; and overall impression.

Evaluation based on these categories can often be done in one or two sips. Unlike wine drinkers, beer judges swallow the beers to experience it in the throat.

Making recommendations is not part of a beer judge's job description, although it often is for beer-tasting panels run by publications. A beer judge's role is to try to pick the best beers of each category.

The effort of defining beer styles is ongoing and critical to judges who must determine whether a beer fits its professed style. If a beer labeled a porter is presented, its score should rightly be marked down — even if it is a delicious beer — if it tastes like a Bavarian dunkel.

After the score sheets have been completed, the panelists usually discuss their scores and why the points were awarded.

This is the time for correction and adjustment. Several noses and palates are better than one, and what one judge suspected but was not sure of might be confirmed or rejected by another. After review, the points are again added up. In the event of a tie, second samples are often requested and further discussion occurs, with some minor adjustments made to the scores to select the ultimate winner.

A judge must throw out any personal likes and dislikes of particular styles. It simply won't do to have someone who doesn't like Bavarian weizenbier judging that style. An open mind is required.

There are several ways to become a judge. Participating in a beer-judge study group and then passing the exam is one way. The Beer

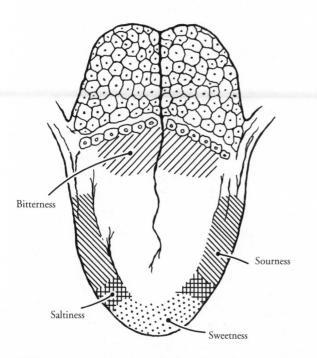

Different parts of the tongue allow the judge to distinguish the unique flavors of the style.

Judge Certification Program, once jointly run by several organizations, is now independent. Another way would be to become an acknowledged expert and be invited to judge based on life experience. (Michael Jackson and Roger Protz fit this category.) It takes time, practice, and much studying to become an expert judge. Knowledge of the breadth and depth of styles, profiles, grains, hops, yeasts, and the brewing process is very important, as is having a keen nose and palate. Having a cooking background helps immensely.

See JACKSON, MICHAEL.

JUPILER BREWERY
LIÈGE, BELGIUM

The Jupiler Brewery dates back to 1853, when it was started by the Piedboeuf family, makers of brewery equipment. The brewery got its water from the Jupille springs, and its barley and hops were grown locally.

In 1966, the company introduced the Jupiler brand, the most popular Pilsner in Belgium. Jupiler has just completed work on a new 4,000,000 hl brewery, which will replace the existing plant. The new brewery has four high-speed bottling lines and is geared to produce just one brand, Jupiler Pilsner.

See BOHEMIAN BEER.

KALEVALA

The epic poem of the Finns. It has more verses relating to brewing than to the creation of the world. In the *Kalevala,* the barley comes from Osmo's field, and his daughter brews the beer. The legend says that a song dealing with the origins of beer must be sung while the beer is brewed.

KAOLIANG

A style of beer made from sorghum in China during the Sung dynasty (A.D. 960–1278). *Kaoliang* is the Chinese word for sorghum, which is farmed in the province of Szechuan.

KEG

A draught beer container usually made of stainless steel. Beer passed into kegs is normally filtered and carbonated to approximately 2.5 volumes. Beer is dispensed from these containers by applying carbon dioxide or carbon dioxide– nitrogen top pressure and opening a liquid outlet

In this illustration from Twenty-five Years of Brewing, *published in 1891, kegs are being scrubbed to prepare them for reuse.*

valve. Modern kegs are of a single-valve, vertical-spear design whereby beer is pushed up through an internal spear through an attached coupling and to a beer line. Two-valve kegs have been used in the past and occasionally still are. On two-valve kegs the carbon dioxide fitting and product outlet fitting are separate features.

Kegs being filled

Normally, kegs are built to a 60 psi (413.57 kPa) internal pressure rating. However, beer generally should be dispensed at 12 to 20 psi (82.71 to 137.86 kPa) depending on beer type, pipe run, and carbonation. Carbon dioxide–nitrogen applications normally call for 25 to 30 psi working pressure.

THOMAS KEMPER LAGERS

See HART BREWING INC.

KENTUCKY COMMON BEER

See COMMON BEER.

KILN

A device used in malting to stop the germination process, so that the malt does not become overmodified and begin a growth cycle. A malt kiln usually consists of a rectangular brick building housing a heat source, or fire room, and draft air controls.

Above the fire room in the kiln is a room acting as a hot-air distribution chamber. A kiln usually has several drying floors located one above the other. Each floor has a device to turn the malt, and often the malt is sifted by way of perforations from one floor to another until the final dried malt is sent to dry malt hoppers. The air circulation through the malt beds reduces the moisture content of the malted barley between 3 percent and 4 percent.

Several different kiln designs are used throughout the world, but the basic function of all of them is the same. New designs have been attempted with attention to increasing energy efficiency.

KILNING

The process of heating germinated barley (or other grains) in a kiln to dry it, cure it, and color it. Kilning is usually done by passing hot air (about 200°F, or 93°C) through a bed of germinated grain. To produce colored grain, such as brown malt, chocolate malt, or black patent malt, the cured grain is roasted at much higher temperatures.

See MALTING.

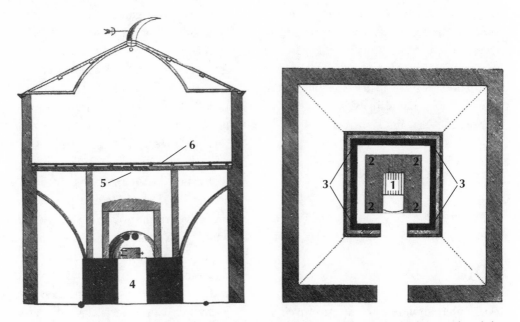

A kiln is a large furnace with a perforated floor. In ancient times, open fire heated the malt, while in more recent brewing times the malt is heated by oil-fire heaters, through which measured amounts of hot air dry and roast the malt to perfection. This illustration is of a malt kiln patented in 1796. 1—fire grate, 2—cellars, 3—brick pillars, 4—fireplace door, 5—kiln floor supporter, 6—kiln floor tiles.

KIRIN BREWERIES LTD. TOKYO, JAPAN

Kirin, Japan's top brewery, was founded by an American, William Copeland, in 1870. The brewery was later purchased by Japanese owners, who gave the brewery its striking Kirin logo — the image of a mythical half-horse, half-dragon.

Currently, Kirin operates 14 breweries, with an overall capacity of more than 30,000,000 hl. The company enjoys an approximately 50 percent market share in Japan and does a substantial export trade.

Kirin produces a wide array of brands, ranging from the flagship Kirin lager to specialty darks and stouts. Kirin beer for the United States market is brewed under license by Molson of Canada. The company's import business is handled by Kirin U.S.A., based in New York City.

See LAGER ALE and STOUT.

KIT

See MALT EXTRACT.

KOJI

An alpha amylase enzyme produced by the fungus *Aspergillus oryzae*. It is used in brewing a Jiu/Chiu type of beverage, similar to sake rice wine, to convert the starches in rice to fermentable sugars.

See ALPHA AMYLASE and JIU/CHIU.

KÖLSCH

An altbier with the pale color of a fine Pilsner and the fruitiness of a fine ale. Cologne (Köln), in Nord Rhein–Westphalen, is an area noted for its luscious white wines. Kölsch is defined by German law as top-warm-fermented and cold-aged, with a very pale golden color, though a little darker than Pilsner (3.3–5.7 SRM), and an alcohol content of 4.4–4.9 percent by volume. According to German law, this must be a vollbier (full beer) with an original gravity of 11.2–11.8/1.045–1.047 mostly from Pilsner and Vienna malts. It also may contain up to 20 percent wheat malt. Mashing is usually by single decoction, and the wort boil lasts 1½ hours or so. The beer has an aromatic bitterness and noticeable hop character (16–34 IBU), is well fermented, and is lagered cold for 14 to 40 days.

Kölsch is a relatively modern style and probably an attempt to compete with the very pale lagers that came into existence in the second half of the 19th century. It is served in a tall, narrow, straight-sided glass about 5 inches (13 cm) tall. The beer is properly served at 55°F (13°C) with a pale white collar about an inch deep. It is rarely imported into the United States, probably because few of Cologne's 13 city brewers and 13 vicinity brewers bottle their product. Nevertheless, it is becoming popular in the United States, where a number of craft brewers are producing it on a small scale.

The Great American Beer Festival guidelines for American Kölsch are 10.5–11.5/1.042–1.046 OG, 4.4–5 percent alcohol by volume, 20–30 IBU, and 3.5–5 SRM.

Original Gravity	Final Gravity	Alcohol by Volume	IBU	SRM
Gaffel Kölsch 1982				
11.6/1.046	1.8	5%	31	4.9
Stecken Kölsch 1982				
11.2/1.045	2.2	4.8%	21	3.4

See ALTBIER, BOHEMIAN BEER, and VOLLBIER.

KQED INTERNATIONAL BEER & FOOD FESTIVAL

By the close of the 1995 festival, San Francisco's public broadcasting station, KQED, will have a baker's dozen of mostly successful events to look back on with pride. A well-organized beer fest usually held the second Saturday of July, the KQED show puts more than 200 beers from around the world before the tasting public, with a number of food booths integrated into the plan. The event lasts only 3 hours, taxing the most ingenious beer sampler.

The festival is a fund-raiser for the TV station, but it is also a fun-raiser. Attendees may see a line of samba dancers leading a conga line around the festival floor — just one example of the eclectic entertainment provided.

Nearly 40 regional microbreweries are featured in the Pavilion of California Small Brewers. Microbrews from other states also

The KQED Festival attracts thousands of beer and food aficionados to its annual event.

are on hand, as well as imports. KQED offers free shuttle service from the event to various mass transit stops.

The sheer diversity of the festival — in terms of domestic and international beers and foods, unusual entertainment, and the attendees themselves — makes this long-running festival a perennial favorite.

KRAEUSEN

The thick rocky foam of flocculating yeast that rests on top of a batch of fermenting beer.

KRAEUSENING

KRAEUSENING

A method of conditioning beer that adds a small quantity of young fermenting wort to a fully fermented lager wort to create a secondary fermentation and natural carbonation.

See KRAEUSENING/WORTING.

Kraeusening is a method of conditioning which adds a small amount of young fermenting wort to a fully fermented wort to create natural carbonation in the beer.

KRAEUSENING/WORTING

An age-old tradition of naturally conditioning (carbonating) and clarifying beer. Kraeusening takes place at the end of the aging cycle when new, freshly fermenting beer in the high kraeusen stage of fermentation is added to aged beer, thus initiating a new ferment. (This stage is characterized by a cauliflower-like head on the brew.) The brewer then bungs the fermenters and conditions the beer by allowing the buildup of carbon dioxide. When the beer is ready, the brewer adds a clarifying agent to settle the yeast and proteins from the new ferment in the tank. This clarifying agent could be egg whites or isinglass, as in wine making, but early brewers used beechwood chips instead. These "chips" are actually shavings that are

6 to 12 inches long, to 1 to 2 inches wide, and ⅛ inch thick. They are boiled twice in water with bicarbonate of soda before being added to the ferment. Brewers also have used hazel chips or even aluminum slats to clarify the beer.

Today only a few brewers practice kraeusening. Among them are Olympia, Budweiser, and San Francisco's Anchor Brewing Co. in the production of its famous Steam brand beer.

British brewers have occasionally used a similar system by adding newly fermenting beer, or even fresh beer wort and yeast, to their fermented beer to create carbon dioxide buildup. Within the British cask-conditioning system, this is done by adding beer wort instead of sugar syrup to start a second ferment in the cask, then venting the carbon dioxide, as is usual for that process.

See BEER IN THE WOOD, CASK-CONDITIONED BEER, COMMON BEER, and FERMENTATION.

KRIEK

See BELGIAN FRUIT ALE.

BRASSERIE KRONENBOURG CHAMPIGNEULLES, FRANCE

Kronenbourg is an Alsatian brewery with fairly high name recognition among Americans. The Kronenbourg brand has had mixed fortunes in the United States but is remembered for an expensive but ultimately fruitless advertising campaign. Kronenbourg beers are still exported to the United States, but they do not have the visibility they did a few years ago.

Kronenbourg is part of France's largest brewing combine. The company operates six breweries with a combined capacity of more than 12,000,000 hl.

KULMBACHER BEER

See BAVARIAN BEER.

KULMINATOR (EKU KULMINATOR) AND THE WORLD'S STRONGEST BEERS

The beer EKU Kulminator Urtyp Hell 28 — which stands for Erste Kulmbacher Union Achtienbräuerei, original type, pale, 28 degrees Plato — was once the strongest beer in the world at 28/1.119 OG and 13.2 percent alcohol by volume. For a time, it was thought to be an Eisbock — that is, concentrated by freezing — but the brewery denies this. The German suffix *-ator* designates a strong doppelbock.

Today Kulminator is the strongest German beer, but the Swiss Samichlaus, a seasonal Christmas beer brewed annually on December 6, is stronger, and an American beer, Samuel Adams Triple Bock, is actually the strongest lager beer in the world (18.3 percent alcohol by volume). The strongest ale in the world is Thomas Hardy's Ale.

Original Gravity	Final Gravity	Alcohol by Volume	IBU	SRM
EKU Kulminator (Germany) 1983				
28.8/1.122	9.2	11.8%	29.5	≈22
Samichlaus Dark (Switzerland) 1987				
28.7/1.122	.14	14.9%	Unknown	≈30
Samuel Adams Triple Bock (Boston, Massachusetts, USA) 1994				
39.5/1.168	9.5	18.3%	17	≈25
Thomas Hardy's Ale (England) 1987				
29.9/1.127	12.5	12%	≈100	≈30

See DOPPELBOCK and EISBOCK.

L

An abbreviation for liter.

LABATT BREWERIES OF CANADA

Labatt Library Services
150 Simcoe Street
Box 5050
London, Ontario
Canada N6A 4M3
519-667-7242; Fax 519-667-7473

This dominating force in Canadian brewing operates a research library that is open to the public by appointment, but mainly functions as a recource for Labatt's legal department, chemists, and brewers.

JOHN LABATT, LTD. TORONTO, CANADA

John Labatt is one of Canada's two dominant brewers (the other being Molson).

John Labatt, Ltd. was acquired by Interbrew A/S, the large Belgian brewer, in June 1995.

John Labatt bought the brewery that would bear his name in 1847 and passed it on to his son, also named John Labatt. The brewery burned down twice in the 19th century, but the company persevered, broadening its markets until Prohibition was enacted in Ontario during World War I.

In the post–World War II era, Labatt began acquiring regional competitors at a rapid pace, adding myriad local brands to its portfolio. Today Labatt runs seven breweries across Canada and brews close to 50 brands, including Labatt Blue, Labatt Genuine Draft, Labatt Ice Beer, Labatt Velvet Cream Porter, Schooner, Kokanee Gold, Kootenay, Oland's Export, and Keith's IPA. Labatt also brews numerous foreign brands under license for the Canadian market, including Budweiser, Bud Light, Carlsberg, Guinness, and Suntory.

See CONTRACT BREWING, ICE BEER, INDIA PALE ALE, and PORTER.

Labels are automatically attached to bottles in most larger brewing operations today.

LABEL

A piece of paper that is glued to a bottle and contains the beer's brand name, brewery, alcohol content, and perhaps other information about the type or style of beer.

LABELER

A machine that applies labels to bottles. Labelers have various capabilities, including application of body labels, neck labels (spot or full wrap), back labels, and code dating. For best performance, labelers require high-quality water-resistant paper or foil labels and a suitable glue.

LACE

The pattern of bubbles sticking to a beer glass once the glass has been partially emptied. Sometimes referred to as Belgian lace, since the pattern resembles this ornamental fabric.

LACTIC ACID

An acid formed by *Lactobacillus* and *Pediococcus* bacteria that is generally unwelcome in beers, except in lambics. Lactic acid gives the beer a tart or sour taste, and certain strains of *Lactobacillus* or *Pediococcus* cause gelatinous or silky formations. Lactic acid does have a place in the brewing process, as it can be used to acidify the mash and sparge water.

LACTOSE

An unfermentable sugar ($C_{12}H_{22}O_{11}$) produced from whey. Often referred to as milk sugar, it is used in brewing to create residual sweetness and body. It is typically used in sweet stouts.

LAGER

One of two major beer types; ale is the other. Lager is fermented at lower temperatures than ale.

We now call ale original beer. It is fermented with a yeast that can work only at temperatures of 58° to 100°F (14° to 38°C). If the temperature of the ferment drops much lower, the yeast goes into a state of hibernation, building a cyst around itself in a process called sporulation.

In the Middle Ages, Bavarian brewers discovered that their yeast actually continued working even at very low (near freezing) temperatures. Indeed, when their beer was kept at these low temperatures, the result was a greatly improved, very smooth, mellow-tasting beverage. Although they had no grasp of how yeast worked, Bavarian brewers took to brewing their beer in the late fall, then storing it in deep caves, which they covered with ice harvested from nearby lakes and rivers. The beer was brought out at the beginning of the spring. This beer, because of its long stor-

age, came to be called lager beer, from the German *lagern*, "to store."

In the late 19th century, when scientists discovered the nature of yeasts and how to use them, they found that this Bavarian yeast lacked the ability to sporulate and continued working to produce alcohol and carbon dioxide at temperatures even below freezing. Moreover, the yeast settled to the bottom of the fermenting vessel at the end of the ferment, where it could be harvested by drawing off the finished beer and leaving the yeast. Because of this characteristic, this yeast came to be called bottom-fermenting yeast, and the beer was known as bottom-fermented beer.

In this cold climate, the chemical changes that yeast brings about are slowed considerably due to the fact that the speed of such activity doubles or halves with each temperature change of 18°F (10°C). Thus, a beer fermented at temperatures near 40°F (4°C) works only half as fast as one fermented at 58°F (14°C). The result is a beer with a much mellower and less assertive taste profile. Not only that, but the cold-fermenting and aging process keeps the beer from being infected with souring bacteria, so that it can be brewed lower in alcohol content and with fewer hops. A person can drink more of it without becoming inebriated, and the lower hop levels appeal to a larger segment of the population.

During the second half of the 19th century, developments in temperature control allowed the introduction of very pale malts, and thus very pale beer. Refrigeration was invented (allowing year-round cold fermenting and aging), and high-quality glassware allowed people to appreciate the aesthetic qualities of pale beer. All these factors came together, and a new beer was invented in Bohemia (now the Czech Republic). It was a cold-fermented, very pale, moderately hopped, mild beer that came to be called Pilsner, after Plzen, the city of its birth. This new beer type swept the planet. It was *the* beer to drink, and it made beer a popular drink of the masses. By the middle of the 20th century, the lager beer revolution had come to dominate beer drinking around the world. This dominance continued as brewers made lager ever paler, blander, less hoppy, and weaker. Only in England and Belgium did brewers continue producing the old-fashioned ales.

See ALE, REAL ALE, and REFRIGERATION.

LAGER ALE

A very pale, warm-fermented (58° to 75°F, or 14° to 24°C), cold-aged beer. After the introduction of Pilsner Urquell in 1843, very light-colored beers became quite popular in Europe and the United States. The Industrial Revolution and continental strife brought central European immigrants to the United States, an extraordinary number of whom were brewers. Their first desire was to make Pilzen-style beer — light, clean, and very pale. But proper cold/bottom-fermenting yeast was often lacking. American brewers had to make do with what they had. They tried to make the light-colored

Bohemian style ale using warm/top-fermenting yeasts in a warm ferment, followed by cold aging in the lager tradition. This was an improvement over the darker, less popular ales of the time, and the style was labeled "cream ale."

Cream ale was a paler pale ale. The warm ferment in the English tradition and the cold storage in the German tradition provided for convenience. As American lager developed, so did American cream ale, and along the same lines. After the introduction of steam beer in California, the cream ale method of brewing was adapted to the steam beer style, and American lager ale was born.

American lager ales were called "bastard ales" in the industry, but until the recent onset of the craft beer revolution, many of the more famous American "ales" were made in this fashion. Many of these lager ales taste almost identical to their lager counterparts: minimal taste profile, minimal hopping, and lacking in hop bouquet.

Traditionally, this beer type had an original gravity over 13/1.052, but today we find 11–14/1.044–1.056 OG, 1.7–2.8 final gravity, 4.4–5.6 percent alcohol by volume (medium, almost identical to that of the standard American lager), 10–22 IBU, and 2–4.4 SRM. The ingredients used are similar to those in American premium beers.

The Great American Beer Festival guidelines for American lager ale or cream ale are 11–14/1.044–1.056 OG, 4.2–5.6 percent alcohol by volume, 10–22 IBU, and 2–5 SRM.

Original Gravity	Final Gravity	Alcohol by Volume	IBU	SRM
Carling Red Cap Ale (Maryland) 1946				
12/1.048	2.7	4.9%	≈16	5.25
Labatt's 50 Ale (Canada) 1986				
11.6/1.046	2.1	4.9%	14	≈3.5
Little King's Cream Ale (Ohio) 1989				
12.2/1.049	2.5	5.1%	14	2
American sparkling ale 1901				
13.9/1.057	2.1	6.2%	≈60	≈6

See AMERICAN BEER, AMERICAN LAGER, and BOHEMIAN BEER.

LAGERING

The process of aging a beer at cool temperatures (35° to 50°F, or 2° to 10°C) for several weeks or months. Lager beers are often described as having a "clean" or "crisp" character. During the slow cold-aging process, many of the yeast by-products that contribute to off-flavors are reduced, and the proteins and polyphenols that create chill haze can settle out of the beer.

LAGER YEAST

A type of yeast (*Saccharomyces uvarum*) that ferments more slowly than ale yeast, forms smaller colonies, and tends to settle to the bottom of the fer-menter. Lager yeasts produce far fewer esters than do ale yeasts, and they result in a beer that is crisper in character and less fruity in aroma.

Lager yeasts ferment best at temperatures from about 40° to 50°F (4° to 10°C). They form small colonies not as easily supported by surface tension as ale yeasts; consequently they settle to the bottom, giving them their common characteristic as bottom-fermenting yeasts. They readily ferment fructose, galactose, glucose, maltose, maltotriose, mannose, melibiose, raffinose, sucrose, and xylulose.

See YEAST.

Holding tanks used in lagering

LAMBIC

A style of beer brewed only in Belgium. Also called wild beer because it is fermented by naturally omnipresent atmospheric yeasts. Most beers are fermented with the careful, totally sanitary addition of top-fermenting or bottom-fermenting yeasts. Lambic brewers add no yeast but allow the beer to ferment naturally with whatever yeast is in the air. Spontaneous fermentation is the oldest of all the fermenting styles.

Lambic beers are wheat beers made only in the area southwest of Brussels. This is the Bruegel country of Payottenland, in the River Zenne valley. The style probably originated in the village of Lembeek (current population 4,000), which once had 40 to 45 breweries. There is now one (Frank Boon, who has run the Breuwerij Frank Boon in Lembeek since 1989), but for a time there were no lambic brewers in Lembeek.

Originally, these wild beers were of three varieties: Mars, a low-alcohol (2 percent by volume) beer brewed only until March (hence the name) and no longer commercially made; faro, a medium-gravity blended beer often drunk mulled with a sugar cube, which has mostly gone out of style (a variation of it is still brewed, with sugar added: 6–8/1.025–1.032 OG/2.5–3.2 Belge); and lambic, a stronger beer that is still quite popular in Belgium but is being replaced by gueuze-lambic.

Since 1965, lambic and gueuze-lambic have been protected names in Belgium. Lambic beers are required to be brewed to an original gravity at least 12.9/1.052 OG/5.2 Belge, but in the old days they were often a good deal heavier. An 1839 sample had 21/1.084 OG/8.4 Belge, 9.8 percent alcohol by volume, 1.1 percent sugar, and 1.1 percent lactic acid. An 1871 sample had 17/1.070 OG/7 Belge, 8.1 percent alcohol by volume, 0.7 percent sugar, and 1.1 percent lactic acid. A faro from the same era was described as 13.8/1.056 OG/5.6 Belge, 4.3–5.4 percent alcohol by volume, 0.7 percent sugar, 0.9 percent lactic acid. Modern gueuze-lambic has a little over 6.3 percent alcohol by volume and similar acidity.

According to old brewing texts, lambic beers were made from about 50 percent raw wheat mixed with barley malt. Beginning in the early part of this century and up to 1946, many changes were made in the ancient process. Decoction mashing replaced the old infusion system, with 30-minute boils at each step. In the decoction system, a portion of the wort is converted (unfermentable starches converted to fermentable sugars), boiled, and returned to the mash, with the process repeated two or three more times.

Today at least 30 percent wheat is required; brewers typically use 30 to 35 percent wheat. The wort boil has been shortened to 4 hours, and hops have been reduced to 8 g/L. These are *surannes* hops — that is, hops that have been aged for 1 to 3 years, at which point they smell like cheese, are quite oxidized, and have lost their bittering properties. The hops retain their resin character and are very strong in bactericidal power. This protection is important to the final product, since it is such a long process from start to finish.

The hop rate is still about four times that used by most United States brewers, yet the resulting bitterness is quite similar to that of modern American lagers: 12–22 IBU. Modern lambic brewers use mostly English hops rather than Belgian hops, which are becoming rare.

In the old days, faro and mars were brewed from the second and third runnings from the kettle and boiled for 12 to 15 hours with spent hops from the lambic boil. Today faro is brewed from low-gravity (2.4–3.2 Belge) lambic.

The fermenting rooms in lambic breweries are dark and filled with cobwebs. Brewers dare not clean their brewing cellars for fear of losing the natural yeasts. Control of bacteria-bearing fruit flies is maintained by the resident spiders, and killing a spider in a lambic brewery is very bad form indeed.

The ferment is quite similar to that described in an old account. The beer is cooled overnight in shallow troughs, often located in the gables of the brewery's roof. The ferment, at 50° to 54°F (10° to 12°C), is by wild yeasts. In some breweries, if the ferment is slow to start, some top-fermenting ale yeast is added. The beer is run into relatively small oak fermenters about the size of wine barrels (55 to 80 gallons, or 2 to 3 hl). The fermentation method is almost identical to the British Burton Union System and continues throughout the winter.

When spring comes, the beer begins to work again. At first it is called young beer. After a second ferment during the summer, the beer rests for another winter. After two summers, it is still. At that time it is called old beer. The finished beer is highly acidic (over 1 percent lactic acid, pH 3.2 to 3.5) and 77 to 86 percent attenuated. The final gravity sometimes drops as low as 1 degree Plato, at which point it is a still beer.

Lambic is very expensive to make, particularly because of the long ferment and aging cycle, but also because the brewer must pay government taxes within the year after the beer is brewed, not when it is ready for sale. Lambic has an original gravity of 11.8–13.5/1.047–1.054/4.7–5.4 Belge. It has an alcohol content of about 4.5 percent by volume.

Gueuze-Lambic

Gueuze-lambic is a blend of young (one-third) and old (two-thirds) lambics. The taste is dry, tart, and fruity, yet sweeter than regular lambic. The art of blending is very important in the production of high-quality gueuze. There is a strong secondary ferment in the bottle, and gueuze is finished like champagne, with a cork (or in some cases a cork *and* a crown cap) and aged another year in the bottle, when it is sometimes rebottled, or even filtered and rebottled. The champagne finish is said to have the most character and the filtered gueuze the least character. Brussels is the home of most *gueuzestekers* (gueuze blenders). Sadly, only about 20 of the 80 lambic brewers making gueuze at the start of the century are still brewing this remarkable beer style, but it is gaining popularity in the United States and in other parts of Europe as well.

The Great American Beer Festival guidelines for Belgian-style gueuze-lambic are 11–14/1.044–1.056 OG, 5–6 percent alcohol by volume, 11–23 IBU, and 6–13 SRM. It should have a sour, acidic flavor and be brewed with some unmalted wheat and old hops.

See ALE, BELGIAN BEER, BURTON UNION SYSTEM, FARO, FERMENTATION, LAGER, and SPONTANEOUS FERMENT.

LAMBSWOOL

A beverage made by mixing together the pulp from 6 roasted apples, some raw sugar, a grated nutmeg, and a small amount of ginger. To make Lambswool, one quart of strong ale is heated until moderately warm, then combined with the other ingredients. If it is sweet enough, it is fit to drink. This concoction is sometimes served in a bowl, with the addition of sweet cakes floating in it.

In Old England, the first day of November was dedicated to the angel presiding over fruits, seeds, and the like. It was called La Mas Ubal (The Day of the Apple-Fruit), pronounced "lama-sool." According to Vallancey, these words were soon corrupted by country folk into "lambswool." The liquor associated with this day was called by the same name.

Lambswool was also a tradition followed in Ireland on Holy Eve and the evening before All Saint's Day (November 1). Sometimes milk was substituted for ale.

LA ROSSA

See MORETTI.

LATIN AMERICAN BREWERIES

Traditionally, historians have located the birthplace of beer in Mesopotamia. However, if it is true that cultivation of the starchy tuber manioc began 10,000 years ago in the Amazon region of South America, then this area may be the real birthplace of beer. German voyager Hans Staden, a 9-month captive of the Tupi Indians of Brazil, penned the first detailed account of native brewing along the Amazon River in 1557. Staden described an ancient process that is still used by traditional brewers in Latin America today.

South American Indian beers are of two main types. The principal type, *Masato* beer, is brewed from the manioc tuber. The second most common variety is *chicha*, or corn-based beer. Hiram Bingham, the American explorer who discovered Machu Picchu in Peru, noted that the lost city might have been built to house the Inca women who made this ancient corn beer.

The taste and texture of Latin American beers vary across the region. Masato beer is usually milky white and porridgelike in texture. Chichas have a greater range of colors, from pale yellow to dark red, due to the degree to which the corn and other grains used in the beers are roasted.

During the 17th, 18th, and 19th centuries, European colonists brought to Latin

America the brewing techniques and beer styles found in their homelands. Over the years, scores of European beer dynasties were established in Latin America. By the year 1800, an estimated 1,000 breweries were in operation in South America. Today only about 100 breweries remain, most producing run-of-the-mill lager styles. Nearly gone are the porters, stouts, bocks, Malzbiers, and Negra and Escura beers that once made this region a beer drinker's paradise.

LATROBE BREWING CO. LATROBE, PENNSYLVANIA

Founded in 1893, Latrobe Brewing Co. is one of America's regional brewery survivors. In recent years, however, Latrobe has been doing a lot more than just surviving. The company's production surpassed a million barrels in 1993, making it the first new million-barrel brewery in the United States in decades. It is also the first brewery to revive a declining brand — Rolling Rock — and make it even stronger than before.

Back in the 1980s, things were looking grim for Latrobe. The company's traditional markets were under assault by powerful mass-market brands, and sales were declining. In 1983, dissent in the ranks triggered a devastating strike, and production plummeted further.

In 1987, the company was purchased by Labatt's U.S.A., the United States importing arm of Canadian brewer John Labatt, Ltd. The importer brought new marketing resources and sales savvy to the beleaguered

Rolling Rock

A very pale lager with a light, crisp character. Rolling Rock is a refreshing beer and one of the better examples of a light American lager. Part of its appeal lies in the familiar green bottle with the retro label. The label on the returnable bottles is applied ceramic, once a common practice. Rolling Rock is one of the few brands to use this somewhat costly labeling method, but it has paid off, as the package is instantly recognizable. In recent years, the company has found a less expensive way to apply a similar label to its nonreturnable bottles. As a result, consumers can now get the familiar long-neck bottles in supermarkets and liquor stores as well as in bars.

brewer, and things quickly began to turn around. By 1991, Latrobe posted sales of 830,000 barrels, up from its 1985 low of 420,000. In 1994, the brewery sold 1,100,000 barrels of beer.

At the heart of this story is Rolling Rock, the beer that has made Latrobe a byword in trendy bars on both coasts. Labatt's gave the Rolling Rock brand high-quality marketing, something Latrobe had never been able to do on its own.

In essence, however, Rolling Rock is still the same beer. It is still sold at "popular" (low) prices in its local Pennsylvania markets, but an ever-larger percentage of it is destined for more affluent urban and suburban markets. In a dance club in New York City, a bottle might cost five to six dollars, whereas in a rural Pennsylvania beverage store, you could get two six-packs for the same price.

Latrobe and Labatt's have provided a case study in how to turn a tottering regional brewery into a roaring capitalist enterprise, all in a few short years.

See MARKET SHARE and REGIONAL BREWERY.

LAUTER TUN

A circular, stainless-steel vessel that receives the entire mash from the mixer after the suitable conversion time has passed. It has a

A lauter tun is a large vessel fitted with a false slotted bottom and a drain into which the mash is placed and the grains are removed through a straining process. The sweet wort remains.

slotted false bottom with "valleys" arranged in concentric circles. The mash bed sits on the false bottom. To enable wort runoff to the brew kettle, rakes with knives rotate slowly, cutting the mash. The desired depth of the mash bed is 12 to 18 inches. The bed is sparged during runoff.

See INFUSION MASH TUN.

JACOB LEINENKUGEL BREWING CO.
CHIPPEWA FALLS, WISCONSIN

Jacob Leinenkugel Brewing Co. entered the eighties as a family-owned brewery but emerged as a subsidiary of Miller Brewing Co. (and Miller, of course, is a subsidiary of Philip Morris). To lend a human face to the brewery, Miller has recruited the young scions of the Leinenkugel clan to work for the company, and the energetic Jake Leinenkugel serves as president.

The company was originally founded by Jacob Leinenkugel and a partner in 1867. Leinenkugel became sole owner in 1889, when the company got its current name. Several generations of Leinenkugels later, the brewery is still churning out beer, and ground was recently broken for an expansion. The new Leinenkugel brewery will have a capacity substantially larger than its current 175,000 barrels.

The company produces Leinenkugel's, Leinenkugel Genuine Bock, Leinenkugel Light, Leinenkugel's Limited, and Leinenkugel's Red. In the past, the main line comprised light lagers, typically in the American style. More recently, the compa-

Leinenkugel's Limited

A firm-bodied, somewhat dry lager with a pleasant malt-hop balance.

ny has rediscovered all-malt brewing and is expanding its specialty offerings.

See LAGER ALE, MILLER BREWING CO., and REGIONAL BREWERY.

BROUWERIJ LIEFMANS N.V.
OUDENAARDE, BELGIUM

The founding date of the Liefmans brewery is not known, but an excise tax registry lists it as being in full operation in 1679. The company is now owned by the Riva brewing group of Dentergems.

The wort is made by Riva, then sent to Liefmans, where it is fermented, aged, blended, and bottled. First fermentation takes place in open tanks. Fermentation is slow, and as the yeast collects on the top of the tanks, it is skimmed off daily. At the end of the fermentation, the young beer is cellared at the brewery for several months. Once it is judged to be mature, it is bottled (with a dose of yeast) and laid down to bottle-condition for a time. The beer is very long-lived, aging comfortably in the bottle for years.

Another Liefmans specialty is kriekbier, not to be confused with its distant kriek lambic cousins. Each year, at the end of July, *Schaerbeek* cherries are picked, washed, and sorted. They are then added to casks of 1-year-old Goudenband. Six to seven months later, this beer is filtered and bottled as kriekbier. The company also makes a similar Frambozenbier using raspberries.

Liefmans beers are represented in the United States by Phoenix Imports of Ellicott City, Maryland, and Manneken-Brussels Imports, Inc. of Austin, Texas.

See FRUIT, VEGETABLE, HERBAL, AND SPECIALTY BEERS.

LIGHT ALE

A term common in Great Britain that refers to a beer that is lighter in color than a mild ale, lower in alcohol content than a pale ale, and that may or may not be lower in calories. In England, this type of ale is often called Scottish light or session beer, since a person can drink it throughout an evening without becoming too inebriated.

See BROWN ALE and SCOTTISH ALE.

LIGHT BEER

In the United States, a low-calorie beer with a lower original gravity (less than 12.5/1.050) than regular beer (more than 12.5/1.050). In the United States, the term light beer was used to describe any beer with a very pale color. Currently, there is no descriptor for very pale regular beer.

Light beers generally have less taste than regular beers and a medium alcohol content (3.1 to 4.1 percent by volume). Regular beers have about 155 calories per 12-ounce bottle. Light beers have either one-half, one-third, or "somewhat" fewer calories than regular beers. The United States government has yet to specify what brewers may call light beer. Canadian regulations specify that light beer, ale, stout, porter, and malt liquor must have 3.2 to 4 percent alcohol content. In Germany, such beer is in the *schankbier* category, under 7.5/1.030 OG.

Light beer can be made in one of two ways: special enzymes are used to convert unfermentable dextrins (at 4.1 calories per gram) to fermentable sugars, which will convert to alcohol; or water is added to reduce calories. There is no way around the fact that alcohol contributes 7.1 calories per gram. If a beer is to become popular, it can only be watered down so much before it loses its appeal.

The final gravity is usually very low in light beers (about 0.1 degrees Plato, or even negative — that is, lower than water). Bitterness is usually under 20 IBU and original gravity around 7/1.028.

A quick calorie count of any beer may be made by multiplying the original gravity (in degrees Plato) by 13.5, although the container will usually state the number of calories, along with the grams of carbohydrate (4.1 calories per gram), grams of protein (5.65 calories per gram), and grams of fat (no fat in beer). If you add the calories in the list together and subtract that from the total calories claimed for the beer, you will have the number of calories from alcohol. There are 7.1 calories in each gram of alcohol, so divide the alcohol calories by 7.1 to find the grams of alcohol. The label also will give the metric weight (a 12-ounce bottle contains 355 ml, or 3.55 cl). Divide the grams of alcohol by metric bottle size (in centiliters) — 3.55 in this example — to find the alcohol percent by weight. Then multiply that figure by 1.256 to find the percent of alcohol by volume.

The Great American Beer Festival guidelines for American Light Lager are 6–10/1.024–1.040 OG, 3.5–4.4 percent alcohol by volume, 8–15 IBU, and 2–4 SRM.

Original Gravity	Final Gravity	Alcohol by Volume	IBU	SRM	Calories
Bud Light 1987					
7.8/1.031	1.7	3.3%	≈14	3	108
Coors Light 1979					
8.7/1.035	0.3	4.4%	9	1.9	117
Miller Lite 1985					
7.8/1.031	−0.4	4.2%	19.5	3	96
Labatt's Light (Canada) 1985					
8.1/1.032	0.3	4.1	13	2.8	109
Original United States low-calorie beer, Gablinger's Meisterbräu, later bought by Miller and called Miller Lite. 1967					
8.3/1.033	−0	4.6%	14	2.2	107

LIGHT-STRUCK

See BOTTLES AND BOTTLING.

BROUWERIJ LINDEMANS SINT-PIETERS-LEEUW, BELGIUM

The Lindeman family has been farming in the area for centuries and brewing since 1816. The brewery is now overseen by René Lindeman. Like most lambic breweries, it is a small operation, producing only 19,700 hl a year (roughly comparable to an American microbrewery in size). Lindemans has developed an international market out of proportion to its size, however, with exports shipped throughout Europe and to the United States.

Lindemans, like many lambic breweries, considers poor housekeeping a virtue. The brewery is located in an 18th-century barn that is laced with cobwebs and heavy with

René and Gert Lindemans discuss one of their lambics.

The grist mill at the Lindeman farm brewery

CONTENTS: 750 ML (25.4 FL OZ)

KRIEK

LAMBIC

BELGIAN CHERRY FLAVORED ALE
BREWED WITH NATURAL INGREDIENTS

BROUWERIJ
LINDEMANS
VLEZENBEEK, BELGIUM

Sole U.S. Agents Merchant DuVin Corp. Seattle, WA 98121

Lindemans Kriek

Kriek, or cherry lambic, gets its name from the whole fresh cherries *(krieken)* that are added to the casks. In addition to flavoring the beer, the fruit gives it a pinkish tinge. Lindemans kriek is a sweet, palate-cleansing beer that is per-

dust. A thorough cleaning would destroy the wild yeasts, the brewers believe, and with them the unique character of Lindemans' spontaneously fermented products. Microbes also abound in the wooden kegs used for aging.

When the brewery is making its lambics, it uses only aged hops, which add preservative properties but little bitterness. After boiling, the wort is transferred into a large, shallow copper vessel that exposes the hot wort to fresh air and presumably wild yeasts. After an initial wild yeast fermentation, the beer is placed in casks and matured for 2 years. While aging, the lambic undergoes a slow secondary fermentation.

Lindemans makes both a filtered and an unfiltered gueuze. The filtered product is available in the United States. Rene Lindeman has made a specialty of fruit lambics: kriek, framboise, and pêche. When the brewery makes kriek, whole fresh cherries are added to the casks, triggering a third fermentation and promoting a spritzy carbonation that gives the finished beer a champagnelike character. All the lambics are bottle-conditioned, with the addition of brewer's yeast cultivated from wild strains. The Lindemans products are imported into the United States by Merchant du Vin of Seattle, Washington.

See FRUIT, VEGETABLE, HERBAL, AND SPECIALTY BEERS and LAMBIC.

LINTNER

A system for measuring malt strength. Diastatic power is the potential power or energy that a given malt has. It is measured in degrees Lintner. High enzyme malts such as varieties of American 6-row barley have high diastatic power.

See DIASTATIC POWER and MALT.

THE LION WILKES-BARRE, PENNSYLVANIA

Over the course of United States brewing history, there have been any number of Lion breweries, but The Lion of Wilkes-Barre is the only one that has survived. The Lion began in 1906 as Luzerne Brewing Co., a company that soon went bankrupt. The company was renamed The Lion, but no sooner had it got its house in order than Prohibition was passed.

Since Prohibition, the brewery has done a modest regional trade and has outlasted all of its competition in Pennsylvania's Wyoming Valley. As those other regionals have gone bust, The Lion has acquired a slew of great old brand names and still brews Stegmaier, Bartels, and Liebotschaner, as well as the Gibbons and Esslinger labels.

The Lion has a capacity of 300,000 barrels but only brewed about 50,000 in 1994. The underutilization of the brewery has attracted many contract brewers, and several well-known contract brews are made there.

As of 1994, the company is under new management and is aggressively moving to build on the specialty potential of many of its brand names.

See PORTER.

Stegmaier Porter

A rather good porter from this old-line regional brewer. It is a roasty, malty brew with a nutty, coffeeish flavor. Some consumers even detect a hint of licorice, although the brewers say they do not use any. Produced as a revivalist specialty brand, it is the equal of several of its microbrewed competitors and better than many.

LIQUID SMOKE

An additive occasionally used by homebrewers to imitate beers produced with smoked malt. This is usually a mixture of water, smoke essence, and brown sugar, although some brands also contain vinegar. Liquid smoke can produce off-flavors in beer.

See SMOKED MALT.

LIQUOR

In brewing, the water used for mashing and brewing. This water tends to contain large amounts of calcium and magnesium salts.

LOCAL STYLE DEVELOPMENT

Local beer styles developed in Europe for two reasons: the brewing guilds specified the composition of the beers, and only certain ingredients were available. At that time, goods were transported by cart, by ship, or both. Transportation was expensive. Manufacturers, out of necessity, used locally produced goods as much as possible to hold down costs.

Daily transport might have averaged perhaps 12 to 15 miles per day. Market towns, therefore, were naturally spaced about that distance apart.

People were much more apt to stay put in one location for their entire lives. They knew their neighbors and were leery of "foreigners." This maintained the stability of local enterprises. Breweries were no exception. Since there was so little contact outside one's local area, the introduction of new styles was hampered. Over time, cultural habits led people to settle on their "own" style to the exclusion of others.

This way of life existed up until the 20th century when motorized transport developed. Today hops and grains are shipped all around the world in huge container ships or by airplane, then trundled several hundred miles per day to their final destination by motor transport.

Much of the diversity of beer styles was swept away in certain countries, especially the United States, by the huge commercial breweries, who narrowed their offerings to a very few brands. Pub brewers and microbrewers have reintroduced many of these styles, and are developing new styles, as well. It is conceivable that beer localism will arise anew, even in the presence of national brands.

LONDON ALE

An ale characterized by its softness, due to the soft water of London, as opposed to the very hard mineral water of Burton-on-Trent. London ales typically have a distinct hop character due in part to London's proximity to the hop fields of Kent to the south and Londoners' traditional desire for some hop bite and sharpness in their ales.

The two remaining great London brewers are Young & Co. (The Ram Brewery), of Wandsworth, and Fuller, Smith & Turner (Griffin Brewery), of Chiswick, both of whose ales are available in the United States. That London has only two major ale-producing breweries left is a shame, as it once set the trend for beer in Britain and as far abroad as Russia and the American colonies. London's brown and dark ales were once copied the world over.

LONE STAR BREWING CO. SAN ANTONIO, TEXAS

See HEILEMAN BREWING CO.

LOUVAIN WIT

See BELGIAN WHITE BEER.

LOVIBOND

See COLOR.

LOW-CALORIE BEER

See LIGHT BEER.

LOWENBRÄU A.G. MUNICH, GERMANY

Lowenbräu was once one of the top imported brands in the United States, competing with Heineken for the number one sales position. The S. A. Miller Brewing Co. began brewing Lowenbräu under license in the United States, altering the recipe in the process, and the brand soon went into severe decline.

Lowenbräu remains one of Munich's top breweries, with production of more than 1,000,000 hl per year. The company produces Lowenbräu Helles, Export, Weisse, Schwarz Weisse, Pils, Oktoberfest, Heller Bock, Triumphator, and Märzen.

See IMPORT and MARKET SHARE.

LUDA

A beer of ancient Ossetia in the Caucasus Mountains region of Europe. Also called ludi. The Ossetians, an Aryan-language tribe of Iranian descent, are credited with having built, in Tappakallah, the largest beer tank in antiquity (600 L, or 156 gallons). It dates to 600 B.C.

LUPULIN

The sticky, yellow granular substance around the base of each flower petal on hop cones. It contains the essential oils and bitter resins that give the hop its bittering and preservative properties and aromatic character.

MAGNESIUM

A metallic element. When magnesium ions are diluted in water, they make the water "hard." Magnesium is more soluble than calcium and as such does not boil out with bicarbonates as readily as calcium does. It will lower the mash pH but not as well as calcium. At levels of 10 to 20 ppm, it is an important yeast nutrient. Levels above 20 ppm impart a sharp, bitter flavor to beer.

MAIZE

See CORN.

MALT

A cereal grain that is allowed to germinate but then is heated in a kiln to cut the germination process short. The term *malt* usually refers to malted barley, even though other cereal grains, including wheat, oats, and rye, can be malted. Malted wheat is commonly available and used in a number of specialty styles, including weizens and many Belgian ales.

Pictured here is caramel malt, also known as crystal malt.

Many maltsters also sell malted rye, which can be used in the grist, usually in small proportions. As a source of fermentable sugar, pale malt yields a specific gravity of about 1.025 to 1.030 (4 to 5 degrees Plato) per pound per gallon, depending on the efficiency of the extract, with dextrin or crystal malts producing a lower specific gravity than other varieties (about 1.015 to 1.020).

Measuring Colors

The color of malt is measured in degrees Lovibond. On this scale, very light-colored malts have ratings of 1 or 2, most crystal or caramel malts have ratings of 10 to 100, brown malts (generally not available today) have ratings of up to 200, chocolate malts have ratings of about 300, and very black malts (dark roasted) have ratings of 500 to 700 or more.

Types of Malts

Classifying and understanding malt types may seem a formidable task. Brewers refer to many aspects of the malt when they describe it or record it in their recipe logs. They may refer to the original strain of barley used to make the malt, the type of kilning used, and even the name of the malthouse that produced it. For example, a recipe may call for "Briess 2-row Klages pale malt," meaning that the malt was produced at the Briess Malting Company of 2-row Klages barley and that it is a pale malt. Generally, it is the malt type that is most important.

In general, brewers use some form of pale malt for the bulk of their grist. When people refer to specialty malts, they are referring to stewed malts (caramel or crystal), wheat malts, or high-kilned malts, which are darker malts used in smaller quantities in the grist.

Some of the terms referring to malt are listed in the following table.

Malts are generally characterized as either pale malt or kilned malt. All malts are kilned, which is the process of drying and curing the malt, but pale malts are dried at fairly low temperatures over long periods of time so that they have a very light color with almost no caramelization of their sugars. When a brewer refers to kilned malt, he or she generally means the darker roasted malt types. In most beers, pale malt makes up the bulk of the grist.

Barley Types	Malt Types	Malthouses
Harrington	Crystal	Hugh Baird (United Kingdom)
Klages	Pale	DeWolf-Cosyns (Belgium)
Maris Otter	Black patent	Briess (United States)
Prisma	Munich	Minnesota Malting (United States)
	Cara-Pils	Great Western (Canada)
	Vienna	Munton & Fison (United Kingdom) Schreier (United States)

In addition to being identified as a pale or a kilned malt, malts are generally identified as either 2-row or 6-row. This refers to the number of rows of kernels when the barley is on the stalk. Two-row malts are often lower in enzymes than 6-row malts.

Terms such as *pale malt* and *6-row malt* are used to classify malts. Other terms, such as *Klages* and *Harrington,* are used to identify the strain of barley.

Pale Malts

All pale malts are very light in color, generally 1 to 3 degrees Lovibond. They

Table of Common Brewing Malts

Malt Type	Yield (SG PTS./ LB./GAL.)	Typical Color (Degrees Lovibond)
Pale 2-row (domestic)	35	1.7
Pale 6-row (domestic)	33	1.7
British pale ale	36	3
British mild ale	33	5
Vienna malt (domestic)	32	4
Munich malt (domestic)	28	10
Cara-Pils malt (domestic)	30	1.7
Crystal malt (domestic)	24	10–120
British crystal malt	26	55
Chocolate malt	24	350
Black malt (domestic)	24	540
Roasted barley	24	500
Flaked maize (corn)	40	0
Flaked barley	30	0
Brown sugar	45	15
Malt extract (syrup)	35	varies*
Malt extract (dry)	45	varies*

*Pale malt extracts can be anywhere between 3 and 10 degrees Lovibond.

are all fully modified and have enough enzymatic power to convert any adjunct grains that may be added to the mash. Pale malts constitute most of the malted barley produced throughout the world. Some specific pale malts follow.

Pale Ale Malt. Fully modified with enough enzymes to convert up to 15 percent adjunct content in the mash, this malt is best for single-step infusion mashes. With its light color (2 degrees Lovibond), this malt is used in pale ales and makes up the bulk of the grist for other styles as well.

6-Row Lager Malt. With a high protein content and thick husk, this malt is also known for its high tannin content, which can produce haze and off-flavors. High in enzymes (100 to 200 degrees Lintner), it can convert adjunct grains at 25 to 50 percent of the grist. Best used with a multiple-step (two or three temperature intervals) mash, this malt is often used in light lagers. Modern lager malts are fully modified, although older texts often say that ale malts are more fully modified than lager malts.

2-Row Lager Malt. Commonly identified as Pilsner malt, this variety sometimes is lower in enzymes than its 6-row cousin, although this also depends on the type of barley used to make the malt. Lager malts today are often more modified than they were in the past. Light in color (1.4 degrees Lovibond), this malt is high in proteins (again, this is changing with some modern malts). It is often used with a step mash that includes a protein rest (122°F, or 50°C). It has less tannin content than 6-row lager malt and is less likely to produce astringency and other off-flavors. This malt is commonly used in European lagers. Recipes calling for 2-row Klages or Harrington usually refer to 2-row lager malt.

German Pale Malt. At 1.8 degrees Lovibond, this malt is light in color with a smooth flavor. Suitable for any lager.

Belgian Pils. Light in color (1.8 degrees Lovibond), this is an excellent base malt for Belgian ales and other European styles.

Vienna Malt. A lightly kilned malt (about 4 degrees Lovibond), Vienna malt is kilned at slightly higher temperatures than pale malt, but it retains enough enzymes (high diastatic power) to be used for most or all of the grist. Vienna malt is typically used in Märzen, Oktoberfest, and other Vienna-style beers to give them a deeper red color and a somewhat nutty malt aroma and flavor.

Wheat Malt. Characterized by the lack of a husk, wheat malt does not form a good filter bed when sparging. Because of this, it also does not tend to contribute tannins to the beer. Wheat malts have enough enzymes to fully convert starches to sugars, but they must be mashed with at least 30 percent barley because of their inability to form a proper filter bed. Wheat malt is high in protein, so wheat beers often have a haze. Wheat also can be used to increase the head retention of the beer; when used at about 5 percent of the grist, it contributes no flavor. When making wheat beers, the grist is typically about 50 percent wheat and 50 percent barley if an infusion mash is used. German-style weizens are made using a decoction mash with 50 percent to 70 percent wheat. The color of wheat malt is about 2 to 3 degrees Lovibond.

Raw (Unmalted) Wheat. Used in wits at up to 45 percent of the grist and in lambics at up to 30 percent of the grist. The wheat contributes a characteristic haze in the beer.

Kilned Malts

Kilned malts are dried and then roasted at higher temperatures than pale malts. These higher temperatures give the malts a darker color and sharper flavor, but they reduce the amount of enzymes, so the malts are generally unable to be mashed by themselves in a grist. Kilned malts are generally used for special purposes and in small quantities, usually with a substantially larger percentage of pale malt constituting the bulk of the grist. Colored specialty malts account for only about 1 percent of the malt produced. However, they allow the brewer to choose from a wide palette of colors, to create special flavors such as the rich roasted flavor of dark grains, and to add special properties such as increased head retention or body.

Amber Malt. An ale malt that is dried slowly and then cured in a roasting drum at high temperatures — usually about 200°F (93°C) for the first 15 minutes or so, then up to 300°F (149°C), producing a Lovibond of 30 degrees.

Biscuit Malt. At 23 degrees Lovibond, this is sometimes referred to as "pale roast." Biscuit malt is known for lending malty characteristics similar to those produced by chocolate malt to light-colored beers. It is used to improve the malt aroma and flavor of light-colored lagers and ales.

Black Patent. Over 500 degrees Lovibond, this is a very dark roasted malt with almost no extractable sugars. It is a germinated, dried malt that is roasted for

1 to 2 hours at 375° to 400°F (174° to 204°C) in a revolving drum. It can contribute very sharp and sometimes excessively harsh flavors if used at more than about 3 percent of the grist.

Brown Malt. At 100 to 200 degrees Lovibond, brown malt is a normal ale malt dried at a high temperature over a wood fire. It is kilned at 350°F (177°C) for 2 to 5 hours. The malt retains a flavor of wood smoke and is seldom found today.

Porter Malt is also known as brown malt. Green malt is spread thinly (about 1½ inches, or 3.81 cm) during the drying stage. Before being fully dried, it is cooled. The rest of the drying is done at high temperatures, causing the grain to pop open from expanding moisture.

Chocolate Malt. About 350 to 400 degrees Lovibond, chocolate malt adds a dark color and smooth roasted malt flavor to beers. A small amount (about 3 percent) creates a nutty flavor and light brown color; larger amounts (up to 10 percent or so) create a black color and smooth roasted flavor. It is often used in porters, mild ales, and brown ales, and occasionally in darker-colored lagers. Chocolate malt has a smoother flavor than darker malts such as black patent and is a good choice for adding black color to a beer. It is made by roasting plump germinated barley that has been dried to about 5 percent moisture in a rotating drum at a temperature of 400° to 450°F (204° to 232°C).

Dextrin Malt. Malted barley that has a lower fermentable sugar content but a higher dextrin content than other malts.

Therefore, dextrin malts contribute to the head retention, sweetness, and body of the final beer.

Munich Malt. Imported varieties are roasted to about 6 to 8 degrees Lovibond, domestic varieties to about 10 degrees Lovibond. Munich malt is used to give a darker, fuller malt flavor to dark and amber lagers. It is typically blended with a pale malt such as Klages or German Pils, with anywhere from 10 to 60 percent of the grist being made up of Munich malt (higher percentages are possible).

Peated Malt. A smoked malt produced in Scotland by Hugh Baird. It is intended primarily for whisky distillers but also is used by some homebrewers and microbreweries in very small percentages (typically no more than 5 to 10 percent of the grist). Excessive amounts will contribute a phenolic flavor to the beer, rendering it undrinkable.

Roast Barley. A black, roasted, unmalted barley. The unmalted barley is roasted in a drum, in a manner similar to that used for chocolate and black malts. It is used at about 5 to 10 percent of the grist to lend a roasted flavor to stouts. It is seldom used in styles other than stouts, although small amounts may be used in porters or dark ales.

Special Roast. About 50 degrees Lovibond, special roast is pale roasted to create a toasted malt flavor and aroma and a reddish amber color. It is used at the rate of 3 to 10 percent of the grist in Vienna beer, altbier, or any beer calling for amber-colored malt.

Victory Malt. About 25 degrees Lovibond, this is a lightly roasted malt used at 5 to 15 percent for flavor and aroma in ales, porters, and darker lagers where malt character without residual sweetness is desired.

Crystal Malts

Crystal malts are fully modified malts with delicious, sweet flavors. Crystal malts are available in colors ranging from fairly light (about 10 degrees Lovibond) to fairly dark (about 120 degrees Lovibond). Crystal malts contribute unfermentable sugars and provide a way of producing residual sweetness and body. The most common variety of crystal is caramel malt, which is 40 degrees Lovibond.

Caramel malts are roasted green malt. After soaking, the malt is left to germinate on the floor for about 5 days and is heavily watered (a process known as stewing). It is then roasted for 3 hours at temperatures up to 300°F (149°C).

Light Crystal Malt. About 10 degrees Lovibond, this is used much like Cara-Pils — to add color and residual sweetness. Pale crystal (about 40 degrees Lovibond) is typically used at rates of 5 to 20 percent of the grist to add light coloring, sweetness, and body.

Cara-Vienne. A light-colored crystal malt of about 22 degrees Lovibond.

Caramel Malt. At 37 to 40 degrees Lovibond, caramel malt is used at ratios of about 5 to 20 percent of the grist. Caramel malt can be made from either 2-row or 6-row barley. Most United States malthouses

Malts

	Color (degrees Lovibond)	Diastatic Power
Pale Malt		
Pale ale	2	36
2-row lager	1.7	60–70
6-row lager	1.7	100–200
Munich malt	10	22
Vienna malt	4	30
Mild ale	2.5–3.5	33
Wheat malt	2.0–3.0	50
Kilned Malt		
Biscuit malt	23	10
Brown malt	100–200	0
Chocolate malt	350	0
Black patent	500+	0
Roast barley	500+	0
Caramel Malt		
Light crystal	10	0
Medium crystal	60	0
Dark crystal	100	0
Dextrin	2	0

use 6-row, whereas most European malthouses use 2-row. Caramel malt is one of the most commonly used malt varieties.

Medium Crystal Malt. With a Lovibond of 60 degrees this malt lends a bit more color than pale crystal and is often used by homebrewers at rates of 5 to 15 percent of the grist. It adds caramel flavor and color, as well as residual sweetness, to ales.

Cara-Munich. A medium-colored crystal malt of about 70 degrees Lovibond, this malt is used to create a deep color in lagers. It also lends a full flavor and contributes to foam stability.

Scottish Crystal. At 90 degrees Lovibond, this malt lends a deep amber or red color and a full-bodied, toasted-caramel flavor to beers. It is used in Scottish ales.

Dark Crystal Malt. With a Lovibond of 120 degrees, this malt contributes a complex bittersweet caramel flavor to beers. Used at 5 percent, it adds color and a slight sweetness. Used at rates up to 15 percent, it contributes substantial sweetness to heavier beers such as barley wines.

Cara-Pils. Also known as dextrin malt, Cara-Pils is used to give a maltier profile to beer. It lacks enzymes and must be mashed with other malts. Cara-Pils is typically used at rates of 5 to 20 percent of the grist. At rates over 10 percent, the malt contributes noticeable residual sweetness.

MALT EXTRACT

Malted barley that has been mashed so that the starches and sugars are converted to fermentable sugars and then reduced by evaporating excess liquid. Extracts are widely available in two forms: liquid syrups, typically packaged in cans or poly bags, and dry powders. The syrups often have hops added and are sold as "kits" to which only water and yeast need be added to make beer. Regardless of what the instructions say, extracts should always be boiled in a wort.

Malt extracts are sold in various forms and packages. Left to right: dry malt extract powder; Northwestern malt extract syrup (packed in a plastic bag inside a box); and Alexander's malt extract syrup (canned, as are many brands of syrup).

One pound of dry extract per gallon of water will yield a specific gravity of about 1.040 to 1.045. One pound of extract syrup will yield a gravity of about 1.030 to 1.038.

When canned syrups are used, corn sugar or any other type of sugar should not be added to the beer, regardless of what the instructions say. Doing so can create a cidery off-flavor.

Buying and Brewing with Extracts

Some of the things to think about when choosing an extract are suitability to style, color, freshness, attenuation, and bitterness (if hopped).

Many extracts are labeled for a particular style. Others, particularly unhopped extracts, often are labeled simply as "gold," "amber," or "dark." A moderately experienced homebrewer will have no problem matching these labels to styles. Most unhopped extracts are, for the most part, interchangeable in most recipes. This is not true of the kits, which are hopped and can have significant differences in flavor. When using extracts, most brewers choose a light or amber extract and combine it with some adjunct grains, such as a pound or so of pale malt or crystal malt, or perhaps a bit of chocolate to give the beer more character, flavor, and a different color than they would get by using the extract alone.

Brewers should buy fresh ingredients. Malt extracts tend to darken with time, and although older cans of extract may be usable, they may not produce the beer a brewer expects.

The term *attenuation* refers to the ability of the yeast to ferment out the sugars in the malt. Some extracts are known for producing beers with more residual body and sweetness than others. In *The Home Brewer's Companion,* author Charlie Papazian recommends Munton & Fison light dry extract or Alexander's pale malt extract syrup to produce a drier beer with less residual sweetness and body. He suggests Laaglander dried malt extract for a sweeter, more full-bodied beer.

The bitterness of an extract is of interest when the brewer is buying a hopped extract (the kits).

Many of the extracts labeled gold, pale, or light will produce a darker-than-expected beer. Alexander's tends to produce lighter-colored beers (4.5 to 4.8 SRM); most other brands of "light" extract produce light amber beers (9 to 11 SRM). To brew a light beer, brewers also should consider doing larger-scale boils. Many extract brewers boil only about 1½ to 2 gallons (5.7 to 7.6 L) of water when making their wort, then dilute it later. This tends to produce darker beers than when the same quantity of extract is used in two to three times as much water.

Another factor to consider is the stove and its heat. Direct heat, especially on electric stoves, tends to caramelize the sugars on the bottom of the pot, forming a crust that darkens beer and is hard to clean. A gas burner or indirect heat is preferable.

MALTING

The process by which grain is allowed to begin germinating until it develops the enzymes needed to convert starches to sugars. Two basic methods are used in commercial malthouses: floor malting and pneumatic, or mechanized, malting. Homebrewers can make their own malt, but the process takes 1 to 2 weeks and requires frequent monitoring and much work. In addition, the results are likely to be inconsistent and to vary in quality.

Floor Malting

The traditional method of malting raw barley is floor malting. The process is fairly straightforward: (1) Soak the raw barley. (2) Allow the barley to germinate. (3) Kiln dry the barley to stop the germination from progressing.

In the first step, the grain is soaked for 40 hours or more in a large vat, or cistern. (In the 19th century, the time ranged from 40 to 72 hours, although the range today is about 40 to 45 hours.) During the soaking period, the water is changed periodically to avoid stagnation. Modern practice calls for aeration during the soaking, often achieved by spraying water continuously as the malt soaks in the vat. The water needs to be changed at least once every 24 hours, so a single malting run may need only one or two changes of water. At the end of the soaking stage, the malt should contain approximately 45 percent water by weight.

In the second step, the water is drained from the vat. The barley is removed from the vat and spread across the floor. (Traditional methods called for an additional step known as couching, in which the grain was piled in a heap and allowed to germinate before being spread.) The depth of the grain bed should be 3 to 12 inches, depending on temperature. The grain bed needs to be turned often to provide fresh oxygen, remove carbon dioxide, and prevent growing roots from becoming entwined. Water is often sprinkled on the germinating grain to stimulate growth. Floor germination takes 8 to 15 days at temperatures of about 50° to 60°F (10° to 15.5°C). Malt intended for roasting may take fewer than 8 days. A maltster knows the germination is finished by examining the grain. Each young shoot, called an acrospire (or plumule), should be about ¾ the length of the grain. A longer acrospire indicates overmodified malt, a shorter acrospire undermodified malt.

In the third step, the grain is kiln dried to stop the natural growth process and to stabilize the enzymes. The kilning process also adds color and flavor. There are two steps in the kilning process: drying and curing.

Drying is done at temperatures of 90° to 100°F (32° to 38°C) and reduces the malt from 40 percent moisture to 5 percent; this usually takes about 2 days. Warm air flows around the grain to carry away excess moisture.

When the grain is dry, it is placed on a perforated floor at a bed depth of 9 to 12

The malting floor of the Cardiff Malting Company at East Moors, Cardiff, is depicted in this sketch from Barnard's Noted Breweries of Great Britain and Ireland, *ca. 1890.*

inches, and hot air (180° to 220°F, or 82° to 104°C) is pumped through it. The malt must be turned while on the floor to ensure even color. Curing usually takes about 2 days. The total time for the entire kilning process is 3 to 5 days.

The temperatures listed preserve the enzyme content of the malt. If higher temperatures are used, they will reduce the enzymatic power of the malt, which means that it will be unable to contribute fermentable sugars to the beer unless it is mashed with high-enzyme malts. To produce darker malts, the drying temperature is generally increased. For very dark malts such as black malt and black patent malt, the grain is roasted in a revolving drum for up to 2 hours at a temperature of 375° to 400°F (190.5° to 204°C).

Floor malting was the predominant malting method through the 1940s, but pneumatic malthouses have predominated in the past 50 years. However, a number of commercial brewers find that the quality of malts from floor malting is higher than that of malts produced pneumatically, so the demand for floor malts has kept quite a few floor malthouses in business. Floor malts are considered superior for brewing ales, as floor malting produces a more uniform, plumper malt.

Pneumatic Malting

Pneumatic malting is a term used to refer to mechanical malting processes and is the type of malting most common today. The environment is strictly controlled by placing soaked grain in tanks or sealed drums through which air, maintained at a constant temperature, is circulated. Aeration is done by rotating the drum or through other mechanical means, such as turning screws. Warm, humid air is pumped in; old air and carbon dioxide are pumped out. The most common mechanical device used today is the Saladin box. Other designs use towers or conveyor belts as variations on the mechanized malting scheme. Most of the malthouses that have been built in the past 50 years are pneumatic malthouses.

See MALT and SALADIN BOX.

MALT LIQUOR

A very pale, cold-fermented, strong American lager beer. Malt liquors were originally designed to be strong in alcohol content (up to 8.1 percent by volume, possibly even higher). By definition, this beer style has a minimal taste profile, is lacking in hop bouquet, and has only subthreshold hop levels (5 to 14 IBU). Ingredients include 50 to 60 percent malt, 30 to 40 percent corn grits, 10 to 20 percent dextrose, and cluster hops at 12 to 14 (or lower) IBU.

Originally, an enzyme such as amyloglucosidase was added to convert the unfermentable dextrins in the beer to fermentable sugars, thus increasing the alcohol and decreasing the final gravity (the flavorful dextrins). Malt liquors, with less body and more alcohol, are an unseemly, poorly balanced product at best and may be described as basically light beer with high alcohol. The ferment is with lager yeast but at warm temperatures for 6 to 8 days. The beer is lagered for 1 to 5 weeks at 32°F (0°C) and processed as lager beer. Final gravity is 0.7–2.7 or even lower. The name *malt liquor* has no significance except to allow strong beer to be sold in those states that require beer above a certain alcohol content (usually 5 percent alcohol by volume) to be called something other than "beer."

Of course, there have been a few malt liquors with substance, mostly European imports. In Germany, for example, regular beer usually has slightly more than 5 percent alcohol by volume and, for that reason, must be labeled as a malt liquor in some states. Since most American beer enthusiasts shun the malt liquor category, such European beers often suffer in sales. As a result, they are often reformulated (by adding water) so that they have less alcohol. The result is usually a beer that has less character than its European original but is actually more suitable for most Americans. Closely related to malt liquors in manufacture are light beers, dry beers, and ice beers.

The Great American Beer Festival guidelines for American Malt Liquor (lager) are 12.5–15/1.050–1.060 OG, 6.25–7.5 percent alcohol by volume, 12–23 IBU, and 2–5 SRM.

Original Gravity	Final Gravity	Alcohol by Volume	IBU	SRM
Skyball Malt Liquor 1941 (prototype malt liquor)				
11.9/1.047	0.56	5.9%	14	3.25
Champale Malt Liquor 1946				
12.3/1.049	1.7	5.6%	5	1.9

Original Gravity	Final Gravity	Alcohol by Volume	IBU	SRM
Colt 45 Malt Liquor 1987				
14/1.057	2	6.3%	15	3.5
Labatt's Extra Stock Malt Liquor (Canada) 1985				
13.6/1.054	4.1	4.9%	22.5	≈4
Old English 800 Malt Liquor 1980				
17.0/1.070	1.6	8.3%	15	3.5

See DRY BEER, ICE BEER, LAGER BEER, and LIGHT BEER.

MALT MILL

A grinder used for crushing malt. There are four major types of malt mills.

A malt mill, roller mill, or grinder is a machine which generally consists of two or four pairs of cylinders through which malted barley is crushed for brewing. This malt mill was used at Hell Gate Brewery, New York, in the late 19th century.

1. A *two-roller mill* is used in micro-breweries and brewpubs for cracking open malt kernels. It is a small, compact unit comprising two rollers generally 6 to 10 inches long, depending on throughput. The two-roller mill is most effective with well-modified, uniformly screened malt.

2. A *four-roller mill* includes a feed chute with a magnetic separator for removing iron and steel objects. The first rollers are fluted, and they tear open the husks. The malt is then fed to the second pair of rollers, which are less fluted and break the hard unmodified ends. In sophisticated mills, a pair of revolving beaters in cylindrical screens allow finer husks and grits to bypass the second pair of rollers. This type of mill is used in large breweries and some microbreweries.

3. A *six-roller mill* has three pairs of rollers allowing for very effective separation and differential size reduction. This type of mill is especially useful for malts that are not well modified or well screened. Only grits from the second pair of rollers find their way to the third pair. Vibrating screens allow for the separation and direction of fine and coarser grits. Six-roller mills are found in large breweries and some microbreweries.

4. A *hammer mill* consists of a horizontally rotating spindle with disks that have a series of "hammers" fixed on them. These disks are surrounded by a housing with precisely constructed sieve plates.

MALTO-DEXTRIN

An intermediary product in the conversion between starch and sugar. Malto-dextrin is not fermentable by normal brewer's yeast. It can be used to increase wort density and add smoothness to a thin beer.

MALTOSE

A sugar ($C_{12}H_{12}O_{11}$) derived from malt that is the primary constituent (after water) of wort. Maltose constitutes about 50 percent of the total sugars in wort. It consists of two joined glucose molecules.

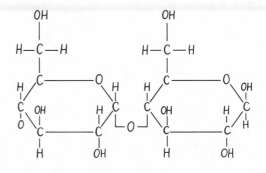

Diagram of maltose

MALTOTRIOSE

A sugar containing three molecules of glucose.

MALT WORM

An insect that feeds on and infects malt. The Latin scientific name for the malt worm, also known as a grain weevil, is *Calandra granaria*.

MALZBIER

In Germany, a malt beverage of very low alcohol content and high nutritional value. It was originally brewed for nursing mothers and children. In France, it is called *bière de malt*.

MANGANESE

A metallic element. Manganese ion is found in trace amounts in malt and is sufficient to ensure proper enzyme action in the mash. Excess manganese is undesirable.

W. T. MARCHANT

The author of *In Praise of Ale* (London, 1888), a beer anthology. Along with Bickerdyke's *Curiosities of Ale and Beer*, published a year later, Marchant's book ranks as one of the significant works of its time.

In Praise of Ale contains close to 700 pages of "songs, ballads, epigrams, and anecdotes relating to beer, malt, and hops." It was last reprinted in the United States in 1968.

MARKET SHARE

The size of the beer market has been relatively stable or "flat" for a number of years. This has made competition for share all the more intense.

The United States beer industry has been shaped by decades of fierce competition and consolidation. Earlier in the century, most United States breweries were family concerns that distributed their products locally or regionally. After World War II, the drive for national market presence began in earnest.

In the postwar era, the industry was racked by a series of "beer wars," and large national brewers came to the fore at the expense of smaller regionals.

Only three brewing companies have succeeded in becoming truly "national" brewers — the Anheuser-Busch Brewing Co. of St. Louis, Missouri, the Miller Brewing Co. of Milwaukee, Wisconsin, and Adolph Coors Brewing Co. of Golden, Colorado. In today's United States beer market, the dominant percentage of the beer is sold by those three companies — 81 percent in 1994.

Among the top three, Anheuser-Busch has the lion's share of the market. The St. Louis–based company held 46 percent share of the market in 1994 (Anheuser-Busch is also the largest world brewer, followed by Heineken, Miller, Kirin, Brahma, and Interbrew). Miller Brewing company held 23.7 percent share of the market in 1994, while Coors Brewing held 10.7 percent of the market share in 1994.

The Stroh Brewery Co. and the G. Heileman Brewing Co., two companies that verge on "national" presence, accounted for another 11.8 percent of United States sales in 1994. In recent years, the market presence of these two companies has declined, and larger and smaller brewers have seized their share.

Altogether, the top five United States brewers held 92.8 percent of the United States market in 1994, leaving just over 7 percent of the market for other players.

The giants have left a few niches in the market, however, that have been profitably filled by beer importers and small United States brewers.

Imported beer made up approximately 5 percent of the market in 1994. The dominant importers are divisions of major international companies. In 1994, the top importers, ranked by market share, were Heineken U.S.A., Molson Breweries U.S.A. (a division of the Miller Brewing Co.), Labatt U.S.A., Guinness Import Co., and Beck & Co. All of these importers are now divisions of their parent breweries.

The strong market presence of imports is an unusual trait of the United States market. International brands are now commonplace on the world market, but in most countries, foreign brands are brewed under license by domestic breweries. In the United States market, most brands are made by their home breweries and shipped ocean freight to the United States.

The smallest part of the United States market is held by regional and microbreweries, roughly two percent. There are now approximately 40 regional United States breweries (defined as those brewers producing over 15,000 barrels a year that are not in full national distribution). A substantial number of these regional breweries got their start as microbreweries within the past ten years. Many are now distributing their products in broader markets, and a few distribute nationally, although on a small scale.

The United States microbrewing segment has been the fastest growing part of the United States beer industry for the past ten years. The ranks of microbreweries have grown steadily since the first scattered microbreweries began opening in the early 1980s. Many of the early players are now substantial regional brewers, but myriad new small breweries continue to open.

There are now over 500 microbreweries (breweries producing fewer than 15,000 31-gallon barrels a year) and brewpubs (small restaurant/breweries, selling an average of 1,000–2,000 barrels a year).

These small companies hold about one percent of the market, but that percentage continues to grow, and new small breweries continue to open at a rapid pace.

See ANHEUSER-BUSCH, BREWPUB, COORS BREWING CO., MICROBREWERY, MILLER BREWING CO., and REGIONAL BREWERY.

MARS BIÈRE

A style of beer produced from the second mashings of the grains during the brewing process. The first (and stronger) wort was used to produce gueuze beers.

Mars bière was so named because March (*Mars* in French) signified the month in the brewing season when mars brewing stopped. Mars is no longer produced since modern brewing practices do not utilize this splitting of the wort.

See LAMBIC.

MÄRZEN

See OKTOBERFEST BEER.

MÄRZENBIER

See OKTOBERFEST BEER.

MASATO

A South American beer brewed from the starchy manioc tuber.
See LATIN AMERICAN BREWERIES.

MASH

A mixture of hot water and ground barley malt that forms the sweet wort after straining.

MASH FILTER

In some cases, a mash filter press replaces the lauter tun. The mash filter requires less sparge action and hence yields stronger wort. However, the filter press is not as flexible as a lauter tun from a throughput standpoint. The filter comprises hollow frames alternating with grooved metal grids covered with cloth or plastic sheets. The frames and grids are gasketed and, when sealed, provide channels for mash and wort. The mash filter may be regarded as a series of mini lauter tuns with 2½-inch beds. When the runoff is complete, the press is opened, and the grain falls into a trough for removal.

See LAUTER TUN.

MASH-IN

The first step in the mashing process: mixing the grains with water.

Mixing ground malt with water is commonly known as mashing-in.

MASHING

The process of mixing water with grains at specific temperatures for specific periods of time to promote enzyme activity that converts starches to fermentable sugars and breaks down complex proteins. The most common mashing methods are infusion mashes, step (or program) mashes, and decoction mashes.

Single-step Infusion Mash

The single-step infusion mash is the simplest of the three methods because it involves only one temperature step. The water and malted barley are mixed (usually referred to as doughing-in or mashing-in) at temperatures of 148° to 158°F (64° to 70°C). Temperatures in the upper part of that range produce more dextrins (unfermentable sugars) and will yield a more robust body, while those near 148°F (64°C) produce more maltose (fermentable sugars). Converting starches to sugars is called saccharification and is the most important step in the more complicated mashing methods.

Infusion Mash

In an infusion mash, the grains are usually put into a single mashing vessel. Then hot water (about 170°F, or 77°C) is added and mixed with the grains until the desired temperature (about 150°F, or 65.5°C) is reached. The mixture is held as close as possible to this constant temperature for 30 minutes to 2 hours. Shorter periods are used with mashes at higher temperatures, longer periods at lower temperatures. A typical mashing schedule might call for maintaining a temperature of 152°F (67°C) for 60 minutes.

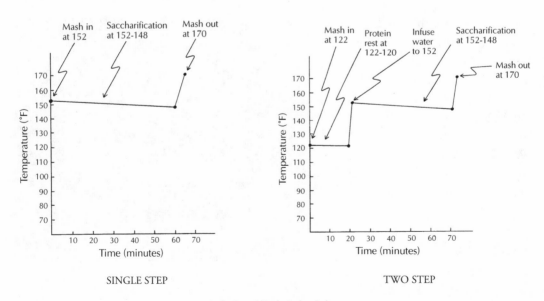

Infusion Mash Schedules

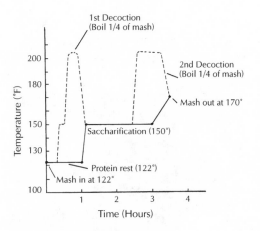

Two-Decoction Mash Schedule

Step Mash

The step mash is basically an infusion mash with one or two additional steps. It differs from the single-step infusion mash in that it begins at a lower temperature — typically 120° to 125°F (49° to 52°C) — and is held at that temperature for about 30 minutes before the temperature is raised to 148° to 158°F (64° to 70°C) by applying direct heat. The lower-temperature step is called the protein rest, and its purpose is to break down complex proteins.

Mashing schedules are often used to describe the variation of temperature over time for each mashing method. The figure on page 318 shows a typical mashing schedule for a two-step infusion mash.

Decoction Mash

The third method, decoction mashing, is the most complex of the three methods, but is the one most commonly used by European lager breweries. The crux of decoction mashing is that at the end of each rest, part of the mash is removed from the mash tun and boiled (typically for about 15 minutes), then returned to the brew pot to bring the mash temperature up to the next step (or at least close). Decoction mashes break down proteins and starches in the boiling phase. The actual step of removing part of the mash and boiling it is called the decoction.

Typical schedules call for one, two, or three decoctions. The two-decoction process is probably the most common and consists of a protein rest at about 122°F (50°C), followed by a decoction that brings the temperature to the sac-charification rest at about 150°F (65.5°C) and then another decoction that brings the mash temperature to the lauter-rest temperature of about 170°F (77°C). The lauter rest stops enzymatic activity. When a three-decoction mash is used, the process begins with an acid rest at about 97°F (36°C). The acid rest corrects the pH. This rest may be skipped, with the pH being balanced through the addition of gypsum. The figure above shows a mashing schedule for a typical two-decoction mash.

The pH of the mash should be 5.2 to 5.8, with 5.3 being optimum. Thicker mashes will convert more starches to sugars.

MASH-OUT

The last step in the mashing process: heating to kill the enzymes. A 5-minute rest at a temperature of 170°F (77°C) is sufficient to stop all enzyme action positively.

A brewmaster stands before his mash tun.

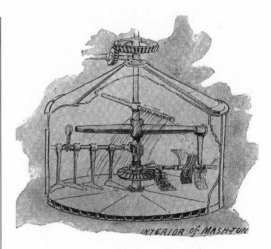

The interior of a mash tun at Hell Gate Brewery, New York, in 1891

MASH TUN

A large vessel, usually made of copper, brass or stainless steel, used for holding the mash.

Mash tuns at the F. X. Matt Brewing Co., Utica, NY

Depending on the type of mash method used, mash tuns are fitted with either perforated false bottoms and sparging arms (infusion mashing) or a propeller (decoction) for letting steam out the top.

See MASH.

MASH TUN RAKES

The part of a mash tun used to loosen the mash. Also called mash tun knives. Rakes also can be used for grain discharge. They are usually used with less modified, more gelatinous malts.

MASS. BAY BREWING CO. BOSTON, MASSACHUSETTS

Mass. Bay Brewing Co. was the first true microbrewery in Boston. The company

Harpoon Light

Harpoon Light is definitely a "light," but it is more interesting than most. It is firm-bodied, with hints of hops dancing in the background and a light malt finish. It is darker than any mainstream light and has a nice balance.

Harpoon India Pale Ale

There may be a soft, malty beer hiding beneath Harpoon IPA's deceptively golden surface, but it is not immediately apparent. What is apparent are hops. This IPA has a floral hop aroma, with a hint of spiciness, and a sharp hop edge to the palate. It is full-flavored, with a lot of citrusy hop character. The bitter finish serves its purpose admirably, leading the drinker from one sip to the next.

had the dubious fortune to start up at the same time and in the same city as beer marketing wunderkind Jim Koch, whose Boston Beer Co.'s Samuel Adams was just breaking into the market. The two Boston brewers engaged in fierce competition, and perhaps both ended up the stronger for it. Samuel Adams became the best-known nationally distributed specialty brand, and Mass. Bay became a strong regional microbrewery/contract brewery.

To get to that point, Mass. Bay has had to endure a few slings and arrows, and only one of the original partners, Rich Doyle, is still participating in day-to-day operations at the brewery. To compete head-to-head with its competition, Mass. Bay suspended its labor-intensive bottling operations and

contracted them out to Upstate New York's F. X. Matt Brewing Co. The new arrangement allowed Mass. Bay to broaden its line of bottled seasonal beers.

The company also hired Nick Godfrey (formerly of Smartfood Popcorn) as marketing director, with the task of increasing the visibility of its Harpoon line. Godfrey did just that, with revamped, more uniform bottle graphics and new local market promotions. Boston is the ultimate college/young professional city, and Mass. Bay soon targeted that market,

sponsoring frequent seasonal fests at its Boston brewery and almost-nightly beer tastings in its taproom.

Today Mass. Bay offers a full line of year-round and seasonal Harpoon beers, including Harpoon Ale, Harpoon Stout, Harpoon Oktoberfest, Harpoon Light, Harpoon India Pale Ale, and Harpoon Winter Warmer. The Company also is planning to bring a bottling line back to its Boston brewery, which will become a full-service brewing operation once again.

See ALE, BOSTON BEER CO., CONTRACT BREWING, MATT BREWING CO., INDIA PALE ALE (IPA), and LAGER ALE.

MASTER BREWERS ASSOCIATION OF THE AMERICAS

Douglas R. Babcock, President
4513 Vernon Boulevard, Suite 202
Madison, WI 53705
608-231-3446

The Master Brewers Association of the Americas is dedicated to the needs of large and small brewers operating in the Americas. It holds an annual conference and convention and caters to the educational needs of the brewing industry.

MATHER OF LEEDS

The last brewery producing British black beer, a somewhat syrupy, opaque brew that is yet another casualty of the lagering of Western civilization.

See BLACK BEER.

F. X. MATT BREWING CO. UTICA, NEW YORK

The F. X. Matt Brewing Co. is one of a handful of old American breweries to remain in the founding family's hands today. The current brewmaster is Francis Xavier Matt II, grandson of the founder, F. X. Matt.

The company was founded in 1888, one of 12 breweries in Utica at the time. In those days, it was known as the West End Brewery, since it served the west end of

The Saranac family of beers is brewed at the Utica, NY-based F. X. Matt Brewing Co.

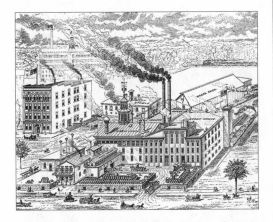

The West End Brewing Company of Utica, New York, which today is known as the F. X. Matt Brewing Company

Utica. Matt outlasted all of its Utica competitors (and just about everyone else in the region) and still distributes its Matt's Premium and Utica Club brands widely in New York State.

Over the years, the company has brewed many styles of beer, including bock, porter, dark lager, India Pale Ale, and stock ale. During Prohibition, the company even produced a nonalcoholic stout.

During the 1950s, the company expanded, building its capacity to 800,000 barrels. But ongoing beer wars sapped the company's strength, and by the 1980s it was in dire straits. Some of the family members wanted to sell the

Season's Best

F. X. Matt started producing Season's Best before seasonal beers made their recent comeback. This seasonal is a clean, crisp, malty beer in line with the F. X. Matt character. More recent versions of Season's Best seem to have even more character than earlier versions.

brewery, but a core group of relatives, led by F. X. Matt II, bought them out. Today Matt family members run the brewery. Nicholas Matt, formerly head of Procter & Gamble's Vicks division, is company president. Fred Matt, son of F.X. II, is the marketing director.

F. X. Matt has recently looked to broader markets with a line of Saranac specialty beers, including Saranac Pilsner, Adirondack Amber, Saranac Pale Ale, Saranac Black & Tan, Saranac Black Forest, and Season's Best. The company also produces a staggering array of con- tract-brewed brands, including Dock Street Amber, Harpoon Ale, Brooklyn Lager, and Helenboch.

See CONTRACT BREWING, PROHIBITION, and REGIONAL BREWERY.

Founder F. X. Matt in his new brewery in 1951.

MENDOCINO BREWING CO. HOPLAND, CALIFORNIA

Mendocino Brewing Co. is the oldest brewpub in California and the second oldest in the United States. When Michael Laybourn, Norman Franks, John Scahill, and Don Barkley started the oper- ation in 1982, they used the equipment

The aging tanks at F. X. Matt Brewing Co. in Utica, NY

The brewhouse of the Mendocino Brewing Co.

and grapevines.

The popularity of Mendocino's beers quickly forced it to become more than a brewpub. In 1987, the company increased its capacity from 800 barrels to 11,000 barrels per year. Further expansion brought capacity to 14,000 barrels. It was clear to Laybourn and his partners that further expansion was both necessary and desirable, and they decided to take an increasingly popular route — a public stock offering. Projected capacity of a new plant, once financed, is 150,000 barrels.

Mendocino Brewing Co. produces several well-regarded ales, including Red Tail Ale and Blue Heron Ale.

See ALE and BREWPUB.

and yeast strain from New Albion Brewing Co., the first, ill-starred United States microbrewery.

In its original incarnation, Mendocino Brewing Co. was an unprepossessing saloon in a small town in California wine country. The brewery included a gravity-flow brewhouse and a restored pub in an early-1900s building once known as the Hopvine Saloon. An enclosed beer garden also was built, garlanded with hop vines

MEUX DISASTER

A disaster that took place at the Meux Brewery in London on October 16, 1814. That afternoon a 22-foot-high vat of strong ale burst, releasing the equivalent of 4,000 barrels of beer. Rupturing additional holding vessels, the flood of ale hit the slum dwellings surrounding the brewhouse like a tidal wave. Between the riots resulting from the thirsty and curious trying to obtain their share and those drowned or crushed by debris, the death toll exceeded 20.

MICHELOB

See ANHEUSER-BUSCH.

MICROBREWERY

A small brewery traditionally defined as producing under 15,000 barrels of beer each year. By the end of 1995, there were approximately 600 microbreweries and brewpubs in the United States. The microbrewery segment is the fastest-growing part of the North American brewing industry, with almost 100 new United States brewery openings in 1994. In the past, most microbreweries were concentrated on the West Coast, but the movement has spread throughout North America.

A differentiation is often made between microbreweries and brewpubs. Microbreweries package the bulk of their beer for off-premises sale. Brewpubs sell most of their beer on the premises, serving it to customers in their own taprooms.

Microbreweries usually have a bottling line, allowing them to package their beer in a cost- and time-efficient manner. Quality control is an important factor in microbrewery operations, since the beer produced must be shipped off the premises. The need for shelf stability adds complexity to microbrewery operations. Brewpubs, in contrast, are able to serve their beer immediately.

See BREWPUB, CONTRACT BREWING, and MICROBREWERY MOVEMENT.

MICROBREWERY MOVEMENT

The microbrewery movement started in Great Britain in the 1970s as a revolt against the homogenization of the British brewing industry. In 1976, what might be called the first American "microbrewery" was incorporated by John McAuliffe. McAuliffe had been stationed with the Navy in Britain and had developed a taste for British-style ales and stouts. His New Albion Brewing Co. in Sonoma, California, was a bit ahead of its time and soon closed. However, New Albion's yeast strain and brewing vessels helped start one of today's more successful small breweries, Mendocino Brewing Co. of Hopland, California.

At the same time that New Albion's star was rising and falling, another small brewery was quietly plugging away in San Francisco. Fritz Maytag had purchased Anchor Brewing Co. in 1965. Anchor was a long-established San Francisco brewery, but its sales had dwindled to around 1,000 barrels a year, and it was floundering when Maytag bought it.

Though a brewing neophyte, Maytag set out to brew authentic, traditional beers. In the early years, his team of amateur brewers probably dumped more beer than they sold, but they carefully preserved the methods of the old Anchor Brewing Co. and gradually mastered the art of brewing. The revived Anchor Steam Beer carved a niche for itself in the Bay Area market, and by 1976 the company was selling 7,000 barrels a year. By 1980, volume had topped 20,000 barrels, and Anchor had become a model for a new generation of brewers to follow.

Anchor and New Albion had scouted the terrain, and others followed. In the vanguard were Sierra Nevada Brewing Co. of Chico, California (1981); Redhook Ale Brewery of Seattle, Washington (1982); Yakima Brewing & Malting Co. of Yakima, Washington (1982); and Mendocino Brewing Co. (1983). These pioneers paved the way for others, and microbreweries and brewpubs began to open all over the United States and Canada. The early microbreweries were concentrated on the West Coast, in a belt running from northern California to Seattle, Washington. Early brewery entrepreneurs found that San Francisco, Portland, and Seattle were especially fertile markets.

The enthusiastic consumer response to microbrewed beers ensured the success of the movement, and aspiring brewers all over the country began to hatch plans for small breweries of their own. By the mid-to-late 1980s, the movement had spread to the East Coast. New Amsterdam Brewing Co. of New York City (1982) started as a contract brewer and later opened a small brewpub in Manhattan. This brewery was forced to close, but other openings followed. D. L. Geary Brewing Co. of Portland, Maine (1986); Commonwealth Brewing Co. of Boston, Massachusetts (1986); and Catamount Brewing Co. of White River Junction, Vermont (1987) were among the earliest in the region.

Now there are small breweries throughout the country. The combination of microbreweries and restaurants, called brewpubs or pub breweries, has proved particularly successful. The repeal of prohibition–era laws aimed at preventing on-premises production of beer has allowed brewpubs to open in almost every state. This is one of the fastest-growing parts of the microbrewery movement. Today, there are prominent microbrewers who began as successful homebrewers, such as Dave Miller of St. Louis Brewery and Pete Slosberg of Pete's Brewing Co., producer of Pete's Wicked Ale.

Microbreweries now account for approximately 1.3 percent of United States beer sales — not an especially large proportion but big enough considering that the United States is the world's largest beer market. Microbreweries continue to open at a rapid pace, and although they will not supplant the country's largest brewers, they are an important part of a more diverse United States brewing industry.

See ANCHOR BREWING CO., BREWPUB; CONTRACT BREWING, GEARY BREWING CO., MENDOCINO BREWING CO., MICROBREWERY; NEW AMSTERDAM BREWING CO., REDHOOK ALE BREWERY, and YAKIMA BREWING & MALTING CO.

MICROBREWING

The practice of brewing small quantities of beer for commercial sale. Microbrewing takes place in a small brew plant with a capacity of under 15,000 barrels per year. The practice of microbrewing has grown in popularity in the United States, as small brewers compete to produce traditional beer styles and create new ones.

See BREWER, BREWERY, and MICROBREWERY.

MICROSCOPE

An optical instrument used for viewing microorganisms under high magnifications. Microscopes are used in the brewing industry for checking brewer's yeast viability and general appearance, as well as the presence of bacteria.

MID-ATLANTIC SMALL BREWERS ASSOCIATION BEER AND FOOD FESTIVAL

The first Mid-Atlantic Small Brewers Association Beer and Food Festival was inaugurated in 1994 in Washington, D.C., and the second annual festival was held in September 1995, in the streets near the Washington, D.C. Convention Center.

MILD ALE

See BROWN ALE.

MILK STOUT

An English stout that usually contains lactose (milk sugar, hence its name) and is much lower in original gravity, and therefore lower in alcohol content, than

dry stout: 1.044–1.048 OG, 3.7–3.8 percent alcohol by volume. Also called sweet stout. The color is very dark amber. Milk stout is sweet because ale yeast cannot digest lactose, which remains in the beer as a nonfermentable sugar. Commercial examples are Mackeson Stout from Great Britain and Louwaege Stout and Wilson Mild Stout from Belgium.

Recently the designation "milk stout" was challenged in both the United States and Great Britain. Regulators successfully complained that since milk was not actually used in the brewing process, the use of the word *milk* was misleading and could

Mackeson's Milk Stout is the standard for milk, or sweet, stouts, which tend to be less alcoholic than dry stouts.

possibly lead children to believe that they were drinking milk. Because of this, the term *milk stout* is now obsolete.

MILLER BREWING CO. MILWAUKEE, WISCONSIN

The Miller Brewing Co. is the second-largest brewing firm in the United States, with five breweries located around the country. The company traces its roots back to the mid–19th century, when it was founded by members of the Best family of Milwaukee (who also founded another of America's extant brewing companies, Pabst).

Part of the Best operation was sold to Frederick Miller in 1855, and the company was renamed the Frederick Miller Brewing Co. in 1888.

The company remained in the hands of the Millers until the late 1960s, when the scion of the Miller family was killed in a plane crash. The company was purchased by Philip Morris & Co. in 1970.

Philip Morris revolutionized the beer industry by taking an obscure light beer brand, renaming it "Lite" and building it into one of the hottest brands in the industry. In the process, light beer joined the pantheon of popular beer styles (today, five of the ten top brands in the United States market are "light" beers). The success of the Lite franchise propelled Miller Brewing Co. from a moderate-sized regional brewer into a big national player. In ten short years, output rose from under 5,000,000 barrels to 45,200,000.

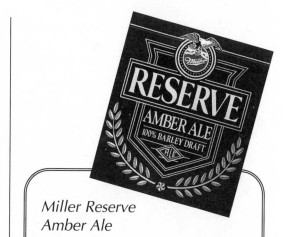

Miller Reserve Amber Ale

A few years ago, beer enthusiasts would have scoffed at the idea of the Miller Brewing Co. producing an ale (or a stout, for that matter). Now, they do both, and very credibly. Miller Reserve Ale is an amber beer with a malty aroma and good, pronounced ale flavor. The beer is brewed with a true top-fermenting ale yeast, which produces the fuller, rounded flavors that ale drinkers expect. Reserve Amber Ale is representative of the new specialty-type beers coming from America's major brewers, although it has more character than most of the other producer's early efforts. Products like Reserve Amber Ale could have an impact on the nascent microbrewery segment in coming years, since Miller (or any big brewer) has the economies of scale to put a specialty beer on the shelf at a price a couple of dollars below any microbrewery product.

Today, the Miller Lite brand is eroding as other brewers' light beers grow in popularity (last year, Anheuser-Busch's Bud Light unseated Lite as the number two brand in the nation, behind number-one brand Budweiser).

The Miller Brewing Co. remains an iconoclast among United States brewers and continues to look for the next major trend. In 1993, Miller test-marketed a clear beer; in 1994, a lime-flavored beer; who knows what the future holds? The Miller Brewing Co. has also created its Reserve product line, including several interpretations of traditional beer styles, including an ale, a stout, and an all-malt lager.

The Miller Brewing Co. is gradually building a strong position in the broader North American market, having purchased a stake in Canada's Molson and Mexico's FEMSA (owners of Cuauhtemoc and Moctezuma).

MILLING

The process of reducing the whole kernels of malted barley to grist by grinding them in a malt mill. This process is also known as crushing. The purpose of milling is to maintain the shape and integrity of the original husks while simultaneously pulverizing the creamy white, starchy endosperm of the malt so that it can be mixed with water in the mash tun.

CERVECERIA MODELO MEXICO CITY, MEXICO

Modelo's Mexico City brewery was founded in 1925. Today the company operates seven breweries, which produced more than 26,000,000 hl in 1994. It is currently building another plant in Zacatecas, which will be the largest plant in Latin America when it is completed.

Modelo has achieved remarkable vertical integration. The company owns its own barley fields, malts the barley at its own malthouses, produces its own cardboard for packaging, and makes bottles in glass factories that are supplied by company silica mines. The company also has a highly integrated distribution system, operating

Negra Modelo

A dark beer with a smooth, malty body and traces of coffee and chocolate flavor. Negra Modelo's lineage has been traced back to Vienna beers brought to Mexico by Austrian brewers in the 19th century. It is one of Mexico's best.

9,000 company-owned vehicles, plus thousands of vehicles owned by independent retailers and wholesalers.

Modelo currently has 72 percent share of Mexican beer exports, shipping beer to Europe, Australia, and Africa, in addition to North and South America. Helping complete the internationalization of the firm, Anheuser-Busch, the largest brewer in the world, purchased a minority interest in Modelo in 1993. Modelo produces the Corona and Modelo lines.

See BARLEY and MALT.

MOLASSES

The syrup that is left behind in the process of making ordinary table sugar from either sugar cane or sugar beets. It is called treacle

Ingredients such as molasses are sometimes added in brewing to enhance color and flavor.

in Great Britain. Molasses is separated from the crystallized sugar in a centrifuge. It contains impurities left over from the sugar cane or sugar beets. Molasses made from sugar cane contains about 14 percent invert sugar; beet molasses contains about 1 percent invert sugar. Blackstrap molasses has had most sugar removed in the crystallization process and has a much stronger flavor than other types of molasses.

Molasses can be added during the boil to provide fermentables and character to the beer. It is not recommended for lighter beers, as 1 cup (237 ml) in 5 gallons (19 L) of beer can have a prominent effect on the character. Used in excessive amounts and depending on the style of beer, molasses can give a butter or wine flavor to beer. It also can be used as a priming agent at the rate of 1 cup (237 ml) per 5 gallons (19 L) of beer.

MOLSON BREWERIES
TORONTO, CANADA

Molson is the oldest continuously operating brewery in North America, founded in 1786 by John Molson. The company has nine breweries with a total capacity of more than 13,400,000 hl. It brews more than 60 brands, including both Coors and Miller beers for the Canadian market. Miller now holds a minority stake in the company.

Molson uses Canadian malted barley, roasted malt, and other grains in the production of its beers. Its products are typically light-bodied golden lagers, much like their mainstream American counterparts to the south.

Popular misconceptions to the contrary, Molson and other Canadian beers are not appreciably stronger than comparable United States beers. Most Molson lagers have an alcohol content of 5.0 percent by volume, roughly equivalent to United States lagers from Anheuser-Busch, Miller, and Coors. Molson has been experimenting with some bolder products, including Rickard's Red, a flavorful ale brewed to an original gravity of 12.6 Plato, and several Molson Classic specialty beers. Molson

Molson Export

A smooth beer, somewhat more full-bodied than its brethren, with some fruity ale character. The "Ex," as it is familiarly called, is fairly typical of the Molson line, although slightly more characterful than the company's lagers. It is brewed to an original gravity of 11.2 with a top-fermenting yeast.

Breweries U.S.A., a subsidiary of Miller Brewing Co., imports Molson beers into the United States.

See EXPORT and IMPORT.

MOLSON BREWERIES INFORMATION CENTRE

Information Centre
2486 Dunwin Drive
Mississauga, Ontario
Canada L5L 1J9
416-828-1786

Open by appointment only. The Molson Breweries Information Centre contains extensive information on Molson Breweries' operation within Canada and throughout the world, with historical information on this, the oldest continuously operating brewery in the world.

BRASSERIE MOORTGAT BREENDONK, BELGIUM

The independent Moortgat brewery is best known for its flagship beer, Duvel. This potent golden ale undergoes three fermentations: the first warm, the second cold, and the third warm, in the bottle. Big red letters on the outside of the brewery read, *"SSST . . . Hier rijpt dev Duvel"* (Shhh, Duvel is ripening). The brewery was built in 1871 by Jan Moortgat. Today it is run by his grandchildren.

The noted brewing chemist Jean De Clerk once worked for Moortgat as a consultant. He spent much of his time refining the company's trademark dark ales. Upon sampling one of De Clerk's creations, a Moortgat brewer remarked that it was "a devil *(duvel)* of a beer." In the early 1970s, Moortgat replaced its dark Duvel with a pale version. This is the Duvel consumers know today.

See ALE, BOTTLE-CONDITIONED BEER, and ENGLISH STRONG ALE.

Duvel

Duvel is brewed with Danish summer barley, malted to stringent Moortgat specifications, and uses whole Styrian Goldings and Saaz hops. The beer undergoes three fermentations at the brewery and is bottle-conditioned. According to the producer, the yeast in the bottle carbonates Duvel in a process identical to that used for champagne, giving Duvel its trademark towering creamy head. Duvel is a strong ale (8.5 percent alcohol by volume) with the appearance of a light golden Pilsner. Its latent power is concealed by its smooth, malty body and sweet, slightly spicy aromatics.

BIRRA MORETTI
UDINE, ITALY

Moretti is brewed in Udine in northern Italy, and its beers betray its proximity to Austria. Until the early 20th century, Trieste and the surrounding coast were part of the Hapsburg Empire, and Austrian brewers left their distinct brewing

La Rossa

A malty, dark amber beer much in the style of a German doppelbock. It is rich and full-bodied, with a spicy hop character that sets it apart from its German cousins. It is brewed to a gravity of 18 degrees Plato, and is said to be the favored beer of actor Paul Newman.

styles behind when the Hapsburg tide receded.

Moretti was family owned until recent years, when it was bought by Canadian brewer John Labatt, Ltd. As a result, its beers are now imported into the United States by Labatt's U.S.A. of Darien, Connecticut. Marco Moretti, scion of the brewing clan, lives and works in Connecticut, helping to spread the word of his family's beer in the New World.

The Moretti trademark bears the distinctive visage of the "mustachioed man." According to the story, a member of the Moretti family spotted this gentleman savoring a beer in a local trattoria and asked to take his picture. He agreed, and his image has adorned every Moretti bottle since 1942. For the Italian market, Moretti produces an all-malt lager called Boffo D'Oro (Golden Mustache) in honor of the anonymous gentleman.

Birra Moretti is also brewed at Castello Brewery in San Giorgio di Nogaro.

Labatt's U.S.A. imports Moretti Pilsner and La Rossa Double Malt into the United States.

See LABATT, LTD. and LAGER ALE.

MOROCCO ALE

A very strong ale, brewed in England at Levens Hall, Cumberland, that uses beef or other meat as an ingredient. The recipe has been kept a secret. It is said that the original recipe was brought by a Crusader named Howard from "beyond the seas."

The recipe was buried during the parliamentary wars of the 1600s and was dug up many years later.

Morocco ale is served to first-time visitors in an immense glass of a curious shape. Drinkers are expected to toast "to the health of the Lady of Levens."

MOTHER-IN-LAW

A British term for a beer mixture of equal parts bitter and old ale.

MOUTHFEEL

A descriptive word used in the judging of beer samples to denote the amount of body a sample contains. Generally, a "good" mouthfeel rating would have appropriate consistency and thickness.

See BODY.

Mugs come in a variety of sizes. These hold more than enough beer to quench a thirst.

MUG

A drinking vessel, usually cylindrical, that has a handle of some sort. While mugs traditionally hold 12 ounces (355 ml) of beer, they can be found in any number of sizes.

See GLASSWARE.

MUMM

A strong, nonhopped ale brewed in Bräunschweig (Brunswick), Germany, in the 18th century. It was apparently first brewed by Christian Mumme in the late 15th century. It is not to be confused with Mumme, a Malzbier still brewed in Germany.

MÜNCHENER

See BAVARIAN BEER.

MÜNCHENER HELLES

A pale Munich beer similar to Munich dunkel developed in the 20th century to compete with the lighter Bohemian beer known as Pilsner. As in its dark parent (Munich dunkel), malt is the primary flavor element, and the impact of hops is minimized (20 to 30 IBU). Munich dunkel has mostly replaced the Dortmunder export style in popularity, at least in southern Germany. It was the model for American and Pacific Rim brewers in developing the style that has become known as American lager, although of the two the Munich beer is a little stronger.

Münchener Helles is maltier and less hoppy than Munich dunkel, with smooth, almost caramelly undertones. It has the following characteristics: 11.5–13.5/1.046–1.055 OG, about 3 final gravity, 4.5–5.5 percent alcohol by volume, 20–30 IBU, and 2.6–4.5 SRM. The usual ingredients are pale 2-row European barley malted at low temperatures to produce the pale Munich malt, Hallertauer or Northern Brewer hops, and medium-hard water (about 200 ppm hardness). This beer style is popular throughout Germany, mostly in the south. It is often a little heavier than the Pilsner found in the north. Compare the Paulaner No. 1 export (lower alcohol content to meet the requirements for distribution in the United States) with the Paulaner Original Münchner Hell (the product sold in Germany).

The Great American Beer Festival guidelines for Münchener Helles and Export (lager) are 11–13/1.044–1050 OG, 4.5–5.5 percent alcohol by volume, 18–25 IBU, and 3–5 SRM (pale golden color).

Original Gravity	Final Gravity	Alcohol by Volume	IBU	SRM
Altenmunster 1981				
12.7/1.051	5.6	1.7%	≈21	≈4
Kulmbacker Schweitzerhofbräu 1982				
12.7/1.051	4.9	2.8%	≈23	≈4

	Original Gravity	Final Gravity	Alcohol by Volume	IBU	SRM
Paulaner No. 1 1989 (export for United States)					
	11.5/1.046	4.9	2.1%	22	3.8
Paulaner Original Munchner Hell 1989 (for consumption in Germany)					
	12.4/1.050	5.5	2%	27	3.65

See BOHEMIAN BEER.

MUNICH BEER

See BAVARIAN BEER.

MUNICH DUNKEL

See BAVARIAN BEER.

MUSEUMS

American Beer Museum
Fort Mitchell, Kentucky

The world's largest collection of beer and brewing memorabilia. Also the site of Beer Camp.

Biermuseum de Boom
Alkmaar, Netherlands

An old brewery. On exhibit are displays of brewing, malting, and cooperage.

Brauereimuseum
Lueneburg, Germany

Contains a working brewery that dates as far back as 500 years. Much original equipment in the exhibit.

Brasserie Cantillon Brewery Museum
Brussels, Belgium

A lambic brewery run by Jean-Pierre Van Roy, a member of the Cantillon family that dates back to Belgian brewers in the 1700s. Brasserie Cantillon is unusual in that it occasionally bottles a lambic in its unblended, still form. Much of the beer they brew is sold in champagne bottles.

Brasserie de Monceau St. Waast
Aulnoye-Aymeries, France

Originally a cheese dairy in the 1870s, the building was converted to a brewery in 1891. It was acquired by the municipality of Aulnoye-Aymeries recently to serve as a working museum of artisan brewing. Some of the brewing equipment — the grist mill and cast-iron mash tun — may date back to 1891. The brewmaster is Patrick Duquesne, who ferments beer with Belgian top yeast.

Brugs Brouwerij-Mouterij Museum
Bruges, Belgium

An old malt-house. The museum in the malt-house holds the history of old Bruges breweries.

City Brewery Museum
Galena, Illinois

Until 1881, the City Brewery. Now it is a museum with displays of brewing and visits to lagering cellars.

Confederation of Belgian Brewers Museum
Brussels, Belgium

This brewers' museum is in the Brewers' Guildhouse and is laid out like a brewery. It includes a small sampling bar.

Guinness Museum
Dublin, Ireland

Historical brewing equipment, coopers' tools, and beer advertising from the history of brewing in Ireland.

Oud Beersel 1882 Museum
Beersel, Belgium

Located in the Vandervelden Brewery. Exhibit includes brewing artifacts.

See BEER CAMP and SAPPORO BREWERIES.

NATIONAL BEER WHOLESALERS ASSOCIATION, INC.

Ron Sarasin, President
1100 South Washington Street
Alexandria, VA 22134-4494
703-683-4300

The National Beer Wholesalers Association acts as the unified voice of the wholesale beer distributors in the United States. Its focus is often legislative, targeting matters that directly affect the business of distributing beer in the United States.

NATURAL CONDITIONING

A secondary fermentation that occurs while the brew still contains live yeast cells. Natural fermentation may occur in the brewing vat or in a maturing vat.

NEAR BEER

A beer having a very low alcohol content, usually under 2.5 percent alcohol by volume. In the United States, near beer must have under 0.65 percent alcohol by volume. In Germany, the limit is a bit higher at 0.7 percent alcohol by volume. During Prohibition, these beers were produced by distilling the alcohol out of the beer.

NEGRA MODELA

See MODELO, CERVECERIA.

NEW AMSTERDAM BREWING CO. NEW YORK, NEW YORK

New Amsterdam Brewing Co. was the seminal contract brewer, founded in 1982 by Matthew Reich. The company pioneered the concept of contract brewing in the early 1980s, producing beer at F. X. Matt Brewing Co. of Utica, New York, and marketing it in New York City and its suburbs.

Reich's tactics are now familiar. He created a brand, wrote an historical story to put on a hangtag, and sold the beer as a microbrewed specialty product. It was a brilliant business strategy, picked up on and carried to fruition by Jim Koch of Boston Beer Co., among others.

Some of New Amsterdam's current family of beers

New Amsterdam Ale

A dry-hopped version of the pioneering New Amsterdam Amber. Dry hopping (the addition of dry, clean hops after fermentation is complete) adds an aromatic character to this full-flavored beer.

Reich stumbled when he tried to build an upscale brewpub in the Chelsea section of Manhattan. The costs of building and operating the plant soon drained the company's coffers, and Reich sold his interest in the company to his contract producer, F. X. Matt. Matt stabilized the business and eventually sold it to the Peerless Beverage Co. Under its new management, New Amsterdam has benefited from increased market support, including TV and magazine advertising. The company sold an estimated 36,000 barrels in 1994.

See ALE BEER, AMBER AND RED BEERS, CONTRACT BREWING, and MICROBREWERY.

NEW INDUSTRIAL BEER

See AMBER AND RED BEERS, AMERICAN BEER, and AMERICAN LAGER.

NEW YORK BEERFEST

Also called the International Beer & Food Tasting Under the Brooklyn Bridge, which makes patrons thirsty just saying it. A non-profit fund-raiser for Brooklyn cultural organizations held in mid-September, the festival matches beers with food from area restaurants. Held in outdoor tents under the Brooklyn Bridge, the first event took place in 1993 with about 3,500 attendees; the 1994 festival was, by most accounts, overwhelmed by upward of 10,000 people, prompting the possibility of split sessions in the future. The beer selection is diverse, with international and domestic specialty beers available.

NINETY-SHILLING ALE

See SCOTCH ALE.

NINKASI

The first definitive beer goddess; literally, "the lady who fills the mouth." Like most Sumerian gods and goddesses, Ninkasi had many manifestations and roles. The literature dating from 5,000 years ago portrays this goddess as the giver and protector of beer and brewing. Ninkasi preceded a long line of female deities that would establish beyond question the femininity of beer. In 1990, Fritz Maytag of Anchor Brewing Co. became the first United States brewer to try to replicate the beers of Sumerian women, and called his sample "Ninkasi." He brewed this Ninkasi sample again in 1993 for the Book and the Cook event.

See ANCHOR BREWING CO. and SUMERIAN BEER.

NITRATE

A salt, or ester, of nitric acid. If a water analysis indicates more than 25 ppm nitrate ions, the water is being contaminated by organic compounds or fertilizer runoff, and a different water supply for brewing should be found. The problem with using water with high levels of nitrate ions is that certain bacteria can reduce nitrates to nitrites, which will adversely affect the metabolism of the yeast.

NITRITE

A salt of nitrous acid (containing less oxygen than nitrate). Any nitrites in a brewer's water supply are a problem, but if the level is above 25 ppm, they can seriously hamper the metabolism of yeast during the fermentation process and will produce dimethyl sulfide (DMS). If the brewing water has elevated levels of nitrites, a new water supply should be found.

See DIMETHYL SULFIDE.

NITROGEN

An element contained in malt and used as an essential nutrient for yeast growth.

See YEAST NUTRIENTS.

NOBLE HOPS

Certain hops grown in Europe that are prized for their aromatic and flavor characteristics. The definitive noble hops, which are named for their places of origin, are Saaz, Hallertauer Mittelfrüh, Spalt Spalter, and Tettnang Tettnanger. Any other hop is measured against these four. Why these are considered "noble" is subject to debate, but there is no argument that brewers value them highly.

See HOPS.

NONALCOHOLIC BEER

A malt beverage that does not contain more than 0.5 percent alcohol by volume. *See* NEAR BEER.

NORTH AMERICAN GUILD OF BEER WRITERS

Rob Haiber, Co-chairman
Reilly Road
La Grangewille, NY 12540
914-223-3269
Fax: 914-227-5520
Internet address:
Rob BBC1@eWorld.com

Formed in 1993 by Robert Haiber and Benjamin Myers, the main objectives of the North American Guild of Beer Writers (NAGBW) are to increase media coverage of beer and brewing, to enhance public knowledge and appreciation of those subjects, and to increase job opportunities for Guild members by informing media and breweries of the Guild's existence. The NAGBW has professional links with the British Guild of Beer Writers, after which the NAGBW is loosly modeled.

The Guild has a presence in Beer and Brewing Central, in World, Apple Computer's online service.

Guild membership stands at 75, and has been steadily increasing with the rising popularity of homebrewing, microbrewing, and specialty beers.

NORTHWEST MICROBREW EXPO

In 1995, the second annual Northwest Microbrew Expo combined the traditional elements of a trade show and convention with the hubbub of a public beer festival. Held in February at the Lane County Convention Center in Eugene, Oregon, the event attracted about 8,000 beer lovers anxious to sample some of the more than 70 beers from 36 microbreweries. The breweries were limited to those from Washington, Oregon, Idaho, northern California, and Alberta, Canada, with the 1995 guest brewer slot going to the Red Ass Ale Brewing Company of Fort Collins, Colorado.

The 1995 festival, which claims to be the largest annual winter microbrew celebration in the country, featured beer tours, a homebrewing school, and a free shuttle between the expo and participating local pubs. The tours were 15-minute walks around the grounds to familiarize participants with specific beers, brewing history, and brewing techniques. The Expo Brew School consisted of miniseminars led by writers Fred Eckhardt, Larry Baush, and other brewing talents.

The 2-day event includes continuous live music, a sports bar area, a food court (the Hungry Brewer Cafe) with offerings from several of the region's restaurants, and the typical commemorative glass ready for those 2-ounce pours.

See GREAT NORTHWEST MICROBREWERY INVITATIONAL.

NOSE

A descriptive word used to judge the total fragrance, bouquet, and aroma of a given beer sample.

See AROMA and BOUQUET.

OASTHOUSE

The traditional structure for hop drying. Modern oasthouses are often called kilns. Generally, an oasthouse is a round building with slotted floors 15 feet above the ground. The hops are spread over horsehair cloths and dried in a draft of warm air. After drying, the hops are sent to a separate room for cooling.

Modern kilns have more than one floor. The green hops are spread 2-feet deep on an upper floor. At various intervals, the hops drop down through up-to-three more floors prior to being collected dry. This is obviously a lot more efficient than the traditional method because hot air percolates through several floors of hops before they leave the oasthouse.

See KILN.

OATMEAL STOUT

See STOUT.

OATS

A grain that is occasionally used in brewing as an adjunct, especially in stouts.

Commercial examples include Samuel Smith's Oatmeal Stout and Anderson Valley Barney Flats Oatmeal Stout. Oats also are used as an adjunct in some Belgian ales, such as wit. Homebrewers typically use steel-cut oats, which are available at most health food stores, although oats can be malted and then mashed as a source of fermentable sugars.

See BELGIAN WHITE BEER and STOUT.

OFF-FLAVOR

Any unpleasant or undesirable flavor that develops in a beer. This off-flavor might be caused by sanitation problems, oxidization, stale ingredients, or poor storage.

OKTOBERFEST BEER

A lager or bottom-fermented beer that is aged (lagered) for longer than usual and made in March for the Oktoberfest, a harvest celebration held in Germany during the last 2 weeks of September. Also called Märzenbier (March beer). This was traditionally the last beer of the winter brewing season. Made stronger than other beers, it was packed in the last ice of winter, stored all through the summer, and consumed in the fall. Even after the invention of refrigeration, the special Märzenbier tradition continued.

Today Märzenbier is amber in color and paler than the traditional dark Munich beers, yet darker than today's pale beers. Märzen is produced annually by each of Munich's breweries. The style is duplicated, on a seasonal basis, by many other breweries around the world, especially those in Germany.

The original Oktoberfest beer dates only from the 1840s and was brewed by Gabriel Sedlmayr in his Munich Spätenbräu Brewery as a tribute to his friend, brewer Anton Dreher of Vienna. The beer was in what we now call the Vienna style, which had just been introduced by Dreher. Spaten Ur-Märzen Oktoberfest Malt Liquor is now available in the United States. (The beer is called a malt liquor because it has an alcohol content [5.5 percent alcohol by volume] that is higher than allowed for beer sold in the United States.) This beer is made according to the ancient *Reinheitsgebot* (pledge of purity).

Märzen is amber or pale copper in color, with medium to strong alcohol content (5 to 6 percent by volume). Although the style originated in Vienna, it is rarely made there today. Some Märzens are made seasonally. Others are labeled "Oktoberfest" but made year-round. Original gravity is 12.5–14.9/1.050–1.061, bitterness 22–35 IBU, and color 8–14 SRM.

The traditional malt in this beer is Vienna malt, which is dried at temperatures higher than the much paler Pilsner malt and lower than the darker Munich malt. Some brewers mix darker malts with pale malts to achieve the proper color standard. The hops used in Ur-Märzen Oktoberfest are from Munich's own Hallertauer district.

The Great American Beer Festival guidelines for all of the Amber Lager Märzen/Oktoberfest beers are 12.5–14/ 1.050–1.056 OG, 5.3–5.9 percent alcohol by volume, 18–25 IBU, and 4–15 SRM.

Original Gravity	Final Gravity	Alcohol by Volume	IBU	SRM
Capital Gartenbräu Oktoberfest (Wisconsin) 1989				
13.11/1.053	3.7	4.7%	18	≈9
Paulaner Oktoberfest (Germany) 1986				
13.6/1.055	2.8	6.7%	22	8.7
Spaten Ur-Märzen Oktoberfest Malt Liquor (Germany) 1985				
13.3/1.054	2.9	5.3%	21	8.3

See VIENNA BEER.

OKTOBERFEST — MUNICH

Living in one of the world's great brewing nations, Germans do not need an excuse to drink beer. Luckily, they have come up with some good ones anyway, as well as the beers to go with them: holiday beers for Christmas, doppelbocks for Lent, bocks in the spring, wheat beers in the summer. Fall is the time for Oktoberfest beers, also called Märzen (March), or Vienna beers. There are many festivals held in October, but as beer festivals go, Munich's

Oktoberfest, an annual beer festival held in Munich's Theresienwiese for sixteen days and nights in late September and early October, is perhaps the most widely known beer festival in the world.

Oktoberfest is the mother of them all, the world's biggest celebration of beer.

It all began in 1810 as a celebration of the marriage of Crown Prince Ludwig I and Princess Therese. Oktoberfest has been going strong ever since. It begins in mid-September, a fortnight before its finish on the first Sunday in October. The festival begins with the lord mayor of Munich, Germany, driving a tap into the first keg of beer at noon under the Spaten brewery tent and bellowing, *"O'zapft ist!"* (The beer is tapped!)

The first celebration was apparently a fairly sober affair, with a horse race held at Theresienwiese (Theresa's Meadow), on October 17, 1810. After almost 200 years, the festival has evolved into a carnival, food orgy, and no-holds-barred beer blast with all the traditional trappings: oompah bands with musicians in lederhosen and beefy waitresses in dirndls hauling up to 14 sturdy, liter mugs of brew at a time.

On the first Sunday, a huge parade of brewery drays pulled by horses ends at the fairgrounds, where the major breweries have worked for 6 weeks setting up vast tents to hold the thousands of tourists. Close to a million thirsty partygoers show up. British beer writer Michael Jackson has said, "The Oktoberfest is quite a spectacle, an impressive display of Teutonic excess. Everyone interested in beer should go at least once. But once may be enough."

The endless fascination with Oktoberfest frequently centers on just how vast a pig-out it is. In 1994, 10 million pints of beer were consumed, along with 60 whole oxen, 750,000 chickens, 65,000 pig knuckles, and more than 830,000 wursts of all shapes, sizes, and colors.

Considering the numbers involved and the amount of beer consumed, the Oktoberfest is a relatively orderly affair. It may not look that way to the casual tourist, bowled over by noise, frequent encouragements to toast *("Prosit!"),* and dancing on tables. But the vastness of the enterprise is carefully regulated by the Munich City Council and the six major brewers. The halls are laid out in a predictable order, the waitressing positions and food stalls handed down from generation to generation, and there are relatively few arrests for drunkenness, thanks in part to strategic sobering-up tents.

Besides Spaten, the only other brewers permitted tents at the festival are Paulaner, Hacker-Pschorr (a subsidiary of Paulaner), Hofbräu, Augustiner, and Lowenbräu, since they brew within the city limits. The brew offerings obviously have changed over the years. Oktoberfest, the beer, did not show up until the Spaten brewery introduced it in 1872, which is why Spaten can call its offering Ur-Märzen, the "original"

Märzen. The beer grew out of a collaboration between Spaten's Gabriel Sedlmayr and Anton Dreher of Vienna, hence the term Vienna beer. The Märzen tag stems from pre-refrigeration days. March was the last month of good brewing weather, so the hardy Vienna beers were brewed then and stored in caves. They were drunk throughout the summer and ceremoniously polished off in the fall — just in time for Oktoberfest! In general, the style is a medium- to full-bodied lager, amber to brown in color, with a pronounced malty-sweet nose and a somewhat lighter malty flavor. The best examples have a spicy bite and compensating hop bitterness to balance the sweetness. The Märzenbiers are still available in the city, but the beers at the festival tend to be lighter these days, supposedly a reflection of consumer tastes.

See CANSTATTERWASAN, FRÜHJAHRS STARK-BIER-FEST, and OKTOBERFESTS.

OKTOBERFESTS

The original Oktoberfest in Munich, Germany, has spawned a goodly number of American descendants. None of the American festivals can match the original, but they are fun nonetheless, with the usual oompah bands, dancers in lederhosen, sizzling wursts, and, of course, beer. The beer may be far from the Oktoberfest style and is usually an American lager made by a major brewer that may be the festival sponsor.

Some larger Oktoberfests around the country are in Covington, Kentucky;

The broad term Oktoberfest *is used today to refer to any beer festival held in late September or early October, but it is derived from the original Oktoberfest, held annually in Munich's Theresienwiese.*

Denver, Colorado; Grand Prairie, Texas; Poughkeepsie, New York; Fort Lauderdale, Florida; Amana, Iowa; and Cincinnati, Ohio. Many begin, like the original, in September. Some are 1-day affairs, like the Calistoga (California) Beer & Sausage Festival, celebrating its 12th year in 1995.

OLD ALE

See ENGLISH STRONG ALE and SCOTCH ALE.

OPEN-TOP COOLING BOX

A shallow rectangular vessel of large surface area in which a thin layer of wort is spread. Also called a coolstrip. Exposing the wort promotes cooling and evaporation of water and volatile oils. The hot break from the brew kettle settles to the bottom, and when the temperature reaches 140°F (60°C), the wort is removed, avoiding the disturbance of any sediment. The wort then passes through an open or closed heat exchanger prior to flowing into a fermenting vessel.

The cooling box is still found in a few breweries in Great Britain and many on the continent and is often located on the top floor of tower breweries. Obviously, this type of cooling, though economical for precooling, is subject to infection.

ORDINARY BITTER

See BITTER.

OREGON BREWER'S FESTIVAL

Hosted by three Portland breweries (Bridgeport Brewing, Portland Brewing, and Widmer Brothers Brewing), the Oregon Brewer's Festival has been held since 1988. The Festival is the largest presentation of handcrafted beers in the United States and, if one is to judge by attendance, one of the world's largest. About 70,000 people attended the 1994 festival, and they consumed 12,245 gallons of beer, from 63 micro and regional breweries, served by some 900 volunteers. The festival takes place outdoors (under large circus tents) on the last weekend of July, at Portland's Willamette Waterfront Park. The Oregon Brewer's Festival is noted for the fact that no judging of beers takes place and there are no awards. The festival management buys (and sells) all of the beers from the breweries it invites. All of America's small brewers are invited. None of the nation's larger old-line brewers are invited, and no contract beers are presented. The first seventy-odd brewers to accept are invited to send beer. Admission to the festival is free, and families with children are welcome. Visitors purchase a plastic beer mug for two dollars and beer chips at one dollar (4-ounce sample). Accompanying exhibits encompass the arts of brewing, homebrewing, hop culture, and barley growing and malting. Food tents offer soft drinks and a variety of pub fare from eight of Portland's finest restaurants, and there's music, too.

London beer critic Michael Jackson has called Portland (now with 20 breweries and brewpubs) the Beer Capital of the Americas. There are another ten breweries in nearby towns (within 30 miles), and, except for the Bamberg area of Northern Bavaria, there is no greater concentration of breweries anywhere. Portland brewers produce over 100 brands, with styles ranging from Adambier to Pilsner, from altbier to doppelbock, from porter to double stout, from Scottish to ESB (Extra Special Bitter) to IPA (India Pale Ale), and lemon lager, raspberry-weizen, and rye beer.

ORIGINAL BEER STYLES

Almost all the distinctive classes of beer made around the world originated in Europe.

Today the British style of ale is making a comeback from near extinction in the late 1960s. It forms the backbone of the new beer counterrevolution. British ale styles were developed beginning around the 5th century and reached their peak during the second half of the 19th century, which was the pinnacle of European beer creativity.

The most impressive European contribution to brewing science and beer styles came from Bavaria, where a special yeast was developed with the ability to ferment beer at very low, nearly freezing, temperatures (below 40°F, or 4°C). The unique cold ferment was carried on in deep caves, which were kept at low temperatures by using ice harvested from frozen lakes in winter. Such beer was called lagered beer, from the German *lagern*, "to store." Munich beer was the first of the great central European beer styles to be developed in the 19th century.

"Pilsner" is a name found on many beers today. The original Pilsner beer was made in Plzen, Czechoslovakia, and was known as Bohemian beer.

Vienna beer was first brewed by Anton Dreher, the great Hungarian brewmaster in Budapest.

Dortmunder export was the last beer type to be developed in central Europe in the 19th century.

The wonderful beer styles of Belgium are just now becoming familiar to the rest of the world.

Gruitbier (spiced beer) was quite popular before the introduction of hops, and variations may have been brewed in most countries from Scandinavia to Switzerland and northern France.

The United States originated the style we now call American lager, which has become the most popular style in the world, despite its lack of substance. American light beer is another popular brew, as is malt liquor.

See AMERICAN BEER, BAVARIAN BEER, BELGIAN BEER, BOHEMIAN BEER, BRITISH BEER, and LAGER.

ORIGINAL GRAVITY

A measure of the specific gravity of the wort prior to fermentation as compared to the density of water. Also referred to as the starting specific gravity. This figure is a measure of the total amount of solids dissolved in the wort, and is used in conjunction with the final gravity to measure the alcohol level in a beer and the degree of attenuation of the yeast.

See DENSITY.

BRASSERIE D'ORVAL FLORENVILLE, BELGIUM

One of Belgium's famed Trappist breweries, Orval produces only one beer — Orval. The current brewery dates from the early part of this century, but abbey records trace the brewing tradition back to the 11th century.

Belgian postage stamps from 1928 feature the Brasserie d'Orval.

It is said that the abbey was originally built because a young countess lost a gold ring in a lake near the village of Florenville. She promised God that she would build him a monastery if he found the ring for her. When a trout jumped from the water with the ring in its mouth, she fulfilled her promise. In her gratitude,

The current buildings at the abbey of Orval were constructed in the 1920s and are, with the exception of the cloister, open to the public.

she set aside land for the church to build a monastery.

The abbey was started by Benedictines in 1070, pillaged sometime later, and rebuilt in the 12th century by Cistercians. In those times, the abbey was somewhat akin to a pharmacy, and one of its tonics is said to have been an ale.

Eventually, the abbey fell into disuse. It lay in ruins for more than a century before the current buildings were completed in 1929. Since that time, the brothers at Orval have brewed their famous ale. It uses Kent Goldings and Hallertauer hops, which are added twice during the brew. It is fermented twice with a strain of top-fermenting yeast, then bottom-fermenting yeasts are added to the bottle. To allow for its bottle-conditioning, the beer is said to age well for up to 5 years.

Orval is packaged in a distinctive brown bottle bearing the trout and gold ring motif. It is imported into the United States by Merchant Du Vin of Seattle, Washington.

See ABBAYE, ALE, BOTTOM-FERMENTING YEAST, and TOP-FERMENTING YEAST.

OXYGEN TESTER

An instrument designed to measure the level of dissolved oxygen in beer samples, specifically in bottled beer, where shelf life is linked to oxygen content. An oxygen level under 0.5 ml is desirable.

OYSTER STOUT

"He was a bold man that first eat any oyster." So said Jonathan Swift. It would take time and an even bolder person to add the delectable mollusk to his beer.

With the birth of Guinness Stout in 1759, a bond between Guinness and a platter of oysters began. This remains one of the truly great culinary combinations of all time, due to the two contrasting but complementary flavors: the oyster's delicate ocean tang and the wondrous malt of the rich Dublin stout.

Such a combination figured in the memories of the great English statesman Benjamin Disraeli. The man who would become British prime minister wrote of an early election victory in 1837, "I dined — at the Carlton — of oysters, Guinness, and boiled bones. Thus ended the most remarkable day of my life."

It was only a matter of time before some enterprising brewer tried to combine the two flavors in a bottle. Around the turn of this century, the Colchester Brewing Co. in England began producing Oyster Feast Stout to mark the yearly oyster harvest. By the early 1940s, due to wartime shortages, powdered oyster shells were used to clarify beer. They also reduced acidity, making smoother-tasting brews with longer-lasting heads.

In 1929, Young & Son Portsmouth Brewery, New Zealand, became possibly the first commercial firm to brew a stout using oysters in the recipe. It was called Victory Oyster Stout.

The last and best known of the oyster stouts came from Castletown Brewery on the Isle of Man. Beginning sometime in the late 1930s and continuing until the late 1960s, Manx Oyster Stout sold well enough to be shipped to England, Asia, Africa, and the United States.

Many Guinness advertisements, especially during World War II, have capitalized on the tremendous popularity of oysters and stout. One slogan from that time reads: "Guinness makes the oysters come out of their shells."

PABST BREWING CO. MILWAUKEE, WISCONSIN

Pabst Brewing Co. is the sixth-largest brewing concern in the United States. Housed in a grand old brewery in Milwaukee, the company is a subsidiary of the S & P Co., which also owns the Falstaff, Pearl, and General Brewing Companies.

Pabst can trace its origins to the Best family, the same family prominent in Miller Brewing Co.'s early history. Best Brewing Co., founded in 1844, was the first company to brew lager beer in Milwaukee, in 1851. Frederick Pabst, a

Aerial view of the Pabst Brewing Co. of Milwaukee, Wisconsin

Ballantine
India Pale Ale

The Ballantine brands came to Pabst through a convoluted path that led from Peter Ballantine Brewing Co. (once of Albany, New York, later of Newark, New Jersey) to Falstaff Brewing Co. (of Cranston, Rhode Island, and Fort Wayne, Indiana), and then to Pabst. For a time in the 1970s (and into the early 1980s, in the East), Ballantine India Pale Ale was the most popular ale brewed in the United States. In an age when light-bodied pale lagers were de rigueur, Ballantine IPA was a shining example of a real, old-time ale. It was deep copper color and potently aromatic, with a full, malty body. When it was brewed at the old Falstaff breweries, it was aged in wood. Since its last move to Pabst's Milwaukee brewery, it seems to have lost some of its character. (For one thing, there are no wooden aging vats in Milwaukee.) It is still a noteworthy ale, however.

Frederick Pabst was a steamer captain when he married into the Best family, ultimately to become a partner in their brewery.

steamer captain, married into the Best family in the early 1860s and eventually became a partner in the brewery, then called Philip Best Brewing Co. Pabst proved a canny businessman, and Best expanded rapidly under his direction. By 1889, the board voted to change the company's name to Pabst Brewing Co.

Frederick Pabst's crowning achievement came in 1893, when Pabst was recognized as "America's Best Lager Beer" at the World's Columbian Exposition. Soon thereafter, the company began affixing a blue ribbon to its bottles, giving the company's flagship beer its now-familiar name.

Pabst Brewing Co.'s sales in the United States market have been on the decline, and the company has gradually closed some of its United States plants, including grand old breweries that once brewed Narragansett and Ballantine beers. In spite of these setbacks, the company is now doing a land-office business in China. Pabst has actually disassembled some of its shuttered United States breweries and shipped them lock, stock, and barrel to China. In that market, Pabst Blue Ribbon sales are booming, and the company is projecting potential sales of 3,000,000 barrels per year.

See BALLANTINE ALE, EXPORT, IMPORT, and MARKET SHARE.

PACKAGE

A term used to describe the many and varied containers used to market and sell

Beer being packaged in bottles, which will be put into 6-packs, 12-packs, and cases, for sale to the consumer.

beer, such as six-packs, kegs, 22-ounce (650.5 ml) bottles, cases, variety packs, and beer balls.

See GLASSWARE.

PAD FILTER

A plate and frame structure using filter sheets made of diatomaceous earth and cellulose fibers, compressed between plastic or stainless-steel plates. Pad filters are used to filter out solid matter and reduce chill haze. Sizes vary from 12 by 12 inches (32 by 32 cm) to 39 by 39 inches (100 by 100 cm). A filtration system may have anywhere from 10 to 200 plates.

Due to a low output, a pad filter is generally used as a polishing, or final, procedure except in very small breweries. The benefit of this type of unit is ease of setup and operation.

See CHILL HAZE.

PALE ALE

The classic beer type of the British Isles, ranging from heavy black beers such as stout to paler, lower-alcohol beers variously called pale ales, mild ales, and bitters. Most English pale ales are not very pale, and some are quite dark, but they are all clear and brilliant. That is, in fact, what identifies them: They are not pale in the way that

Budweiser and Pilsner Urquell are. Beer critic Michael Jackson puts it quite well: "A true pale ale is not golden: it has a dash of color in its cheeks." Still, many American brewers label their blond, golden, or light amber ales "pale ale."

The origins of pale ale are obscure, but it is apparent that the style has always had hops, so it must have been introduced after the early 16th century, when hops were first used in England. The name *pale ale* came about sometime after the demise of "ale" (hop free) as a style in the 17th century. Burton ale has been around since about 1630, and that may be the original beer of this type. In any case, pale ale became popular in the 18th century as a counterpoint to porter. There is some question about whether this beer was called bitter before it was called pale ale, but the two beer styles are now closely intertwined.

Pale ale is brewed in Australia, New Zealand, South Africa, Canada, the United States, Belgium, the Netherlands, and even Malta and the Falkland Islands. The popularity of the new American micro brewing movement ensures that it will be taken up soon in the Far East and probably Latin America as well.

In Britain, these beers are usually called bitter ales when served on tap. Because of their assertive taste profile, they should be served warmer than most beers — 50° to 60°F (10° to 15.5°C) — so that the taste may be savored.

Pale ales are expected to be amber to dark in color (8 to 12 SRM). They have medium alcohol content (less than 6.2 percent by volume) and an original gravity of 11.6–14.9/1.046–1.061. They have an assertive to strong taste from the use of fully modified British 2-row pale malts plus darker malts (such as amber, brown, and even chocolate). A single-step infusion mash is used. The mash is brought to the conversion temperature of 155° to 158°F (68° to 70°C) as quickly as possible. Pale ales have a medium to intense hop flavor and a noticeable to intense bouquet (20 to 50 IBU) from the use of British hops such as Kent Goldings, Fuggle, and Bullion. They also might include one or more kinds of sugar. The brewing water should be medium to very hard (250 to 1,700 ppm hardness).

True pale ales are heavier than bitter ales, are bottled, and are sometimes bottle-conditioned. This product is dry, hoppy, and well fermented, with a lower apparent extract. A 1900 London pale ale had an original gravity of 14/1.057 and bitterness at 76 IBU. A modern British brewing text quotes best pale at 10.1–12.6/1.040–1.050 OG, 4.3–6.6 percent alcohol by volume, and 19–55 IBU.

American Pale Ale

American brewers have probably brewed an English-style pale ale since the beginning of the beer style. Toward the end of the 19th century, lager styles and German brewers dominated the American brewing scene, and ales were brewed less frequently. By Prohibition, the American pale ale tradition had been seriously eroded. This erosion continued after Prohibition, so that by 1960 only one American brewer, now under Pabst/General Brewing, was brewing a pale ale, Ballantine. When the craft brewery revolution began to take off in 1986, the style began a modest comeback. Today about one-quarter of the brands being introduced by craft brewers are in the pale ale genre.

The Great American Beer Festival gives guidelines for Classic Pale Ale as 11–14/1.044–1.056 OG, 4.5–5.5 percent alcohol by volume, 20–40 IBU, and 4–11 SRM. It should be estery and fruity, with medium maltiness (from English malts) and English hops. The guidelines for American Pale Ale are similar: 11–14/ 1.044–1.056 OG, 4.5–5.5 percent alcohol by volume, 20–40 IBU, and 4–11 SRM. It should be hopped with aromatic American hops. Diacetyl should not be evident (or not above minimal) in either of these pale ales.

Original Gravity	Final Gravity	Alcohol by Volume	IBU	SRM
Bass White Shield 1989				
12.9/1.052	2	5.8%	26	9.1
Bass Pale Ale 1978				
11.8/1.047	2.9	4.7%	19	9.8
Boulder Pale Ale 1986				
12.5/1.050	2.3	5.3%	29	≈18
Sierra Nevada Pale Ale 1990				
12.8/1.051	3	5.2%	30	≈10
Whitbread Pale Ale 1978				
13.4/1.055	2.7	5.8%	25.5	≈9

Belgian Pale Ale

Two world wars and a long association between the Belgian and British peoples have led to the popularity of British and Scottish ales in Belgium. Some Belgian brewers have taken to brewing similar pale ales. The Belgian pale ales are similar in style and production to Scottish pale ale, although they usually have a distinctly Belgian flair resulting from the Belgian yeast strains.

The Great American Beer Festival guidelines for Belgian Pale Ales are 11–13.5/1.044–1.054 OG, 4–6 percent alcohol by volume, 20–30 IBU, and 3.5–12 SRM.

Original Gravity	Final Gravity	Alcohol by Volume	IBU	SRM
DeKoninck 1985				
12/1.048/4.8 Belge	2.4	5%	≈20	≈16
Palm Ale 1985				
13.6/1.055/5.5 Belge	3.8	5.5%	≈20	≈14

See BITTER, BLOND OR GOLDEN ALE, BOTTLE-CONDITIONED BEER, BURTON ALE, CASK-CONDITIONED BEER, INDIA PALE ALE, IRISH ALE, PORTER, REAL ALE, SAISON BEER, and SCOTTISH ALE.

PALLETIZER

A piece of equipment designed to take full packaged cases of beer or kegs arranged on a pallet, shrink-wrap the pallet, and deliver the pallet to a forklift loading station.

PALM BREWERY
LONDERZEEL, BELGIUM

The Palm Brewery, located not far from Brussels, dates back to 1747. This company produces the top-fermented Palm

Special, which is marketed throughout the region. The brewery currently has a capacity of 800,000 hl, and has completed an extensive modification of its brewhouse and packaging capability.

See BELGIAN BEERS and TOP-FERMENTING YEAST.

BIÈRE DE PARIS

Beers similar in style to Bière de Gardes. They are a distinctly parisian style. Like Bière de Gardes, Bière de Paris are bottled in wine bottles, but they are lagers rather than ales. This style was previously known as brune de Paris (Paris Brown).

While France is known primarily as a nation of wine drinkers, the history of beer brewing in Paris dates to Roman times. At the time of the French Revolution, there were 28 active breweries in the city, in a section called La Glacière (The Ice-house).

The beers were strong and amber-colored. This tradition continues today. One example is beer brewed by Brasserie Nouvelle de Lutéce, near Douai, which is lagered for 60 days.

See BIÈRE DE GARDE.

PARTI-GYLE BREWING

A method of brewing in which two or more batches of beer at different densities are made from the same mash. Typically, this is done by taking the first runnings from the sparging process and creating a heavy beer, then using later runnings to make a lighter beer. Variations are possible, such as mixing some part of the various runnings to achieve a target density.

See DOUBLE, TRIPLE, AND QUADRUPLE BEERS AND ALES.

LOUIS PASTEUR

The great French scientist who made modern brewing possible. Pasteur's wonderful book *Etudes sur le Bière,* written in 1876 and translated into English in 1879 (reprinted in 1945 by American Library Service under the title *Studies on Fermentation — The Diseases of Beer, Their Causes, and the Means of Preventing Them),* was dedicated to improving French beer. French brewers ignored him, however, and the Germans, against whom the book was directed, took his methods to heart. Their beer improved, as did that of the British. In 1895, the great British brewing scientist Walter Sykes wrote in the *Journal of the Institute of Brewing,* "More to him [Pasteur] than to any other man living or dead do we owe much of our present knowledge of that difficult, maybe even mysterious process carried on by the agency of living organisms *viz.* fermentation."

Pasteur was the first to establish the scientific role of yeast in the fermentation process in his studies from 1857 to 1868. Emil Christian Hansen, a Danish brewer from the Carlsberg Brewery in Copenhagen, expanded on the information. By 1890, Hansen had established procedures for isolating and cultivating a pure yeast culture from a single cell and had determined its use in the production of better beer.

See BIÈRE DE GARDE.

PASTEURIZATION

The application of heat to beer for a specific period of time to stabilize it by killing bacteria, halting fermentation, and therefore extending the shelf life of the bottled, canned, or kegged product.

PASTEURIZER

A piece of equipment that heat treats (pasteurizes) beer to destroy all biological contaminants. There are two types of pasteurizers: flash pasteurizers and tunnel pasteurizers.

Flash pasteurization involves a plate heat exchanger with four sections: regeneration, heating, holding, and cooling. Beer is pumped countercurrent to hot water and steam to achieve the desired pasteurization temperature, held for a predetermined amount of time, and then cooled via brine or glycol coolant counterflow.

The advantages of flash pasteurizers are that they take little space, are cheap to operate, and require less time at elevated temperatures because chemical changes are rapid. The obvious disadvantage is that sterile beer requires sterile kegs, cans, bottles, and filling conditions, and overall sterility is not guaranteed in this system.

Tunnel pasteurization is used with

A pasteurizer is an apparatus for pasteurizing beer, or exposing the beer to intense heat for a period of time in order to stabilize it, halt fermentation, kill any germs or bacteria, and therefore prolong its shelf life. Shown above is an early pasteurizer.

filled bottles and cases of beer. These machines can have one or two decks and comprise multiple compartments: first preheat, second preheat, pasteurizing zone, precool, and cool. Typical times and temperatures for pasteurizing bottled beer is as follows:

- First preheat, 5 minutes, 110°F (43°C)
- Second preheat, 10 minutes, 130°F (54°C)
- Pasteurization, 20 minutes, 140°F (60°C)
- Precool, 5 minutes, 120°F (49°C)

- Cool, 10 minutes, 100°F (38°C)
- Discharge cool, 2 minutes, 70°F (21°C)

Times are normally shorter for canned products.

The ultimate effect of pasteurization is to extend the beer's shelf life for up to 1 year. However, a biscuity flavor may prevail after 2 to 3 months in beers with a high oxygen level.

PATRON SAINTS OF BEER

Many saints are featured on beer bottles even though most of these holy men and women were neither patrons of beer nor even beer drinkers. Most of them were put on beer labels through commercial monastic brewing.

During the Middle Ages, nearly every abbey brewed beer for the faithful flock within its walls. But soon the church made its way into the business of beer, selling it to people outside the abbeys. Each abbey used its patron saint to create brand recognition. Many pubs, especially those in Britain, pictured saints on their signboards.

Today saints appear on scores of beer labels. England produces Saint Austell's Brewery, Saint Edmund's Ale, Saint Christopher, and Saint Neots Bitter. Wales offers Saint David's Porter, and Scotland has Saint James Scottish Ale. France produces Saint Landelin, Saint Armant, Saint Leonard, and Saint Hildegaarde. Belgium is perhaps best known for beer brands such

Saints were frequently pictured on pub signs, especially in Britain.

as Saint Sixtus, Saint Bernardus Pater, Saint Benoit, Saint Hubert, Saint Idesbald, Saint Louis, Saint Amands, Saint Feuillion, and Saint Christoffel.

The first full-fledged saint of beer was Saint Columbanus (612 A.D.). This missionary priest is said to have interrupted a group of men about to sacrifice a vat of ale to the god Wodan. When he blew on the ale cask from across a clearing, the cask flew into pieces with an awful explosion. Columbanus then explained that they were wasting good ale and that his God loved ale, but only when drunk in His Name. Saint Columbanus is credited with a beer lover's favorite blessing: "It is my design to die in the brew-house; let ale be placed to my mouth when I am expiring, that when the choir of angels come they may say: 'Be God propitious to this drinker.'"

Saint Adrian (ca. 303 A.D.) is perhaps chief among the saints of beer, being recognized as such throughout the world. Saint Adrian's Day, celebrated on September 8, is the occasion for much Christian beer drinking in Europe.

A more worthy saint was Saint Florian, who in the 8th century saved Nürnberg, Germany, from burning down in a great fire. It seems Saint Florian extinguished the flames with — you guessed it — beer.

Saint Brigid (439–521 A.D.) was a beer-loving woman. She worked in a leper colony, which one day found itself almost out of beer: "For when the lepers she nursed implored her for beer, and there was none to be had, she changed the water, which was used for the bath, into an excellent beer, by the sheer strength of her blessing and dealt it out to the thirsty in plenty."

Saint Hildegard, the abbess of Diessenberg, was an herbalist whose writings include the earliest-known references to the use of hops in the brewing of beer. According to her, "[Hops], when put in beer, stops putrification and lends longer durability."

Saint Arnold of Soissons got the credit as the patron saint of hop pickers. Legend also holds that he was able to end a plague when he submerged his crucifix into a brew kettle and persuaded people to drink only the beer the kettle held.

Saints Augustine of Hippo, Luke, Nicholas of Myra (Santa Claus), and Armand were all said to have been saloon keepers before their conversion to Christianity. Saint Matthew, the apostle, whose beer festival day is September 21, also was a publican.

St. Arnou is widely considered to be the patron saint of brewers. Born in 580 in the French diocese of Toul, St. Arnou was declared the bishop of Metz in 612, a role he maintained for 15 years. After his retirement from the role of bishop of Metz, St. Arnou moved to a monastery where he died in 640. In 641, the citizens of Metz apparently requested that his body be moved to Metz, where it could be ceremoniously buried. During this voyage, while the citizens were carrying the body of St. Arnou from the monastery to Metz, a miracle is said to have occurred. The porters were tired and thirsty and stopped for a drink. Although there was only one mug of beer, it never ran dry and quenched everyone's thirst.

This Saint's name is also commonly spelled St. Arnould, Saint Arnolds, but should not be confused with Saint Arnou de Oudenaarde, (sometimes called Saint Arnouldus) a Belgian saint who is said to have appealed to God for cold beer during a battle in Flanders in the 11th century.

See CHRISTIAN TRADITION, BEER AND ALE IN; ST. ARNOU; and ST. ARNOU DE OUDENAARDE.

PAULANER-SALVATOR-THOMASBRAU A.G. MUNICH, GERMANY

The Paulaner combine, founded in 1886, has become the largest brewing company in Munich, having now acquired Hacker-Pschorr. The brewery traces it origins to monastic brewers of the 1600s, who brewed a strong Lenten beer called Sankt Vaters (Sacred Father). This rich, dark beer, later called Salvator or Savior, is the ancestor of today's doppelbock style. In tribute to Salvator, most other doppelbocks made in Germany end in *-ator*. Among them are Spaten's Optimator, Ayinger's Celebrator, and Augustiner's Maximator.

Salvator is unique among doppelbocks in that it is available year-round. The brewery pours the world-renowned beer at the Salvator Keller, an enormous beer garden–restaurant near the brewery. The complex can accommodate up to 6,000 people.

Paulaner-Salvator-Thomasbrau A.G. produces the Paulaner, Salvator, Thomas, and Waitzinger brands. The conglomerate brews around 2,000,000 hl annually. The Paulaner beers, including Salvator, are imported to the United States by Paulaner–North America Corp. of Englewood, Colorado.

See BOCK BEER, DOPPELBOCK, and IMPORTER.

PEACHES

See FRUIT.

PEARS

See FRUIT.

PECTINASE

An enzyme that breaks down pectin in fruit.

See ENZYMES.

PEG TANKARD

A communal drinking tankard popular in the 17th century in Britain. The tankard was fitted with a row of pegs (usually eight, but the number varied with the size of the vessel) on the handle side. For example, a 2-quart tankard was fitted with eight pegs, each indicating a gill's worth of beer. Each peg marked an individual share.

This custom may have originated as a means of controlling excessive drinking. In 969 A.D., King Edward, in part instigated by

A 2-quart peg tankard was divided by pegs into eight draughts.

Saint Dunstan, archbishop of Canterbury (959–975), issued a royal decree ordering that pins or nails be fitted inside each tankard and that whoever drank beyond his mark would be severely punished. This gave rise to expressions such as "nick the pin," "to drink to pins," "take him down a peg," and "pin-drinking."

P'EI

A style of beer popular in China during the Tang dynasty (618–907 A.D.).

PELLETS

A form of hops in which whole hops are crushed and compressed into small, round pellets that resemble rabbit food. Pellet

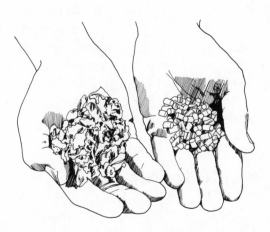

At left are dried hops, consisting of pieces of the hop blossom. At right are hops in pellet form.

hops get better utilization rates than whole hops and are easier to store.

See HOPS.

PENNSYLVANIA BREWING CO., PITTSBURGH, PENNSYLVANIA

Pennsylvania Brewing Co. is one among an increasing number of hybrid brewing operations. The company is at once a brewpub selling beer in its own taproom, a microbrewery shipping beer off-premises, and a contract brewer, having bottled beer produced for it at a larger brewery. This hybridized business style has allowed Pennsylvania Brewing Co. to sell more beer than most breweries its size and some that are larger.

The brewery is the inspiration of Tom Pastorius, an American who had worked in Europe and embraced German culture, particularly *gemütlichkeit,* which means "hospitality." Pastorius returned from Germany in the early 1980s, barely conscious of the United States microbrewery movement but eager to open his own small German-style brewery.

The idea of German-style brewing was not new to Pittsburgh, a city that once boasted 65 breweries, many of them producing lagers for a large German immigrant population. Although pockets of German immigrants remained, the breweries were long gone by the 1980s.

Pastorius was fortunate to have a perfect brewing site close at hand — the shell of

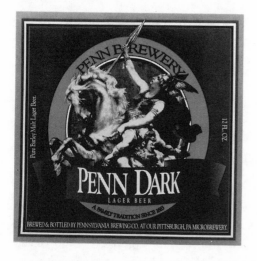

the old Eberhardt & Ober Brewing Co., located in an area of Pittsburgh still called Deutschtown. The old brewery had closed in 1952, and the buildings were in serious disrepair. The city of Pittsburgh had actually condemned the site shortly before Pastorius arrived on the scene.

Pastorius and his partners came up with $4 million to refurbish the complex, renovating the bulk of it as office space and retaining about one-quarter for a brewery. Pastorius imported a 30 hl brewhouse from Germany, along with most of the other brewing components. Despite all his careful planning, however, he ran out of money, and he and his brewmaster, Alex Deml, had to finish the project themselves, spending New Year's Eve 1988 rigging up the tanks.

The brewery opened in April 1989 and soon began selling prodigious quantities of beer through its taproom. Although Pastorius had not had the money to put in a kitchen, it was soon evident that customers wanted more than pretzels to accompany their lager.

Today Pennsylvania Brewing Co. boasts a kitchen and expanded dining area. The brewery hosts frequent seasonal fests, complete with German cuisine, oompah bands, and plenty of it own German-style beers. The company brews several brands on-premises, and also markets its contract-brewed Penn Pilsner.

See BREWPUB, CONTRACT BREWING, and MICROBREWERY.

PENNSYLVANIA SWANKEY

See COMMON BEER.

PEORIA INTERNATIONAL BEER FEST

The annual Peoria International Beer Fest is co-sponsored by a local beer distributor (Specialty Imports) and the Peoria, Illinois, Jaycees as a fund-raiser for the community organization. (Admission is lower for those bringing canned food donations.) The 1995 edition was held in March at the Peoria Exposition Gardens. Over 75 beers — imports as well as craft brews — were poured for more than 2,500 tasters.

PEPPERED AND SPICED BEERS

The marriage of hot spices and cold beer is an ancient one indeed, perhaps older than 10,000 years. Ages before the dish known as chili was born, primitive humans routinely blended hot spices with beer. This custom survives today in many corners of the world. Today chili beers are available from U.S. microbrewers, such as Oregon Trader Brewing's Chili Beer.

Pleistocene hunter-gatherers, who first banded together in settlements, did so to farm the grains used in beer. Dried spices were used to jazz up the taste of the communal stew pot as well as the village beer vats. Some of the first beers made were lagered (aged) with hot spices.

About 4000 B.C., Sumerian brewsters made pepper beers under the divine protection of the goddess Ninkasi. With the advance of Egyptian civilization, brewers developed a host of spicy brews to satisfy the thirst of the pharaohs. Pungent spices figured into no less than eight varieties of "hot" beer.

During the 8th through the 10th centuries A.D., Norse brewsters used a wide variety of spices in their beers. Their favorite spices were heather and garlic. The latter was believed to protect against evil spells and general bad luck.

The peoples of Central and South America were the first to use peppers (as we know them) in beer. This is a practice that has been traced back thousands of years to the Amazon region of South America.

See NINKASI.

PEPTIDASE

An enzyme that breaks down proteins in the early stages of a mash.

See ENZYMES.

BIRRA PERONI
ROME, ITALY

Peroni is Italy's biggest brewer, operating plants in Rome, Naples, Bari, Padova, S. Cipriano, and Battipaglia. The company has a capacity of 5,100,000 hls. It is family owned, but Kronenbourg holds a stake in the firm.

Peroni produces numerous brands, including Birra Peroni, Nastro Azzurro, Black, Red, Itala Pilsen, Raffo, Wuhrer, Crystall, Simplon, and Peroni Analcolica. Nastro Azzurro and Raffo are premium

products (brewed to an original gravity of 12° Plato or higher). Nastro Azzurro is a lager with a long hop aftertaste characterized by a little sour malt far in back. Raffo Beer is a brilliant pale tawny-gold with a malt and bitter hop flavor. Birra Peroni is a slightly lighter-bodied variation.

Peroni is imported to the United States by Barton Beers of Chicago, Illinois.

See IMPORTER.

PERRY

A fermented alcoholic beverage made from the juice of pears. Perry may be fermented using champagne yeast (sometimes it is a modified yeast that is used) or through spontaneous fermentation, and is served on draught.

Perry is a traditional drink in Britain, where it has been actively promoted by the Campaign for Real Ale (CAMRA), a consumer group that promotes traditional cask ale. To show their commitment to cider (made from the juice of apples) and perry, CAMRA started APPLE (Apple Cider and Perry Product Liaison Executive) to promote the two alcoholic beverages made from fruit juice.

Perry is most frequently mentioned in the same breath as real cider. Perry is not as widely known as cider. Perry sells for about half as much as cider when both are available at the same British pub.

In England, perry was sold at drinking establishments called cider houses, analogous to alehouses. There is a newly renovated cider house at Dunkertons Cider Company at Luntney, Pembridge, Herefordshire. It is claimed that Dunkertons is the first cider house that has been built in centuries.

In 1995 at the Great British Beer Festival (GBBF), cider and perry had their own awards for the first time. They were not judged as part of the Champion Beer of Britain selection process (which is done prior to the public opening of the five-day festival) but were voted on by those who attended the GBBF.

In England there is a National Association of Perry Makers, and a similarly named one for cider-makers.

See CAMPAIGN FOR REAL ALE (CAMRA).

PET

A polyethylene container with a capacity of 2.0 L (45 ounces). Very common for soft drinks in the United States, and in England for 1.5 liter beer containers.

pH

A measure of the acidity or alkalinity of a solution, which ranges from 1 for strong acids to 14 for strong alkalines. In brewing, a pH of 7 (neutral) reflects an ideal water source. In mashing, slightly acidic values are ideal — in the range of 5 to 5.5. If the pH is higher than 5.5, it can be lowered by adding gypsum.

Any given amount of pure water contains a certain number of hydroxide ions (OH^-) and hydronium ions (H_3O^+, or simply H^+). At a temperature of 77°F (25°C), the concentration of these hydroxide ions and hydronium ions in pure water is 0.0000001 moles per liter for each ion. This is said to be neutral pH or pH 7. The pH scale is simply the number of moles per liter of hydronium ions raised to the power of 10 (minus sign ignored). (See the table that follows.) A pH of 5 is ten times as acidic as a pH of 6, which is ten times as acidic as a pH of 7, and so on.

pH Scale

Moles per liter H$^+$		pH		Moles per liter OH$^-$
0.1	10^{-1}	1	10^{-13}	0.0000000000001
				Very strong acid
0.01	10^{-2}	2	10^{-12}	0.000000000001
0.001	10^{-3}	3	10^{-11}	0.00000000001
0.0001	10^{-4}	4	10^{-10}	0.0000000001
0.00001	10^{-5}	5	10^{-9}	0.000000001
0.000001	10^{-6}	6	10^{-8}	0.00000001
0.0000001	10^{-7}	7	10^{-7}	0.0000001
				Neutral
0.00000001	10^{-8}	8	10^{-6}	0.000001
0.000000001	10^{-9}	9	10^{-5}	0.00001
0.0000000001	10^{-10}	10	10^{-4}	0.0001
0.00000000001	10^{-11}	11	10^{-3}	0.001
0.000000000001	10^{-12}	12	10^{-2}	0.01
0.0000000000001	10^{-13}	13	10^{-1}	0.1
0.00000000000001	10^{-14}	14	10^{0}	1.0
				Very strong alkaline

PHARAONIC EGYPT

See EGYPTIAN BEER.

PHENOLIC

A medicinal or chemical taste that occurs in beer. This is an undesirable effect often caused by sanitation problems during brewing.

pH METER

An instrument used to measure pH levels of products. A pH meter uses a potassium chloride–saturated electrode and a temperature compensation tube. A pH meter is vital for quality control of brewing liquor, wort, and beer production. These instruments range from simple pen meters, which are acceptable for rough testing, to sophisticated fully compensating models.

PHOSPHORIC ACID

An acid that is often used by soft drink manufacturers and can be used in brewing, as well. It is excellent as a mash and sparge-water acidifier.

PHYTIN

A salt found in malted barley that forms phytic acid in mash.

See ACID REST.

PICTS AND HEATHER ALE

In the history of Western civilization, no beer has aroused so much speculation and curiosity as the "lost" heather ale of the Picts. About the year 250 B.C., the Greek navigator Pytheas first explored and wrote of the land we now know as Scotland, an area that was home to a fierce, independent group of tribes collectively called the Picts. Legend describes Picts as living in villages deep underground. The Picts were supposedly so ferocious that even the legions of Julius Caesar could not subdue them. In A.D. 361, the Roman emperor Julian witnessed the Picts in battle and said of the wild, ale-drunken tribes that they sounded like "the bellowing of oxen and the cawing of the raven." Anthropologists such as Margaret Murray believe that the myths about leprechauns stem from the Picts.

The Picts' heather ale was the first beer brewed in the British Isles. It became famous for its potency and hallucinogenic power.

Heather, or ling, is a low-growing evergreen shrub of the species *Caluna vulgaris*. These beautiful plants are found throughout the Scottish Highlands.

According to accounts from the first through the eighth centuries, the process of heather ale brewing was the most closely guarded secret of the Picts, whose chieftains were the sole keepers of the recipe. The Pict ale was made using the flowers and tops of heather, whose blossoms were gathered, washed, and then placed at the bottom of the brew vats. Wort, the liquid extract from malted grain, was then added to the blooms. Two parts heather to one part malt gave the ale its supposed narcotic property. Heather performed the same function as hops — as a bittering agent and preservative for the beer. Many ancient authors mentioned the extreme bitterness of heather ale. They reported the use of other bitter ingredients such as bog-beans and yarrow. Corn or barley was used in malting, and honeycombs were the primary source of fermentable sugar. Ambient,

airborne yeast completed the fermentation process.

Heather ale brewing survived in small, isolated areas of the Highlands as late as the early 19th century. However, the real stuff died out sometime in the 4th century, when the Scottish king Niall led his forces to exterminate the Picts in Galloway. There, according to the most common version of the legend, the secret of heather ale died with Trost of the Long Knife, the last king of the Picts. Robert Louis Stevenson is one of the many writers who have retold this tale.

PIKE PLACE BREWERY
SEATTLE, WA

Pike Place Brewery is one of America's smallest microbreweries, though its reputation greatly exceeds its production. On the occasion of its opening, in October of 1989, it sponsored the world's shortest nonmotorized uphill parade to wheel their first keg of draught up the hill in the Pike Place Public Market to Cutter's Bayhouse, their first account. Since then, Pike Place beer has spread throughout Seattle, becoming the beer of choice of local beer aficionados.

Established by John Farias, proprietor of a Seattle malt store, and Charles Finkel, founder of Merchant du Vin Corporation and one of the most influential people in the beer-marketing world, Pike Place has been nurtured carefully and lovingly, placing more emphasis on quality than on quantity. Its cask-conditioned ales have

The Pike Place Brewery is located in Seattle's Pike Place Public Market. The brewery uses Northern Brewer and Canadian B. C. Goldings hops and 2-row Maris malt to make its beers.

Hops being added to the copper brew kettle at Pike Place Brewery

been praised by the likes of Michael Jackson and *BEER:the magazine.*

Pike Place brews about 2,500 barrels each year. Among the styles they have brewed are Pike Place East Indian Pale Ale, Pike Place XXXXX Stout, Pike Place Porter, Pike Place Old Bawdy Barley Wine, and Pike Place Pale Ale, the only one of their beers marketed nationally.

See BARLEY WINE, MICROBREWERY, PALE ALE, PORTER, and STOUT.

PILGRIMS AND BEER

An example of the colonial American attitude toward beer can be found in the logbook of the *Mayflower,* where the Plymouth landing is revealed as a desperate result of a lack of beer: "For we could not now take time for further search [for a place to land our ship] our victuals being much spent, especially our beer." The first Thanksgiving was graced with ale brewed and fermented with whatever ingredients the settlers could grow, gather, or otherwise procure locally, including corn.

PILS/PILSNER/PILSENER

See BOHEMIAN BEER.

PILSNER URQUELL
PLZEN, CZECH REPUBLIC

Plzensky Prazdroj, in Plzen, Czech Republic, is the source of Pilsner Urquell (the "original Pilsner"). The brewery has operated since 1842, producing a bottom-fermented pale beer that has become the model for Pilsners the world over. A story, perhaps apocryphal, traces the origins of Pilsner to a strain of bottom-fermenting yeast stolen from Bavaria and smuggled to a Bohemian brewer. Whatever its provenance, this yeast, when combined with Bohemian hops and soft local water, made for quite a beer.

Just as dry and ice beers have swept through contemporary markets, the Pilsner craze of the 1850s soon spread far and wide. The first shipment of Pilsner Urquell arrived in the United States in 1856, but local American brewers were already hard at work trying to duplicate this most fashionable of beers.

Pilsner Urquell

A pale beer with a spicy bouquet and dry finish. Slightly maltier and more full-bodied than most contemporary Pilsners, Pilsner Urquell maintains the mystique that made it the world's most imitated beer.

Many of the world's most popular beers today descend from these Bohemian originals. For instance, Adolphus Busch was very taken with Czech beers, which inspired his flagship product, Budweiser.

In the century since, the Pilsner Urquell brewery has maintained very traditional practices in producing its beer. The company traditionally fermented the beer in open, wooden vessels and aged it in pitch-lined oak casks. Some beer enthusiasts might selfishly feel that the "velvet revolution" that freed the Czech Republic was a mixed blessing, for it has brought technological progress to a brewery that was allowed to pursue its traditional (albeit labor-intensive) methods under communism. The brewery has undergone substantial modernization, with an eye to increasing export production. It is said that most of the Pilsner Urquell made for export is fermented and aged in steel vessels.

In the United States, Pilsner Urquell is imported by the Guinness Import Co. of Stamford, Connecticut. Both bottled and draught versions are available.

See BOHEMIAN BEER.

BRAÜEREI PINKUS MÜLLER MÜNSTER, GERMANY

The Müller family has been brewing beer in their Münster brewery since the first half of the 19th century. The operation of the brewery and brewpubs has been passed along for generations. From the early decades of this century until the end of the sixties, the brewery was run by Carl Pinkus Müller, who came to be known as the "singing brewer" because of his trained voice and the contention that altbier helps one develop a good singing voice.

In 1970, Carl Pinkus Müller handed the brewery over to his oldest son,

Carl Pinkus Müller, the "singing brewer,"
in his lager cellar in 1935

Hans, who with his wife, Annemarie (herself the daughter of a brewer), oversees the brewery and pubs. The Pinkus Müller Brewery is best known for its altbier, and Hans Müller is now the last altbier brewer in Münster. But the brewery produces other beers, including an Ur Pils and a Weizen.

Pinkus Müller beers are imported in the United States by Merchant du Vin Corporation of Seattle, WA.

PINT

A measure for a glass of beer. One-eighth of a United States gallon, the pint has survived from an ancient Roman unit of corn.

PITCHING

The process of adding yeast or a yeast starter to the boiled and cooled wort to begin the fermentation process.

PITTSBURGH BREWING CO. PITTSBURGH, PENNSYLVANIA

A large, independent brewery that was part of the G. Heileman empire for a few years. When debt-laden Heileman looked for assistance, a local financier named Michael

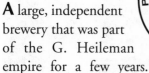

Iron City

A rather ordinary beer that is slightly meatier than some of its mainstream competition, but not by much. All in all, Iron City is a typical American light lager beer.

Carlow bought Pittsburgh. Unfortunately, the new ownership has its own financial troubles.

Pittsburgh Brewing Co. was one of the country's first brewing conglomerates, a combine of 16 breweries formed in 1899. Most of the smaller breweries in the company were gradually closed. Of the remainder, only the big Pittsburgh plant survives (although the shell of one other, Eberhardt & Ober, now houses a microbrewery, Pennsylvania Brewing Co.).

The company has become a large-volume contract producer of beers and nonalcoholic products, including packaged teas. It was once the only contract brewer for Samuel Adams Boston Lager, but Boston Beer Co. now contracts production at a number of other breweries as well.

The Pittsburgh Brewing Co. maintains its team of horses and delivery wagon. Founded in 1861, the company is one of the oldest continuously operating breweries in the country.

The brewery has a capacity of 1,200,000 barrels and has brewed a staggering array of brands over its long history. In contemporary times, the brewery's best-known product (aside from Samuel Adams) is probably Iron City beer. Iron City was a brand long before Pittsburgh Brewing Co. was incorporated, perhaps as far back as the 1860s. The company is experimenting with some more interesting specialty brews, including J. J. Wainwright Lager (Wainwright Brewing Co. was a member of the original Pittsburgh conglomerate).

Although the brewery's financial picture is troubled, the company enjoys an enviable depth of brand loyalty in Pittsburgh and beyond. It is not by accident that most of the country's surviving regional breweries are located in Pennsylvania. The region's beer drinkers seem to value tradition and local production more than most.

See CONTRACT BREWING and PENNSYLVANIA BREWING CO.

PIVOVAR GAMBRINUS
PLZEN, CZECH REPUBLIC

Pivovar Gambrinus, in the shadow of the great Pilsner Urquell, brews a fine lager beer called Gambrinus. This brand is imported into the United States by Stanley

Stawski Importing Co. of Chicago, Illinois. It is a smooth, golden, malty beer with an assertive hop finish, much in the style of its more famous cousin.

See LAGER ALE.

PLATO

A measurement of the density of a wort (dissolved sugars) in which 1 degree Plato represents 1 percent dissolved sugar in solution. This is equivalent to the Brix scale used by wine makers.

PLOUGH MONDAY

In old England, a minor festival held the first Monday after Twelfth Night. Villagers would decorate a plough (plow) with ribbons and take it from house to house. Some would dress up in various mummers' guises and chant, "God speed the plough." The main characters were Bessy (a man dressed up in fantastic female garb) and the Clown. A variety of strange dances and vulgar antics completed the entertainment for the day. During the rounds, the revelers would ask for ale, bread, and cheese at the houses. They were seldom refused.

PLUG

A form of hops in which whole hops are compressed into a ½-inch-thick (1.27 cm) by about 1-inch-diameter (2.54 cm) cake.

Plugs are less susceptible to oxidation than whole hops.

See HOPS.

PLUMS

See FRUIT.

POLYCLAR

A type of plastic used as a fining agent to reduce chill haze. The molecular charge of Polyclar is such that proteins, tannins, and even yeasts are attracted to it and precipitate out of solution. It is used at a rate of 1 tablespoon (14.79 ml) per 5 gallons (19 L) of beer. A major drawback to Polyclar is that it can reduce head retention.

See CHILL HAZE and FININGS.

POLYPROPYLENE AGINATE

A compound that serves as a heading agent when added to beer, improving head retention. It is made from seaweed and is available in either liquid or powder form. Generally, it is mixed in with the priming sugar prior to bottling.

POMBO

A low-alcohol millet beer made by women in Guinea, Africa. Also called *pombé*. It is drunk during ceremonies and purification rites. People believe that the sensation produced by the alcohol is a sacred means of rejecting disorder of the spirit and achieving serenity.

To make pombo, millet (or sometimes sorghum) is steeped, germinated, and sun-dried. The grain is then crushed into flour, mixed with gombo stems and water, and simmered in large clay pots for an entire day. The mixture is transferred to a second vessel in which it is boiled overnight. More flour and water are added the next morning. After another day has passed, the wort is drawn off, and medicinal herbs are added. Rich in vitamin B, when finished, pombo is slightly hazy, yellow, and foamy.

A variant is made in Rwanda and Uganda using bananas that are neither too green nor too ripe in addition to millet. Fermentation takes about 48 hours.

POPERINGE HOPPESTOET

Every third year, in the third week of September, a beer and hop festival is held in Poperinge, near Ieper, Belgium. This is the main hop-growing region of Belgium, where the hop shoot is considered a delicacy and is often used in food recipes. The festival lasts a week and includes parades, hop-picking contests, and many barrels of beer.

During the Middle Ages, Poperinge was an important cloth-producing center. Quarrels with the neighboring weaving town of Ieper resulted in a decline of the cloth trade, but thanks to the Abbey of Saint-Omer, the hop plant found its way to town and gradu-

ally took root in the fertile soil.

Now three-quarters of Belgium's national hop harvest is from the area. The first pageant took place in 1956, and since 1960 the festival has been held triennially.

PORTER

A robust beer with an alcohol level somewhere around 5 to 6.3 percent by volume. The beer is strongly hopped and allowed to mature for up to 6 months. The style became popular in England when it was introduced in 1722 by Ralph Harwood, an East London pub brewer.

In the early 18th century, English beer was essentially of three types: small (weak) beer, strong pale ale, and strong brown ale. Those beers were usually fermented from fairly strong and highly hopped worts. The strength and high hop levels protected the beer from souring. The pale and brown ales were often mixed. In the Shoreditch area, around East London, a mixture came into favor among the market porters. It was called "three threads" and consisted of equal parts pale ale, new (actively fermenting) brown ale, and aged brown ale (sometimes called stale ale). To satisfy his patrons, the pub keeper had to keep all three beers on hand.

In 1722, Harwood produced a beer from scratch to match the taste of "three threads." He called this new beer "entire." Everyone else called it porter, because of its popularity with that group of workers. It became England's first national beer. Richardson described an 1805 porter as

Porter was first brewed by an East London pub brewer, Ralph Harwood, in 1732.

in Denmark, the Czech Republic, Germany, Poland, Hungary, Russia, and France. Recently, a small Austrian brewery also began producing this intriguing style. In addition, porter is brewed in Canada, China, and the United States. German porter is brewed from 7 to 10 percent black patent malt and caramel malt; bitterness is 51 IBU.

American Porters

The Yuengling Brewery in Pottsville, Pennsylvania, made a porter before Prohibition, but after Prohibition Yuengling Porter was made by the lager ale method. Typically, post-Prohibition porters were brewed with 3 percent caramel malts (80 to 120 degrees Lovibond), 12 to 18 percent American black malt, 1 percent dextrin malt, 17 percent high dried malt (Munich or amber), and 20 percent corn grits. Licorice and/or molasses also were added, to produce original gravity of 12–15/1.048–1.061 and an alcohol content over 5 percent by volume.

In 1974, Fritz Maytag of the Anchor Brewing Co. in San Francisco, changed his dark steam beer to a porter formula, at a robust original gravity of 17/1.070 and about 7.5 percent alcohol by volume. Originally fermented as a California common beer (steam beer), Anchor Porter has been brewed as a genuine top-fermented ale in recent years. It is a truly authentic American porter. For example, an American porter in 1887 had 18/1.074 OG and 6.2 percent alcohol by volume. Another in 1889 had 13.5/1.054

having 15.8/1.065 OG, 6.3 percent alcohol by volume, and 20 percent molasses in the kettle.

From England, the style spread to the continent and to Ireland, where it was slow to take hold. Irish porter came to be brewed much stronger and was called stout porter, later simply stout. The Guinness Brewery in Dublin produced both plain Porter and Extra Stout Porter; by 1800 Guinness was producing only porter and stout.

The last British porter was brewed in Dublin in 1973, but the style has survived

OG and 5.3 percent alcohol by volume. In 1908, porter was defined by brewing authority Robert Wahl as a dark beer with an original gravity of at least 13 degrees Plato and a hop rate of 18 per United States gallon (4.75 g/L), resulting in a bitterness of about 60 IBU at an estimated 25 percent utilization rate (60 mg/L).

In the United States, porters are now being made in craft breweries, and the style is coming back into favor.

The Great American Beer Festival guidelines for Porter are 10–15/1.040–1.060 OG, 4.5–6.5 percent alcohol by volume, 20–40 IBU, and 20–35+ SRM (deep color from black malt rather than the roasted barley common to stouts).

Original Gravity	Final Gravity	Alcohol by Volume	Bitterness	Color
Anchor Porter (California) 1989				
16.2/1.066	4.6	6	35.5	≈35
Black Hook Porter (Washington) 1989				
11.8/1.047	2.2	5	49	≈35
Narragansett Porter (Rhode Island) ca 1960				
13/1.052	2.7	5.4	≈25	≈25
Sierra Nevada Porter (California) 1982				
14/1.057	3	5.8	34	≈38
Samuel Smith Tadcaster "Taddy" Porter 1982 (first British porter since 1970s; brewed for United States market)				
12/1.048	2.2	5.1	≈25	≈25

See BROWN ALE, SMALL BEER, and STRONG PALE ALE.

POTASSIUM

A metallic element. During the mash, excessive potassium levels can inhibit enzymes and lead to a salty taste in the beer. Potassium levels should be below 10 ppm for brewing water. Potassium is very soluble in water, so reducing this ion is best done by dilution with distilled water.

Potassium also is a very important yeast nutrient. There is an adequate supply of potassium in normal wort.

PPM

An abbreviation for parts per million.

PREEVACUATION PUMP

A pump used with a bottle filler to facilitate the preevacuation of bottles at the start of the filling cycle. These pumps work on a negative pressure and use a water-assisted mechanism. Their function is to suck all the air from a valve-sealed bottle to create a vacuum.

PRESSURE RELIEF VALVE

A safety valve used on tanks that come under pressure, such as enclosed fermenting vessels, univessels, conditioning tanks, and bright beer tanks. In the event of the internal pressure exceeding preset limits, the valve relieves the excess pressure, preventing the possibility of a tank eruption. The pressure relief valve is often combined with an anti-vacuum valve.

PRIMA MELIOR

The name given to the best monastic beers of the 7th to 9th centuries. Literally translated, *prima melior* means "first quality." Second-rate, or "blue-collar," brews were designated *secunda*. The poorest quality beers, which were doled out to people of the lowest classes, were given the name *tertia*.

Jan Primus was also known as King Gambrinus or, more simply, the King of Beer.

PRIMING

A method of carbonating beer in the bottle or keg by adding fermentable sugar to a beer containing active yeast and then filling and sealing the container. This creates a second fermentation. The yeast that is still in suspension in the beer will convert the sugar to ethanol and carbon dioxide. Since the container is sealed, the carbon dioxide will remain dissolved in the beer, thereby carbonating it.

See CARBONATION.

JAN PRIMUS

The "King of Beers." Primus was the fourth duke of Brabant, Louvain, and Antwerp, Belgium. He is known as Jean Primus in France and as Gambrinus elsewhere in Europe. Primus is credited with introducing the toast as a social custom. Several breweries and beers bear the name Gambrinus.

PROHIBITION (THE VOLSTEAD ACT)

A 1919 act of the United States Congress that culminated a centuries-long effort by religious and moralist factions to stamp out alcohol consumption in the United States. Prohibition movements began in the first half of the 19th century, with the enactment of local and state prohibition laws in Maine in 1829, Indiana in 1832, and Georgia in 1833. These laws were referred

On April 7, 1933, Prohibition was repealed in the United States. Happy people are seen here unloading beer—legally!

to as "local options," and permitted local government, at the county, city, town, village, or even municipal district levels, to restrict or ban alcohol.

It wasn't until after the Civil War that small local efforts originating in New England developed into broader national campaigns such as the National Temperance Society, National Prohibition Party (1869), Total Abstinence Brotherhood, and the Women's Christian Temperance Union (1874). For a short period from 1880 to 1890, eight states were "signed up" for Prohibition, but by 1904, the number had dropped to three.

A third revival of the Prohibition efforts occurred during the first two decades of the 20th century, led mostly by Southerners and Westerners. Anti-saloon leagues reached their peak at this time. By the time the Volstead Act was passed, and the 18th Amendment to the United States Constitution was proposed, 33 states had already enacted state Prohibition laws, more than the two-thirds vote required for constitutional ratification.

National Prohibition was adopted in the United States with the ratification of the 18th Amendment to the Constitution on January 16, 1919. It went into effect one year later, and lasted just short of 14 years, ending on December 5, 1933, with the adoption of the 21st Amendment. Prior to this, several states — Montana, New York, and Wisconsin — had repealed their enforcement statutes, effectively ending Prohibition in those areas. By 1942 only Kansas, Mississippi, and Oklahoma retained statutory Prohibition.

Prohibition had serious economic implications for the United States. By prohibiting the manufacture and sale of alcoholic beverages, the government forced breweries and distilleries to close and lay off thousands of workers in a specialized industry, forcing them to learn new trades. Farmers who supplied the barley and wheat for the brewing industry lost valued markets. The transport industry, the auto industry, the restaurant industry, the advertising industry, the timber industry, the clothing industry, and the support industries that comprised the total brewing industry all suffered serious declines. Finally, government itself suffered revenue losses when it could no longer tax the industry from which it got major support.

PROTEIN

A class of organic compounds containing amino acids. In beers an excessive amount of protein leads to chill haze. A good hot and cold break are required to remove (coagulate) excessive proteins.

See CHILL HAZE, COLD BREAK, and HOT BREAK.

PUB

An abbreviated form of public house.

Street view of the Old Tabard Inn in Southwark, London, in the early 1900s.

PUBLIC HOUSE

In England, an establishment where beer and other alcoholic beverages are served. Also called a pub.

PUMP

A piece of equipment designed to move liquids from one place to another. There are numerous types of pumps. Those normally used in brewing are categorized as follows: centrifugal pump, positive displacement pump, and peristaltic pump.

Centrifugal Pump

Centrifugal pumps are most commonly used for liquid transfer between brewhouse tanks and fermentation tanks. They come with either a closed or an open impeller and generally need to be primed. Impeller selection is determined by the liquid being pumped. If the liquid contains particulate matter an open impeller is generally used.

Positive Displacement Pump

Positive displacement pumps are used

when pumping liquid against a pressure and where the pump needs to build up pressure to maintain flow. They are used when transferring beer to a bottle filler or in filtration systems.

The Hell Gate Brewery pumping station in New York is captured in this 1891 photograph.

Peristaltic Pump

Peristaltic pumps are used where a pulsing/dosing action is required — for example, for dosing diatomaceous earth onto the septa of a diatomaceous earth filter.

PURL

A hot, spiced ale that was popular in England in the 1800s and was the precursor to coffee as a morning beverage. This beer cocktail was very popular with dockworkers and sailors. The men who sold Purl from small boats were called Purlmen.

QUART

A unit of liquid measure equal to 32 fluid ounces (0.9463 L).

RACKING

The process of removing the clear liquid from settled trub by pumping or siphoning the liquid from one vessel (in which solids have been allowed to settle) to another vessel. *See* TRUB.

Fermented beer being racked from the maturation vat into casks

RACKING ARM

A device through which beer is transferred from a bright beer tank to a keg or, in the case of naturally conditioned beer, from a fermenting vessel back into a cask. It is designed in such a way that when the keg or cask is filled, the beer fobs over into another keg or a tank and is then recycled.

RAILROAD TRANSPORT OF BEER

The use of the railroad system to transport beer was a natural progression from using the tramways and wagon-ways to haul minerals to rivers and ports. The development of rail transport began with Richard Trevithick's invention of the steam engine, first tested in 1802, although it did not replace horse-pulled conveyances for at least another 20 years.

In England, the expansion of the railroads directly led to the expansion of breweries and the establishment of many more pubs. This growth was most pronounced during the years from 1840 to 1870. Before the railroads, 15 to 20 miles was about the greatest distance beer could safely be transported in one day by horse-drawn wagon, since going too fast on bumpy, rutted roads could cause the barrels to explode, especially on warm days. Rail transport opened up opportunities for breweries, particulary for those located at important rail junctions, to market and distribute their beers over an area never before imagined.

By 1837, the Bass Brewery at Burton-on-Trent had reached an annual output of about 10,000 barrels. By 1847, following the establishment of the Midland railroad, the brewery's output had increased to 60,000 barrels. By 1853, a second brewery had to be built to handle the increase in demand, and annual output reached 130,000 barrels. Within ten years, a third brewery was built when output reached 400,000 barrels. By 1876, production had reached 900,000 barrels and the brewery site had grown to encompass 12 miles of track with 11 rail-engines. By 1880, beer was the second largest industry in England.

German immigrant brewers in the United States also took advantage of the railroads. Instead of siting breweries on the coastal periphery, they placed them centrally in the American midlands, at the heart of one of the world's greatest grain-producing areas. The central location also eased blanket distribution — moving goods from the center of the country out to its borders. A brewer in New York would have to ship beer at least 1,000 miles farther to California than would a brewer in St. Louis. Centrally located brewers had

markets in all directions by land: Coastal brewers had ocean on one side. Brewers in Cincinnati, St. Louis, and Milwaukee had a competitive advantage over breweries established in New York, Dallas, or Los Angeles. Brewers at the periphery were also at a tremendous cost disadvantage because they had much higher expenses shipping the grains and hops to their breweries from the interior.

The railroad's positive impact on brewing was further enhanced by the establishment of depots and warehouses along the rail routes where beer could be kept cool until it was delivered to its final destination.

RAINIER BREWING CO. SEATTLE, WASHINGTON

Seattle subsidiary of the G. Heileman Brewing Co.

See HEILEMAN BREWING CO., G.

RAUCHBIER

A beer made from malt that is fire-dried. Fire-drying is a process in which smoke penetrates the drying room. Also known as smoked beer. This was the normal malt drying method used into the 18th century, much as peat is used to fuel the kilns in Scotland to make Scotch whiskey. In the northern Bavarian city of Bamberg, where most of this beer is made today, moist beechwood logs are used. They give the beer a very distinctive smoky flavor. The only sample of Bamberg rauchbier found in the United States is Kaiserdom Rauchbier, produced in Eltmann. Rauchbier is a *Reinheitsgebot* (pledge of purity) beer brewed by a very distinctive method; it is a bottom-cold-fermented and lagered beer.

The direct-fired kilning process not only partially roasts the barley but also adds a dark smoky color to the beer and imparts a very distinctive taste. The beer goes well with German smoked sausage, Westphalian smoked hams, and any other smoked food or cheese, such as smoked salmon and outdoor barbecue. Smoked beer is an acquired taste and may take several bottles before one gets used to it.

Kaiserdom Rauchbier is made with malt kilned by smoking.

Stone Beer — *Rauchenfels Steinbier*

Stone beer is both the oldest style of beer and one of the newest. The method dates back to before there were metal brew kettles and wort could be boiled only by heating stones and placing them in the kettle.

In 1982 Gerd H. Borges was an executive of the Sailer Maktoberdorf Brewery in North Germany, when he found an article from 1906 discussing stone beer brewing. Entranced with the idea, Borges decided to revive the style. At length, he located the son of the last brewmaster, who had died in 1965. The old man had made a tape recording to preserve the priceless information. His son gave the tape to Borges in return for the latter buying the stone quarry where the special stones were to be found. These were the graü-wacke stones, a type of sandstone, from Kütschachtal, which could stand being heated to 2200°F (1200°C) and then cooled to 212°F (100°C) without exploding and without leaving any of their character in the beer wort.

In 1982, Borges reintroduced stone brewing at his own Ewald Werner Brewery in Neustadt near Coburg, where the exceedingly soft water (0-degrees hardness) was ideally suited for brewing this style of beer. A large open fireplace was constructed so that a steel basket holding 880 pounds (396 kg) of stones could be heated to the desired temperature in a beechwood fire. The fireplace held 212 cubic feet (6 m$_3$) of wood. The steel basket and stones were heated for 4 hours. Then the basket was lifted out of the fire and transported by an overhead monorail to the brew kettle. At that point, the beer wort, which had been preheated to about 203°F (95°C), came to a full boil. The stones were then coated with caramelized sugar. They were cooled and stored, then placed in the beer during the secondary ferment. The renewal of the fermenting action peels the sugar off the stones, imparting a delicate smoky flavor to the finished beer. Rauchenfels Steinbier is one of the world's unique brews.

Peat Smoked Beers

There is one style popular in some areas, particularly in Europe, where the malt is Scotch whiskey malt, and the product has a definite tinge of "Scotch" flavor to it. There are presently at least two of these, both lagers: Adelscott by Fischer from France (Alsace), and another by Heineken. Both are a bit sweet on the palate.

American Smoked Beers

Several American craft brewers have taken up smoked beer production. The best known of these is the Alaska Brewing Co. Alaskan Smoked Porter, which is made with malt that has been smoked over alder wood in a nearby salmon smokehouse. The annual production takes place after a triple cleaning of the smokehouse to rid it of any fish odors. The beer itself has wonderful lasting qualities, as witnessed in a recent vertical (annual by years) tasting. London beer critic Michael Jackson has rated this beer with four stars (one of only six American beers so honored). Another American smoked beer, Vermont Smoked Porter

from the Vermont Pub and Brewery in Burlington, is smoked with apple, hickory, and maple wood.

The Great American Beer Festival recognizes two smoke-flavored beer categories: Bamberg-Style Rauchbier Lager, with 12–13/1.048–1.052 OG, 4.3–4.8 percent alcohol by volume, 20–30 IBU, and 10–20 SRM; and a general smoke-flavored beer (lager or ale), for which they ask for a balance between the style's character and its smoky properties, gravity, and so on.

Original Gravity	Final Gravity	Alcohol by Volume	IBU	SRM
Alaskan Smoked Porter 1989				
13.6/1.055	4.1	5%	54	≈40
Kaiserdom Rauchbier 1982				
12.7/1.051	3.2	5%	25.5	≈30
Rauchenfels Steinbier 1985				
11.3/1.045	2.2	3.8%	27	12.5
Vermont Smoked Porter 1991				
12/1.048	4.1	4.1%	28	≈35
Adelscott Malt Liquor 1985				
16.2/1.066	4.2	6.5	unknown	~7

See REINHEITSGEBOT and SMOKED MALT.

REAL ALE

A beer that has been conditioned by having its final fermenting activity carried out in its serving container. Thus, both bottle-conditioned and cask-conditioned beers are real ales, even though the results in these two cases are quite different. Bottle-conditioned beers are saturated with carbon dioxide under pressure from a closed ferment; cask-conditioned beers are merely saturated with carbon dioxide, from a restricted-opening ferment. The former are gassy, the latter are not.

Most people, especially those in Great Britain, consider only the beer that has been cask-conditioned to be true real ale. As beer critic Michael Jackson says, "In its most traditional form, British ale is cask-conditioned. This is what is meant by 'real ale.'" Cask-conditioned beer is alive, with some carbon dioxide saturation, and not flat.

The Campaign for Real Ale (CAMRA) originated in 1971 as a consumer reaction in England to the British brewing industry's effort to change the drinking habits of pub drinkers. (The British consume about 80 percent of their beer in public houses, compared to 10 to 15 percent in the United States). The major brewers had been cutting back on their real ale production in an attempt to replace real ale with keg beer (American-style beer service). CAMRA was organized to combat that effort. This was the first blow in the beer counterrevolution, which spawned a whole new generation of craft brewers in England, as well as in the United States, and all around the world. Real ale was saved as a national heritage in Britain and has even gained a toehold in the United States, where an increasing number of pubs are offering this choice.

See BOTTLE-CONDITIONED BEER, CAMPAIGN FOR REAL ALE (CAMRA), and CASK-CONDITIONED BEER.

REAL ATTENUATION

The attenuation of beer that is devoid of carbon dioxide and alcohol.

See ATTENUATION.

RED BEER

See AMBER AND RED BEERS, BELGIAN BROWN AND RED ALE, and IRISH ALE.

REDHOOK ALE BREWERY SEATTLE, WASHINGTON

The Independent Ale Brewery was founded in 1981 by Paul Shipman (a wine industry entrepreneur) and Gordon Bowker (one of the founders of Starbuck's Coffee). By 1982, the renamed Redhook Ale Brewery was producing beer out of a former transmission garage in Ballard, a small Scandinavian neighborhood of Seattle.

In the first year, the company brewed about 1,000 barrels of beer, all of it sold within a 5-mile radius of the brewery. The company became known for its Redhook Ale, a brew brimming with fruity esters (some of these esters, notably the strong banana flavors, were perhaps unintentional). But what might be considered faults in an industrial beer were perceived as endearing quirks in an upstart micro-brew. The company's beers developed a following, and the portfolio soon included Blackhook Porter, Ballard Bitter, Redhook ESB, and Wheathook.

In 1989, the brewery moved to a new location — a converted trolley barn about a mile from the old transmission shop. The new brewery pushed capacity to 40,000 barrels a year and allowed the construction of an on-site taproom, the Trolleyman Pub. By 1991, the brewery was facing a familiar dilemma — demand was exceeding capacity. As a result, a $4 million expansion took place, providing the expanded trolley barn site with a 75,000-barrel capacity.

Founder Paul Shipman realized that the original brewery site was running out of expansion room and made plans to move to the next level. In 1992, the company purchased a 22-acre tract in Woodinville, Washington, about 18 miles outside Seattle. Construction on the new Woodinville brewery was completed in September 1994. Initial capacity was 60,000 barrels, but even that addition soon appeared insufficient, for Shipman signed an agreement in the fall of 1994 to give Anheuser-Busch, the largest brewing company in the world, a minority stake in the company. The agreement also plugged Redhook into the Anheuser-Busch distribution network, the most powerful and efficient network in the United States.

The bottling line at Redhook Ale Brewery in Seattle, Washington

To keep itself from getting too corporate (and its brewers from stagnating), Redhook has started what it calls a Blue-Line brewing program, in which brewers produce limited runs of draught-only seasonal and specialty beers. The Blue-Line beers help keep the suddenly large brewer in tune with the dynamic Seattle beer market.

By late 1994, the Anheuser-Busch deal was putting Redhook beers on store shelves throughout the United States. That is when Shipman announced plans to build another new brewery in New England, at the former Pease Air Force Base in New Hampshire. The brewery broke ground at Pease in June, 1995. The announcement positioned Redhook as the first craft brewer with nationwide reach and a major new player in the U.S. brewing industry.

See ALE, ANHEUSER-BUSCH, BITTER, MICRO-BREWERY, and PORTER.

REFRIGERATION TECHNIQUES

The Dreher family of Wien had been involved with brewing since the 1630s when Anton Dreher, while studying brewing at München, met Gabriel Sedlmayr and a lifelong collaborative friendship developed. Dissatisfied with their lack of control over temperature (one of the key physical factors in beer production, especially for lagers), the two launched an effort to improve refrigeration techniques.

In the early 1860s, Gabriel Sedlmayr introduced the first refrigeration plant at his München brewery. Anton Dreher, seeing what his friend was accomplishing, installed an entirely new refrigerated brewing plant at a preexisting brewery, which he bought at Trieste, located at the top of the Adriatic Sea. It had been said that good beer could never be brewed there, but with his new methods, Dreher's brewery flourished.

These innovations in refrigeration equipment brought three enormous changes to brewing. First, operations could be conducted year-round, instead of having to close between May and September. This also meant that brewing could be done in equatorial countries, where it is seldom cool enough to brew. Second, by accurate temperature control, brewers were able to produce a consistently high-quality product, especially lagers, which are much more sensitive to temperature than ales. Third, refrigeration for the first time permitted long-distance transport via railways, and long-term storage of beer in any season — particularly significant for a continent the size of North America.

REGIONAL BREWERY

A company that distributes its beer in a circumscribed area. Most United States regional brewers produce anywhere from 15,000 to 1,000,000 barrels of beer each year.

The United States brewing industry includes only three truly national brewers (Anheuser-Busch, Miller, and Coors) and two brewers that come close (Stroh and G. Heileman). All others are regional or local, although that is changing. Fritz Maytag,

A drawing of the early Jacob Schmidt Brewing Company in St. Paul, Minnesota

Straub Brewing, Inc. of St. Mary's, Pennsylvania, is a regional brewery that has strong local loyalty.

founder of Anchor Brewing Co., has announced his intent to become the first "small national brewer." His company and others like it are indeed approaching national status as they build their distribution networks to encompass the entire country. For the time being, however, only the larger brewers have the market penetration to give them truly national reach.

The growth of microbreweries has swelled the ranks of regional brewers, which had been thinned by the beer wars of the postwar era. Many once-tiny microbreweries are now becoming significant regional players, as their volume climbs into the 50,000-barrel range.

Dozens of old-line regional companies were driven out of business during the 1960s and early 1970s, as the major brewers brought their economies of scale to bear. The number of regional brewers went from several hundred down to a couple of dozen, and those surviving did so only tenuously. During the 1980s, the surviving regionals began to recover, replacing volume lost to the mass-market brands with contract brewing.

The Val. Blatz Brewery of Milwaukee, Wisconsin, was one of the many regional breweries acquired by G. Heileman in the 1960s.

Given local market loyalty, regional brewing can be viable even in today's mass market. In certain areas of the country, consumer loyalty has proven stronger than mass-market advertising dollars. Pennsylvania is perhaps the best example of this. A majority of the regional brewers that survived the beer wars were located in Pennsylvania, including Pittsburgh, Yuengling, The Lion, Straub, Jones, and Latrobe. The same kind of regional loyalty seems to be developing in California and the Northwest, where local producers are retaking market share from national brewers for the first time in memory.

See ANCHOR BREWING CO., JONES BREWING CO., LATROBE BREWING CO., THE LION, MICROBREWING, PITTSBURGH BREWING CO., STRAUB BREWING CO., and YUENGLING & SONS BREWING CO.

REINHEITSGEBOT

A German standard for brewing was established by Duke Albert IV in 1847. In 1516, German beer purity law —*Reinheitsgebot*— decreed that the only ingredients allowed in the brewing of beer are water, hops, malt (barley and wheat), and yeast. Chemical additives, sugar, rice, corn, and unmalted barley are prohibited.

Several other countries, such as Finland and Norway, have similar regulations. Many breweries, especially microbreweries and brewpubs, brew under the *Reinheitsgebot*, which is a strong marketing claim.

RESIN

See HOPS.

RESPIRATION

The absorption of oxygen and the production of carbon dioxide by germinating barley. The respiration is caused by an acid rest during steeping.

RHODE ISLAND INTERNATIONAL BEER EXPOSITION

The second annual Rhode Island International Beer Exposition was held in late September 1995 at the Providence Convention Center. Two 4-hour sessions were held, with beers from around the world represented. The exposition is being planned as a yearly event.

RICE

A cereal grass *(Oryza sativa)* grown in flooded marshy areas. Rice is usually used in brewing as an adjunct in very light bodied United States commercial beers. It is appropriate when trying to duplicate the light body beers typical of pale American lagers or cream ales. Rice also is used in brewing sake (Japanese rice wine).

When used in brewing, 25 to 50 percent rice is mixed with 6-row pale malt.

The 6-row malt is used because it has high enzyme levels and can convert the unmalted grains. When 6-row malt is used without adjuncts, however, the beers produced tend to develop haze due to their high protein and tannin levels. Rice is sometimes preferred as an adjunct because it imparts little flavor. Although many major breweries add rice and corn to beers, their primary motivation for doing so is cost, and the result is a blander, lower-quality beer than one brewed with only 2-row pale malt.

Rice is most commonly used in its whole-kernel form, although other forms, including flaked rice or grits, may be used. If used in whole-kernel or grit form, the rice must be cooked before being used. Rice extract is sold as both a syrup and a powder. Homebrewers, particularly extract brewers, often use rice extract to increase the fermentable sugars without adding body to beer.

See SAKE.

RINGNES A/S OSLO, NORWAY

A Norwegian brewing company that operates four plants. Ringnes produces a dry, crisp lager often seen in export markets. Ringnes beer is imported to the United States by Seemayer Asso-

ciates of Stamford, Connecticut, and Rader Co. of Boyertown, Pennsylvania.

See EXPORT and IMPORT.

BROUWERIJ RIVA N.V. DENTERGEMS, BELGIUM

Riva owns both Gouden Carolus and Liefmans, and the company operates a midsize regional brewery in its own right (capacity 115,000 hl). The company is best known in the United States for its Dentergems wheat beer, brewed in the "Hoegaarden" style. It is a top-fermented, bottle-conditioned, unfiltered beer brewed from a mash of wheat and malt. Dentergems Riva Blanche is imported into the United States by Phoenix Imports of Ellicott City, Maryland.

Dentergems

A foggy gold in the glass, this beer is topped with a creamy white head. Yeast swirls through the beer as the glass is lifted. The beer has a spicy, yeasty aroma and some of the characteristic clove flavor, but more maltiness than one would expect. Dentergems is crisp and light-bodied, with a clean maltiness and some apple notes.

See Gouden Carolus, Hoegaarden Brewery, and wheat beer.

ROASTED BARLEY

Unmalted barley that is roasted at high temperatures to give it a dark color (about 700 degrees Lovibond). Roasted barley has a drier flavor than roasted malt and is often used in dry (Irish-style) stouts.

ROASTING DRUM

A small metal drum heated with gas burners mechanically turned to create specialty malts (black patent malt, chocolate malt, and so forth).

See MALT.

ROCK, RHYTHM & BREWS

This annual early October weekend festival is held in Newport, Oregon and boasts more than 10,000 attendees, who are presented with 100 brews to taste from 30 brewers.

The Rock, Rythm & Brews festival is a major fund-raiser for local charities, especially the Lincoln County Food Share, which receives both funds and food from attendees, who could shave a dollar off the admission price if they donated two cans of food).

Music is an equal partner with beer at the festival and a major draw. Music offerings range from Seattle blues queen Duffy Bishop to classic rock groups such as Iron Butterfly, Rare Earth, and the Spencer Davis Group.

RODENBACH N.V. BROUWERIJ ROESELARE, BELGIUM

Located in West Flanders, the Rodenbach brewery boasts more than 300 wooden

Rodenbach

Rodenbach is brewed from four malts — one pale from summer barley, 2- and 6-row varieties of winter barley, and a red Vienna malt. Corn grits also are used. Brewers add East Kent Goldings and Brewer's Gold hops, as well as five different strains of yeast. Rodenbach is deep amber in color, reddish when held up to the light. It is rich in fruity aromas that lead the drinker into a beer of great complexity. Although it is known as a sour beer, the sourness does not overpower, but rather quenches. This is a beer that must be tried.

casks, each more than 20 feet high. Within these great tuns, Rodenbach's ale ferments for up to 2 years, emerging as a sour red beer acclaimed by beer critics. Four coopers labor fulltime to maintain the wooden vessels, at least one of which has been in continuous use since before the Franco-Prussian War. The brewery was founded in 1836, and a malthouse from that time has been turned into a museum. Much of the current brewhouse dates from the early 20th century.

Rodenbach beer is imported into the United States by Vanberg & DeWulf of Cooperstown, New York.

See ALE and BELGIAN BROWN AND RED ALES.

ROLLING ROCK

See LA TROBE BREWING CO.

ROMAN EMPIRE AND BEER

The Romans were a wine culture and, as such, were not overly anxious to promote beer. Archaeologists, however, have found the remains of a regimental Roman brewery in Germany. The Roman legions recruited locally from a Romanized German population which kept its identity in beer. This does not contradict the theory that brewing in Europe was done from the top down, as evidenced by beer jugs discovered at Kulmbach, Germany, which were dated to 800 B.C., long before the Romans came to Germany.

Pliny, the Roman orator and writer (c A.D. 62–144), wrote:

"The nations of the west have their own intoxicant from grain soaked in water; there are many ways of making it in Gaul and Spain, and under different names, though the principle is the same. The Spanish have taught us that these liquors keep well."

Pliny's statement confirms the theory that nowhere does he say that the Romans introduced beer or brewing to the West. The inference is that the locals had the grain, and they had prior brewing experience.

RUSSIAN IMPERIAL STOUT AND RUSSIAN STOUT

See STOUT — IMPERIAL.

RYE

A strongly flavored grain *(Secale cereale)* used in brewing the *roggenbier* (German for rye beer) style and occasionally in specialty beers. Rye also is used in fermented beverages that are common in countries outside North America and Great Britain. For example, rye accounts for a significant percentage of the grist for the Finnish brew called sahti.

When mixed with malted barley in the grist, rye is usually added in fairly small quantities — typically 10 to 20 percent — although it can (cautiously) be increased to 30 to 40 percent to create a pronounced rye flavor, which is often characterized as crisp and slightly spicy. When rye is used at the 15 percent level, the character is not at all pronounced. The form of rye used also influences the strength and character of the flavor. A sharp rye flavor can be ameliorated to some extent by using rye in conjunction with malted wheat.

Rye is noted for having high protein and beta glucan levels, so homebrewers may want to experiment with smaller proportions of rye to barley at first. They also must be aware that rye lacks the husks of barley, and thus longer runoff times may be needed and extra water may be added to the mash. A low-temperature step mash works well with rye. Mash-in takes place at 105° to 110°F (40.5° to 43°C), the acid rest at 122° to 130°F (50° to 54°C), the saccharification rest at 152°F (67°C), and mash-out at 170°F (77°C).

Rye is usually available in five forms: whole, rolled, roasted, malted, and flakes. The best option for brewing is rye flakes, although all forms are usable. All-grain brewers may combine malted rye with their grist.

In the malting process, rye is significantly more difficult to handle. It is very fragile, is steeped for shorter times, and uses less water. It also causes problems with modern malting equipment. Still, larger malthouses do malt rye.

See RYE ALE.

RYE ALE

A beer made with rye malt and having a tangy flavor that is quite intriguing. Craft brewers have begun experimenting with this style, although the use of rye malt is not really new. In medieval times, brewers used whatever was at hand, including rye, particularly in the Baltic region, where it grows readily. Rye grains have no husks, so they present brewing problems similar to those encountered with wheat.

The Russians have long used rye bread to make homebrewed kvass, a popular low-alcohol drink that is currently being overshadowed by increasingly available Euro-American soft drinks.

The classic rye beer is Schierlinger Roggenbier from Bavaria. This beer is brewed from 60 percent dark rye malt. The brewery has a special mash tun with revolving knives to deal with the sometimes sticky and gelatinous mashes.

In the United States, several northwest brewers are making rye ales, notably the large Redhook Ale Brewery, which brews a seasonal rye. This beer has 10 percent flaked organic rye, 85 percent 2-row barley malt, and 5 percent Munich malt. It is very pale in color. The Tugboat Brewpub in Portland, Oregon, uses one-third rye malt to two-thirds barley malt, a ratio that many

craft brewers are trying. In addition to being malted, rye is available to brewers rolled or roasted, as well as in the whole-grain form.

Rye ale is a very new beer type, and brewers are experimenting with different ingredients and methods. Most brewers seem to be following their wheat formulations and methods, although rye may be expected to add much more flavor than wheat. Rye ale is made with pale malt plus about 30 to 40 percent rye malt and has a low hop level (about 15 to 20 IBU), a normal original gravity of 11–12/1.044–1.048, and a relatively pale color. Dark rye ales probably will appear soon.

Original Gravity	Final Gravity	Alcohol by Volume	IBU	SRM
Big Time Hefe-Ryzen (Washington) 1991				
13/1.052	4.2	4.7%	Unknown	≈4.5
Schierlinger Roggenbier (Germany) 1991				
12/1.048	2.7	5%	Unknown	≈21
Tugboat Rye Ale (Oregon) 1995				
11.2/1.045	2.2	4.8%	≈20	≈4.5

See REDHOOK ALE BREWERY, RYE, SAHTI, and WHEAT BEER.

SACCHARIFICATION

The conversion of starches to sugars by enzymes. The term is usually used to refer to the rest (or step) in a mash during which starches are converted to sugars. A saccharification rest takes place at approximately 147° to 158°F (64° to 70°C) and usually ranges in time from 30 minutes for a higher-temperature rest, to 90 minutes for a lower-temperature rest. A higher saccharification temperature creates more dextrins (unfermentable sugars).

See INFUSION MASH.

SACCHAROMYCES

The genus of yeasts that can ferment sugar into alcohol and carbon dioxide. These yeasts are used in baking and in beer and wine making. The word means "sugar fungus" and is derived from the Greek words *sakcharon* (which means sugar) and *mykes* (fungus).

See YEAST.

SAHTI

A popular Finnish beer brewed commercially and homebrewed in saunas. Sahti contains rye, which imparts a harsh taste, as well as hops, traditional berries, juniper branches, and straw. Sahti is often strong, up to about 12 percent alcohol by volume, although most sahti is about 5 percent by volume. Whitbread of Great Britain recently introduced a sahti ale as part of its specialty line. Women in Finland still make sahti, just as they have always done, usually in the sauna. The brewing process takes all day. The straw and juniper branches are used to filter the mash, which is carried out in a cradlelike vessel called a *kuurna* (leaving a juniper flavor in the wort). After the wort boil, the beer is fermented in milk cans for about a week. There are some commercial sahti breweries. Their products have a modest, unmalted rye increment but are mostly barley malt. The original gravity is 19.5–24.4/ 1.080–1.100, with much unfermentable extract remaining (8 percent), and the alcohol content is about 8 percent by volume.

See RYE and RYE ALE.

ST. ARNOU

Often referred to as the patron saint of brewers, this 6th century French bishop spent his holy life warning the peasants about the dangers of impure drinking water. Beer was safe according to Saint Arnou, because "from man's sweat and God's love, beer came into the world."

Saint Arnou is often confused with Saint Arnou of Oudenaarde. The name is also sometimes spelled St. Arnould or St. Arnolds.

See PATRON SAINTS OF BEER.

ST. ARNOU DE OUDENAARDE

A Belgian saint (Arnoldus the Strong, from Oudenaarde) who appealed directly to God for some cold beer during a droughty battle in Flanders in the 11th century. Like Saint Columbanus, Saint Arnoldus had a Christ-like, God-given ability to multiply beer into vast quantities at the saying of a prayer. He is often confused with the French bishop of Metz, Saint Arnou.

See PATRON SAINTS OF BEER.

ST. JAMES'S GATE

The old entrance to the city of Dublin, Ireland. Arthur Guinness leased a brew-house there in 1859 for the extraordinary term of 9,000 years at an annual rent of 45 Irish pounds.

See GUINNESS PLC.

SAISON BEER

Saison beers are what might be called "family" brews. Usually they are only about 50 percent attenuated, due to the ingredients and methods used in brewing them. Saisons

St. Arnou is considered to be among the most prominent patron saints of brewers. He was born in 580 in the French diocese of Toul.

are from the French-speaking Walloon region of southern Belgium. They were originally old-style ferments (often combinations of malt with raw wheat, oats, or rice) brewed to modest original gravities (11.3–12.5/1.045–1.050/4.5–5 Belge) for family and work consumption. They were made in the early summer (April–May) but not consumed until wintertime, so they had to be brewed with some strength to survive, yet be mild enough to be drunk by working farmers. Modern saison beers have a distinctive and easily recognized Belgian character, but they are produced mostly with pale malts, good hop levels, and multiple yeast strains, giving them the typical fruity Belgian character that is so appealing. Some of these beers are spiced, some are dry hopped, and most are golden to amber or even copper in color.

SAISON DUPONT

See DUPONT.

SAKE

Japanese rice wine. This distinctive beverage is really neither beer nor wine, although it is technically a beer because it is made from grain (rice) but is called a wine. The United States government licenses and taxes the six American sake breweries as beer breweries. However, sake is much stronger than beer in alcohol content, and it behaves more like wine than beer. That may be why most states license their sake breweries as wineries.

Sake is easily the most complex alcoholic beverage, with the highest alcohol content (usually 16 percent, but may be as high as 21 percent by volume) of any naturally fermented beverage. It contains some 600 elements and is the best-known example of a whole class of Oriental rice beers, encompassing a wide range of distinctive styles.

Sake making is the least understood brewing process in the world. Sake is made by fermenting rice, a cereal grain. However, rice is mostly starch and is not directly fermentable by yeast. The key to this ferment lies in the use of natural starch-conversion enzymes produced by a mold called *Aspergillus oryzae,* which is closely related to *Penicillium* and is cultured on rice. The moldy rice is called *koji,* which is essential to making sake.

The sake-brewing process today is almost identical to ancient brewing methods, allowing for modifications and improvements resulting from modern technology. The production of sake begins by making koji. The rice used to make koji is polished to remove the outer hull. The polishing process usually removes about 25 to 30 percent of the rice grain. This has the effect of removing some fatty acids, proteins, and minerals that can ruin the delicate flavor of sake. After being polished, the rice is steeped in cold water for about 18 hours. This soaking process softens the cell walls, which makes the next step (steaming) much more effective in preparing the rice for the ferment. After soaking, the rice is steamed for about 45 minutes, then spread on mats to cool. The *Aspergillus oryzae* mold is sprinkled on the rice and grows for 2 days. During that time, the rice is kept warm to encourage mold growth.

When the koji is ready, actual sake production may begin. First, more rice is polished, soaked, steamed, and cooled as described above. Rice, koji, and water are combined, and a special sake yeast is added to make a starter. When the starter is fermenting nicely, the main or primary ferment *(moromi)* begins. This is a three-stage process in which successive mixtures of rice, koji, and water are added, each doubling the size of the ferment. By the fifth day (the third such doubling), the primary ferment is at its height. This ferment is followed by a second 3-week ferment at temperatures below 50°F (10°C). The koji converts the starches in the rice grains to sugars, which are almost immediately fermented to alcohol. This ensures a very strong product. At that time, the young sake is pressed, separated from the spent rice grains, and filtered.

The resulting clear sake is then pasteurized. Pasteurization is necessary to prevent bacterial damage to the final product. Sake may be aged in the brewery for 6 months to 1 year, but most brewers claim that sake does not improve much with age. Sake is light-sensitive, however, and must be kept in the dark.

Springtime may be the best of all sake seasons. The Japanese are fond of viewing early spring cherry and plum blossoms, or the stars and the moon, while sipping sake very slowly and perhaps reading haiku. In warm seasons, sake is drunk chilled or at room temperature from *masu,* small square cypress or lacquerware measuring boxes. The cypress boxes add a refreshing touch of flavor to the sake.

Premium sake is made using the highest-quality rice and then polishing the rice to a very high level by removing 40, 50, or even 60 percent of the grain. Such high-grade sake is expensive to make. When rice is polished, the grains take a severe beating. Many of them crack and disintegrate. Only the best grains survive intact, and much rice is wasted, resulting in the high cost. Premium sakes are called *Ginjo* (literally "poetic" sake). There are even super premium sakes, called *Dai Ginjo* (super poetic). These expensive premium sakes are becoming more popular in both the United States and Japan.

See KOJI and JIU/CHIU.

SALADIN BOX

A germination method invented by Jules Alphonse Saladin in France in 1880. The term is now used interchangably with germination box.

See GERMINATION SYSTEMS FOR BARLEY and MALTING.

SALTS

See WATER.

SAPPORO BREWERIES TOKYO, JAPAN

Japan's third largest brewer. With about 20 percent of the home market, Sapporo Breweries produces Sapporo Lager, Sapporo Draft Yebisu, and Sapporo Black and has an annual capacity of 16,500,000 hl.

SCHANKBIER

See GERMAN BREW STRENGTHS and SMALL BEER.

The Sapparo Breweries museum

AUGUST SCHELL BREWING CO., NEW ULM, MINNESOTA

August Schell Brewing Co. was founded in 1858 in the immigrant German community of New Ulm, Minnesota. The brewery survived the Sioux uprising of 1862, reportedly because the Schell family had treated the Indian population with unusual fairness. Much of the rest of New Ulm went under the torch.

The town quickly recovered and by 1866 had four other breweries. By 1880, however, August Schell had become the dominant brewery in the region. As a sign of his success, Schell built an elaborate mansion and beer garden in 1885, a site that is now on the National Register of Historic Sites and is open to the public.

During Prohibition, the company made near beer and soft drinks. It is also one of the few breweries to admit to having made some alcohol during that period, a practice that was said to be commonplace.

The company is still family owned and has a capacity of 40,000 barrels. Schell was one of the first American regional breweries to rediscover the virtues of revivalist specialty beers and now produces a full range of traditional

Founder August Schell

The August Schell Brewery of New Ulm, Minnesota, in 1881

August Schell Weizen

A dry, light-bodied wheat beer with a fruity tang. Schell was probably the first old-line regional brewery to notice the growing consumer interest in specialty beers, and the company quickly began turning out a line of characterful seasonal and specialty beers. August Schell Weizen is a good example of the brewery's craft. Schell kraeusens several of its specialty beers, including the Weizen.

brands. In addition to the company's mainstream Schell's Deer Brand (30 percent corn), Schell's Light (20 percent corn), and Schell's Export (30 percent corn), Schell brews several characterful revivals: August Schell Pils (100 percent barley malt, Hallertauer and Cascade hops), August Schell Weizen (60 percent wheat malt, 40 percent barley malt, Hallertauer and Cascade hops), and Octoberfest (four types of malt; Cascade and Nugget hops). The company also produces the all-malt Ulmer Lager, Ulmer Braun, and Schmaltz's Alt (five types of malt; Chinook, Mt. Hood, and Hallertauer hops).

See REGIONAL BREWERY and WHEAT BEER.

SCHÜTZENFEST

Literally a "festival of shooting," which is what it once was, this July festival in Hannover, Germany, now concentrates on beer. Custom calls for downing a beer along with a glass of corn schnapps, which is shooting prowess enough.

SCHWARZBIER

See BLACK BEER.

SCOTCH ALE

A strong ale closely related to English old ale. These extra-strong versions of Scottish ales are quite popular in Belgium, where they are called "Scotch" ales (hard liquor may not be sold in Belgian cafés). One such brand is Gordon's Finest Gold Blond Ale, which is exported to the United States after being bottled in Antwerp. It is not sold in the British Isles. In Scotland, these ales were formerly called 90/ ("ninety shilling," from the 19th-century price of a barrel). Original gravity is usually above 18/1.074.

The Great American Beer Festival guidelines for Strong Scotch Ale are 18–21/1.072–1.085 OG, 6.2–8 percent

alcohol by volume, 25–35 IBU, and 10–25 SRM.

Original Gravity	Final Gravity	Alcohol by Volume	IBU	SRM
McEwan's Scotch Ale 1983				
21.5/1.088	5.2	8.5%	≈28	30
Traquair House Ale 1983				
19/1.078	2.7	11%	≈32	34

See ENGLISH STRONG ALE and SCOTTISH ALE.

SCOTTISH ALE

A variant of the basic pale ale style made with British malts. In the early part of this century, the malts were dried with peat moss kilning, as is still the case with Scotch whisky malts. This imparted a smoky flavor to the beer. Modern Scottish ales have a sweeter maltiness, with little of the smoky character that endeared them to folks in the beginning. Scottish ales differ from those in the rest of Britain, especially in the use of caramel or crystal malts. They usually include darker malts, notably amber and brown, plus some chocolate malt, and perhaps treacle (molasses) or brown sugar in the kettle. Scotch ales are less hoppy than their English counterparts and a good deal sweeter. *Diacetyl* and sulfur esters may be present. These ales are found frequently in Belgium, France, and the United States (among American craft brewers). Some Scottish ales are more like mild brown ales or even bitters.

Scottish light ale is closest to the mild ale category. The Great American Beer Festival guidelines for it are 7.5–9/1.030–1.035 OG, 2.8–3.5 percent alcohol by volume, 9–20 IBU, and 8–17 SRM.

In Scottish heavy ale, maltiness is the key, with 9–10/1.035–1.040 OG, 3.5–4 percent alcohol by volume, 12–17 IBU, and 10–19 SRM.

Scottish export ale is similar to Scottish heavy ale but a little stronger and slightly hoppier at 10–12.5/1.040–1.050 OG, 4–4.5 percent alcohol by volume, 15–20 IBU, and 10–19 SRM.

Original Gravity	Final Gravity	Alcohol by Volume	IBU	SRM
Grant's Scottish Style Ale (Washington) 1982				
13.5/1.054	2.7	5.6%	45	15
Portland McTarnahan Ale (Oregon) 1992				
13/1.052	3.3	5.2%	40	15

See BROWN ALE, PALE ALE, and SCOTCH ALE.

SCOTTISH BEER FESTIVALS

The Campaign for Real Ale (CAMRA) sponsors two beer festivals in Scotland in the fall. The Glasgow Ale Festival is held in mid-September at the Arches Theatre and offers more than 100 cask-conditioned ales, ciders, and perries sold in pints and half-pints. Imported beers from the United States, Germany, and Belgium also are available. A few weeks later at Meadowbank Stadium in Edinburgh, the Traditional Beer Festival eschews the imports and ciders but offers more than 75 cask-conditioned ales.

Independent breweries also have annual cask festivals that highlight, but are not limited to, their own beers. The first is usually the Traquair House Beer Festival in late May, at Traquair House, Innerleithen. In early June, the Caledonian Brewery Ale Festival takes place in Edinburgh. Then the scene shifts to Dunbar in early September for the Belhaven Brewery Scottish Beer Festival.

See CAMPAIGN FOR REAL ALE (CAMRA).

SCOTTISH & NEWCASTLE EDINBURGH, SCOTLAND

The core of the present-day Scottish & Newcastle was formed more than a century ago, but the current corporation owes its existence to the 1931 merger of Wm. McEwan & Co. and Wm. Younger and Co., both of Edinburgh. The firm merged with Newcastle Breweries of Newcastle-on-Tyne in 1960, and during the 1980s, Scottish & Newcastle acquired Home Brewery PLC and Matthew Brown PLC. In June 1995, Scottish & Newcastle acquired Courage Brewing, making it one of Britain's largest brewers.

The company now operates five breweries and four malthouses and has approximately 1,900 tied public houses. It produces the McEwan's, Younger's, Newcastle, Matthew Brown, and Theakston's labels.

See ALE.

SCURVY–GRASS ALE

A medicinal drink formerly prepared by adding an infusion of watercress to ale.

This was one of many attempts to combat and find a cure for scurvy, which especially plagued seamen. Scurvy was the main cause of the ill health and low morale of seafarers around the world. Although scurvy grass ale was nutritious and healthful, it was not the solution to this problem. Eventually, scurvy was attributed to the lack of vitamin C and could thus be prevented by eating vitamin C-rich foods.

SEAMER

A piece of equipment located at the end of a can filler that blows carbon dioxide over the surface of the beer as the pull-tab can end is positioned. The carbon dioxide helps reduce the air content of the can. The can end is sealed onto the can by two rolling operations. Fill heights can be checked by gamma radiation techniques.

SEASONAL BEER

A beer that is made for a particular season or occasion, to be consumed at a special time of the year.

For example, many brewers make special beers for the harvest season in Germany. That is a time for stronger (5.7–6.3 percent alcohol by volume), darker, more full-bodied beers. Such beers are called Oktoberfest or Märzenbiers. They are made in the spring, aged during the summer, and served at fall harvest festivals. These amber beers go especially well with the heavy foods of the season.

The Christmas-New Year season also has many special beers — called fest, holiday, or winter beers — that are stronger (up to 10 percent alcohol by volume), and sometimes have spices added to them. Anchor's Our Special Ale, a Christmas ale, is one example. This beer has cinnamon, nutmeg, ginger, and other spices added (every year's recipe is different). It and other spiced winter beers are delicious served warm, at about 120°F (49°C).

There are also special spring beers (bock beers are usually winter-spring beers) and summer beers. These seasonal beers are for sipping, in the fashion of fine wines.

Some brewers produce particular beers annually, but without designating them as "seasonals." This is especially true of brewers (mostly American) who brew barley-wine-style ales.

Original Gravity	Final Gravity	Alcohol by Volume	IBU	SRM
Anchor Our Special Ale (California) 1987 (Christmas spiced ale)				
16.5/1.068	4.3	6.4%	55	≈30
Paulaner Oktoberfest (Germany) 1989				
13.6/1.055	2.8	5.7%	22	8.7
Sierra Nevada Pale Bock (California) 1990				
16.5/1.068	3.8	6.8%	47	≈7.5

SECONDARY FERMENTATION

See FERMENTATION.

SEDIMENTATION

One method of clearing a beer and removing unwanted solid matter (trub). In this method, the solids are allowed to settle out of the beer, and then the clear beer is pumped or siphoned off. In commercial practice, solids are usually removed by filtration rather than sedimentation.

See FILTRATION and TRUB.

GABRIEL SEDLMAYR SPATEN-FRANZISKANER-BRAU MUNICH, GERMANY

The Spaten company can trace its roots to the late 14th century. The name Spaten, German for "spade," is a play on the name of one of the 17th-century owners, a man named Spaeth.

The modern Spaten brewery did not take shape until the early 19th century, under the guiding hand of Gabriel Sedlmayr, whose family had served as brewers for the Bavarian royal court. Sedlmayr is recognized as one of the first professional brewing chemists, bringing science to bear on the technique of brewing. His Munich lagers were dark beers (all beers were dark in those days) made with bottom-fermenting yeasts. These dark Munich lagers were the immediate predecessors of the lighter-colored bottom-fermented beers that have become the world standard.

The company produces more than 1,000,000 hl of beer each year and brews a number of brands, including Spaten Hell, Spaten Lager, Spatengold, Ludwig Thomas Dunkel, Spaten Pils, Spaten Ur Märzen, Doppelspaten Optimator, Spaten Premium Bock, Spaten Light, Franziskaner Hefe-Weiss, and Spaten Ocktoberfest. Spaten beers are imported into the United States by Sieb Distributors of Ridgewood, New York (in the East), and Spaten West of Brisbane, California.

See BOCK BEER, BOTTOM-FERMENTING YEAST, LAGER ALE, OKTOBERFEST BEER, and WHEAT BEER.

SESSION BEER

See LIGHT ALE.

SHANDY

Originally, a drink made of beer and ginger, ginger beer, or ginger ale. Today Shandy is a mixture of beer and lemonade (English style) or lemon juice.

SHEKAR

A beer consumed by the biblical Noah's son Shem (Isaiah 5:11) and made from corn, honey, dates, and spices. From the Jewish word meaning "to become inebriated."

SHELF LIFE

A measure of the amount of time a packaged beer product can remain on a shelf or in a cooler before spoilage occurs.

SHIMEYANE

A subequatorial African tribal beer made from corn and raw sugar.

SHOT AND A BEER

A small glass of liquor other than beer, traditionally chased with a tall glass of beer. A popular American practice.

SHU BEER

A millet-based beer. Shu beer was brewed in China during the Han dynasty (207 B.C. to 200 A.D.).
See JIU/CHIU.

SICERA

A strong, hopped drink. Sicera was made by the Jews during their captivity in Babylon. It was believed to ward off leprosy. Sicera, which comes from the Latin *Cicera ex lupulis confectam,* now refers to any intoxicating liquor other than wine that is made from corn, honey, or fruit.

Some scholars maintain that the Hebrew word *sicera,* which is translated as "strong drink" in the Bible, is really the barley wine mentioned by the Greek historian Herodotus and that the Israelites brought knowledge of its use from Egypt. The Israelites certainly knew how to brew sicera shortly after the Exodus, the book of Leviticus states that the priests were forbidden to drink wine or strong drink before they entered the tabernacle. Furthermore, in the book of Numbers, the Nazarenes were required to abstain from both wine and strong drink, and even from vinegar made from either.

In every biblical passage, sicera is mentioned separately as being distinct from wine.

SIEBEL INSTITUTE OF TECHNOLOGY

4055 West Peterson Avenue
Chicago, IL 60646
312-463-3400
Fax 312-463-7688

The Siebel Institute of Technology was founded and incorporated by Dr. John Ewald Siebel in 1901. Dr. Siebel was born in Germany in 1845. He studied physics and chemistry at the University of Berlin before moving to Chicago in 1866. In 1868, he opened the John E. Siebel Chemical Laboratory, which developed into a brewing research organization and eventually a brewing school.

The name of the laboratory was changed to the Zymotechnic Institute in 1872. Most acknowledge 1872 as the beginning of the education and service business that continues today at the Siebel Institute of Technology. Several of Dr. Siebel's sons joined the company in the 1890s, which led to its incorporation in 1901. In the early 1900s, courses were conducted in both German and English.

The mission of the institute is to "promote the progress of the industries based on fermentation, through instruction, investigation, analysis and otherwise." Today it offers the general public various courses designed to expand their knowledge of the brewing industry. Students include both experienced and inexperienced brewers, allied industry personnel, wholesalers, importers, brewery executives from marketing departments, homebrewers, microbrewers, pub brewers, and those interested in starting a brewing business. Courses range from 3 days to 3 months in length.

SIERRA NEVADA BREWING CO., CHICO, CALIFORNIA

Sierra Nevada Brewing Co. was one of the earliest American craft breweries, founded in 1980 by a pair of former homebrewers, Ken Grossman and Paul Camusi. After brewing their own beers for years, the pair cobbled together a brewhouse from used dairy tanks, with an ultimate goal of selling 3,000 barrels a year.

Sierra Nevada Pale Ale

A fresh, crisp beer that is rich with malty, fruity flavors. Its brisk American character can almost make its ancestral British pale ales seem stodgy and tired by comparison. When the bartender pours out a glass of Sierra Nevada Pale Ale, a great gust of floral hop aromas waft from the glass.

The Sierra Nevada Brewing Co. was founded in 1978 by Ken Grossman and Paul Camusi.

Fifteen years later, the company has thrived, and Sierra Nevada has grown into one of the top United States producers of specialty brands. In recent years, the compa-

ny has expanded its brewing plant almost continually, and in 1994 Sierra Nevada sold more than 154,000 barrels of beer.

Sierra Nevada is an example of what happens to a brewery when it gets everything just right, and the most clear-cut example of how microbrewing has turned the old brewing order on its ear. Most professional brewers look askance at their homebrewing brethren. To be sure, brewing on a commercial scale is an entirely different proposition than brewing on a stovetop. In the commercial arena, inconsistency is no longer charming, and quality control takes on new importance. Quite a few early microbreweries were not able to make the leap, but Grossman and Camusi assuredly did.

The Sierra Nevada Taproom & Restaurant opened in 1989.

The brewhouse of the Sierra Nevada Brewing Co. is capable of producing over 80,000 barrels per year.

Sierra Nevada made its mark producing bottle-conditioned ales, a practice in which live yeast is added to bottles before packaging. The yeast adds a variable to the process, which could affect carbonation, and also rules out pasteurization and sterilization. On the plus side, the yeast can act as an antioxidant and stabilizer. In practice, care in production and packaging have provided the brewery with a consistent, highly individual product.

See ALE, CASK-CONDITIONED BEER, HOME-BREWING, MICROBREWERY, and PALE ALE.

SIGN BOARDS

Pub signs can be directly traced to ancient Rome where it was customary to hang grapevines, leaves and all, from the fronts of their *tabernae* which served wine. The English word tavern derives from this Latin word. The wreath of grapevines was a signal that new wine was available.

The Roman Empire operated on a commercial basis. Along the main routes throughout the empire, taverns were established to sustain travellers. Since the vast majority of people in the Empire were illiterate, and of many nationalities, symbols or signs were the best way of communicating the nature of an establishment.

When the Romans occupied Britain (A.D. 43) they naturally brought their customs with them, including the taverns or wine shops. For the next 500 years, other people — Anglos, Saxons, and Danes — invaded Britain. These people brought with them their ale- and mead-drinking

A sign painter's craft was important because of the high rate of illiteracy.

customs, which replaced the wine-drinking habits of Roman rule.

The development of local ale houses, limited to one per village by order of King Edgar (A.D. 959–975), spurred the development of pub signs. They began with sticks or stakes mounted on the front of the house. Since pubs did not have individual names, the stake, which came to be known as an ale-stake, was the only indication that ale was on sale inside. This changed in the 18th century, when pubs began to adopt names. Ale houses were then called "public houses" because they were open to the entire public. Since many of the names were of animals, saints, royalty, trades, and common objects such as hammers and nails, it is easy to see that a simple sign of a white horse hanging from the outside of the building would be sufficient to identify the public house as the White Horse.

Because the illiteracy rate remained high in Britain until the end of the 18th century, virtually all pubs had picture signs. The tradition continues to this day.

See ALE-STAKE.

SIKARU

An ancient Sumerian beer made from loaves of bread.

SILO

A container used for bulk storage of unmalted or malted grains. Unmalted grains are usually stored at the malthouse, malted grains at the brewery. All large breweries have silos. Some microbreweries also have them to save space and ease grain handling.

Silos are generally made of steel or concrete, with smooth sides and hopper bottoms (80 degree cones for movement). A silo must be constructed to maintain the proper moisture level of the unmalted or malted grains. This prevents insect infestation and biochemical changes in the grain due to increased moisture. Silos are generally fitted with electric temperature probes to maintain temperature and humidity at preset levels. Depending on weather conditions (if located outside) or internal atmosphere (if located inside a building), a dryer may be needed in the silo.

Silos have a topmanway for augering in grain and human access. They also may be fitted with an external blowpipe (4 to 6 inches in diameter) for blowing in grain from a bulk grain truck. This has been deemed unsatisfactory in some cases because of the potential for more damaged kernels (versus conveying or augering). The only way to minimize this is to gravity-feed grain (that is, build the silos below the grade).

SINGLE-STAGE FERMENTATION

A term used for the fermentation process in homebrewing whereby complete fermentation is carried out in a single container that is fitted with an air lock to prevent the beer from getting contaminated.

See FERMENTATION.

SIPHONING

The process of pumping liquid from one container to another by creating a vacuum. The siphon is a tube in the shape of an inverted U. One end of the tube is placed in the liquid and the other in a vessel to which the liquid is to be transferred. The second vessel must be at a lower height than the first.

SMALL BEER

A weak beer served in the past to servants, monks, agricultural workers, children, and the poor. In those days, sanitation was nonexistent and water a dangerous drink. Small beer was made from the final runoff of the brewer's mash. The first-run beer would usually be a Dubbel or Tripel or a strong ale. The second run would be ordinary beer, and the final run small beer. Small beer had 6.7/1.026 OG, 1.9 final gravity, and 2.5 percent alcohol by volume. It was probably very dark and consumed quickly after a short brewing cycle. In the Middle Ages monasteries produced a lot of small beer, which often took the place of drinking water.

The Belgian single beer and the German schankbier are two other examples of this type of beer. These generally have an original gravity of about 7.5–9/1.030–1.036 and a low alcohol content (2–2.5 percent by volume).

SAMUEL SMITH

Samuel Smith's Old Brewery is the smallest brewery in Tadcaster, England, and the oldest brewery in Yorkshire. Sam's takes great pride in preserving the old-fashioned Yorkshire method of brewing the highest-quality classic styles of traditional British beer.

Copper mash tuns are used to mix the malts with the hard crystalline "liquor,"

or brewing water, which is still drawn from the original well, sunk almost 250 years ago.

The beers are fermented in traditional stone Yorkshire Stone Squares (huge fermenting vessels made of solid blocks of slate). These squares have to be cleaned out by hand and have always been known to produce a particularly full-bodied beer.

The yeast at the Samuel Smith brewery has not been altered since the turn of the century, and it is probably the oldest unchanged strain of yeast at any brewery in England. It is still as healthy and active as it has ever been, frothing up into rich, creamy heads.

Many modern breweries use hoop pellets or extract, but Samuel Smith uses the finest whole-dried Kent hop flowers. A hop blender, whose skill has been handed down from generation to generation, blends and weighs each batch of hops, which are added twice during the brew.

Samuel Smith is one of the few breweries still in existence that has its own cooperage, where a team of skilled craftsmen makes the wooden casks in which the beer is naturally conditioned. Tools such as a jack shave, a patsy, a chive, an adze and a heading swift are used by the coopers and their apprentices. An apprenticeship lasts four years, after which time

Samuel Smith's grey shire horses are kept in the stables at the Old Brewery.

the apprentice must go through an initiation ceremony and make a hogshead (a 54-gallon cask), leaving its end open; he is then covered in wood shavings, drenched with beer, and rolled around the cooper's shop inside the barrel he has made.

Samuel Smith stables between six and eight shire horses at the brewery, and the team regularly wins prizes at shows throughout the country. These horses weigh one ton each and can pull half as much again as their own weight.

Five generations of Smiths have managed the brewery and its tied estate, making it a family firm in the truest sense of the word, and generations of Taddy (Tadcaster) families continue to serve as employees. Families of serious Yorkshire beer enthusiasts consider the taste of all Samuel Smith beers a national treasure.

Since its introduction to American beer drinkers a decade and a half ago, the range of Samuel Smith beers has become popular wherever it is sold. A range of five of Samuel Smith's top-fermented specialties—including World Champion Old Brewery Pale Ale, Classic Nut Brown Ale, The Famous Taddy Porter, Celebrated Oatmeal Stout and festive Winter Welcome (seasonal) — are now available in the United States in 550 ml "Yorkshire Pints," exactly as they are served in Samuel Smith's pubs , such as Ye Olde Cheshire Cheese on Fleet Street in London, or the Angel and White Horse in Tadcaster. Old Brewery Pale Ale, Nut Brown Ale, The Famous Taddy Porter, Celebrated Oatmeal Stout, Pure Brewed Lager and Imperial Stout are also available in standard United States sizes and 6-packs

Samuel Smith is imported into the United States by Merchant du Vin Corporation, of Seattle, WA.

See YORKSHIRE STONE SQUARE.

SMOKED BEER

See RAUCHBIER.

SMOKED MALT

Malt that is smoked before it is used to make beer. The German rauchbier style uses malt smoked over a beech fire. Beech-smoked malt is not widely available, although some homebrew supply shops do carry it. In Scotland, malt smoked over a peat fire is used to make whisky. A few

Malt can be smoked or dried over an open fire to impart a smoky flavor to beers such as rauchbiers.

commercial breweries, such as the Alaskan Brewing Co., produce beers made with smoked malt. Homebrewers have begun experimenting with the widely available Hugh Baird peat-smoked malt in Scottish

ales, although the smoky flavor is often regarded as phenolic and is not a true component of the style. Some homebrewers also experiment with smoking their own grains in backyard barbecues or use liquid smoke, which is often sold in supermarkets. However, some brands of liquid smoke contain vinegar, which may impart undesirable characteristics to the beer.

See RAUCHBIER.

SODIUM

A metallic element that is very soluble in water. For good brewing water, the sodium level should be less than 150 ppm. In excess of this, it can lend a harsh taste to beer and be poisonous to yeast. At lower levels, it can enhance the flavor, especially when paired with chloride ions.

SORA

A variety of chicha made from special strains of corn. Sora was a royal brew reserved for Inca leaders.

SORGHUM BEER

A beer made primarily from sorghum but also containing other sorghum grains collected from a variety of grasses. Sorghum is a grain used to produce thick beers in Africa. These beers are often referred to as Bantu or Kaffir beers. Sorghum is usually brewed with millet and corn. The sorghum is malted, as barley would be in most breweries. Then it is mixed in a grist with water, heated, and allowed to sit overnight. The beer is soured using lactic acid. The sorghum is then typically mixed with corn and boiled. It is cooled overnight, then mixed with more corn to a gruel consistency. The beer is fermented by using naturally occurring microflora or by adding bread. Sorghum beer is consumed before fermentation is complete. It forms the basis for many African tribal beers, including commercial versions packaged in waxed cardboard cartons. Sorghum beers taste a bit like raisins in cider.

SOUBYA BEER

An Egyptian/Sudanese tribal beer that is made from rice. This beer is nearly extinct today.

SOUTH BAY BEER FESTIVAL WINTERFEST

The annual Winterfest, featuring specialty beers from more than 35 California breweries, is held in late February at the Redondo Beach Brewing Company. The 6-hour event, broken into three sessions, is a fundraiser for local charities. Admission includes a souvenir pint glass; beer samples are purchased individually.

SOUTHEASTERN MICROBREWERS' INVITATIONAL

This invitational festival, a 1-day, 4-hour festival, is attended by about 2,500 people, and is cosponsored by the Southeastern Microbrewers' Association (SMA) and the Carolina Brewery, both of Chapel Hill.

Close to 40 breweries attend, including representatives from both the growing number of southern microbreweries and other small breweries nationwide. Speakers include Michael Jackson and Steve Johnson (publisher of the *World Beer Review*), and the winner of a raffle to benefit a local scholarship receives a round-trip ticket to the Great American Beer Festival.

The SMA promotes the production, distribution, and responsible consumption of American microbrewed beers. Besides organizing the festival, the group publishes material about southern brewing and lobbies for more sensible legislation concerning beer alcohol levels in North Carolina and surrounding areas.

SPARGE GEAR

A central rotating pivot installed at the top of a mash tun. Two arms, one on either side of the central pivot, extend to just off the edge of the vessel wall. These are drilled in spiral fashion. This enables them to rotate around the mash tun under water pressure, spraying sparge water evenly over the mash bed and thus allowing for the rinsing of sugars from the bed.

See MASH TUN.

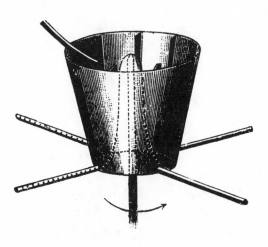

Sparging has always been a part of the brewing process, in one form or another. Here, an old Scotch turning cross sparger is illustrated.

SPARGING

The rinsing of grains after a mash to extract as much sugar from the grains as possible. Sparging is usually done with 168° to 176°F (75.5° to 80°C) water.

SPARKLING LAGER ALE

See LAGER ALE.

SPECIAL BITTER

See BITTER.

SPECIALTY BEER

See FRUIT, VEGETABLE, HERBAL, AND SPECIALTY BEERS.

SPECIFIC GRAVITY

Also called original gravity, it is the measure of the density of a liquid or solid as compared to the density of water. Water is given the specific gravity value of 1.000 at 39.2°F (4°C).

See DENSITY and ORIGINAL GRAVITY.

Taking a measurement of specific gravity of the ale

419

SPEZIALBIER

See GERMAN BREW STRENGTHS.

SPICED ALE

See FRUIT, VEGETABLE, HERBAL, AND SPECIALTY BEERS; SEASONAL BEER; and FESTBIER.

SPICES

See HERBS.

SPOETZL BREWING CO. SHINER, TEXAS

A small local brewery in Shiner, Texas, that is now a subsidiary of the Gambrinus Importing Co. of San Antonio (importers of Corona for the Western United States).

Spoetzl was founded in 1909 as the Shiner Brewing Association, but was taken over by brewer Kosmas Spoetzl in 1914. Spoetzl kept the brewery going during Prohibition by brewing near beer and selling ice. When he died in 1950, Spoetzl passed the brewery on to his daughter Celie, who ran it until the mid-1960s.

The brewery changed owners several times before Gambrinus bought it in 1985. The importer's resources have enabled the brewery to expand its production capacity and broaden its marketing efforts. The brewery continues to produce only two beers: Shiner Premium and Shiner Bock. The Bock has become quite celebrated in parts of the West, and is now available more widely, thanks to Gambrinus' distribution connections.

Shiner Bock

Shiner Bock is not an especially robust example of the bock style. Over the near century since Kosmas Spoetzl founded the brewery, the Germanic brewing traditions that inspired him have lost something in the translation (which could be said about most of America's German-inspired lagers). Shiner Bock is a dark amber, slightly sweet beer with a light malty palate. Its light body seems appropriate for the sweltering clime, however, and served as it is in Texas, ice cold, it can be quite refreshing.

SPONTANEOUS FERMENT

A natural ferment from atmospheric yeasts and other microflora that are present everywhere on earth. The brewer adds no yeast but allows the beer to ferment naturally. If a liquid containing fermentable extract is left standing at a temperature of 60° to 100°F (15.5° to 38°C), a ferment will begin. This will change the fermentable sugars to alcohol and carbon dioxide. Most brewers and wine makers add a particular yeast strain to their worts and musts early on to prevent this from happening. Their preference is for a particular yeast to work in a specific way to produce an alcoholic beverage with specific characteristics. Spontaneous ferments allow a wide range of wild yeasts and other bacteria to work, which can lead to unpredictable results.

Pure yeast culturing is a relatively recent phenomenon, dating only from the mid-19th century. By the turn of the century, most lager brewers in Germany and the United States, were using pure yeast cultures. Pure yeast culturing was less effective with top-fermented beers, and brewers in those countries, as well as in Great Britain and Belgium, concluded that the distinctive character of many of their beers was a direct result of the action of these bacteria.

In the United States, Prohibition resulted in the loss of these special yeasts because nearly all U.S. yeast banks were purged of such "contaminants" during that time. World War II had a similar effect on the German brewing industry. Thus, American and German beers today are clean and sterile, lacking the special character that is so charming in some British and Belgian beers. Belgian beers, particularly Belgian red and brown ales, are most noted for their multiple-yeast ferments. Belgian lambic beers rely entirely on spontaneously fermenting (wild) yeasts. Most prominent are *Brettanomyces lambicus* and *B. bruxellensis,* along with *Saccharomyces bayanus* and *S. cerevisiae,* the latter two a wine and a beer yeast, respectively.

One other spontaneously fermented hopped beer type came from Gdansk, Poland. Danziger Jopen-bier has not been made since well before World War II. Its very long (10-hour) wort boil resulted in 9–12/1.036–1.048 OG, 2.5–7 percent alcohol by volume, 1–2 percent lactic acid, and a very low hopping rate (about 10 IBU).

See BELGIAN BROWN AND RED ALES, BROWN ALE, and LAMBIC.

SPRAYBALL

A stainless steel ball fitted into a stainless steel brewery tank for in-place cleaning. These balls also can be found on cask washers and some keg washers where the spears are removed. The balls may be stationary, with holes drilled accordingly to give upward, downward, or 360-degree spray jets depending on the application. Or they may be designed to spin around an axis to create complete cleaning coverage. Both cleaning detergent and clean rinsing water are pumped at high velocity through these units.

SPRAYMALT

Dry malt extract (powder).
See MALT EXTRACT.

SPRECHER BREWING CO. MILWAUKEE, WISCONSIN

When a traveler entered Milwaukee via its modern gateway (the airport) in recent years, the first brewery to be seen was not

SPECIAL AMBER

University of California at Davis, where he studied chemistry and fermentation. Pabst recruited him directly from Davis, and he worked for the big brewery for 4 years.

When the company announced cutbacks in 1984, it asked for voluntary layoffs, and Sprecher jumped at the chance. He started Sprecher in 1985 with $40,000 and a bunch of old dairy tanks. He soon began brewing quite respectable German-style microbrews.

Among Sprecher's brands are Special Amber, Hefe-Weiss, Milwaukee Weiss, Mai Bock, Octoberfest, Winter Brew, Bavarian Black, Milwaukee Pils, Dunkel Weizen, and Fest Bier. Sprecher also runs the occasional batch of Irish Stout and bottles a large quantity of his own gourmet root beer.

See ALE, AMBER AND RED BEERS, BOCK BEER, OKTOBERFEST BEER, STOUT, and WHEAT BEER.

the vast Miller plant nor the stately Pabst brewery. It was tiny Sprecher, announcing itself with a towering smokestack emblazoned with its logo, a heraldic shield with griffin rampant.

Sprecher has moved its operations to a larger building, but the company remains a gnat among the Milwaukee giants. Still, Sprecher is becoming one of the largest small breweries in the Midwest, with sales of 8,800 barrels in 1994.

Founder Randall Sprecher developed his interest in good beer while serving in Europe with the U.S. Army. Once back in this country, he tried a couple of different careers but found his calling at the

SPRUCE

An evergreen tree of the genus *Picea*. Although spruce is rarely used in commercial brewing, historically it was used in some ales, and it has become an interesting experimental flavor for homebrewers. Young shoots from the spruce tree are clipped and added during the later stages of the boil.

SPRUCE BEER

An alcoholic beverage made from the shoots of the black or red spruce tree that was popular in North America in the 17th and 18th centuries. The shoots were used in lieu of hops, and the resulting mild beer was thought to protect against scurvy.

SRM

Standard Reference Method.
See COLOR.

HANS STADEN

A German gunner held prisoner by Brazilian Indians for 9 months in the mid-1500s. In 1557, he wrote one of the first accounts of beer brewing in the jungles of South America, *Veritable histoire et description d'un pays habité*, from which this passage is taken:

The women make the beer. They take the manioc roots and cook them in huge pans and let it cool. Young girls chew the manioc and put it into containers. After the roots have been chewed [they] put the paste into a pan and put water in and heat containers that are buried in the floor and are considered vats for beer. Pour the manioc and cover the vats tightly. It will ferment on its own and like this, will become strong. Leave it buried for two days. Drink it and you'll get drunk. It's thick and tastes good. Each of the huts prepares its own beer and when the village wants to have a celebration they sit around the containers that they are drinking from, some on pieces of logs, some on the bare floor. The women

serve the beer as custom demands. They drink all night long. They also dance, at times around their instruments, and they make a terrible noise once they are really drunk.

STARCH

A tasteless white carbohydrate ($C_6H_{10}O_5$) produced by barley and other plants. Starches are converted to fermentable sugars by enzyme action.

STARCH CONVERSION

The transformation of starches to sugars by enzyme action. Also called saccharification.
See SACCHARIFICATION.

STARTER YEAST

To provide the optimum yeast count for the fermentation process, a yeast starter is normally made up ahead of time. This gives the yeast a chance to multiply up to the proper count required to ferment the beer, while developing the lowest amount of fermentation by-products. Pitching too little yeast is often a problem because with a low initial cell count, the yeast has a very long period of exponential growth to achieve a vigorous fermentation.

For most ales, an initial cell count of 5 x 10^6 cells per milliliter, to about 20 x 10^6 cells per milliliter is required. (That's 5 to 20 million cells per millilitre, for the math-

423

impaired.) For lagers, the initial cell count varies depending on initial gravity. The gravity (in degrees Plato) is multiplied by 10^6 to get the cell count per milliliter. For most homebrewers, this works out to about 1 quart (0.9 L) of fully fermented, decanted slurry per 5-gallon (19 L) batch (or ½ ounce [14 ml] of thick slurry per gallon [3 L] of wort when repitching).

STEAM BEER (CALIFORNIA COMMON BEER)

Many say steam beer is the only indigenous American beer style. It was first brewed in California during the Gold Rush towards the end of the 1800s.

The name is trademarked by Anchor Steam Brewing Company, and the style name, to keep other brewers from infringing upon the trademark, is California Common Beer.

It is brewed as a hybrid, using lager yeast but fermenting at ale temperatures. This developed because the temperatures were too warm to conduct proper lager fermentation.

Fermentation is done in long shallow pans called clarifiers, followed by warm conditioning and then kraeusening with young beer.

At one period, there were 53 breweries in San Francisco brewing steam beer. The name developed from the sound of escaping carbon dioxide when the kegs were tapped.

See ANCHOR BREWING and COMMON BEER.

STEAM BOILER

A piece of equipment used to generate steam for sterilizing brewing equipment, kegs, and casks. Also used in bottle washers and pasteurizers. These boilers can range in size from very small to huge depending on the number of BTUs per hour required in the brewery. Normally, a water-fed system and blow-down tank are associated with the boiler. Steam boilers are usually either gas or oil fired. Electric boilers are available, but they are more expensive to run. Boilers can be low pressure or high pressure and generally require a fully qualified boiler operator for safe operation and maintenance.

STEEL MASHER

A piece of equipment used for mixing crushed malt with hot brewing liquor. A steel masher comprises a large base tube that comes out of the crushed malt grist case with a right-angled bend. The crushed malt from the grist case meets the hot liquor before falling onto a short screw conveyor with mixing rods, which mixes and conveys the wet malt to the mash tun.

STEEP TANK

A stainless steel tank used for steeping barley during malting prior to passing it to the germination floor. Steep tanks are cylindrical or rectangular in cross-section and have a conical bottom. The steep tank is partially filled with water, then barley is loaded from the top. Water sprays at the grain outlet minimize dust on transfer. The steep water is heated to a set temperature to break the barley's dormancy. Air pipes and nozzles allow for uniform aeration during steeping.

Conical steeps may be discharged wet or dry-cast by draining the water off first. Flatbed steeps also are used. In this case, the grain is mechanically discharged.

Beer steins come in all shapes, sizes, and materials, with varying amounts of decoration.

STEGMAIER PORTER

See Lion, The.

STEIN

A German drinking vessel usually made of earthenware and traditionally having a capacity of 0.5, 1, or 3 L (15, 30, or 90 fluid ounces). The German word *stein* means stone.

Today, these large, capped flagons serve mostly a ceremonial purpose, but their design originated to perform a serious function. The lid prevented flies from drowning in the brew, a precaution that was necessary during the Black Death plague that swept across Europe in the 14th century.

STEINBIER (STONE BEER)

See Rauchbier.

STEP MASH

An infusion mash with one or two additional time and temperature steps. It differs from the single-step infusion mash in that it begins at a lower temperature — typically 120° to 125°F (49° to 52°C) — and is held at that temperature for about 30 minutes before the temperature is increased to the 148° to 158°F (64° to 70°C) range. This lower-temperature step is called the protein rest, and its purpose is to break down complex proteins.

See Mashing.

STEVENS POINT BREWERY
STEVENS POINT, WISCONSIN

Stevens Point is a small regional brewery known for its Point Special brand. The company is now owned by Barton Beers, a beer importer that is a subsidiary of Canandaigua Wine Co.

The original Stevens Point was founded in 1857. The name was changed to Stevens Point Beverage Co. during Prohibition. After Prohibition, the company went back to making Point beer.

The company traditionally brewed Point Bock in season. It also produces Point Light, Point All-Malt, and Spud Beer. Stevens Point has an annual capacity of about 60,000 barrels.

See BOCK BEER and IMPORTER.

STINGO

A very old Yorkshire term for strong ale or beer. This beer was held in high esteem by all who drank it.

Stingo, or stingoe, is referred to in a concluding verse from *In Praise of Ale,* where Bacchus and his wine drinkers are bested in a drinking contest by Colonus and the beer crowd. After first drinking the bacchanalians under the table, Bacchus and his court retire south to Yorkshire where they again taste:

> Both from North Allerton and Easingwold,
> From Sutton, Thirke, likewise from Rascal Town,
> Ale that is called Knocker-down —
> They tasted all; And swore they were full glad,
> Such Stingoe, Nappy, pure ale they had found,
> Let's loose no time said they but drink round.

However, the Yorkshire ale proves too strong for Bacchus, and a final adjournment of their massive drink-up is called. They retreat farther south:

> Bacchus swore to come he would not fail,
> To glut himself with Yorkshire Nappy ale.
> It is so pleasant, mellow too and fine,
> That Bacchus swore he'd never drink more wine.

STOCK ALE

See ENGLISH STRONG ALE.

STONE BEER (STEINBIER)

See RAUCHBIER.

STOUT

An ale beer that originated in Ireland in the 1770s, when Guinness began calling its porter "stout porter." Porter came into being in the 18th century in London as a robust, aged beer. The porter style spread to Ireland, where it was slow to take hold. Irish porter came to be brewed much stronger than English porter.

Arthur Guinness opened his brewery west of Dublin in 1759, but he did not brew porter until 1778. Ultimately, Guinness "stout porter" became synonymous with stout, the Irish national drink. By 1886, Guinness, brewing only stout porter, had become the largest brewery in the world.

A 1908 American brewing text defined stout as a beverage with an original gravity of at least 16/1.064 and twice the hopping rate of porter. The Guinness found in the United States today has an original gravity of 13.2/1.052 from pale English 2-row malt, 9 percent each of flaked barley and dark roasted barley, used in a two-step infusion mash. It is hopped at 50 IBU with Bullion bittering and Goldings aromatic hops and has an alcohol content of and 5.5 percent by volume. Today's Guinness would have been a porter in 1908. In this day, Guinness is the role model that many other stouts follow.

Stout has become one of the American microbrewery movement's most popular beers. Most microbreweries brew one or more stouts, some of which are very fine.

Whitbread's entry into the stout market was heralded by promotional materials extolling the virtues of Whitbread versus its unmentioned competitor, Guinness Stout.

Dry Stout

Dry stout should have an original gravity of at least 13.5/1.055, a final gravity of around 2.8/1.011, alcohol content over 5.4 percent by volume, bitterness above 25 IBU, and color at 35–70 SRM. Ingredients include pale English 2-row barley malt, dark caramel malt (80 to 120 degrees Lovibond), chocolate and black malts, and sometimes sugar and flaked barley. Stout production starts with British-style infusion mash and may have a forced attenuation to reduce the apparent extract or final gravity (dry). There is an overlap between stouts and porters, and the brewer is the final arbiter in such matters.

Dry Classic Irish Stout

The Great American Beer Festival guidelines for this style are 9.5–12/1.038–1.048 OG, 3.8–5 percent alcohol by volume, 30–40 IBU, and 40+ SRM. The beer is expected to have a lot of roast

Stouts are now available in many varieties, all based upon the original Extra Stout produced by Guinness.

property but not much hop or malt character.

Foreign-Style Stout

Guinness Foreign Extra Stout sets the pattern worldwide for the many Guinness stouts brewed by Guinness and other contract breweries. This Guinness is rarely found in the United States (Texas being the exception). In 1908, double stout was defined as having an original gravity of 18.3/1.075. Double stout is defined as having 19/1.076 OG and 109 IBU.

The Great American Beer Festival guidelines for double stout are 13–18/1.052–1.074 OG, 6–7.5 percent alcohol by volume, 30–60 IBU, and SRM 40+.

Specialty Stouts

Sweet stout is the English style epitomized by Mackeson, which is somewhat sweet and lower in alcohol than other stouts, though full-bodied nonetheless. This style is described as 11.1–11.9/1.044–1.048 OG, more in the range of porter but with a higher final gravity (3+) from the residual sweetness, which comes from the addition of unfermentable lactose sugar and oatmeal. Other specialty stouts include oyster stout, which has some oyster extract in its composition.

The Great American Beer Festival guidelines for sweet stout are 11–14/1.045–1.056 OG, 3–6 percent alcohol by volume, 15–25 IBU, and 40+ SRM. Guidelines for oatmeal stout, which has oat flakes or rolled oats in the mash, are 9.5–14/1.038–1.056 OG, 3.8–6 percent alcohol by volume, 20–40 IBU, and 20+ SRM.

Original Gravity	Final Gravity	Alcohol by Volume	IBU	SRM
ABC Extra Stout (Singapore) 1982 (bottle-conditioned)				
15.9/1.065	3.3	6.8%	49.5	≈40
Barclay and Perkins Double Stout (England) 1884				
18.8/1.077	4	7.5%	125	Unknown
Guinness Extra Stout (England) 1978				
13.2/1.052	2.8	5.5%	50	≈40
Guinness Extra Stout (Ireland) 1901				
18.2/1.075	3.4	7.9%	90	≈40
Guinness Extra Stout (Ireland) 1933				
17.7/1.072.6	3.2	8%	≈90	≈40
McMenamin Hillsdale Terminator (Oregon) 1987				
14.1/1.058	3.6	5.1%	60	≈40
Mackeson Stout (England) 1978 (sweet stout)				
11.5/1.046	4.4	3.7%	29	≈40
Sierra Nevada Stout (California) 1982				
16/1.066	3.8	6.4%	44	≈40

See MILK STOUT, PORTER, and STOUT — IMPERIAL.

STOUT — IMPERIAL

The most famous of all Imperial Stouts is that made by Barclay and Perkins, now of the Courage Brewing chain in England. The original Imperial Stout was what we now call a barelywine-style ale. Originally brewed and shipped to the Baltic area as

Imperial stout was originally called Russian stout, and was brewed from 1780 to World War I by what is now the Courage Brewery for consumption in St. Petersburg in Russia.

early as 1780, it was popularized by Catherine the Great, empress of Russia, in 1795. Barclay and Perkins continued to ship this stout to Russia until World War I. The beer had an original gravity of 24–24.5/1.099–1.102. The alcohol by volume was about 8.4–10.5 percent. The original Imperial Stout is still brewed annually by the same company. It is matured for 2 months in wooden casks, then aged for 1 year in bottles, which are about the size of a champagne split. Originally, they had wired corks, but now they are simply crown-capped. The beer will keep for 7 years or longer. There are many imitations, but the real thing is still very difficult to obtain and is not available in the United States.

American Imperial Stouts

The most famous American Imperial Stout is craft-brewed Grant's Imperial Stout from Yakima Brewing & Malting in Yakima,, Washington. It was slightly "Imperial" when first introduced in 1982, but only "princely" by 1990. At least one Imperial Stout, Samuel Smith Imperial Stout, has been introduced into the United States market from England. It, too, is on the "princely" side but is a credible double stout.

Original Gravity	Final Gravity	Alcohol by Volume	IBU	SRM
Grant's Russian Imperial Stout 1982				
19.5/1.080	3.4	7.1%	54	≈40
Grant's Imperial Stout 1990				
15.5/1.064	2.75	6.8%	61	≈40
Samuel Smith Imperial Stout (England) 1986				
17.6/1.072	3.1	7.6%	Unknown	≈40

See BARLEY WINE and STOUT.

Straub

A light-bodied beer with a firm palate and a sweet, malt character. There is evidence of some drying hops at the finish.

The copper kettle once used by the Straub Brewery, Inc.

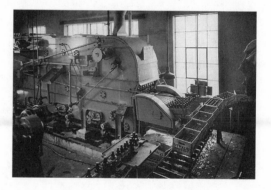

An early Straub bottling line

STRAUB BREWERY INC. ST. MARY'S, PENNSYLVANIA

Straub is a small family-owned brewery about 100 miles north of Pittsburgh. The company used to brew just one beer, Straub, but now it also brews Straub Light. Straub enjoys strong local loyalty but has never tried to expand its market. This is as much due to fiscal conservatism as to the fact that the Straub family has always put

The Straub family has been brewing since 1872.

hunting and fishing on an equal footing with business. Straub is perhaps the last brewery that runs a public tap, offering two glasses of free beer to anyone who stops in for a taste.

See LIGHT BEER, MICROBREWERY, and REGIONAL BREWERY.

STRIKE HEAT

The temperature of the water being added to grains during the mashing process. This temperature varies depending on the mashing method. A strike heat of about 170°F (77°C), or perhaps a bit higher, works well with a single-step infusion mash. A lower temperature, per-

haps 140° to 150°F (60° to 65.5°C), works better for a mash that begins with a protein rest step.

STROH BREWERY CO. DETROIT, MICHIGAN

Stroh Brewery Co. remains one of America's largest brewing companies, although its market share has gradually declined from a high point in the early 1980s. Stroh remains a family-owned company, with great pride in the business of brewing beer. It operates five large breweries.

Bernhard Stroh founded the Stroh Brewery Company of Detroit, Michigan, in 1850.

Original premises of the Stroh Brewery Company, Detroit, Michigan.

431

Augsburger Red

Part of the Augsburger family of beers, acquired by Stroh from Joseph Huber Brewing Co. in the late 1980s. Since buying the Augsburger franchise, Stroh has expanded it exponentially, with new German-style seasonal brands, such as a wheat beer, a bock, and a doppelbock. Rot means "red" in German, and Augsburger Rot is typical of the new wave of red beers made by American brewers. It is not a bold departure from Stroh's mainstream lagers, but it is somewhat more full-bodied. It is one of the better red beers, with crisp, firm-bodied character and toasted malt flavors.

Stroh was founded by Bernhard Stroh in 1850, but the brewing roots of the Stroh family go all the way back to 18th-century Germany, where an individual named Stroh may have brewed beer for the tavern he owned.

The company's brands bear the heraldic lion rampant, first used in the late 19th century, when Stroh was known as the Lion Brewery. The name was changed to Stroh Brewery Co. early in this century. Stroh endured Prohibition by making near bear, malt extract, and anything else that it could.

The company advertises its beer as "fire brewed," a reference to the direct-fire kettles first used by Stroh before Prohibition. According to some brewing experts, the direct-fire method can slightly caramelize the wort during brewing.

See MARKET SHARE.

STRONG ALE

See BARLEY WINE, BELGIAN STRONG ALE, ENGLISH STRONG ALE, KULMINATOR, and SCOTTISH ALE.

STRONG BEER

See ABBEY BEER, DOPPELBOCK, EISBOCK, GERMAN BREW STRENGTHS, KULMINATOR, and STOUT — IMPERIAL.

STRONG BITTER

See BITTER.

STRONGEST BEER

See KULMINATOR.

SUCELLUS

A Celtic god of brewing. "The Good Striker" is depicted with a hammer in one hand and a beer jug in the other. He is one of the few male deities associated with beer and fertility. This minor god survived until about A.D. 400.

SUCROSE

A fermentable sugar ($C_{12}H_{22}O_{11}$) produced from sugar cane, sugar beets, or maple sap. Sucrose consists of one molecule of glucose joined with one molecule of fructose. The table sugar sold in supermarkets is sucrose. Occasionally, it is used in some forms of brewing, such as the candy sugar used in certain Belgian ales. Used in excessive amounts, sucrose imparts a ciderlike flavor to beer. Sucrose ferments, but at a slower rate than glucose or maltose.

SUDDEUTCHE WEIZENBIER

See WHEAT BEER.

SUDS

A slang word for beer, probably derived from the German word *sud,* which means to brew.

SUGARS

Any of a number of water-soluble compounds that are relatively sweet. Probably the most important sugars to beer and wine makers are the fermentables: fructose, galactose, glucose, mannose, maltose, maltotriose, sucrose, melibiose, raffinose, and xylulose. Not all yeasts can ferment all of these sugars, and many nonfermentable sugars also are desirable, as they impart a residual sweetness to the final product. Most of these are dextrin sugars.

Sugars are carbohydrates, which means that they are chemical compounds consisting of carbon, hydrogen, and oxygen. Simple sugars are called *monosaccharides,* and they include dextrose and fructose. More complex sugars are built of two or more monosaccharides and are called *polysaccharides.* Maltose is a polysaccharide that is composed of two glucose molecules. An *oligosaccharide* is a sugar consisting of several joined molecules of one sugar.

See YEAST.

SULFATE

An ion that has no chemical effect on beer but gives a sharp, dry edge to highly hopped beers. Sulfate should not be added to water that is high in sodium, as a harsh, overly bitter beer will result. Brewing water should have no more than 150 ppm sulfate.

SUMERIAN BEER

"I feel wonderful, drinking beer, in a blissful mood with joy in my heart and a happy liver." These words were written by a Sumerian poet about 3000 B.C., at a time when goddesses were firmly established as the protectors and providers of beer. Ama-Gestin, the "Earth Mother," and Ninkasi, the "Lady Who Fills the Mouth," were the Sumerian goddesses of beer.

The women of ancient Sumer brewed and sold beer and ran the taverns under the spiritual protection of Siduri, goddess of the brewery and wisdom. The dominance of women in the brewing arts is confirmed time and again in cuneiform poems and prayers. Common greetings of the time were "May Ninkasi live with you — let her pour your beer everlasting," and "My sister, your grain — its beer is tasty, my comfort." Sabtiem — brewsters and tavern keepers — were the only tradespeople of the era with private deities who spiritually guided the making of their products. Among the bewildering variety of beers were black and white beers, beers of two parts, beer from the world below, beer of sacrifice, supper beer, horned beer, wheat beer, and the apparently foamy beer with a head.

At the height of the Sumerian Empire, beer was made from *bappir*, half-baked, crusty loaves of bread. Crumbled by hand and mixed with water, the bread would form a soupy mash to be filtered through a basket into a beer pot below. Some ancient recipes called for pepper, spices, tree bark, and powdered crab claws to season the beer. In Mesopotamia, as much as 50 per-cent of each grain harvest went to beer production. During the first Ur dynasty, about 3000 B.C., the welfare system of the time daily dispensed to each needy person one gallon of beer.

The Assyrians and Babylonians would age beer in wide-bottomed, narrow-necked pots. Dispensing the brew was a challenge. Grain husks, yeast, and other debris made drinking this muddy mixture unpleasant, until some creative soul used a hollow reed to pierce the flotsam in the brew vessel and reach the clear beer below. Kings and notables went to beer shops carrying straws of gold inlaid with lapis lazuli. These exquisite utensils were routinely buried with their owners for the enjoyment of beer in paradise.

Among the myths of Sumer was a precursor of the Christian tale of Noah and the Flood. Atrahasis brought beer aboard his ark when God told him that humankind was to be drowned for being too noisy. Atrahasis wrote, "For our food, I slaughtered sheep and oxen, day by day; with beer, olive oil and water, I filled large jars."

Records indicate that beer shops, called *Bit Sikari*, and taverns were common in cities and villages. As drunkenness was a spiritual state, beery transactions were not to be sullied by the exchange of money. In the Code of Hammurabi, the sale of beer for silver or gold was forbidden: "If a beer seller do not receive barley as the price for beer, but if she receive money or make the beer a measure smaller than the barley measure received, they [the judges] shall throw her [the brewster] into the water." In this fashion, the Marduk-Ibni, the brewster and tavern keeper, made her profit only by barter.

Archaeological sites throughout the Tigris-Euphrates Valley have yielded thousands of cuneiform tablets containing recipes for and prayers in praise of beer. *Kassi* (black beer), *Kassag* (fine black beer), *Kassagasaan* (finest premium beer), and *Kassig* (red beer) were not only savored as beverages but also formed the basis for most medical treatments for ailments from scorpion stings to heart conditions.

Every human culture that enjoyed beer also suffered a vocal minority who viewed malt beverages as a threat to public morals.

Cuneiform tablets cautioned the young with homilies such as these: "Oh, Lord, thou shalt not enter a beer shop!" and "The beer drunkard shall soak your gown with vomit." Other social sanctions prohibited high priestesses from loitering in beer halls, under penalty of death by burning. Despite such restrictions, beer endured as a joyful part of life. Drinking songs sung by all classes reflect the happiness of time spent out in beer halls.

Although priestesses were forced to drink in secret, the use of attractive bare-breasted women for the purpose of advertising beer brands and shops was coming into vogue. Images of curvaceous barmaids invited patrons to sample the delights of both beer and, sometimes, brothels. Similar tablets, leaned against city gates, conveyed messages such as "Drink Ebla — the beer with the heart of a lion."

See BI-KAL, NINKASI, and SIKARU.

SUMMIT BREWING CO.
ST. PAUL, MINNESOTA

Microbrewers are an eclectic lot, and their résumés reflect it. Mark Stutrud is no exception. Before starting off on a brewing career, he worked as a social worker for 9 years, counseling adolescents on substance abuse. If he is now a substance producer, it is of the most benign sort: fine ale.

Stutrud founded his brewery in 1984, when there were no more than 15 microbreweries in the country. It took him two years to do business planning and market research, to gather a group of partners, and to arrange the financing for the endeavor. Stutrud and his partnership began refurbishing their chosen site — a former truck-rebuilding shop in St. Paul — in

Summit Great Northern Porter

Dark brown in color with a cream-colored head, this beer greets the nose with a roasty aroma and some coffee notes. Great Northern Porter has a lot of hop character richly melded with its full malty body.

SUMMIT BREWING CO.

A worker hammers in a new bung to seal a keg racked at the Summit Brewing Co.

Ingredients added to the combination mash tun/brew kettle at Summit Brewing Co. are of the finest quality.

The bottling line at the Summit Brewing Co. of St. Paul, Minnesota

1986, and a 30-hl copper kettle and lauter tun was acquired from a German brewery. About half the equipment for the brewery was purchased used.

In July 1986, the company began test-brewing its Summit Extra Pale Ale. Two months later, it began shipping beer. Shortly after that, area wholesalers began contacting the brewery about distribution.

In 1987, the partners made a $100,000 stock offering to fund the purchase of a bottling line and other equipment. Summit has enjoyed a measured but impressive expansion in the years since, with sales of 14,028 barrels in 1994.

Summit also makes India Pale Ale, Heimethingen Maibock, and Hefe Weizen.

See MICROBREWERY and PORTER.

SWAN-NECK

A stainless steel or copper tube attached to the side of a fermentation vessel, then bent back over the yeast head. Normally associated with open-top fermentation vessels in which a certain yeast type might require further aeration. The outlet of the swan-neck is flattened to create a fine spray when fermenting wort is pumped from the vessel through the pipe and over the yeast head. This enables oxygen pickup to occur, allowing fermentation to continue.

SWEET STOUT

See MILK STOUT and STOUT.

TAFELBIER-BIÈRE DE TABLE

A sweet, low-alcohol, Flemish beer style that is in danger of being replaced by non-alcoholic and low-alcohol beers. Called *Bière de table* in France, *tafelbier* is Flemish for table beer. It is made with the second or last spargings of grains in the mash tank. The result is a low-gravity wort, which in turn produces a low-alcohol beer with 3.0 percent alcohol by volume. In Belgium, tafelbiers account for about 3.5 percent of total beer production.

This style is similar to the English mild, but tends to be even less alcoholic.

TALLA BEER

A double-fermented beer once brewed in Ethiopia by fermenting roasted barley, millet, and corn, and flavoring it with twigs from a local tree. Talla was the tree whose bark and leaves were used for bittering.

TANNIN

A naturally occurring, polyphenolic, astringent acid ($C_{76}H_{52}O_{46}$) found in tea, the bark of some trees, and other sources. Although it is useful in the leather industry, tannin from polyphenols in barley can result in harsh flavors in beer. Tannin also can combine with proteins and may settle out of solution or contribute to haze. One benefit of the hot break is that tannins, which have a negative charge, are attracted to proteins, which have a positive charge. The tannin and protein join together and fall out of suspension. In this way, a brewer can reduce the possibility of haze in the final brew.

Tannin can be extracted from the barley husks by boiling the malt. It also is extracted during sparging if the sparge time is too long, the temperature is too high, or the water is too alkaline.

TAPROOM

A room in a tavern or pub where beer is served on draught.

TAP-UP SUNDAY

An old English name for the Sunday preceding October 2, when a fair was held at St. Catherine's Hill near Guildford. So called because any person, with or without a license, might open a tap or sell beer on the hill for that one day.

TASTE TEST

A tasting or judging carried out by a group of knowledgeable judges to evaluate a new product or changes made to an existing product. The results are designed to help the brewer improve the beer being tasted.

TAVERN

Today, any location where alcohol is served. Traditionally, a tavern was a place

Tavern and alehouse signs

where only wine was served; beer was served in an alehouse.

TAXES ON ALE

Levies on beer for specific purposes appear to date back to the establishment of governments. For example, in 1363 the inhabitants of Abbeville, France, were granted a tax on ale for the purpose of repairing their fortifications. For each "lotus of ale of gramville, the tax was one penny Parisien; for each lotus of God-ale the tax was ½ d."

In present-day Britain, excise and value-added taxes on beer are so high that smuggling of British beer back into Britain from France has reached alarming proportions. The resale of this smuggled beer is endangering the existence of many pubs and creating new opportunities for organized crime.

TAYLOR, JOHN

The poet laureate of beer and ale. Taylor (1580–1653) was born in Gloucester, England. A master of self-promotion, he fancied himself a poet with such relentless conviction that he soon became accepted as one. Although he extolled the virtues of a pot of good ale in more than 100 tracts and pamphlets, both he and his books are now all but forgotten.

Taylor was a customs agent, an adventurer by land and sea, a saloon keeper, a publisher, and, for 40 years, the greatest advocate of good beer. Upon entering a town, he would inquire as to where the best ale was to be found. He believed that where one could find the best beer one would find the best lodgings. If he was unable to locate adequate lodgings or beer, Taylor would present himself at the front door of the local bigwig and ask for lodging for the night. Representing himself as the "Queen's Waterman" and the "King's Water-poet," Taylor explained that, in return for cakes and ale, he would immortalize his host in his next book.

Once ensconced free of charge at a home or an inn, John Taylor would regale patrons and guests with tales of his travels and satires on the leading events and figures of the day. His entertaining presence more than compensated a host for the expense of a few pots of ale.

TEETOTALER

A person who abstains from drinking any alcoholic beverage whatsoever.

The term originated in England in September 1833, when Richard Turner (1790–1846), drunk on ale, stumbled into a temperance meeting and took the pledge, swearing off alcohol forever. In declaring to the crowd his total abstinence, Turner, who had a speech impediment, stuttered, "Tee-tee-total." As fate would have it, attending members of the press reported this verbal slip and lampooned Turner's "teetotal," which passed into common usage.

TEMPERATURE-PROGRAMMED MASH TUN

A mash-mixing vessel heated by a steam jacket or coil to raise the mash temperature through a predetermined step program. Generally used where poorly modified malts are used. Normally, a protein rest at 125° to 130°F (52° to 54°C) is achieved first, followed by a saccharification rest at 149°F (65°C) and then maybe a progressive rise to 165°F (74°C).

TEWAHDIDDLE

A beer cocktail of Old England that consists of one pint of ale, a tablespoon of brandy, a teaspoon of brown sugar, a bit of grated nutmeg or ginger, and some very thinly shaved lemon peel. Tewahdiddle had the reputation of being an excellent drink in old England.

THERMOMETER

An instrument used to measure the temperature of gases, liquids, and solids and very important in all brewery operations. Two types of thermometers are used: fast-acting mercury types and slower spirit types. Fixed-dial thermometers or digital readout thermometers are used in fermenting vessels and conditioning tanks, as well as in brewing vessels. Fixed thermometers are located in the beer bowl of a bottle or can filler.

THERMOMETER WELL

A stainless steel protective sheath built into a tank or fixture where the thermometer is a permanent feature. The well protects the thermometer stem from damage and provides a sanitary, cleanable surface.

TIED HOUSE

A given pub, tavern, or inn that is tied to a single brewery by mutual agreement. Tied houses serve only that brewery's products or guest beers determined only at the discretion of that brewery.

T'IEN TSIOU

A Chinese Jiu, or beer, made from millet that dates to 2000 B.C. It is a green, or young, beer that is not completely clarified or fermented. Tsiou is the clarified, fully fermented version.
See JIU/CHIU.

TISWIN

See APACHE CORN.

TITHE ALE

A meal of ale, bread, and cheese that was provided by the recipient of a tithe to the tithe payers. For example, in Berkshire, England, after a Christmas Eve church ser-vice, the parishioners who were able to pay the tithe retired to the vicarage and were entertained there with ale, bread, and cheese. This was not considered a benefaction from the vicar but a right of the tithe payers. The vicar was required to brew 4 bushels of malt in ale and small beer and to provide 2 bushels of wheat for bread and half a hundredweight of cheese. Whatever remained unconsumed was given to the poor. Variations of this custom could be found in every parish throughout Great Britain, through the mid 1800s.

TOASTING

The custom of drinking to one's health and pledging. The term may be connected to the British custom of putting toast in ale

The tradition of toasting can be traced back many centuries, although its origin is not certain.

cups. Another theory is that the term derives from a corruption of the German drinker's cry *"Stoss an!"* (Knock glasses!).

In the reign of Charles II, Earl of Rochester wrote:

Make it so large that, filled with Sack
Up to the swelling brim,
Vast toasts on the delicious lake,
Like ships at sea, may swim.

TOMBS AND BEER

Inasmuch as most civilizations regarded beer as essential to life, the custom of placing beer in the grave with the dead is an ancient business. In pharaonic Egypt, beer to nourish the ka, the spirit of the dead, could appear in the form of a pictorial representation on the tomb wall. In some cases, even miniature wooden breweries and brewsters were placed within the tomb.

The oldest beer vessels found in tombs, still containing traces of brew, date to 8,000 years ago. Some cultures, such as

Hieroglyphics from Mesopotamia illustrate the importance of beer to ancient cultures.

ancient Egypt, provided special beers as offerings to the gods who would sit in judgment over the souls of the deceased. "The beer that does not sour" and "the beer of truth" were but two varieties designed to soften the sternest of gods. The ritual pouring of beer on graves and the offering of opened containers of beer to the thirsty spirits of the dead remains common throughout Africa, South and Central America, and Asia.

Ancient Egyptian drawings from tombs show us that beer was thought to be important to the gods and goddesses.

Top-fermenting yeast rises to the surface of the wort during fermentation. Also called ale yeast, it ferments more rapidly than bottom-fermenting yeast and has a higher alcohol tolerance.

TOP-FERMENTING YEAST

A yeast that exhibits the characteristic of forming dense colonies on the surface of fermenting beer. Also known as ale yeast. These yeasts are *Saccharomyces cerevisiae*, and they ferment best at temperatures of 55° to 70°F (13° to 21°C). Since they ferment very quickly, they impart more esters and fruitiness to the beer.

See YEAST.

TRADITIONAL BITTER

See BITTER.

TRAPPIST BEER

See ABBAYE.

TRAQUAIR HOUSE PEEBLESSHIRE, SCOTLAND

Any trip to Scotland deserves a visit to romantic Traquair, where Alexander I signed a charter over 800 years ago and where the "modern" wings were completed in 1680. It was a pleasure ground for Scottish kings in times of peace, then a refuge for Catholic priests in times of terror. The Stuarts of Traquair supported Mary, Queen of Scots, and the Jacobite cause without counting the cost. Though they were imprisoned, fined and isolated for their beliefs, their home — untouched by time — reflects the tranquility of their family life.

Today their descendants, the Maxwell Stuarts, who still live here in a wing of the castle, have opened their home so that visitors can also enjoy its unique atmosphere and history. Enjoy a day reliving the past.

Enter the long drive from the main road to the castle and you will enter a time machine. From the famous Bear Gates to the castle itself, Traquair radiates an ageless beauty and charm.

See the secret stairs which led Bonnie Prince Charlie to safety; the ancient cellars where the very finest potables, including Traquair House Ale, were stored before being served to royalty; two extraordinary libraries covered with leather-bound books, rare furniture, paintings, embroideries and important letters displayed as they have been during family occupancy for over 500 years.

Romantic Traquair House, known for its Bear Gates, has been home to the Stuarts since the 15th century.

When Mary, Queen of Scots visited in 1566, a strong ale was already a favorite with visiting royalty. In 1739, a 200-gallon copper was installed in the brewhouse beneath the chapel and probably served a weary Bonnie Prince Charlie during his stay in 1745. For over 200 years the copper, mash tun, open coolers, fermenters and wooden stirring paddles lay idle.

It has been 500 years since the first Stuart took up residence in this remarkable family home, and it was a Stuart, Peter Maxwell Stuart, 20th Laird of Traquair, who renovated the brewhouse and, using the original vessels and recipes, began to brew again. He established a worldwide reputation for his ale and the special contribution to living history that it makes.

Beer writer Michael Jackson rates Traquair House Ale as "A World Classic," awarding it his highest rating. He describes the ale as "rich and full with its sweetness balanced by oakey dryness." It has a deep golden-amber color with an exquisite hop balance.

Brewing the strong, barleywine-style ale takes about 10 days, after which the ale is stored in casks for 3 to 4 months before being bottled. Total annual production runs from 50,000 to 60,000 bottles.

Traquair House Ale was certainly an inspiration for Bonnie Prince Charlie who visited Traquair in 1745 before leading a

Traquair House Ale

A dark, strong, and heady brew with a port-wine character. There are rich aromas of malt, hops, dark chocolate, fruit, and spices. The ale leaves a winey, grainy, hoppy taste, and the finish — which is intense and bitter — leaves hints of pineapple and chocolate.

The ale is made from roast and pale malts, with Goldings and Red Sell hops, and uses top-fermenting yeast. It is 7 percent alcohol by volume and has an original gravity of 1.075.

Traquair House Ale is the only British ale to be brewed in uncoated wooden vessels.

A draught version is sold in Britain in the winter. The bottled version is popular in such far-flung and unlikely countries as Japan and the United States.

rebellion to restore the estate. The Earl of Traquair vowed not to open the famous Bear Gates until the handsome prince succeeded in regaining the monarchy. They remain closed to this day.

The 20th Laird renovated the brewhouse and used the original vessels, which include a 200-gallon copper, an oak mash tun, open coolers and fermenters, and wooden paddles. He began to brew in 1965, using the recipe of his ancestors for traditional strong Scotch ale.

Catherine Maxwell Stuart, 21st Lady of Traquair, inherited the property from her father in 1990. She is continuing to follow in her father's footsteps in running the brewery with utmost concern for quality and tradition. "Many Americans visit the castle yearly, and we are delighted to make limited quantities of our beer available to them at home," Ms. Stuart reported.

Merchant du Vin Corporation of Seattle, Washington, is the sole American importer of Traquair House Ale.

TREACLE

The British name for molasses.
See MOLASSES.

TRIHALOMETHANE (THM)

A derivative of methane that is also known as chloroform. When large amounts of chlorine are added to drinking water, a certain amount of this compound will form. It is harmless at low levels, but may not be in higher concentrations. It can be used as an indicator of a municipal drinking water system's treatment. If high levels of THM are indicated in the water analysis, the water is not being filtered as well as it could be, and large amounts of chlorine are being added to the water. Low levels of THM indicate well-filtered water and less chlorine. THM can be removed with a carbon sink filter.

TRIPEL

See ABBEY BEER.

TRUB

Any solid matter that settles out of beer. Trub forms at various times in the brewing process. In the brew kettle, proteins and other matter coagulate at high temperatures, forming what is called hot trub, or hot break. Similarly, chilling the hot wort quickly causes more proteins to drop out of suspension, forming what is called cold trub or cold break. Trub can form a thick layer at the bottom of the fermentation vessel. This trub will consist of yeast cells, hop particles, and additional protein matter. Trub should not be left in contact with the clean beer for extended periods of time (more than about 2 weeks). It is removed from the beer by filtration or by allowing solid matter to settle out and then pumping or siphoning the clean beer to another vessel (racking). Trub can include the materials listed in the following table.

MATERIAL	TRUB TYPE
Hop solids	Fermenter
Yeast cells	Fermenter
Protein	Hot, cold, fermenter
Carbohydrates	Hot, cold, fermenter
Polyphenols	Hot, cold
Alpha acids	Hot
Fatty acids	Hot

TSIOU

See T'IEN TSIOU.

TURBIDITY METER

An instrument used to measure beer haze. Haze, not being a quantitative substance but an appearance that varies with illumination, beer color, and other factors, is measured against a predetermined standard. Absolute turbidity varies with wavelength, so turbidity changes when illuminated by different-colored light. Bottle imperfections also may cause inconsistent results, so several samples are generally required and a mean average is calculated. The units of measurement are European Brewery Convention (EBC) or Association of Brewing Chemists (ASBC) units. A simple scale illustrates their meaning:

	EBC UNITS	ASBC UNITS
Almost brilliant	0.5	35
Very slightly hazy	1.0	70
Slightly hazy	2.0	140
Hazy	4.0	280
Very hazy	8.0	560

TWO-STAGE FERMENTATION

The process of fermenting beer in two separate vessels. The primary fermentation takes place in the first vessel. This typically lasts from 2 to 6 days for ales and up to 8 or 9 days for lagers. During this stage, the yeast does most of its work, breaking down the sugars into alcohol, carbon dioxide, and other by-products. A thick head of creamy foam, called the kraeusen, forms on top of the beer during the primary fermentation. When the kraeusen subsides, the beer is transferred to a second fermentation vessel. This separates the clean beer from the settled yeast cells, hops, and protein particles that formed a layer of trub on the bottom of the first vessel. By removing the beer from the trub, the risk of developing off-flavors can be reduced. The second fermentation is a slower stage that typically takes a week or more.

TYPELLAR

A medieval English name for a seller of ale. At that time, ale was known as typhyle.

U.K. GALLON

A synonym for imperial gallon.
See GALLON.

ULLAGE

The empty space at the top of a bottle, cask, or barrel between the liquid and the seal or top of the container. Also referred to as headspace.

UNHOPPED

A nonhopped malt.

UNITED STATES BREWERS' ASSOCIATION

This now-defunct organization was in high gear in 1941, when it was establishing committees to deal with the legislative issues of concern to smaller brewers in the United States. For the next 35 years it championed the idea that brewers under a certain size be taxed on a

Delegates to the 17th Annual Convention of the United States Brewers' Association

smaller scale than larger brewers. A bill proposing an excise tax differential for smaller brewers was signed into law in October 1976. This was the association's crowning achievement, after which it

449

Fred Lance, honorary president of the United States Brewers' Association

unofficially merged with the Brewers' Association of America, an organization that continues to function as the voice of small brewers in the United States.

See BREWERS' ASSOCIATION OF AMERICA.

UNITED STATES BREWING INDUSTRY

The United States brewing industry is one of the most productive in the world. Although American per capita consumption of beer is not especially high, the sheer size of the United States population makes this the world's largest beer market (although China will likely assume this status in the near future). United States beer sales in 1994 were 197,190,000 barrels, up 0.9 percent over 1993 figures. Exports also rose to an estimated 7,000,000 barrels.

The United States brewing industry dates to colonial times. By the early 20th century, thousands of breweries were operating in the United States. Most were fairly small by today's standards, but many large regional plants also thrived.

Legal beer brewing in the United States came to an abrupt halt with the enactment of Prohibition in 1919. During Prohibition, some brewers subsisted by producing near beer (nonalcoholic beer), malt extract, and brewer's yeast. Most breweries went out of business.

The repeal of Prohibition in 1933 triggered a brewery boom, and in 1938 more than 500 breweries were in operation. Some post-Prohibition breweries were short-lived efforts undertaken by profit-minded businessmen, but many old brewing families also returned to the trade.

In the post–World War II era, mass marketing changed the face of the United States brewing industry. Some brewers transcended regional status and became national in scope. Scale and cost-efficiency favored these larger producers, and consolidation of the brewing industry began in earnest.

By the 1970s, small regional brewers were going out of business in droves, and larger brewers dominated the market. That dominance continues today, with three brewers (Anheuser-Busch, Miller, and Coors) dominating the brewing industry. In 1994, this first tier held 81 percent of the market share. A second tier of relatively large regional brewers (Stroh, G. Heileman, Pabst, and others) held another 14 percent. Imports accounted for about 5 percent of sales and micro-brewers 0.3 percent.

See MARKET SHARE.

UNIVESSEL

An enclosed stainless steel vessel with a conical bottom used for fermenting and lagering beer. A 70-degree–angle bottom is normally favored because it allows compacting of yeast in the cone. Once compacted, the yeast can be gently run off, leaving the beer relatively yeast–free and allowing for lagering to occur in the vessel.

The benefits of this type of system are as follows:

1. Reduced number of tanks require less space than other systems
2. Reduced beer loss due to fewer beer transfers
3. Increased speed of operation
4. Efficient vessel utilization

Vessels are fitted with glycol cooling jackets, a pressure relief/antivacuum valve, a thermometer, a sample cock, and a C.I.P. (clean in place) system.

See GLYCOL JACKETS.

UNPACKER

A piece of equipment used to unload empty bottles from cases and load them onto a bottle washer (if dirty) or a bottle rinser (if clean). Cases are either discarded or reused depending on their condition.

UR-TYPE BEER

Ur means "original of type." Pilsner Urquell, for example, means original Pilzen beer. Many German brewers use the prefix to indicate their original brew type: Spaten Ur-Märzen is their original Märzenbier, and Ayinger Ur-Weisse Dunkeles is their original dark wheat beer.

U.S. GALLON

A unit of liquid measurement.
See GALLON.

U.S. QUART

A capacity measure of 57.75 cubic inches or 32 fluid ounces (0.9463 L).

VALENTINE TUBE

A swinging U-shaped tube, or swan-neck, running wort off from the mash tun. This tube is designed for gentle wort withdrawal, as it is raised to reduce the hydrostatic head. A series of inverted U-shaped tubes, each individually controlled, may be used to drain wort from different areas of the mash tun.

VEGETABLE BEER

See FRUIT, VEGETABLE, HERBAL, AND SPECIALTY BEERS.

VERMONT BREWERS FESTIVAL

An invitational festival sponsored by the brewers of the Green Mountain state. The site borders Burlington's famed Community Boathouse, Lake Champlain, and the Adirondack Mountains.

Three four-and-a-half hour sessions are held, each with its own musical theme (Dixieland, Irish folk, contemporary rock). In addition to the ten Vermont brewers, 20 other craft breweries attend, providing festival-goers the opportunity to sample more than 100 beers.

The New England Culinary Institute signed on as a major sponsor of the festival, so the beers are matched with world-class cuisine as well.

VICTORIA MICROBREWERY FESTIVAL

See GREAT CANADIAN BEER FESTIVAL.

VIENNA BEER

A beer made with Vienna malt. In the mid-19th century, Vienna was the capital and cultural center of the large and decaying Austro-Hungarian Empire, which sprawled from what is now the Czech Republic to the former Yugoslavia on the Adriatic and included Slovakia, Bohemia, most of central Europe, and Trieste, in present-day Italy. At this time, when the great beer styles of Europe were coming into being, the great Austrian brewmaster Anton Dreher introduced a very special brew that came to be called Vienna beer.

The special malt for this beer is Vienna malt, similar in many ways to British pale malt, which was dried at temperatures higher than those used for the very pale Pilzen malt and lower than those for the darker Bavarian malt. This was what determined the amber color of the original Vienna lager.

Dreher had collaborated with Munich brewer Gabriel Sedlmayr in adapting lagering systems and bottom-fermenting methods (1841) for his brewery at Schwechat (founded in 1632 and still in existence), on the outskirts of Vienna. Dreher also had breweries in Budapest, Michelob (Bohemia), and Trieste (Italy).

After the fall of the Austro-Hungarian Empire at the end of World War I, the lovely Vienna lager gradually ceased to be made in Austria or Hungary, but it was still brewed in Mexico (Dos Equis and others). As the years passed, information about this style became difficult to locate. Until Michael Jackson (in his first book, *World Guide to Beer)* described what he thought constituted the style, it was effectively dead. Mainly due to Jackson's efforts, the style is now being revived, even in Vienna. One of the earliest revival efforts was in the United States, with the production of Ambier Genuine Vienna Style Lager in about 1985. The beer was contract brewed by the Huber Brewery in Monroe, Wisconsin, for homebrewer Gary Bauer. Bauer's beer was successful, and amber lagers began to appear under many craft brewers' labels. Vienna beers are now becoming quite the rage.

Vienna lager has been described as having about 13.5/1.055 OG, 5 percent alcohol by volume, and 32–40 IBU with Saaz or Styrian Goldings hops. Vienna's water is a little softer than Munich's, at 150 to 240 ppm hardness. The malt is made from the lightest possible barley. This malt is similar to Munich malt but with lower drying temperatures. It is almost impossible to calculate the color of the original Vienna beer. One estimate is about 10–15 SRM.

The Great American Beer Festival guidelines for Amber Vienna Lager are 12–14/1.048–1.056 OG, 4.8–5.4 percent alcohol by volume, 22–28 IBU, and 8–12 SRM.

Original Gravity	Final Gravity	Alcohol by Volume	IBU	SRM
Ambier Genuine Vienna Style Lager (Wisconsin) 1985				
13/1.052	3.4	5%	25	≈18
Dos Equis Amber (Mexico) 1986				
10.9/1.042	2	4.6%	22	≈18
Kleinschwechat Dreher 1898 (Austria)				
13.1/1.053	4	4.9%	≈36	≈18
Michelober Dreher 1888 (Austria)				
13.3/1.054	3.5	5.2%	≈36	≈18

See AMBER AND RED BEERS.

VIKINGS AND ALE

Ale was perhaps the most important item in Viking life. Consummate seamen and navigators, the Vikings were the terror of the 8th through the 10th centuries. They raped, burned, and pillaged their way through North Africa, Holland, England, Ireland, Wales, France, Germany, and Italy, sacking such cities as Paris, Hamburg, and Cologne. Intrepid explorers, the Vikings discovered Iceland in 861 A.D. and settled that country in 874 A.D. Viking "graffiti" has been found in ancient Constantinople (now Istanbul, Turkey), and written reports tell of Viking activities on Russia's Volga River. Some people believe that the Viking chief Leif Erikson first explored America in the year 1000 A.D. If that is true, you can bet that Eriksson's ships had ale on board.

The act of christening ships was originally a Viking custom, which called for human blood mixed with ale to be sprinkled on a ship's bow. Large amounts of ale were kept in huge casks on every vessel.

Viking brew was called *Aul*. The Danes adapted *Aul* to *Ol*, and from this comes the English word ale. There were at least three styles of Viking ale — clear ale, mild ale, and Welsh ale — all unhopped, slightly sweet, and potent. In Ireland during the 9th century, the Vikings are said to have brewed ale with heather, using honey as the fermentable sugar and adding wormwood as a bittering agent. Ales brewed with oats and bayberries also were common. Historians tell us that Viking ale was often served with garlic to ward off evil.

Many drinking horns bore ale-runes, inscriptions to protect against deceitful women and poisons. Rune sticks covered with magical inscriptions also were thrown into the ale horn to protect against feminine wiles.

When ale horns were in short supply, the Vikings delighted in drinking ale from the boiled skulls of enemies killed in battle. While engaged in this gory bliss, the warriors would often bleed themselves into each other's ale skulls in the brotherhood ceremony only death could undo. Viking custom called for getting one's enemies drunk on ale, then burning down the alehouse with the passed-out foes inside.

During the Vikings' reign, any pledge or statement made while drunk was legally binding. Rents and taxes paid in beer and ale were called *ale-gafol*, and ale tribute was exacted from all conquered tribes. When a Viking died, his or her property was sold off, and one-third of the proceeds were used to buy the funeral ale served at the cremation.

As in most ancient societies, women did all the brewing in Viking culture. Viking law dictated that all brewing vessels, cauldrons, and the like were the exclusive property of the brewsters, and could not be owned by men. Each alewife would bequeath her brewhouse supplies to her nearest female relative.

Religious ceremonies among the Vikings were drunken orgies involving massive amounts of ale. *Minnae*, or memory cups of beer, were drunk to honor the dead. Ale was routinely poured on graves as a sacrifice to the departed spirits. In fact, paradise itself, called Valhalla, was no less than a giant alehouse.

A typical day in Valhalla was said to begin with a prebreakfast battle during which the deceased would hack each other to bits. Their wounds would heal instantly, however, and the warriors then would share a breakfast of boiled boar and ale. This heavenly brew was provided by Heidrun, the goat from whose udders continually flowed a stream of beer that filled a jar so large that "all could drink from it, and not empty it." Tall, beautiful war goddesses called the Valkyries served the ale.

As for the creation of ale, Viking sagas give the following explanation: The gods had been at war with some humans called the Vans. After much killing, a peace conference was called, and at the end of the negotiations, a treaty was sealed by members of both groups spitting into a large jar. To preserve this occasion, the gods shaped the saliva and some dust into a living man named Kvaser. Kvaser was soon murdered by some dwarfs, his blood running into an iron kettle. Honey was added to Kvaser's blood, and the whole mess was brewed into ale.

Copious ale drinking does not seem to have affected Vikings' health and stamina. In 922 A.D., Ion Fadhlan observed, "I have never seen people with a more developed body stature than they. They are tall as date palms, blond and ruddy." The Vikings burned much of Europe to the ground. In return, they gave the world the gift of ale.

See ALE-GAFOL, ALE AS RENT, and TAXES ON ALE.

VOLKSFEST

See CANSTATTER WASEN.

VOLLBIER

German law defines vollbier (full beer) as 11–12/1.044–1.048 OG, 18–24 IBU, and 2.4–4.5 SRM (very pale color) — in other words, the ordinary, everyday beer found in most of the world. In the old German and United States brewing industries, "light" beer was defined as less than 12/1.048 OG and "heavy" beer as more than that.

V. WEDGE WIRE

A heavy-duty slotted wire with V-shaped cuts, sometimes used as an alternative to the false bottom of a mash tun or lauter tun, to enable easy runoff. A V. wedge wire is a less expensive method of providing a vessel with a false bottom, but it is not always as sturdy as a specially made false floor.

See FALSE BOTTOM.

WANDERHAUFEN SYSTEM

See GERMINATION SYSTEMS FOR BARLEY.

WASSAIL

A beverage made with strong ale, sugar, spices, and roasted apples. From the Anglo-Saxon *waes hael,* "Be well."

In 1732, Sir Watkin W. Wynne prepared what is considered to be the first wassail bowl cocktail in Oxford, England. Into an immense silver-gilt bowl was placed a pound of Lisbon sugar, on which was poured 1 pint of warm beer. A little ginger and nutmeg were then grated over

Wassail bowls have been used for thousands of years.

the mixture, and 4 glasses of sherry and 5 pints of beer were added to it. It was stirred and sweetened to taste, then covered and let stand for 3 hours. Three or four slices of toast were placed on the creaming mixture, and the wassail bowl was ready. Two or three slices of lemon and a few cubes of sugar rubbed on a lemon peel were added just before serving.

Groups of young people who would visit the homes of their friends in the early hours

The custom of wassail is quite ancient.

457

of New Year's Day, carrying bowls of spiced ale, were referred to as "wassailing." The original wassail bowl was presented to Jesus College of Oxford in 1732 by Sir Watkin W. Wynne. However, bowls of varying capacities have apparently been used to drink beer and ale for thousands of years, based upon pictograms and ancient writings.

WASSAILING TREES AND CROPS

An ancient pagan custom surviving well into Christian times in which country people poured offerings of ale on prize fruit trees, crop fields, and other agricultural areas. Additionally, prize cattle, sheep, and other livestock were given offerings of holiday brew. The purpose was to ensure fertility in the growing and breeding season to come.

WATER IN BREWING

All water is made up of two hydrogen atoms and one oxygen atom. But, all water is not alike. Suspended chemicals, salts, minerals, and other elements can be present and can alter the characteristics of beer. There is also a difference between well water and surface water, which is prone to contamination from farm use chemicals and other airborn matter. If the water comes from a municipal water supply, it will contain chlorine to control bacteria. Well water is preferred because

it is most likely to contain desired salts, especially calcium. Calcium stimulates yeast growth and fermentation and aids yeast precipitation. Change the water and you change the beer.

Burton-on-Trent, England, and Dortmund, Germany, are two breweries with unique water supplies which have adapted to local conditions to produce unique beer styles.

Water is not the only reason these two cities prospered as brewing centers. Location and easy transport access are important to their brewing success, but the unique waters defined the classic styles of beers. Water's impact on the taste of any beer is subtle, but minerals in water do enhance the sensation of bitterness.

Breweries are often the largest commercial users of water wherever they are located. Brewers use vast quantities of water to make beer, since beer is mostly water.

There has been a movement among brewers in North America and elsewhere to develop ways to decrease the amount of water they use that gets turned into waste-water via their sanitation processes, and waste yeast and trub disposal. Every gallon saved reduces brewery operating costs at both ends. On the front end is their water bill, if on a municipal system, or their electric bill if they are pumping water from their own wells. On the back end are sewerage disposal and treatment charges. Water conservation makes good sense environmentally and is good business practice.

A Question of pH

Water is not as stable as one might think. Any given amount of pure water contains a certain number of hydroxide ions (OH^-) and hydronium ions ($H3O^+$, or simply H^+). At 77°F (25°C), the concentration of both of these hydroxide and hydronium ions in pure water is 0.0000001 moles per liter. This is said to be a neutral pH (power of hydrogen), or pH 7, which is a perfect balance.

In homebrewing, the pH of mash must be within the ideal range of 5.3 to 5.5 for the best possible extraction. If the water contains too high a concentration of bicarbonates, the mash will not reach this pH range unless dark roasted grains, which tend to be acidic, are added or the water is treated. Fortunately, when this becomes a potential problem, bicarbonates can be precipitated out of the wort by boiling or adding slaked lime.

The pH itself is not as important as the ions. As compounds dissolve into the water, they break up, or ionize, into their component elements. For example, sodium chloride (NaCl) will form one sodium ion (Na^+) and one chloride ion (Cl^-). The OH^- and H^+ ions are highly reactive and will react with other ions that are introduced in the solution. When the balance between the OH^- and H^+ ions is changed, the solution is no longer at a neutral pH.

Malt contains complex soluble phosphate compounds, or salts, which are somewhat acidic. They will react with other ions in the water. If the water is high in bicarbonates, the weak acid from the phosphate compounds will be neutralized. If, however, the phosphates react with calcium, they will precipitate out of solution, leaving an increased number of hydrogen ions and acidifying the mash.

See BICARBONATES and pH.

Common Ions Found in Water

Ion	Tolerable Level
Calcium	50–100 ppm
Carbonate/Bicarbonate	50 ppm
Chloride	100 ppm, light beer; 350 ppm, dark beer
Copper	10 ppm
Fluoride	10 ppm
Iron	10 ppb or less
Lead	20 ppb or less
Magnesium	10–20 ppm
Manganese	Trace (do not add)
Nickel	Trace (do not add)
Nitrate	20 ppm or less; has no effect but is not needed
Nitrite	Trace or less
Potassium	10 ppm or less
Silicate	10 ppm or less
Sodium	75–150 ppm; do not use with sulfates
Sulfate	75–150 ppm; do not use with sodium
Tin	Trace
Zinc	Trace

WEIHENSTEPHAN BAYERISCHE STAATSBRÄUEREI, FREISING, GERMANY

Weihenstephan, the state brewery of Bavaria (Bayerische Staatsbräuerei), is said to be the oldest brewery in the world. Historical records show that monastic brewers began producing beer at the site in 1040 A.D., and continuing until modern times.

The brewery was eventually secularized and was owned by the Bavarian royal family for a time. It is now a commercial venture, operated by the state government of Bavaria. A state-run brewing college is also located at the site.

The brewery produces a range of world-renowned wheat beers, some of which are available in the United States through Bavaria House Import Co. of Wilmington, North Carolina. These brands include Weihenstephan Weizenbier Crystal Clear, a golden wheat beer; Weihenstephan Hefe-Weissbier, a Bavarian-style wheat beer sedimented with yeast; Weihenstephan Hefe-Weissbier Dunkel, a dark wheat beer, also sedimented with yeast; and Weihenstephan Lager.

See WHEAT BEER and YEAST.

WEISSBIER OR WEIZENBIER

See BERLINER WEISSE and WHEAT BEER.

WEIZENBOCK

See BOCK BEER and WHEAT BEER.

WELSH ALE

See PALE ALE.

WHEAT

A grain that is used in some beer styles in either malted or unmalted form. Malted wheat is used for approximately 50 to 70 percent of the grist for a German weizen (wheat) beer. Unmalted or raw wheat is used for about 40 percent of the grist for a Belgian wit, or white. American wheat beers are derived from the German styles and use anywhere from 25 to 70 percent wheat in the grist. Wheat is almost always used in combination with barley.

Wheat presents several challenges to the maltster and brewer. It is difficult to malt, grind, and sparge. Much of the problem lies with the lack of husk; this makes the grain fragile during the malting process and makes it form a tighter grain bed, which sometimes results in stuck sparges. Wheat is higher in protein than barley, giving it better head retention properties but also a tendency to produce cloudiness. (Winter wheat is usually preferred because of its lower protein content.) A small amount of malted wheat can be added to the grist of other styles to increase head retention.

See ACROSPIRE, MALT, and WHEAT BEER.

WHEAT BEER

A beer made in the usual fashion but with a significant portion of wheat or wheat malt to replace the usual barley malt and other cereals. There are four major wheat beer styles: Belgian white, north German white, Bavarian white, and American wheat.

Wheat beers (sometimes called white beers) are a throwback to the old days, when both wheat and barley were used to make beer. Wheat beers were so common in the Middle Ages that most of the wheat crop went into beer and frequently little remained for bread. This was one of the reasons for the *Reinheitsgebot* (pledge of purity) of 1516. Partly an effort to force brewers to use barley for beer and leave the wheat for bread, it was notably unsuccessful in that regard.

Belgian White Beers

Many Belgian beers are made up of significant amounts of wheat, most notably those in the lambic group. Another white beer, called *wit*, is similar in some ways to the Berliner *weisse* style. Louvain white, an old style, was traditionally produced with 5 percent oats, 45 percent wheat, and 50 percent green (air-dried rather than kiln-dried) barley malt and rolled wheat. The mash on this style is held for an especially long protein rest. This results in very cloudy beer, lending itself to the name white.

The white beer style is gaining popularity today, especially in the United States and the Netherlands, thanks in large part to the popularity of the microbrewery movement and the experimentation by these brewers with the old styles of beer.

The Great American Beer Festival guidelines for Belgian White beers are 11–12.5/ 1.044–1.050 OG (4.4–5.0 Belge), 4.8–5.2 percent alcohol by volume, 15–25 IBU, and 2–4 SRM.

North German and Bavarian White Beers

In northern Germany, white beers have a faintly tart overlay. Pinkus Weizen is a good example of that type. An organic beer, it is available in the United States. It is especially refreshing on hot days with a slice of lemon or a dash of *schuss,* as is done with Berliner Weisse.

The Bavarian white beer, called Suddeutche Weizenbier, is the most popular of the German white styles. It is the one being exported in large amounts to the United States. Bavarian white beer is made with a mixture of barley malt and about 40 to 60 percent wheat malt. The beer is an ale — that is, top-fermented — but aged as a lager, which helps rid the beer of albuminoids, or heavy proteins. This produces a much clearer product than might have been made in the Middle Ages.

The typical Bavarian white beer has a very distinctive palate because of the special yeast used, which gives it a phenolic taste reminiscent of cloves. This comes from 4 to 6 ppm of *4-vinylguaiacol,* an ester imparted to the beer by the yeast in the fermenting process. The clovelike flavor adds to the charm of this beer.

Bavarian white beers are often served with a slice of lemon so that the drinker can squeeze a few drops of lemon juice into the beer. Many people, however feel that lemon detracts from the beer's flavor.

Wheat beers are always top-fermented by a yeast that works at warm temperatures (58° to 65°F, or 14° to 18°C). They are aged lager–style at near freezing temperatures.

Two finishes are available: *kristalklar,* the filtered version, and *hefe-trub,* with yeast *(hefe)* sediment *(trub).* The latter type is bottle-conditioned by the addition of kraeusen (fresh beer wort) and bottom-fermenting yeast. The wheat in the beer gives this style an especially thick and foamy head. Bavarian wheat beers range in alcohol content from around 5 percent by volume to as high as 7.6 percent in the weizenbocks. Some are amber and even dunkel (dark).

The Great American Beer Festival guidelines for Weizen/Weissbier Ale are 11.5–14/1.046–1.056 OG, 4.9–5.5 percent alcohol by volume, 10–15 IBU, and 3–9 SRM. The phenolic clovelike flavor is necessary, at least 50 percent wheat malt must be used, and the beer should be highly carbonated. The Dunkelweizen subcategory is similar but darker in color (16–23 SRM). Another subcategory, Weizenbock Ale, calls for 16–20/1.066–1.080 OG, 6.9–9.3 percent alcohol by volume, similar hopping rates, and 5–30 SRM.

Original Gravity	Final Gravity	Alcohol by Volume	IBU	SRM
Ayinger Export Weissbier (Bavaria) 1981				
12.7/1.051	2.5	5.2%	10.5	≈7
Hibernia Dunkel Weizen (Wisconsin) 1986				
13/1.052	3.6	4.9%	20	≈18

Original Gravity	Final Gravity	Alcohol by Volume	IBU	SRM
Paulaner Hefe-weizen Alt Bayerisches Brauart (Bavaria) 1986				
13.2/1.051	2.7	5.3%	18.5	≈7
Pinkus Weizen (northern Germany) 1984				
11.1/1.044	1.7	4.9%	25	≈3.5
Schramm Weizenbock (Germany) 1888				
17.9/1.074	6.8	5.6%	20	Unknown

American Wheat Beer

American wheat beers draw on the tradition of the Bavarian wheat style. American wheat is distinctively less assertive in flavor, and it is fermented with regular ale yeast; it therefore lacks the clove taste common to its Bavarian counterpart.

Craft brewers have brewed amber wheat beers, dark wheat beers, and even wheat bocks and fruit-based wheat beers. The style allows for much creativity. Basic ingredients are 50 to 60 percent 2-row barley malt and 40 to 50 percent wheat malt. Characteristics are 9.5–12.5/1.038–1.050 OG, 3.5–5 percent alcohol by volume, modest hop levels of 12–20 IBU, and 2–16 SRM. A wheat bock should be at least 16/1.066 OG and 6 percent alcohol by volume.

The Great American Beer Festival guidelines for American Wheat Ale or Lager are 9.5–12.5/1.036–1.050 OG, 3.5–4.5 percent alcohol by volume, 5–17 IBU, and 2–8 SRM.

See WHEAT BEER.

Original Gravity	Final Gravity	Alcohol by Volume	IBU	SRM
Anchor Wheat (California) 1985				
11/1.044	1.5	5%	25	≈3.5
August Schell Weiss (Minnesota) 1985				
11.5/1.046	3	4.5%	≈16	≈3.5
Pyramid Wheaten (Washington) 1985				
10/1.040	3.2–4.0	2.3–1008%	15	3.5
Widmer Weizen (Oregon) 1986				
11/1.044	2.1	4.4%	18	≈5
American Weissbeer 1900				
9.3/1.037	2.5	3.6%	≈27	Unknown

The most popular of the new American wheat beers is a draught hefe-weizen from the Widmer Brewery in Portland, Oregon. Brothers Kurt and Rob Widmer began their draught-only brewery in the spring of 1984 with the production of a Düsseldorf-type altbier. Their first seasonal beer, a filtered wheat beer called Widmer Weizen, met with almost instant success. It soon became the most popular of the brewery's beers. The following year, Widmer offered the weizen as an unfiltered hefe-weizen and suggested serving it in the Bavarian mode, with the special glasses and lemon wedges. This new brew was even more successful. There was no clove taste, which may have been the reason for the beer's success. It had a mellow, unassertive taste profile and a very pale, cloudy color. It quickly became a gateway beer for anyone wishing to try the new microbrewed beers without worrying about the heavy, hoppy taste of other new "ales," which was quite unfamiliar to Americans at that time.

The Widmer hefe-weizen became a cult beer in Portland and helped make the fledgling Widmer Brewery into the largest producer of draught-only beers in the country. American hefe-weizen has become a popular beer type brewed by most small craft brewers and brewpubs in the country.

See BELGIAN WHITE BEER, BERLINER WEISSE, and BOTTLE-CONDITIONED BEER.

WHIRLPOOL

A cylindrical, vertical, stainless steel tank used for to separate the hop/trub from the boiled wort. This is the separation method when hop pellets, powders, or extracts are used instead of whole hops in the brew kettle.

Wort from the brew kettle is pumped around the circumference of the whirlpool at high speeds to create a whirling effect. Centrifugal force throws all the hop residues and precipitated proteins to the middle of the vessel. These settle to the bottom, allowing the bright wort above the trub to be run off. The bottom of the vessel is generally slightly conical, although some vessels are flat or have a well-shaped bottom.

The brew kettle is often combined with the whirlpool. The boiled wort is taken from the bottom of the cone base and returned about one-third of the way up the straight side through a tangential return. The internal whirling effect that is created results in separation of the boiled wort and the hop residues.

WHITBREAD PLC
LONDON, ENGLAND

Founded in 1842, Whitbread became a public company in 1880. It is now a large combine, operating six breweries. Among its best-known brands are Whitbread Best Bitter, Mackeson Stout, and Boddington's Bitter.

Whitbread beers are imported to the United States by Hudepohl-Schoenling of

Various labels from the bottles of Whitbread PLC brands

Samuel Whitbread, of Whitbread PLC

Whitbread PLC brands from throughout the company's history

Cincinnati, Ohio (Whitbread & Mackeson) and Labatt's U.S.A. of Darien, Connecticut (Boddington's).

WHITE ALE

South Hams, as the southern district of Devonshire, England, is locally known, is remembered for once preparing white ale. It used to be brewed with malt, a small quantity of hops, flour, spices, and grout (also called ripening). As there are different recipes for grout, these ales varied considerably. This beer is not available today from any commercial brewer.

WHITE BEER

See BELGIAN WHITE BEER, BERLINER WEISSE, and WHEAT BEER.

WHITE HORSE IPA

A special Burton-brewed India Pale Ale (IPA) unveiled at The White Horse at Parson's Green, London, on July 31. This memorable event, which provoked much press coverage, developed out of a seminar Mark Dorber, cellar manager (and now publican) at The White Horse, organized in July 1990. Four Burton brewers at the seminar had the idea to try to recreate a late 1800s IPA. In April 1993, in cooperation with Gus Gutherie, technical director of Bass Brewery, they reproduced a classic IPA. Tom Dawson, a retired Bass brewer agreed to act as consul-

---

White Horse IPA

An India Pale Ale with 7.0 percent alcohol by volume, original gravity 1.064, 85 IBU.

It contains 90 percent halcyon malt, 10 percent brewer's sugar, progress whole hops in copper, and Kent Goldings for dry hopping.

The strong hops overpower any other bouquet. It has a long-lasting hop flavor. The color is 18 SRM.

The White Horse IPA boasts a lovely big white head, and because the Progress hops used had a higher–than–normal alpha acid content (7 percent versus a more normal 5 percent), the bittering units imparted were 40% more than what might be expected.

---

tant. To formulate this joint effort, Mr. Dawson consulted Bass's brewing ledgers back to the 1880s.

The White Horse IPA was brewed in the Bass Brewery Museum brewhouse, begun in 1920. This lovely example of a tower-type plant was transported in the late 1970s to the Bass Brewery and installed in an old engine house, now within the confines of the museum. The plant has a 5-barrel capacity. Two brews or batches were necessary to fulfill a White Horse beer festival order of "at least six-hogsheads."

At joint team made up of young Bass brewers and cellarmen from The White Horse assembled at 6:00 A.M. on Saturday, 19 June 1993 at the brewery. Twenty-nine hours, two brews and a clean-up later they were done. Then it was up to the yeast to do its work.

The resulting beer was a hop-lover's delight. To those fortunate enough to have some, it will remain, surely, a most memorable ale.

See India Pale Ale (IPA).

WICHITA FESTIVAL OF BEERS

After the success of the first event in November 1994, promoters planned to make this an annual event and lined up the June 1995 festival for the Century II Exhibition Hall in downtown Wichita, Kansas. The promoters, Standard Beverage Corporation, happen to be beer distributors, but the 65 offerings at the festival were not limited to their beers. The festival raised $22,000 for the local leukemia society.

WIDMER BREWING CO. PORTLAND, OREGON

Widmer Brewing Co. operates out of a sizable draught-only plant and a new building in which bottled beer is produced. The company has built a market for its hefe-weizen (wheat beer with yeast) in its hometown and is now expanding the style into other western metropolises.

The company was founded in the early 1980s by two brothers, Kurt and Rob Widmer. Kurt developed an appreciation for German beer while living and working in Germany during the 1970s. He experimented with homebrewing for several years, then established Widmer Brewing Co. in 1984. The company built a second brewery in Portland in 1988, then 2 years later moved its operations to an historic building in north Portland, expanding its capacity substantially. A 120-keg-per-hour filling line was added in 1993. The company's 40-barrel brewhouse churned out a record 50,000 barrels in 1994.

Widmer Hefe-Weizen

Made with a strain of yeast from Germany's famous Weihenstephan brewing school, Widmer Hefe-weizen has taken the Portland market by storm. A golden, cloudy beer, it is kegged unfiltered directly from the fermenters, leaving yeast in suspension. This beer is rich in flavor and B-complex vitamins. It is a clean, quenching brew.

Most recently, Widmer has contracted to have Widmer beers produced at a state-of-the-art brewery operated by G. Heileman in Milwaukee. This agreement will give Widmer the ability to expand its beer into the midwestern and eastern markets.

In addition to hefe-weizen, the company produces weizen, Märzen, Oktoberfest, and bock, using the traditional German altbier brewing style, which combines ale and lager brewing techniques. Widmer beers are top-fermented and cold-conditioned.

See MICROBREWERY, WHEAT BEER, and YEAST.

WILD BEER

See LAMBIC and SPONTANEOUS FERMENT.

WILD YEAST

Any yeast other than the specific strain of *Saccharomyces* the brewer has chosen to use. Wild yeasts impart off-flavors, as they ferment sugars that *Saccharomyces* strains do not. If they are large enough in number, they can ruin a batch of beer with off-flavors and off-aromas. The best defense is good sanitation procedures, a pure strain of brewing yeast, and high pitching rates.

WINTER BEER

See FESTBIER.

WIT

See BELGIAN WHITE BEER and WHEAT.

WOMEN, BEER, AND BREWING

Until the Middle Ages, the brewing of beer was exclusively the province of the woman in the household. Old laws even went so far as to state that the vessels used in brewing were her personal property. As far back as 2000 B.C., Mesopotamia (part of modern Iraq) acknowledged women as brewers in an industry that even then was held in the highest regard. In Babylon, female brewers, or brewsters (the feminine form, just as baxter and spinster are the feminine forms of baker and spinner), were priestesses in the temple, giving the industry an ecclesiastical flavor that continued to the monastic breweries of medieval

Beer was often advertised as being so nourishing that nursing mothers were encouraged to drink it. Today, some groups still advocate the drinking of stout or porter while nursing, although the medical establishment has not embraced this theory.

England. The ancient Finns preserved their accounts of the creation of the world in a song and story cycle known as the Kalevala. Historians date the beginnings

Depicted here as a tavern sign, original-ly the "good woman" representa-tion referred to some female saint, or a holy or good woman who had met death by the privation of her head. Also called the "silent woman," it evolved to become a tasteless joke.

of these poems and legends to as early as 1000 B.C. For the Finns, beer was born through the efforts of three women preparing for a wedding feast. Osmotar, Kapo, and Kalevatar all labored to pro-duce the world's first beer, but their efforts fell as flat as the brew itself. Only when Kalevatar combined saliva from a bear's mouth with wild honey did the beer foam, and the Finns received gift of ale.

In thirsty post-Roman times, the Anglo Saxon *bredale,* which means "bride," was a prominent part of the marriage ceremony. The bride's family brewed a special ale for the occasion. The term "Bridal Ale" lives on in our present-day usage, *bridal.* During medieval times, as monasteries began brewing beer on a larger scale, women's involvement in the brewing process gradually dimin-ished and finally came to an end, as more and more, the man became the brewer in the home.

The Industrial Revolution struck a final blow to the ale wife, who sold unhopped beer with a shelf life of a few days from her brewpub. Men have tended to do the brewing ever since. Modern marketers, too, suggest that beer is a "man's" beverage. That belief may be changing, however, as more women come to regard brewing as an ancient craft of great culinary value, the successful accom-plishment of which is in no way sexist.

The position of brewer at Pinkus Muller in Munster has been handed down from father to son since 1811. Pinkus now has a brewster, Barbara Muller, daughter of Franz Muller and

Women brewed and enjoyed beer throughout the ages, as this print (ca. 1800) illustrates.

granddaughter of Pinkus Muller. Significantly, Pinkus became the modern world's first organic brewery since Barbara's arrival. She attended Weihenstephan, the oldest brewing university, and reports increased enrollment for women seeking degrees.

WORT

The unfermented mixture of water, sugars from malted barley, and hops. The term usually refers to this mixture during the boiling process. During the sparging operation, before hops are added, the liquid is referred to as "sweet liquor." After the boil is finished and the wort is chilled and moved to the fermenter, it is usually referred to as "unfermented beer." Once fermentation is complete, it is "beer."

WORTING

See KRAEUSENING/WORTING.

YAKIMA BREWING & MALTING CO.
YAKIMA, WASHINGTON

Yakima Brewing & Malting Co. was the brainchild of Scottish-born Bert Grant, a career brewer with a taste for hoppy ales. During a long career with several major North American brewing companies (including Stroh and Carling O'Keefe), Grant harbored a dream: to build his own small brewery.

In 1982 he did just that, opening the first microbrewery in Washington state in the old Yakima Opera House. Since then, Grant has expanded his operations considerably. The company completed construction of a new 12,000-barrel brewery (that can expand as demand warrants) in 1991 and operates a brewpub in a former Yakima railway depot.

Grant has an affection for hoppy, British-style ales and brews a full range of them, including Grant's Scottish Ale, Russian Imperial Stout, India Pale Ale, Grant's Celtic Ale, and occasional seasonals. The company also produces cask-conditioned ales for pouring in the brewpub and at select retail establishments in the Seattle area.

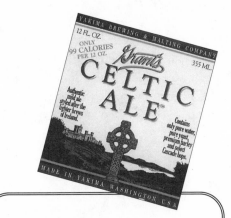

Grant's Celtic Ale

Ostensibly based on the mild ales of the British Isles, Grant's Celtic Ale has that style's light body but a more generous helping of hops. It is a true session beer, with an alcohol content of under 3 percent by volume. This ale is a dark, rich-looking brew with a spicy aroma and pleasing bitterness. Whatever it owes to its mild ale predecessors, it is one of those uniquely American beers that takes the best of Old World brewing traditions and transforms them into something entirely new.

Grant's ales have become widely available, even as far as the East Coast. Unusual among microbrewers, Grant has a pasteurizer, which helps give his ales the shelf stability that many microbrews lack.

See ALE and MICROBREWERY.

YARD OF ALE

A 3-foot-long, horn-shaped drinking glass that holds about a quart (0.9L) of beer. A yard of ale usually has a long fluted neck and sits on some sort of a globular bottom, although shapes and stands vary. Half-yards also are available.

YEAST

A relatively large single-celled fungus requiring 1,000 to 2,000 cells laid end to end to make a string 0.39 inch (1 cm) long. Yeasts reproduce by budding, also known as binary fission or cell division. The mother cell produces a daughter cell that can grow to the size of the mother in 2 to 6 hours. Yeasts are widely distributed in nature, passing the winter in the soil. In spring, wind and other natural agents spread them far and wide. Yeasts have the ability to convert sugars into alcohol and various by-products (such as esters and diacetyl). They are classified by genus, species, and strain. The main genus used by brewers is *Saccharomyces,* and the species primarily used in beer are *cerevisiae* for ales and *uvarum* (also known as *carlsbergensis,*) for lagers. Although some texts claim that yeasts used for wheat beer are *delbruckii,* they are actually *cerevisiae.* The different strains are identified by various attributes in their fermentation. These attributes are usually based on growth rate, temperature tolerance, attenuation, and, most importantly the flavors they impart (or do not impart) to beer. The brewer must weigh these factors when selecting the proper strain of yeast to use for the style of beer being made.

The exact function of yeasts was entirely unknown until the 19th century. In the

Skimming the yeast

years 1837–38, separate publications by C. Cagniard de la Tour, T. Schwann, and F. Kützing indicated that the scientists had discovered that yeast was a living organism that reproduced through a process of budding. Schwann named it *Zuckerpilz,* which means "sugar fungus." *Saccharomyces* is derived from this genus, which includes baker's and brewer's yeasts.

It was not until 1876, when Louis Pasteur summarized fermentation as "life without air," that the exact role yeasts play in the fermentation process was discovered. Pasteur found that yeasts given an ample amount of air did not produce nearly the amount of alcohol as when the air was suppressed. He also noted that in highly aerated wort, yeasts grew more rapidly and were able to absorb into their cells a far greater proportion of the transformed sugars. In wort without air, the growth rate slowed considerably, but production of alcohol increased dramatically.

When yeasts have an abundance of the correct nutrients and an abundance of oxygen, they reproduce through the process of budding. The mother cell forms a lateral protrusion or extension, passing essential cell materials to the daughter cell. Once enough material is passed to the new cell, it is sealed off from the mother cell and begins its own independent life. Some yeasts will produce spores, much like mushroom fungi, which contain half the chromosomes of the parent yeast. When the spore mates with a compatible spore type, the two will eventually grow into a new yeast strain. Yeasts that are capable of this sexual cycle are called perfect yeasts. For the most part, beer yeasts are imperfect and have lost the ability to form spores. This is important to the brewer in that the chances of a new strain of yeast appearing via spores in a fermenting beer and imparting off-flavors are nil.

Depending on the strain of yeast, the temperature range at which it best ferments is quite narrow. One out of a million yeast cells will spontaneously mutate into something other than the original strain. If the pH, temperature, or nutrients are not within the parameters preferred by a particular yeast, the mutation rate will increase dramatically and will most likely ruin the beer with off-flavors.

As long as the yeasts have fermentable sugars to consume, they remain in suspension. When the fermentable sugars have all been used up, the yeasts enter the stationary phase. They begin to form clumps, called flocs, and settle to the bottom of the fermenter. This is called flocculation. How well a particular strain does this depends on several factors. The genetic makeup of the yeast, the available nutrients, and the environment all influence how well or poorly a yeast will flocculate. Certain strains of yeast will not flocculate much, but will settle down to a powdery, easily disturbed layer of yeast. Other strains will group together and create a layer on the bottom of the fermenter that is difficult to remove.

See FERMENTATION and YEAST NUTRIENTS.

YEAST NUTRIENTS

The nutrients needed for yeast to reproduce and ferment properly. Oxygen and nitrogen are also needed for yeast reproduction and fermentation. Adequate aeration of the wort will provide the oxygen that is required, and ammonium ions, amino acids, and polypeptides that are found in the wort will provide the nitrogen that is required.

Soluble proteins are absorbed and broken down into amino acids in the mash. These amino acids are subsequently consumed by the yeast. Substantial quantities of phosphate and sulfate are also needed for proper yeast growth, as are trace amounts of calcium, iron, magnesium, phosphorus, potassium, sodium, and sulfur.

During brewing, if the fermenting beer lacks the nutrients that are needed, the fermentation process will be shortened and it will leave behind fermentable sugars. As the nutrients run out, the yeast will begin to enter a self-preservation stage during which it activates certain enzymes that reduce the yeast cell to amino acids and other substances. These substances will then settle out of solution. The beer needs to be removed from the yeast before the yeast cells begin to feed on themselves (autolysis) which would impart off-flavors to the beer. Autolysis is abnormal, however, and should not be a major concern for most brewers.

See AERATION, FERMENTAION, and YEAST.

YEAST PRESS

A sheet press where entrained beer (barm) is recovered and blended back with racked beer. In large breweries where yeast is removed from open-top fermenting vessels by suction, it is normally sent down to a holding tank. The yeast is normally pumped from this tank to the press. Sometimes yeast is stored in the press, which is kept cool. Otherwise it is discharged into another storage container.

See BARM.

YEAST PROPAGATION TANK

A tank designed for efficient, sterile yeast growth. The setup generally includes a holding/growth vessel, a wort-sterilizing vessel, and a sterile air facility.

To effect infection-free propagation, the yeast cultures must be inoculated with sterile wort. Growth is then promoted by the injection of sterile air into the growth medium. In essence, the propagation is a miniature version of a closed, sanitary fermentation vessel. Many designs and methods are available to accomplish this.

YEAST SUCTION PUMP

A pump used for skimming yeast off the top of an open-top fermentation vessel and guiding it down into a receiving container.

The Yorkshire Stone Square at the Samuel Smith Brewery in Yorkshire, England

YORKSHIRE STONE SQUARE

A type of fermentation vessel originally made of stone and later of slate, but now made of stainless steel. The Yorkshire Stone Square has a lower compartment that is separated from the open upper area by a deck, which allows entry to the lower vessel by a series of pipes and a central manhole. The lower compartment contains wort and yeast. As the yeast head grows, it rises up through the manhole and onto the deck. The beer then drains back through the pipes. This system is used with highly flocculent yeasts that require vigorous aeration. At the end of fermentation, the yeast is recovered by skimming it off the deck. Samuel Smith's Brewery in England is noted for using this fermentation system.

D. G. YUENGLING & SON BREWING CO. POTTSVILLE, PENNSYLVANIA

D. G. Yuengling & Son Brewing Co. is a brewery with a notable distinction: It is the oldest continuously operating brewery in the United States, founded in 1829.

The first Yuengling to arrive in Pottsville was a young German immigrant named David Gottlob Yuengling, a brewer by trade. His first operation was called the Eagle Brewery, but it was destroyed by fire in 1831. Undeterred, Yuengling rebuilt on a hillside overlooking Pottsville, and the brewery has remained there ever since. After the move, the name was changed to the Yuengling Brewery, but the firm kept the eagle as its trademark.

The brewery was positioned on a hillside for a good reason. The nascent art of lager brewing required cool temperatures to ferment and age the beer, and in those prerefrigeration days, it was necessary to dig cellars deep into the earth. In these cool chambers, generations of Yuenglings aged their beers.

In the early days, Yuengling was a draught-only brewery. The beer was put into barrels and transported by horse-drawn wagons to the taverns where it was sold.

The Yuengling Brewery in Pottsville, Pennsylvania, 1843

When Prohibition came, strict limits were put on how many tanks a brewery could have. Yuengling sealed off some of its underground chambers with brickwork to comply. (Yuengling unsealed the cellars in 1976 and put the bottles and papers found there in an on-premises museum.) During the 14 years of Prohibition, the company made Yuengling Special, a nonalcoholic brew. The company also diversified into ice cream, operating an ice cream factory right up to the 1980s.

Yuengling experienced some lean years in the 1960s and 1970s, as mass-market brands started to infiltrate its home base. But as other regional brewers fell by the wayside, Yuengling managed to survive.

The current company president, Dick Yuengling, took over the brewery in the early 1980s, bringing a flair for marketing to a brewery that scarcely knew the word. During his tenure, Yuengling has introduced a number of revivalist products to bolster the brewery's timeless Yuengling Porter and Chesterfield Ale. Today D. G. Yuengling & Son is benefiting from the specialty beer surge, and the old-fashioned beers the company brews are enjoying some celebrity.

See MICROBREWERY and PORTER.

Pottsville Porter

Yuengling's Pottsville Porter, "brewed expressly for the tavern and family trade," might be considered the brewery's trademark product. Yuengling was brewing porter (albeit a bottom-fermented version) when the porter style was all but extinct, even in Great Britain. Pottsville Porter is somewhat lighter-bodied than traditional porters (perhaps a result of the lagerlike production process), but it fits the bill in all the important respects: dark amber color, nice malty aroma, and roasty, coffeeish flavor. It was available into the early 1980s in squat old-style bottles with a label of antique design. For better or worse, the package has been updated, and the beer is now bottled in the popular longneck style.

ZIP CITY BREWING CO.
NEW YORK, NEW YORK

Zip City Brewing Co. brought to the East Coast something the West Coast already had: the sophisticated brewpub. Because the brewery is located in one of America's gastronomic centers, founder Kirby Shyer was not content to offer his patrons simple pub fare, so he brought in a two-star chef and let him loose in the kitchen. As a result, the brewpub serves eclectic fare (yellow-fin chili and Pilsner-steamed clams) and pours a wide range of German-style specialty beers from its gleaming Austrian brew kettles.

Shyer got the notion of starting a brewpub at a 1987 conference sponsored by the Association of Brewers. He had toyed with the idea of starting a contract brewing business, but after the conference he knew that he wanted to do more than just market a beer — he wanted to brew it.

He was soon flying to California to take a brewing course at the University of California at Davis and touring microbreweries around the country, absorbing arcane information on brewhouse construction

In addition to brewing quality beers, Zip City offers patrons a wide variety of gourmet fare.

The lager cellar at Zip City Brewing Co.

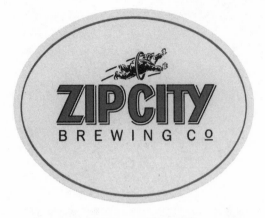

and yeast propagation. In his travels, Shyer narrowed his vision down to a brewpub and began taking restaurant management courses.

He also found a place to locate his pub — a building on a rising block on West 18th Street. The building did come with some unusual karmic baggage, however, having once served as the headquarters of the National Temperance Society.

The brewery name is a literary reference from the Sinclair Lewis novel *Babbitt*. In the novel, the main character refers to his nameless metropolis as "Zip City" because of the ever-accelerating pace of modern urban life.

Zip City focuses on German-style lagers, with four main styles: Pilsner, helles, Märzen, and dunkel. The helles is a light, quaffable, firm-bodied lager with a slight chill haze. The Pilsner is smooth yet assertive, with a relatively high hopping rate that gives the taste buds a jolt. It has a palate-cleansing finish and is remarkably clear for an unfiltered product. Zip City also produces a changing list of seasonal beers, including a warming Eisbock.

See ALE, BREWPUB, and LAGER ALE.

ZUUR (SOUR) BEER

See BELGIAN BROWN AND RED ALES.

ZWICKEL COCK

A stainless steel sample valve designed for taking samples in enclosed containers possibly under pressure. Also known as a trycock. Carbon dioxide-testing units, in particular, are designed to attach to the valve and allow for sampling of carbonated beer without losing carbonation or getting over-foaming. The zwickel cock is built with a highly sanitary design and is generally found on bright beer tanks and univessels.

ZYMOSIS

Fermentation.

ZYMURGY

The science or study of fermentation. The word *zymurgy* is derived from zymase (a yeast enzyme). Also, *zymurgy* is the title of a magazine, published by the American Homebrewers Association.

ZYTHOS

The Greek name for barley wine, from the Egyptian word *zythum*.

APPENDICES

ORGANIZATIONS

Allied Brewery Traders' Association
G. W. C. Lemmens, Chairman
85 Tettenhall Road
Wolverhampton, West Midlands
WV3 9NE United Kingdom
0902 22303; fax 0902 712066
See ALLIED BREWERY TRADERS'
ASSOCIATION.

**American Beer Association
and Gourmet Beer Society**
Box 1387
Temecula, CA 92593
(909) 676-2337
Fax (909) 699-3477
Contact: John S Thomas. E-mail
  Brewbaron@aol.com.
*Supports American beer industry by advo-
cating change in the regulation of federal
and state laws.*

American Brewers' Guild
2110 Regis Dr. #B
Davis, CA 95616
(916) 753-0497
Fax (916) 753-0176

American Homebrewers Association
Karen Barela, President
P. O. Box 1679
Boulder, CO 80306
303-447-0816
See AMERICAN HOMEBREWERS ASSOCIATION.

**American Malting Barley Association,
Inc.**
Michael P. David, Executive VP
735 North Water Street, Suite 908
Milwaukee, WI 53202
414-272-4640
See AMERICAN MALTING BARLEY
ASSOCIATION, INC.

**Asociacion Latinoamericana de
Fabricantes de Cerveza**
Jose-Maria de Ro-mana, Cooridinator
General
Prolongacion Arenales 161 San Isidro
Lima 27 Peru
Apartado Postal 1642
Lima 100 Peru
22-32-25 or 41-55-83; telex, 21022
(025202) PB HCSAR

**Asociacion Nacional de Fabricantes de
Cerveza**
Fernandez de la Hoz
7, 28010 Madrid
Spain
34-1-593 27 70 or 34-1-593 28 13;
  fax, 34-1-448 97 12; telex, 44629
ANFAC E

Association des Brasseurs de France
25 Boulevard Malesherbes
75008 Paris
France

ORGANIZATIONS

Association of Brewers
P.O. Box 1679
Boulder, CO 80306-1679
(303) 447-0816
See ASSOCIATION OF BREWERS.

American Society of Brewing Chemists
3340 Pilot Knob Road
St. Paul, MN 55121
(612) 454-7250
See AMERICAN SOCIETY OF BREWING
CHEMISTS.

Beer Drinkers of America
5151 Golden Foothill Pkwy., #100
El Dorado Hills, CA 95630
(800) 441-BEER
Magazine: *Heads Up*

The Beer Institute
1225 I St. NW, Suite 825
Washington, DC 20005
See BEER INSTITUTE.

**Brewers and Licensed Retailers
Association**
R. W. Simpson, Director
42 Portman Square, London
W1H 0BB United Kingdom
011-44-171-486-4831
Fax 011-44-171-935-3991
See BREWERS AND LICENSED RETAILERS
ASSOCIATION.

Brewers' Association of America
P.O. Box 876
Belmar, NJ 07719-0876
(908) 280-9153

Brewers Association of Canada
R. A. Morrison, President
155 Queen Street, Suite 1200
Ottawa, Ontario, Canada K1P 6L1
613-232-9601
See BREWERS ASSOCIATION OF CANADA.

Brewers' Guild
P. J. Ogie, President
8 Ely Place, Holburn
London, EC1N 6SD United Kingdom
44-171-405-4565
fax: 44-171-831-4495
See BREWERS' GUILD.

Brewing and Malting Barley Research
206 167 Lombard Ave.
Winnipeg, Manitoba, Canada
MAN R3B 0T6

British Guild of Beer Writers
P. O. Box Hemel Hempstead
Herts HP3 0RJ
England
011-44-1442-834-900
Fax: 011-44-1442-934901
See BRITISH GUILD OF BEER WRITERS.

Bureau of Alcohol Tobacco and Firearms
National Laboratory Center Library
1401 Research Boulevard
Rockville, MD 20850
(301) 294-0410
See BUREAU OF ALCOHOL, TOBACCO AND
FIREARMS.

CAMRA
230 Hatfield Road
St. Albans, Hertfordshire
AL1 4LW united Kingdom
011-44-1727-86726
Fax: 011-44-1727-867670

CAMRA Canada
P. O. box 2036
Ottawa, Ontario
Canada K1P5W3
(613) 837-7155

European Brewery Convention
Secretariat General
2380 BB Zoeterwoude
P. O. Box 510
Netherlands
011-31-71-456047
See EUROPEAN BREWERY CONVENTION.

Hop Growers of America
P.O. Box 9218
Yakima, WA 98909
(509) 248-7043
Fax (509) 248-7044

Institute for Brewing Studies
P.O. Box 1679
Boulder, CO 80306-1679
(303) 447-0816
Fax (303) 447-2825
See INSTITUTE FOR BREWING STUDIES.

Institute of Brewing
33 Clarges Street
London
W1Y 8EE United Kingdom
011-44-171-499-8144
Fax: 011-44-171-499-1156
See INSTITUTE OF BREWING.

National Association of Beverage Importers
1025 Vermont Ave. NW, #1205
Washington, DC 20005
(202) 638-1617

National Beer Wholesalers Association
1100 S Washington
Alexandria, VA 22314
(703) 683-4300

National Beverage Retailers Association
5101 River Rd., #108
Bethesda, MD 20816
(301) 656-1494

National Licensed Beverages Association
4214 King St.
Alexandria, VA 22302
(703) 671-7575

North American Guild of Beer Writers
Reilly Road
La Grangeville, NY 12540
(914) 223-3269
Fax (914) 227-5520
Rob Haiber, Co-chairman
See NORTH AMERICAN GUILD OF BEER WRITERS.

COLLECTORS' CLUBS

American Breweriana Association (ABA)
P.O. Box 11157
Pueblo, CO 81001
(719) 544-9267
See AMERICAN BREWERIANA ASSOCIATION, INC.

ABA Bottlecap Exchange
11129 Barman Ave.
Culver City, CA 90230
Contact: David Friedman

ABA Coaster Exchange
1623 N Lindwood Ave.
Appleton, WI 54914
Contact: Kenneth C. Kositzke

ABA Label Exchange
4330 W 152 St.
Cleveland, OH 44135
Contact: Pat Wheeler

ABA Lending Library
5961 E Fountain Circle
Mesa, AZ 85205
Contact: Chris Pastor

ABA Micro Coaster Exchange
298 Charles Rd.
Southampton, PA 18966
Contact: Kevin Bracken

ABA Napkin Exchange
5132 Round Rock Dr.
El Paso, TX 79924
Contact: Jeffrey H. Coolaw

ABA Opener Exchange
448 Crandon Ave.
Calumet City, IL 60409
Contact: Lawrence Biehl

ABA Sports Card Exchange
P.O. Box 1492
Portsmouth, VA 23705
Contact: Hugh O. Griffin, Jr.

ABA Label Source
W 2569 Candlelite Way
Appleton, WI 54915
(414) 687-0752
Contact: Bob Meyer

Beer Can Collectors of America
747 Merus Ct.
Fenton, MO 63026-2092
(314) 343-6486

Just for Openers (JFO)
701 E Audubon Lake Dr.
Durham, NC 27713
Contact: John Stanley

Micro Chapter, ECBA
P.O. Box 826
South Windsor, CT 06074-0826
(203) 644-9582
Contact: Roger Levesque

National Association for Breweriana Advertising
2343 Met-to-Wee Ln.
Wauwatosa, WI 53226
(414) 257-0158
Contact: Robert Jaeger

Stein Collectors International
3530 Mimosa Ct.
New Orleans, LA 70131-8305
Magazine: Prosit, 4/year

Whiskey Pitcher Collectors Association
19341 W Tahoe Dr.
Mundelein, IL 60060

EDUCATIONAL ORGANIZATIONS

American Brewers' Guild
  2110 Regis Dr., #B
  Davis, CA 95616
  (916) 753-0497
  Fax (916) 753-0176

Brewing Courses, University Extension, UCD
  Davis, CA 95616
  (916) 757-8899
  Fax (916) 757-8558

Hands-On Brewing School
  23883 Madison St.
  Torrance, CA 90505
  (310) 375-BREW
  Fax (310) 373-6097
  Contact: Bohemian Brewery Importers

Microbrewers Association of America Short Courses
  4513 Vernon Blvd., #202
  Madison, WI 53705
  (414) 774-8558
  Fax (414) 774-8556

Microbrewery Planning Course, URI Food Science
  530 Liberty Ln.
  North Kingston, RI 02852
  (401) 792-2466

U.S. Brewers' Academy, Siebel Institute
  4055 W Peterson Ave.
  Chicago, IL 60646
  (312) 463-3400
  Fax (312) 463-4962

MAIL ORDER BEER CLUBS

American Beer Club
18395 Gulf Blvd., Suite 202
Indian Shores, FL 34635
(800) 953-BEER

Beer Across America
150 Hilltop Ave.
Barrington, IL 60011-0728
(800) 854-BEER
The original microbrewery beer-of-the-month club. Various subscriptions available.

The Beer Exchange
Chicago, IL
(800) 454-BEER

Beer of the Month Club
(800) 854-2337
Fax (312) 549-0114
Two international selections sent each month.

Beers 2 You
1825 A Johns Dr.
Glenview, IL 60025
(800) 323-BEER

Great American Beer Club
480 Scotland Rd., Suite C
Lakemoor, IL 60050
(800) 879-2747 or
(800) 995-3991

Micro Brew Express
2246 Calle del Mundo
Santa Clara, CA 95054
(408) 748-9090
Fax (408) 748-9099

Premium Beer Club
(800) 671-BREW
Two microbrew four- or six-packs per month. Newsletter.

IMPORTERS OF BEER

US AND CANADA

Acme Food Specialties
P.O. Box 4445
Santa Fe Springs, CA 90670-1457
(310) 946-9494
Fax (310) 944-6809
*Ritterbrau, Einbecker UrBock, Konig
Pilsener, Schultheiss Berliner Weisse
(Germany).*

Admiralty Beverage Co.
2336 NW 21st Ave.
Portland, OR 97209
(503) 240-5522
*Young's, Scottish & Newcastle (England);
Paulaner, EKU, Chimay, Duvel,
Hoegaarden, Sapten, Lucifer, Dentegems,
more.*

All Saints Brands
201 Main St. SE, #323
Minneapolis, MN 55414
*Christoffel Bier Blond, La Trappe (Holland)
many more.*

Amazon
P.O. Box 1466
Brattleboro, VT 05302
(802) 254-3884
Contact: Anne Latchis
Xingu (Brazil). T-shirts available.

Anheuser-Busch
1 Busch Pl.
St Louis, MO 63118
(314) 577-2000
Carlsberg.

Asahi Breweries USA
(310) 541-8680
Asahi Beer Super Dry.

Associated Importers
P.O. Box 2902, Grand Central Station
New York, NY 10163
(212) 972-5111

Barton Beers
55 E Monroe St.
Chicago, IL 60603
(312) 346-9200
Fax (312) 346-2213
*Double Diamond (UK); Tsingtao (China);
Peroni (Italy); San Miguel (Philippines); St.
Pauli Girl (Germany); Corona Extra,
Corona Light, Coronita, Negra Modelo,
Modelo Especial, Pacifico (Mexico).*

Belukus Marketing
(609) 589-2414
Young's Beers (UK).

Bier Haus
Copiague, NY 11726
Hue Beer (Vietnam), Old Growler (UK).

Brand Beer
600 Houze Way, #E6
Roswell, GA 30076
(404) 594-7774
Brand.

Brandevor USA
18211 NE 68th St., #E100
Redmond, WA 98052
(206) 881-5095
Simpatico.

Bulunda Import-Export Co.
Jacksonville, FL
(904) 642-1077
Ngoma (Togo).

Century Importers
11911 Freedom Dr., #1100
Reston, VA 22090-5609
(703) 709-6600
Fax (703) 709-6999
*O'Keefe, Kronenbourg, Old Vienna,
Courage, Caribe, Foster's, more. Taunton
Cider (UK).*

Cherry Company
4461 Malaai St., P.O. Box 1375
Honolulu, HI 96818
(808) 537-5245
Kirin.

Chrissa Imports
50 Cypress Ln.
P.O. Box 548
Brisbane, CA 94005
(415) 468-5770
Spatenbrau, Konig Pils, Goesser.

Condal Imports
2300 Randall Ave.
Bronx, NY 10473
(718) 589-1100
Extracto de Malta.

Crown Jewel Importers
Fairfield, NJ
(201) 575-8886
Monrovia (Liberia).

DAB Importers
770 E Main St., #1A
Morristown, NJ 08057
(609) 234-9400
Fax (609) 234-9640
DAB (Germany).

Domaine Cellars
2040 N Loop W, #200
Houston, TX 77018
(713) 681-5461
Fax (713) 681-8521
Carib.

Dribeck Importers
57 Old Post Rd., #2, P.O. Box 4000
Greenwich, CT 06830
(203) 622-1124
Beck's.

East Coast Importing
P.O. Box 2739
Acton, MA 01720
(508) 692-8466
Bitburger, Maisel, Merrydown Cider.

Efco Importers
P.O. Box 741
Jenkintown, PA 19046
(215) 224-9022
Fax (215) 885-4584
*Brahma, Broyhan, EKU, St. Bernard Brau,
Tyrolian.*

Eidelweiss Imports
3765 Investment Ln.
West Palm Beach, FL 33404
Hofmark (Germany).

L. Fatato
318 Second St.
Brooklyn, NY 11215
(718) 965-7200
Canadian Ace, Malta El Sol.

Fischer Beverages International
393 Totten Pond Rd.
Waltham, MA 02154
(617) 890-3534
Fischer.

Frank's Distributing
2 Adams St.
Denver, CO 80206
(303) 322-2728
Algonquin, Gruner, Upper Canada.

Gambrinus Importing Co.
14800 San Pedro, #310
San Antonio, TX 78232
(210) 490-9128
Corona, Modelo, Pacifico, Cobra, Redback.

Joseph Gies Import
3345 Southport Ave.
Chicago, IL 60657
(312) 472-4577
EKU, Kulmbacher.

Grolsch Importers
1985 N Park Pl.
Atlanta, GA 30339
(404) 955-8885
Fax (404) 955-7571
Dinkelacker (Germany).

Guinness Import Co.
Landmark Sq., 9th floor
Stamford, CT 06901
(203) 323-3311
*Bass, Guinness, Harp, Pilsner Urquell,
Moosehead, Dos Equis.*

Frank M. Hartley
1630 Palisades Ave.
Ft. Lee, NJ 07024
(201) 461-4610
Hennenhauser, Horsy.

HDT Importers
6007 NE Stanton, P.O. Box 13490
Portland, OR 97213-0490
(503) 249-1885
Fax (503) 264-4925
Kulmbacher Schweizerhofbrau.

G. Heileman Brewing Co.
100 Harborview Plz.
La Crosse, WI 54601
(608) 785-1000
Hacker-Pschorr, Swan, Castlemaine.

Highland Distributing Co.
Houston, TX
(713) 862-6364
Mamba (Ivory Coast).

Hilton Commercial Group
P.O. Box 2026
Toluca Lake, CA 91610
(818) 953-4160
Vienna Lager, Giovane, Burgbrau.

Holsten Import Corp.
120 White Plains Rd.
Elmsford, NY 10523
(914) 345-8900
Fax (914) 332-7148
Holsten (Germany).

Hans Holterbosch
375 Park Ave.
New York, NY 10016
(212) 421-3800
Hofbrau Bavaria (Germany).

Hudepohl Schoenling
1625 Central Pkwy.
Cincinnati, OH 45214
(513) 241-4344
Fax (513) 241-2190
Staatliches Hofbraeuhaus (Germany).

Imported Beer Co.
2410 Duncom Dr.
Missisauga, Ontario, Canada
(905) 828-6288

International Beverages
65 Shawmut Rd.
Canton, MA 02021-1461
(617) 821-2712
Aass, Chimay, Holsten, Mamba, Schloss Eggenberg, Timmermans, Upper Canada, Young's, Burghoff, August Schell.

International Brands
441 N Kilbourn Ave.
Chicago, IL 60624
(312) 826-4001
Guinness, Harp, Bass, St. Pauli Girl, Kiwi, Nordik Woll, Ringnes, Dinkelacker, Mamba, OB, Bohemia, Carta Blanca, Kirin, more.

Jacquin International
2633 Trenton Ave.
Philadelphia, PA 19125
(215) 425-9300
Birell.

Kelwil Importers
P.O. Box 1987
Bloomfield, NJ 07003
(201) 748-9010
Silver Dragon, Yin Long, Zhuhai.

Kirin USA
600 Third Ave.
New York, NY 10016
(212) 687-1865
Kirin.

Leonard Kreusch
1 Caesar Pl.
Northvale, NJ 07647
(201) 784-2500
Euler, Kloster, Maximilian Bock.

Labatt Importers
23 Old Kings Way S
Darien, CT 06820
(203) 656-1876
*Labatt's (Canada); Moretti (Italy); Foster's
(Australia); Whitbread, Mackeson (UK);
Dos Equis (Mexico) and more.*

Manneken-Brussel Imports
1602 E Cesar Chavez St.
Austin, TX 78702
(512) 472-1012
Fax (512) 472-1544
Chimay (Belgium)

Markstein Enterprises
101 Park Pl.
San Ramon, CA 94583
(510) 838-1919
EKU.

Merchant du Vin Corp.
140 Lakeside Ave., #300
Seattle, WA 98122-6538
(206) 322-5022
Fax (206) 322-5185
Contact: Ian McAllister
*Lindemans, Orval, St. Sixtus, Watou
(Belgium); Brasseurs (France); Aying,
Pinkus, (Germany); Samuel Smith (UK).
And more.*

Monarch Import Co.
845 Third Ave., 20th floor
New York, NY 10022
(312) 346-9200
Tsingtao (China).

Mosakin Corp.
Matawan, NJ 07747
(908) 566-9443
Guilder, Star (Nigeria).

Oriental Brewery Co.
619 E Palisade Ave.
Englewood Cliffs, NJ 07632-1825
(201) 871-7300
Liefmans (Belgium); OB Beer (Korea).

Pa's Bier
P.O. Box 3243
Long Beach, CA 90803
(310) 421-2818
Edelweiss (Switzerland).

Paterno Imports
2701 S Western Ave.
Chicago, IL 60608
(312) 247-7070
Fax (312) 247-0072
Berliner Kindl (Germany).

Phoenix Imports
2925 Montclair Dr.
Ellicott City, MD 21043
(800) 700-4ALE
*Hexen Braeu, Rubens Red & Gold, Thomas
Hardy's Ale, Royal Oak, Samuchlaus,
Liefmans, Corsendonk, Gouden Carolus.*

Premier Brands Beverage Importers
101 Burnside Dr.
Toronto, Ontario, Canada
(416) 588-7082

Rader Co.
RD 6, Box 12
Boyertown, PA 19512
(610) 367-6075
Brand, Krakus, Kulmbacher, Paulaner,
Gosser, Ringnes, Holsten, Dinkelacker,
Spaten, Rischer, Tiger, Northern Goose.

St. Killian Importing Co.
P.O. Box K
Kingston, MA 02364
(617) 585-5165
Wurzburger.

Sapporo USA
1290 Ave. of the Americas
New York, NY 10104
(212) 765-4430
Sapporo.

Scottish & Newcastle Importers
444 De Haro, #125
San Francisco, CA 94107
(415) 255-4555
Newcastle Brown Ale, McEwan's,
Theakston's Old Peculier.

Sieb Distributors
418 Seneca Ave.
Ridgewood, NY 11385
(718) 386-1480
Fax (718) 821-8120
Spaten, Franziskaner.

Spaten West
50 Cypress Ln.
Brisbane, CA 94005
(415) 468-7240
Spaten Munich (Germany).

Stawski Distributing Co.
1521 W Haddon Ave.
Chicago, IL 60622
(312) 278-4848
Fax (312) 278-5206
Gosser (Austria); Royal, Faxe (Denmark);
Taj Mahal, Golden Eagle, Kingfisher
(India); Okocim, Krakus, Zywiec (Poland);
Golden Pheasant (Slovak); Singha (Thai).

Stroh Brewery Co.
100 River Pl.
Detroit, MI 48207
(313) 446-2000
Toronto.

Stroh
1 Yonge St.
Toronto, Ontario, Canada
(416) 366-7876

Suntory International
1211 Ave. of the Americas
New York, NY 10036
(212) 921-9595
Fax (212) 398-0268
Suntory.

Thames America Trading Co.

714 Penny Royal Ln.
San Rafael, CA 94903
(415) 492-2204
Fax (415) 492-2207

Maes Pils, Double & Triple Grimbergen (Belgium); Golden Promise (Scotland); Taunton Cider (UK); Welsh Ale, Welsh Bitter (Wales).

Vanberg & DeWulf Importers

52 Pioneer St.
Cooperstown, NY 13326
(800) 656-1212

Affligem Abbey, Blanche de Bruges, Boon Lambics, Castelain, Duvel, Jenlain, Mort Subite, Rodenbach, Saison Dupont, Scaldis (Belgium); Jade organic country ale (France).

Van Munching & Co.

1270 Ave. of the Americas
New York, NY 10020
(212) 332-8500

Heineken, Amstel, Grizzly.

Victor Sales

4610 Booth Boyle Ave.
Los Angeles, CA 90058
(213) 583-1864

Oranjeboom, Red Brewster, Gosser.

Warsteiner Importers

Market Tower 1, #500, 3033 S Parker
Aurora, CO 80014
(303) 750-8862

Warsteiner (Germany).

Western International Imports

Los Angeles, CA

Snowflake (China).

Whyte & Whyte

Elk Grove Village, IL 60007
(708) 439-4355

Herout Cider (France).

Wines, Ltd.

Beltsville, MD 20705
(301) 210-4000

Xingu (Brazil).

Wisdom Import Sales Co.

17401 Eastman Ave.
Irvine, CA 92713
(714) 261-5533

Tecate, Bohemia, Carta Blanca, Chihuahua, Watney's Red Barrel.

MAGAZINES, NEWSLETTERS, AND JOURNALS

Alephenalia Beer News
Merchant du Vin
140 Lakeside Ave.
Seattle, WA 98122
Charles Finkel, Publisher
*Published irregularly. Full of
interesting information about beer
styles and beer events.*

Ale Street News
P.O. Box 1125
Maywood, NJ 07607
(201) 368-9100
Tony Forder, Jack Babin, Publishers
*Published 6 times a year.
Covers the East Coast beer world.*

All About Beer
1627 Marion Ave.
Durham, NC 27705
(800) 977-BEER
Daniel Bradford, Publisher
*Published 6 times a year. Reviews, calen
dar; covers cuisine and homebrewing.*

American Brewer, the Business of Beer
P.O. Box 510
Hayward, CA 94543-0510
(800) 646-2701
William Owens, Publisher
*Published quarterly. Business magazine
for the micro- and pub-brewing industry.*

American Breweriana
P.O. Box 11157
Pueblo, CO 81001
(719) 544-9267
Published 6 times a year.

Bartender
P.O. Box 158
Liberty Corner, NJ 07938
(908) 766-6006

BarleyCorn
P.O. Box 2328
Falls Church, VA 22042
(703) 573-8970
George Rivers, Editor
*Published 8 times a year. Covers
Mid-Atlantic region. Includes news,
reviews, calendar, and articles.*

Beer & Brewing Industry International
Schloss Mindelburg, Postfach 14 63
D-8948 Mindelheim, Germany
08261 999 0
*Published twice a year. Includes
brewing news from around the world.*

Beer and Tavern Chronicle
277 Madison Ave.
New York, NY 10016
Gregg Smith, Co-editor
Published 12 times a year.

Beer Drinkers International
P.O. Box 6402
Ocean Hills, CA 92056

Beer: the magazine
P.O. Box 717
Hayward, CA 94543-0717
(510) 538-9500
William Owens, Publisher
Publishes 5 times a year.
International magazine for
beer lovers, aficionados,
and fanatics.

Beer Marketer's Insights
51 Virginia Ave.
West Nyack, NY 10994
(914) 358-7751
Jerry Steinman, Publisher
Published 23 times a year.
Also publishes Alcohol Issues
Insights, published 12 times
a year; Import Insights, published
once a year, reporting on
major development in
the U.S. beer industry.

Beer Statistics News
51 Virginia Ave.
West Nyack, NY 10994
(914) 358-7751
Jerry Steinman, Publisher
Published 24 times a year.
Beer industry update,
published once a year, reports
on major developments in the
U.S. beer industry.

The Beverage Communicator
P.O. Box 43
Hartsdale, NY 10530

Beverage Media
161 Sixth Ave.
New York, NY 10014
(212) 620-0100

Beverage World
150 Great Neck Rd.
Great Neck, NY 11021.

Brew: Traveling America's Brewpubs and Microbreweries
1120 Mulberry St.
DesMoines, IO 50309
(515) 243-4929
Don Walsmith, Publisher.
Published 6 times a year. Featured on
Real Beer Page of Internet.

Brew Hawaii
P.O. Box 852
Hauula, HI 96717
(808) 259-6884
A. S. Tynan, Editor
Published 6 times a year. Newspaper of
the Hawaii Homebrewers Association.

Brew Your Own: The How-to Homebrew Beer Magazine
216 F Street, Suite 160
Davis, CA 95616
(916) 758-4596
Carl Landau, Publisher
Published monthly.

The Brewer
Brewers Guild
8 Ely Pl.
London EC1N 6SD
England
171 405 4565
Published 12 times a year.
Includes technical papers.

Brewers & Distillers International
63 Burton Rd.
Burton upon Trent
Staffs DE14 3DP
England
1283 66784
Publishes marketing and
technical information for the
brewing industry.

Brewers Bulletin
P.O. Box 677
Thiensville, WI 53092-0677.

Brewers Digest
4049 W Peterson Ave.
Chicago, IL 60646
(312) 463-7484
Published 12 times a year.

Brewers Guardian
10 Belgrade Rd.
Hampton, Middlesex
England
TW12 2AZ
181 941 7750
Published 12 times a year.
Includes technical papers.

The Brewing Industry News
P.O. Box 27037
Riverdale, IL 60627

Brewing Techniques
P.O. Box 3222
Eugene, OR 97403
(800) 427-2993
Stephen A. Mallery, Publisher
Published 6 times a year. Technical
resource for small-scale brewers.

Canada's Beer Magazine
102 Burlington Ct.
Ottawa, Ontario, Canada
ONT K1T 3K5
(613) 737-3715
Mario D'Eer, Publisher
Published 4 times a year. Covers
Canadian brewing, micro and amateur.

Celebrator Beer News
564 W Sunset
P.O. Box 375
Hayward, CA 94543
(510) 670-0121
Thomas E. Dalldorf, Editor/Publisher
Published 6 times a year.

Cheers
41 Haddricks Mill Rd.
S. Gosforth, Newcastle upon Tyne
Tyne and Wear
NE3 1QL England
191 284 2742
Published 4 times a year; reports news
of clubs and brewpubs.

Club & Pub News
    Cumberland Ho.
    Lissadel St.
    Salford, Manchester
    M6 6GG
    England
    161 745 8845
    Published weekly. Reports
    news of brewpubs and clubs.

Dionysos
    University of Wisconsin
    Superior, WI 54880-2898
    Published 4 times a year.
    Journal of literature on
    intoxication.

Free House
    47 Church St.
    Barnsley S Yorks S70 2AS
    England
    1226 734333

The Grist International
    2 Balfour Rd.
    London N5 2HB
    England
    171 359 8323
    Publishes news on small independent
    brewers worldwide.

Malt Advocate
    3416 Oak Hill Rd.
    Emmaus, PA 18049
    (610) 967-1083
    John Hansell, Publisher/Editor
    Published quarterly. "Dedicated
    to the discerning consumption of
    beer and whisky."

Matter World Times
    P.O. Box 275
    White Plains, NY 10602
    (914) 633-2973
    Published 6 times a year.

Midwest Beer Notes
    339 Sixth Ave.
    Clayton, WI 54004
    (715) 948-2990
    Mike Urseth, Editor
        and Publisher
    Published 6 times a year.

Moderation Reader
    4714 NE 50 St.
    Seattle, WA 98105-2908
    (206) 525-0449
    Gene Ford
    Published 6 times a year.
    Concerned with drinking
    in moderation.

Modern Brewery Age
    50 Day St.
    P.O. Box 5550
    Norwalk, CT 06856
    (203) 853-6015
    Also publishes "Brewing for Profit
    on a Small Scale."

The New Brewer
    P.O. Box 1679
    Boulder, CO 80306-1679
    (303) 447-0816
    Virginia Thomas,
        Editor and Publisher
    Published 6 times a year by the
    Institute for Brewing Studies.

Northwest Beer Journal
2677 Fircrest Dr. SE
Port Orchard, WA 98366-5771.

Northwest Brew News
22833 Bothell-Everett Hwy., #1139
Bothell, WA 98021-9365
(206) 742-5327
Jim Jamison, Russ Ulrich,
    Pubishers
Published 6 times a year.

Pint Post
12345 Lake City Way NE, #159
Seattle, WA 98125
(206) 527-7331
Larry Baush, Publisher
*Published 4 times a year; subscription
includes membership in Microbrew
Appreciation Society.*

The Sake Connection
P.O. Box 546
Portland, OR 97206-0546
(503) 289-7596
Fred Eckhardt, Editor
Published 4–5 times a year.

Southern Draft Brew News
702 Sailfish Rd.
Winter Springs, FL 32708-0425
(407) 327-9451 or (407) 677-6017
Jerry Gengler, Editor
Published 6 times a year.

Southwest Brewing News
11405 Evening Star Drive
Austin, TX 78739
Joe Barfield, Bill Metzger, Publishers

Suds 'n Stuff
P.O. Box 6402
4764 Galicia Way
Ocean Hills, CA 92058
(800) 457-6543
Mike and Bunny Bosak
Published 6 times a year.

What's Brewing
CAMRA
P.O. Box 2036
Station D
Ottawa, Ontario, Canada
ONT K1P 5W3
*Publishes newspaper with reviews,
and news from around the world.*

What's On Tap
P.O. Box 7779
Berkeley, CA 94707-7779
(800) 434-7779
William Brand

Yankee Brew News
P.O. Box 520250
Winthrop, MA 02152
(617) 461-5693
Published 6 times a year.

Zymurgy
American Homebrewers Association
P.O. Box 1679
Boulder, CO 80306-1679
(303) 447-0816
Published 5 times a year.

BIBLIOGRAPHY

BOOKS

Beaumont, Stephen. *A Taste for Beer.* Pownal, VT: Storey Publishing, 1995.

Briggs, D. E., *et al. Malting and Brewing Science,* vol. 1. London: Chapman & Hall, 1981.

Brown, Jonathan. *Steeped in Tradition: The Malting Industry in England Since the Railway Age.* University of Reading: Whiteknights, 1983.

Burch, Byron. *Brewing Quality Beers: The Home Brewer's Essential Guidebook.* Fulton, CA: Joby Books, 1986.

Cooperrider, Brian. *Road-Map Guides to the Microbreweries.* Silver City, NV: Lone Mountain Designs.

Eames, Alan. *A Beer Dinker's Companion.* Harvard, MA: Ayers Rock Press.

———. *Secret Life of Beer: Legends, Lore, and Little-Known Facts.* Pownal, VT: Storey Publishing, 1995.

Ehret, George. *Twenty-Five Years of Brewing.* New York: The Gast Lithograph and Engraving Company, 1891.*

Endell, Fritz. *Old Tavern Signs: An Excursion in the History of Hospitality.* Cambridge: Houghton Mifflin Company, 1916.*

Erickson, Jack. *California Brewin'.* Reston, VA: Redbrick Press.

Finch, Christopher, and W. Scott Griffiths. *America's Best Beers: A Complete Guide to the More Than 350 Microbreweries and Brewpubs Across America.* New York: Little, Brown and Company, 1994.

Fix, George. *Principles of Brewing Science.* Boulder, CO: Brewers Publications, 1989.

Flynn, Colin T., and Randy DalFranco. *Guide to America's Micro-Brewed Beer.* Washington, DC: Rosehill Ents.

Garetz, Mark. *Using Hops: The Complete Guide to Hops for the Craft Brewer.* Danville, CA: Hoptech, 1994.

Haiber, Robert, and William Paul Haiber. *A Short, but Foamy, History of Beer: The Drink that Invented Itself.* La Grangeville, NY: Info Devel Press, 1993.

Hermann, Dr. Leonard. *Das Bier im Bolfsmund.* Berlin: Verlag von Reimar Hobbing, 1861.*

Hield, Mary. *Glimpses of South America.* London: Cassell & Company, Ltd., 1883.*

Hough, J. S., Briggs, D. E., Stevens, R., Young, T. W. *Malting and Brewing Science*, vol. 2. London, England: Chapman-Hall, Ltd., 1982.

Hulme, A. C. *The Biochemistry of Fruits and Their Products.* New York: Academic Press, 1970.

Jackson, Michael. *Michael Jackson's Beer Companion.* Philadelphia: Running Press, 1993.

————. *The New World Guide to Beer.* Philadelphia: Running Press, 1988.

————. *The Simon & Schuster Pocket Guide to Beer.* New York: Simon & Schuster, 1986.

Johnson, Steve. *On Tap New England: The Beer Connoisseur's Guide to Brewpubs, Restaurant Breweries, Craft Breweries, Cottage Breweries, and Brewery Inns.* Clemson, SC: WBR Publications, 1994.

King, Frank A. *Beer Has a History.* London: Hutchinson's Scientific and Technical Publications, 1947.

Kunze, Wolfgang. *Technologie Brauer and Mälzer.* Liepzig, E. Germany: VEB Fachbuchverlag, 1977.

Lutzen, Karl F., and Mark Stevens. *Homebrew Favorites: A Coast-to-Coast Collection of More Than 240 Beer and Ale Recipes.* Pownal, VT: Storey Publishing, 1994.

Miller, Dave. *Brewing the World's Great Beers.* Pownal, VT: Storey Publishing, 1992.

————. *The Complete Handbook of Home Brewing.* Pownal, VT: Garden Way Publishing, 1988.

————. *Dave Miller's Homebrewing Guide.* Pownal, VT: Storey Publishing, 1995.

Mosher, Randy. *The Brewer's Companion.* Seattle, WA: Alephanalia Publications, 1994.

Nachel, Marty. *Beer Across America.* Pownal, VT: Storey Publishing, 1995.

Narziss, Ludwig. *Abriss der Beierbrauerei.* 4th ed. Stuttgart, Germany: Ferdinand Enke Verlag, 1980.

Noonan, Gregory J. *Brewing Lager Beer.* Boulder, CO: Brewers Publications, 1986.

Nugy, H. L. *The Brewer's Manual.* Bayonne, NJ: self-published, 1948.

BIBLIOGRAPHY

One-Hundred Years of Brewing. Supplement to *The Western Brewer*, 1903. Chicago & New York: H. S. Rich & Co. Reprinted by Arno Press (New York, 1974).*

Papazian, Charlie. *The Home Brewer's Companion.* New York: Avon Books, 1994.

Prouxl, Annie, and Lew Nichols. *Sweet & Hard Cider: Making It, Using It, & Enjoying It.* Pownal, VT: Garden Way Publishing, 1980.

Reese, M. R. *Better Beer & How to Brew It.* Pownal, VT: Garden Way Publishing, 1978.

Richardson. *Science of Brewing* (1805), as quoted in Nithsdale and Manton, *Practical Brewing.* London: Food and Trade Press, 1947.

Robertson, James D. *The Beer Log.* Oceanside, CA: Bosak Publishing Company, 1994.

Salem, F. W. *Beer, Its History and Its Economic Value as a National Beverage.* Hartford, CT: F. W. Salem & Company, 1880.*

Schwimmer, Sigmund. *Source Book of Food Enzymology.* Westport, CT: AVI Publishing, n.d.

Smith, Gregg. *The Beer Enthusiast's Guide.* Pownal, VT: Storey Publishing, 1994.

Timbs, John, F.S.A. *Clubs and Club Life in London.* London: Chatto & Windus, 1908.*

Wahl, Robert, and Henius, Max. *American Handy Book of the Brewing, Malting and Auxiliary Trades,* vol. 2. Chicago, IL: Wahl Henius Inst., 1908.

Wood, Heather. *The Beer Directory.* Pownal, VT: Storey Publishing, 1995.

Yenne, Bill. *Beer Labels of the World.* Secaucus, NJ: Chartwell Books, 1993.

———. *The Field Guide to North America's Breweries and Microbreweries.* Avenel, NJ: Crescent Books, 1994.

*Art from this public-domain work has been reprinted in *The Encyclopedia of Beer.*

ARTICLES

Barchet, Ron. "Cold Trub: Implications for Finished Beer and Methods for Removal." *Brewing Techniques* (March/April 1994).

———. "Hot Trub: Formation and Removal." *Brewing Techniques* (November/December 1993).

Bergen, Roger. "American Wheat Beers." *Brewing Techniques* (May/June 1993).

Bucca, Ralph. "Fruit Beers." *BarleyCorn* (July/August 1994).

Eby, David. "Sensory Aspects of Zymological Evaluation." In *Evaluating Beer*. Boudler, CO: Brewers Publications, 1993.

Farnsworth, Paul. "Yeast Stock and Starter Culture Production." *Zymurgy* (Special Issue, 1989).

Farrell, Normal. "The Enchanting World of Malt Extract." *Zymurgy* (Winter 1994).

Foster, Stephen. "It's Funny What Hops into Your Memory." *Zymurgy* (Special Issue, 1990).

Frane, Jeff. "How Sweet It Is." *Zymurgy* (Spring 1994).

Garetz, Mark. "Hop Storage." *Brewing Techniques* (January/February 1994).

Grant, Bert. "Hop Varieties and Qualities." *Zymurgy* (Special Issue, 1990).

Guzinski, Gus. "Hop Oil Equals Aroma and Flavor." *Zymurgy* (Special Issue, 1990).

Haunold, Alfred. "Development of Hop Varieties." *Zymurgy* (Special Issue, 1990).

Haunold, Alfred, and Gail B. Nickerson. "Factors Affecting Hop Production, Hop Quality, and Brewery Preference." *Brewing Techniques* (May/June 1993).

Hayden, Rosannah. "Brewing with Rye." *Brewing Techniques* (September/October 1993).

Isenhour, John. "A Sterile Transfer Technique for Pure Culturing." *Zymurgy* (Special Issue, 1989).

Korzonas, Al. "Options for Adding Fruit." *Zymurgy* (1989).

Lodahl, Martin. "Malt Extracts: Cause for Caution." *Brewing Techniques* (July/August 1993).

Matucheski, Michael. "Oats: The Right Grain to Brew!" *Zymurgy* (Special Issue, 1994).

Miller, Dave. "Ask the Troubleshooter." *Brewing Techniques* (November/December 1993).

Morris, Rodney. "Isolation and Culture of Yeast from Bottle-Conditioned Beers." *Zymurgy* (Special Issue, 1989), Schloss Mindelburg, Germany.

Mosher, Randy. "Parti-Gyle Brewing." *Brewing Techniques* (March/April 1994).

O'Neill, Carol. "Extract Magic: From Field to Kettle." *Zymurgy* (Winter 1994).

Piendl, Professor Anton. From the series "Biere Aus Aller Welt." *Brauindustrie Magazine* (1982–1991), Schloss Mindelburg, Germany.

Palamand, Raoul. "Training Ourselves in Flavor Perception and Tasting." In *Evaluating Beer*. Boudler, CO: Brewers Publications, 1993.

BIBLIOGRAPHY

Rager, Jackie. "Calculating Hop Bitterness in Beer." *Zymurgy* (Special Issue, 1990).

Rajotte, Pierre. "Collecting and Reusing Live Brewer's Yeast." *Zymurgy* (Special Issue, 1989).

Richman, Darryl. "Running a Yeast Test." *Zymurgy* (Special Issue, 1989).

Tinseth, Glenn. "The Essential Oil of Hops: Aroma and Flavor in Hops and Beer." *Brewing Techniques* (January/February 1994).

Watkins, Milton C. "Sorghum Beers." *BarleyCorn (July/August 1994)*.

Weix, Patrick. "Become Saccharomyces Savvy." *Zymurgy* (Summer 1994).

Wills, Dave. "Assessing Hop Quality." *Zymurgy* (Special Issue, 1990).

TEXT CREDITS:

The CIDER and GLASSWARE entries were written by Matt Kelly.

The BOTTLE CAP entry was adapted from the article by David Friedman "Crowns —Obsolete on 100th Birthday? The Crystal Ball Says It's Just over the Horizon." *American Breweriana Journal* (March/April, 1991). Adapted by Nick Noyes with additional text from Mark Stevens. Used with permission.

The TRAQUAIR HOUSE, SAMUEL SMITH BREWERY, and WOMEN, BEER, AND BREWING entries were adapted from *Alephenalia*. Used with permission of Charles Finkel, Merchant du Vin Corporation, Seattle, WA.

The chart on pages 128–129 was adapted from one provided courtesy of Byron Burch, Great Fermentations of Santa Rosa, 840 Piner Road, #14, Santa Rosa, CA 95403. Used with permission.

PICTURE CREDITS:

NOTE: Art not credited here is in the public domain. *See* BIBLIOGRAPHY.

Page 23, right: Plant Tech. Ltd.; **page 24:** Miller, Dave, *The Complete Handbook of Home Brewing.* Pownal, VT: Storey Communications, Inc., 1988. Illustration by Kay Holmes Stafford; **page 26:** Miller, Dave, *Brewing the World's Great Beers: A Step-by-Step Guide.* Pownal, VT: Storey Communications, Inc., 1992. Illustration by Carl F. Kirkpatrick; **page 35:** Whitbread PLC, *The Story of Whitbread.* London: Talisman Communications, 1992; **page 37, right:** Wykes, Alan, *Ale and Hearty.* London: Juniper Books Ltd., 1979; **page 37, left:** Hermann, Dr. Leonard, *Das Bier im Bolfsmund.* Berlin: Verlag von Reimar Hobbing, n.d.; **page 55:** Jung, Hermann, *Bier-Kunst und Brauchtum.* Dortmund, Germany: Schropp Verlagg, 1970; **page 59:** Merchant du Vin Corporation; **page 60:** Merchant du Vin Corporation; **page 63:** Mark Stevens; **page 64, top:** Mark Stevens; **page 67:** Hermann, *Das Bier im Bolfsmund;* **page 72:** Oldenberg Brewery; **page 73:** Oldenberg Brewery; **page 74:** Patrick Piel, Gamma Liaison; **page 77:** J. Sutton, Gamma Liaison; **page 78:** Hermann, *Das Bier im Bolfsmund;* **page 82:** Jung, *Bier-Kunst und Brauchtum;* **page 91:** Whitbread PLC, *The Story of Whitbread;* **page 95:** Grobecker, Kurt, *O Bier du Schmäckest Fein.* Hamburg, Germany: Holsten Brewery, 1979; **page 101:** Boston Beer Co. (Richard Vanderwarker); **page 103:** Boston Beer Co. (Richard Vanderwarker); **page 104:** Boston Brewers Festival, (Ken Winokuer); **page 105:** Nachel, Marty, *Beer Across America.* Pownal, VT: Storey

Communications, Inc., 1995. Photograph by Nicholas Whitman; **page 107**: Peter Austin & Partners (Contracts), Ltd.; **page 108**: Matthias Müller; **page 113**: Smith, Gregg, *The Beer Enthusiast's Guide*. Pownal, VT: Storey Communications, Inc., 1994. Illustration by Christine Erickson; **page 114, right**: Peter Austin & Partners (Contracts), Ltd.; **page 121**: Smith, *The Beer Enthusiast's Guide*. Illustration by Christine Erickson; **page 123**: Peter Austin & Partners (Contracts), Ltd.; **page 126**: Haydon, Peter, *The English Pub: A History*. London: Robert Hale, Ltd., 1994; **page 131, left and right**: Zahm & Nogel, Inc.; **page 132**: Fisher, Joe and Fisher, Dennis, *Great Beer from Kits*. Pownal, VT: Storey Communications, Inc., 1996. Illustration by Allison Kolesar; **page 134**: Wykes, *Ale and Hearty;* **page 135**: **Merchant du Vin Corporation**; page 136: Hermann, *Das Bier im Bolfsmund;* **page 141**: Chicago Brewing Company; **page 142, right**: Jung, *Bier-Kunst und Brauchtum;* **page 143**: Fisher and Fisher, *Great Beer from Kits*. Illustration by Allison Kolesar; **page 148**: Proulx, Annie and Nichols, Lew, *Sweet & Hard Cider*. Pownal, VT: Storey Communications, Inc., 1980; **page 149**: Ibid.; **page 152**: Wykes, *Ale and Hearty;* **page 157**: Peter Austin & Partners (Contracts), Ltd.; **page 159, bottom**: Merchant du Vin Corporation; **page 161**: Coors Brewing Company; **page 163, left**: Delos, Gilbert, *Les Bières du Monde*. Paris: les Éditions Hatier, 1993; **page 163, right**: Haydon, *The English Pub;* **page 170**: Full Sail Brewing Company; **page 173, left**: Mark Stevens; **page 174**: Dixie Brewing Company; **page 177**: Hermann, *Das Bier im Bolfsmund;* **page 178**: Bridgeman Art Library, Ltd.; **page 184**: Jung, *Bier-Kunst und Brauchtum;* **page 185, top**: Ibid.; **page 193**: Glover, Brian, *Prince of Ales: The History of Brewing in Wales*. Dover, NH: Alan Sutton Publishing, 1993; **page 196**: Jung, *Bier-Kunst und Brauchtum;* **page 198**: Full Sail Brewing Company; **page 207, top and bottom**: Full Sail Brewing Company; **page 214**: Brigita Fuhrmann; **page 215**: Brigita Fuhrmann; **page 217**: Simon, Andre L., *Bibiotheca Bacchica*. London: Holland Press, 1927; **page 219**: Sigloch Bildarchiv; **page 220**: Great American Beer Festival; **page 221**: Great American Beer Festival; **page 222**: Great American Beer Festival; **page 230, top and bottom**: Hart Brewing, Inc.; **page 231**: Hart Brewing, Inc.; **page 234**: G. Heileman Brewing Company, Inc.; **page 238, top**: Metropolitan Museum of Art; **page 238, bottom**: Haydon, *The English Pub;* **page 243**: Miller, *Brewing the World's Great Beers;* **page 244**: Glover, *Prince of Ales;* **page 245, right**: Delos, *Les Bière;* **page 245, left**: IFA-Bilderteam GmbH; **page 246, bottom**: Merchant du Vin Corporation; **page 247, right**: Mark Stevens; page 248: Delos, *Les Bières;* **page 251**: Fisher and Fisher, *Great Beer from Kits*. Illustration by Allison Kolesar; **page 252**: Merchant du Vin Corporation (Darius Kinsey; courtesy Snoqualmie Valley Historical Museum, North Bend, WA); **page 261**: Fisher and Fisher, *Great Beer from Kits*. Illustration by Allison Kolesar; **page 265**: Glover, *Prince of Ales;* **page 271**: The Book and the Cook; **page 274**: Smith, *The Beer Enthusiast's Guide*. Illustration by Christine Erickson; **page 278**: Jung, *Bier-Kunst und Brauchtum;* **page 281**: KQED International Beer and Food Festival; **page 286**: Jung, *Bier;* **page 289**: Ibid.; **page 294**: Haydon, *The English Pub;* **page 297**: Merchant du Vin Corporation; **page 298**: Merchant du Vin Corporation; **page 303**:

Nicholas Whitman; **page 309:** Miller, *Brewing the World's Great Beers.* Illustration by Carl F. Kirkpatrick; **page 311:** Glover, *Prince of Ales;* **page 318:** Mark Stevens; **page 319:** Mark Stevens; **page 320, top left:** Erich Spiegelhalter; **page 321, bottom left:** F. X. Matt Brewery Company, Inc.; **page 323, top:** F. X. Matt Brewery Company, Inc.; **page 324, top right:** F. X. Matt Brewery Company, Inc.; **page 324, left:** F. X. Matt Brewery Company, Inc.; **page 325:** Mendocino Brewing Company; **page 328:** Haydon, *The English Pub;* **page 331:** Jung, *Bier-Kunst und Brauchtum;* **page 334:** J. Sutton, Gamma Liaison; **page 340:** New Amsterdam Brewing Company; **page 347:** Delos, *Les Bières;* **page 349:** Jung, *Bier-Kunst und Brauchtum;* **page 351:** Merchant du Vin Corporation; **page 352:** Merchant du Vin Corporation; **page 357:** IBA-Bilderteam GmbH; **page 364:** Wykes, *Ale and Hearty;* **page 365:** Brigita Fuhrmann; **page 371:** Merchant du Vin Corporation; **page 373:** Merchant du Vin Corporation; **page 375:** Pittsburgh Brewing Company; **page 380:** Jung, *Bier-Kunst und Brauchtum;* **page 381:** Wide World Photos/AP; **page 387:** Merchant du Vin Corporation; **page 390:** Redhook Ale Brewery; **page 392, bottom:** Straub Brewing Company; **page 400:** Jung, *Bier-Kunst und Brauchtum;* **page 403:** Merchant du Vin Corporation; **page 411, left and right:** Sierra Nevada Brewing Company; **page 414:** Merchant du Vin Corporation; **page 415:** Merchant du Vin Corporation; **page 416:** Merchant du Vin Corporation; **page 417:** Simon, *Bibliotheca Bacchia;* **page 419, right:** Helga Lade Fotoagentur GmbH; **page 425, all:** Grobecker, *Bier, du Schmäckest Fein;* **page 426:** Stevens Point Brewery; **page 427, all:** Whitbread PLC, *Story of Whitbread;* **page 428:** Ibid.; **page 429:** Ritchie, Berry, *An Uncommon Brewer: The Story of Whitbread 1742–1992.* London: James & James Publishers, Limited, 1992; **page 430, both:** Straub Brewing Company; **page 431, left:** Straub Brewing Company; **page 436, all:** Summit Brewing Company; **page 442:** Simon, *Bibliotheca Bacchia;* **page 443:** Jung, *Bier-Kunst und Brauchtum;* **page 444:** Gilles Bassigna, Gamma Liaison; **page 445:** Merchant du Vin Corporation; **page 457, top:** Hermann, *Das Bier im Bolfsmund;* **page 457, bottom:** Wykes, *Ale and Hearty;* **page 464, all:** Whitbread PLC, *Story of Whitbread;* **page 467:** Delos, *Les Bières;* **page 468, bottom:** Hermann, *Das Bier im Bolfsmund;* **page 472:** Glover, *Prince of Ales;* **page 475:** Merchant du Vin Corporation; **page 476:** Merchant du Vin Corporation; **page 479:** Zip City Brewing Company

ACKNOWLEDGMENTS

The creation and production of a reference work of this scope can happen only with the involvement of a great many people. Mary Kay Linge, editor at Henry Holt Reference Books, has been an enthusiastic source of direction and encouragement from the beginning of the project to the very end.

Christine Rhodes and Amanda Haar deserve special recognition for developing this ambitious project and enlisting some of the best names in the beer industry to write about their areas of expertise. Christine, who has also written entries for this volume, coordinated the contributing editors and has been involved with every stage of development.

The other contributing editors are acknowledged in a separate section of the front matter.

Many others provided invaluable assistance. Thanks to Barbara Jatkola of Jaffrey, NH, who did an exceptional job of copyediting; Nick Noyes, who pitched in whenever copy needed to be written; Jim Busch, who reviewed the technical and chemical entries for accuracy; and Elizabeth Tinsley, who helped with research. Special thanks to typist Chris Meyer of Arlington, VT, who contributed so much more than keyboarding editorial changes; Wanda Harper Joyce of Colchester, VT, who provided the initial stages of page layout; and Cindy McFarland, not only for a great design, but for coordinating the prepress team in the final weeks of production.

Charles Finkel and Ian McAllister of Merchant du Vin Corporation, Seattle, WA, were extraordinarily helpful in providing artwork for breweries whose products they import (as well as for breweries whose products they don't) and for permission to adapt text from *Alephenalia,* a fascinating and colorful company publication. Thanks also to photographers Joel Sackett of Bambridge, WA, and Gordy Hattori of Seattle, both of whom are employed by Merchant du Vin.

Stu Galloway of the American Breweriana Association acted on our plea for bottle-cap information with much-appreciated speed.

Thanks to the many breweries who responded to our request for photographs, labels, and logos.

Finally, Catherine Gee Graney, managing editor at Storey Communications, Inc., must be singled out for her contribution. She was the glue that kept the project intact and on track.

Pamela B. Lappies
Project Editor